ROYAL HISTORIES

Royal Histories

*The Transformation of the
Royal Bank of Canada, 1864–2022*

JOEL Z. GARROD

UNIVERSITY OF TORONTO PRESS
Toronto Buffalo London

© University of Toronto Press 2025
Toronto Buffalo London
utorontopress.com

ISBN 978-1-4875-4261-0 (cloth)   ISBN 978-1-4875-4262-7 (EPUB)
                                 ISBN 978-1-4875-4263-4 (PDF)

Library and Archives Canada Cataloguing in Publication

Title: Royal histories : the transformation of the Royal Bank of Canada,
   1864–2022 / Joel Z. Garrod.
Names: Garrod, Joel Z., author.
Description: Includes bibliographical references and index.
Identifiers: Canadiana (print) 20240537351 | Canadiana (ebook) 20240537386 |
   ISBN 9781487542610 (cloth) | ISBN 9781487542627 (EPUB) |
   ISBN 9781487542634 (PDF)
Subjects: LCSH: Royal Bank of Canada – History. | LCSH: Banks and
   banking – Canada – History. | LCSH: Globalization – Canada – History.
Classification: LCC HG2708.R6 G37 2025 | DDC 332.1/20971 – dc23

Cover design: Heng Wee Tan
Cover image: Royal Bank of Canada, new branch, Kingsway & Slocan,
Vancouver, approximately 1952; Collection: Leonard Frank Photos Studio
fonds; Photographer: Otto Landauer; Jewish Museum & Archives of BC;
LF.01616

We wish to acknowledge the land on which the University of Toronto Press
operates. This land is the traditional territory of the Wendat, the Anishnaabeg,
the Haudenosaunee, the Métis, and the Mississaugas of the Credit First Nation.

This book has been published with the help of a grant from the Federation
for the Humanities and Social Sciences, through the Awards to Scholarly
Publications Program, using funds provided by the Social Sciences and
Humanities Research Council of Canada.

University of Toronto Press acknowledges the financial support of the
Government of Canada, the Canada Council for the Arts, and the Ontario Arts
Council, an agency of the Government of Ontario, for its publishing activities.

  Canada Council   Conseil des Arts
         for the Arts   du Canada

Funded by the   Financé par le
 Government   gouvernement
  of Canada   du Canada

Contents

Acknowledgments vii

Permissions ix

List of Abbreviations xi

A Brief Timeline of the Royal Bank of Canada xv

1 Introduction 3

2 Making National Capital: The Origin of the Royal Bank of Canada, 1864–1944 44

3 The Expansion of National Capital: The Growth of the Royal Bank of Canada, 1945–1974 95

4 Making Global Capital: RBC in the Digital Age, 1975–2008 130

5 Emerging Tendencies and Trajectories: 2009–2022 227

References 279

Index 341

Acknowledgments

Books, like people, are social creations, and this one is no different. To start, I'd like to thank Gary Teeple, who originally set me on the path of Canadian political economy, and whose work I continually find myself rereading. I'd also like to thank the Department of Sociology and Anthropology at Carleton University. I owe a significant debt to the faculty, staff, and students for creating the sort of collegial environment that allows projects like this one to grow. In particular, I'd like to thank Laura Macdonald and Janet Siltanen, who helped me develop the ideas in this book, as well as Wallace Clement, who not only taught me how to conduct such a study, but steered it through its stormiest passages. I would also like to thank my comrades in the doctoral seminar – especially Mathieu Charbonneau and the late Blake MacMillan – who were always more than happy to engage in friendly debates about the subject matter. A significant chunk of this book was completed at St. Francis Xavier University, so many thanks are also owed to my colleagues there who continue to be supportive of my research. Many thanks to Daniel Quinlan and the staff at the University of Toronto Press for their assistance in getting the manuscript to publication. I am also indebted to my parents, Pam and Bob, for all of their love and support over the years that ultimately made this project possible. Although my dad didn't share my view of political economy, when he passed away in 2018, my doctoral dissertation was sitting open on his kitchen table next to his glasses. This book is dedicated to his memory. The biggest thanks go out to my partner Em, who saw this text through its final stages and all the emotional ups and downs that such a process necessarily entails. They were an immensely thoughtful sounding board while I rambled about the banks, and they offered excellent critical commentary on my ideas. This book would not exist without their love and patience. While all of these people have impacted this book in one way or another, I take full responsibility, as is customary, for all errors or misrepresentations.

Permissions

Parts of chapter 1 were first published in *Studies in Political Economy* in 2017 and 2018 © Taylor & Francis Ltd., available online:
www.tandfonline.com/10.1080/07078552.2017.1393909
www.tandfonline.com/10.1080/07078552.2018.1536359
Reprinted by permission of Taylor & Francis Ltd.
Parts of chapter 5 were first published in *Economy and Society* in 2019 © Taylor & Francis Ltd., available online:
www.tandfonline.com/10.1080/03085147.2019.1678316
Reprinted by permission of Taylor & Francis Ltd.

Abbreviations

ABCP	asset-backed commercial paper
ATS	alternative trading system
BATS	Better Alternative Trading System
BBVA	Banco Bilbao Vizcaya Argentaria
BCBS	Basel Committee on Banking Supervision
BCC	Business Council of Canada
BCE	Bell Canada Enterprises
BCNI	Business Council on National Issues
BIS	Bank for International Settlements
BIT	bilateral investment treaties
BMO	Bank of Montreal
BoC	Bank of Canada
CBA	Canadian Bankers Association
CCB	Canadian Commercial Bank
CCBs	Canadian covered bonds
CCF	Co-operative Commonwealth Federation
CCPA	Canadian Centre for Policy Alternatives
CDIA	Canadian direct investment abroad
CDIC	Canadian Deposit Insurance Corporation
CDO	collateralized debt obligation
CDOR	Canadian Dealer Offered Rate
CERB	Canada Emergency Response Benefit
CETA	Canada–European Union Comprehensive Economic and Trade Agreement
CFTC	Commodity Futures Trading Commission
CIBC	Canadian Imperial Bank of Commerce
CMA	Canadian Manufacturers' Association
CMHC	Canada Mortgage and Housing Corporation
CNR	Canadian National Railway

CPR	Canadian Pacific Railway
CPTPP	Comprehensive and Progressive Agreement for Trans-Pacific Partnership
CRA	Canada Revenue Agency
CSA	Canadian Securities Administrators
CUSFTA	Canada–United States Free Trade Agreement
CUSMA	Canada–United States–Mexico Agreement
DAO	decentralized autonomous organization
D-SIBs	domestic systemically important banks
ECT	Energy Charter Treaty
EPU	European Payments Union
ETF	exchange-traded fund
EU	European Union
FCAC	Financial Consumer Agency of Canada
FDI	foreign direct investment
FECB	Foreign Exchange Control Board
FISC	Financial Institutions Supervisory Committee
FSB	Financial Stability Board
FSF	Financial Stability Forum
FSI	Financial Stability Institute
G7	Group of Seven
G10	Group of Ten
G20	Group of Twenty
GATS	General Agreement on Trade in Services
GATT	General Agreement on Tariffs and Trade
GDP	gross domestic product
GFMA	Global Financial Markets Association
G-SIBs	global systemically important banks
HFT	high-frequency trading
HSBC	Hongkong and Shanghai Banking Corporation Limited
IBC	international business company
IEX	Investors Exchange
IIA	international investment agreement
IIF	Institute of International Finance
IIFA	International Investment Funds Association
IIROC	Investment Industry Regulatory Organization of Canada
IMF	International Monetary Fund
IMPP	Insured Mortgage Purchase Program
ING	Internationale Nederlanden Groep
IPEF	Indo-Pacific Economic Framework
ISDS	investor–state dispute settlement
ISO	International Organization for Standardization

KWS	Keynesian welfare state
LDC	less-developed country
LIBOR	London Interbank Offered Rate
LSE	London Stock Exchange
LTC	long-term care
MAiD	medical assistance in dying
M&A	mergers and acquisitions
MBNA	Maryland Bank of North America
MNC	multinational corporation
MNE	multinational enterprise
MX	Montreal Exchange
NAFTA	North American Free Trade Agreement
NATO	North Atlantic Treaty Organization
NDP	New Democratic Party
NHA-MBS	National Housing Act-Mortgage-Backed Securities
OECD	Organisation for Economic Co-operation and Development
OIGB	Office of the Inspector General of Banks
OMERS	Ontario Municipal Employees Retirement System
OPEC	Organization of the Petroleum Exporting Countries
OSC	Ontario Securities Commission
OSFI	Office of the Superintendent of Financial Institutions
OTF	Ontario Teachers' Federation
p2p	peer-to-peer
PACER	Pacific Agreement on Closer Economic Relations
PwC	PricewaterhouseCoopers
RBC	Royal Bank of Canada
RBTT	Royal Bank of Trinidad and Tobago Financial Group
RCEP	Regional Comprehensive Economic Partnership
Reg NMS	Regulation National Market System
REIT	real estate investment trust
RHOSP	registered home ownership savings plan
RRSP	registered retirement savings plan
SEC	Securities and Exchange Commission
TAR	territory, authority, and rights
TBTF	too big to fail
TCC	transnational capitalist class
TD	Toronto-Dominion Bank
TFW	temporary foreign worker
TFWP	Temporary Foreign Worker Program
THOR	Tactical Hybrid Order Router
TNC	transnational corporation

TNS	transnational state apparatus
TPP	Trans-Pacific Partnership
TSX	Toronto Stock Exchange
TSXV	Toronto Venture Exchange
UBS	Union Bank of Switzerland
UN	United Nations
UNCTAD	United Nations Conference on Trade and Development
WB	World Bank
WTO	World Trade Organization

A Brief Timeline of the Royal Bank of Canada

1864   Merchants Bank founded in Halifax, Nova Scotia.
1867   Canadian Confederation.
1869   Changed name to Merchants Bank of Halifax. Incorporated under federal charter.
1870   Branch opened in Pictou, Nova Scotia.
1871   *Bank Act* passed. Branches opened in Bridgewater, Truro, Weymouth, Antigonish, and Lunenburg, Nova Scotia.
1872   Branch opened in Sydney, Nova Scotia.
1873   Branches opened in Maitland, Nova Scotia; and Charlottetown, Prince Edward Island.
1874   Branch opened in Summerside, Prince Edward Island.
1877   Branch opened in Souris, Prince Edward Island.
1879   National Policy.
1881   Branch opened in Port Hawkesbury, Nova Scotia.
1882   Opened first international branch in Bermuda. Also opened branches in Baddeck and Guysborough, Nova Scotia; and Sackville, Richibucto, Bathurst, Kingston, and Dorchester, New Brunswick.
1883   Branch opened in Newcastle, New Brunswick.
1885   Branch opened in Paspebiac, Quebec.
1886   Branch opened in Moncton, New Brunswick; and St. Pierre and Miquelon.
1887   Branches opened in Fredericton, New Brunswick; Woodstock, New Brunswick; and Montreal, Quebec.
1889   Bermuda branch sold.
1891   Canadian Parliament granted Canadian Bankers Association the right to block charters for new banks.
1895   Branch opened in St. John's, Newfoundland.
1899   Branches opened in Cuba and New York.

xvi   A Brief Timeline of the Royal Bank of Canada

1901   Changed name to Royal Bank of Canada (RBC).
1907   Branch opened in Puerto Rico. Moved head office from Halifax to Montreal.
1910   Branches opened in London, England; Winnipeg, Manitoba; and Trinidad. Acquired Union Bank of Halifax.
1911   Branches opened in Jamaica and Barbados.
1912   Branches opened in Dominican Republic and Belize. Absorbed the Traders Bank of Canada to improve position in Ontario.
1913   Branches opened in Grenada and Guyana.
1914   *Finance Act* passed.
1915   Branches opened in Antigua, Dominica, St. Kitts, and Costa Rica.
1916   Branch opened in Venezuela.
1917   Branches opened in Nevis, Montserrat, and Tobago. Absorbed Quebec Bank.
1918   Branch opened in Spain. Absorbed Northern Crown Bank to give it a better position in Manitoba and Saskatchewan.
1919   Branches opened in Paris, Russia, Haiti, Guadeloupe, Martinique, Argentina, Brazil, and Uruguay.
1920   Branches opened in St. Lucia and Colombia.
1925   Purchased Bank of Central and South America. Opened branch in Peru.
1929   Branch opened in Panama. Black Tuesday.
1934   Bank of Canada created. Bank of Montreal ceases to be the government's bank.
1938   Bank of Canada nationalized.
1940   RBC has 65 operating units in 15 countries outside of Canada.
1944   Bretton Woods agreement signed.
1949   Bank of Canada became sole issuer of currency.
1954   RBC entered into correspondent relationship with Bank of China.
1957   Eurodollar markets created.
1958   Branch opened in Hong Kong.
1959   Branch opened in St. Vincent.
1960   RBC left Cuba.
1961   RBC installed first computer.
1964   Branch opened in Cayman Islands.
1966   Branch opened in Lebanon.
1967   Revision to *Bank Act* disallowed any single investor from owning more than 10 per cent of a chartered bank. It also disallowed the banks from owning more than 10 per cent of another Canadian corporation.
1969   Branch opened in West Germany.

1970	Orion Bank Ltd. formed in London, England. RBC branches opened in Japan and Australia. RBC now has 125 operating units in 30 countries outside of Canada.
1972	Royal Bank of Canada in Trinidad sold 51 per cent of its equity to local nationals on a five-year payment scheme, becoming the Royal Bank of Trinidad and Tobago.
1973	RBC forced to incorporate operations in Jamaica, becoming Royal Bank (Jamaica). Bretton Woods system collapsed.
1974	Branches opened in independent Africa, the Philippines, and Dubai. Basel Committee on Banking Supervision (initially the Committee of Banking Regulations and Supervisory Practices) formed.
1975	Branch opened in Singapore.
1978	Branch opened in South Korea.
1979	Branches opened in Mexico and Egypt. Gains first retail banking operation in England.
1980	Has more than 200 operating units in 45 countries outside of Canada. Acquires Banco de San Juan in Puerto Rico.
1981	Branches opened in Thailand and China.
1983	Branch opened in Taiwan.
1984	RBC left Guyana.
1985	Started to withdraw from most of the Caribbean.
1986	Branch opened in India. England's Big Bang.
1987	Canada's Little Bang.
1989	Canada–United States Free Trade Agreement went into effect.
1990	Has more than 125 operating units in 32 countries outside of Canada.
1993	Sold banks in Puerto Rico and Brazil. Merged operations with Royal Trust.
1994	Royal Trust opened office in Bermuda. North American Free Trade Agreement (NAFTA) went into effect.
1995	Branch opened in Chile.
1996	RBC and RBC Dominion Securities integrated trading functions under RBC DS Global Markets, which operated out of 20 locations including London, New York, Singapore, Montreal, and Toronto.
1998	RBC Dominion Securities opened in a number of Caribbean locations. RBC acquired First Network Bank in Atlanta, the first pure internet bank. Attempted to merge with Bank of Montreal; rejected by minister of finance.
1999	Major restructuring. Closed offices in Asia and Latin America. Acquired firms in Channel Islands.

2000	Has more than 300 offices in over 30 countries outside of Canada. Reoriented strategy around North America. Became one of the largest trust companies in Channel Islands. Acquired Dain Rauscher Wessels, a US brokerage and investment banking firm.
2001	Acquired Centura Bank in North Carolina as well as firms in Australia.
2002	Branch opened in Brunei.
2004	Global private banking offices opened in Spain and Turkey.
2005	Became member of the Australian Stock Exchange. Acquired a number of British financial firms.
2006	Created institutional investment joint venture with Dexia.
2008	Acquired Royal Bank of Trinidad and Tobago, creating one of the largest banking networks in the Caribbean with a presence in 18 countries and territories. Opened wealth management offices in India and Chile.
2009	Acquired Mourant Private Wealth, with operations in Jersey, Dubai, and Cayman Islands.
2010	Acquired London-based Bluebay Asset Management.
2012	Acquired Latin American, Caribbean, and African private banking business Coutts (wealth division of Royal Bank of Scotland). Completed acquisition of Dexia's 50 per cent stake in their joint venture.
2013	Acquired Canadian subsidiary of Ally Bank.
2015	Acquired City National Corporation.
2016	Sold RBC General Insurance Company to Aviva Canada for CAD$582 million.
2019	Acquired WayPay, a cloud-based payments fintech.
2020	COVID-19 pandemic begins. Acquired Dr. Bill, a mobile billing platform for physicians. Launched Aiden, an AI-powered electronic trading platform. Acquired Founded, a technology platform enabling businesses to automate legal tasks.
2021	Completed sale of its Eastern Caribbean banking operations to a consortium of regional banks.

ROYAL HISTORIES

Chapter One

Introduction

Corporate power is not tangential to Canadian society. Corporate power is Canadian society.
— James Eayrs (1975, p. 9)

Nowhere in the world can be found so intensive a degree of close organization as among bank interests in Canada.
— Gustavus Myers (1914/1972, p. ii)

Introduction

In *The Banks Did It*, economic sociologist Neil Fligstein (2021) comments on the vast amount of literature created in the wake of the 2008 financial crisis:

> The search for the "cause" of the crisis brought about an avalanche of books and papers on the subject. Many were journalistic accounts, some were memoirs, and still others were books rushed to press by economists, political scientists, and sociologists. (p. xi)

Just as quickly as these causes were discovered (of which, Fligstein notes, there were many), so too did there emerge a wide range of solutions. Many Marxists argued that the reform of national financial systems was not enough and that the real solution was no less than the total nationalization of the banks (Ackerman, 2012; Lapavitsas, 2013b; Patnaik, 2022; Teles, 2016). In their view, this would turn "the financial institutions that are the life-blood of global capitalism into public utilities that would facilitate, within each state, the democratization of decisions that govern investment and employment" (Panitch & Gindin, 2012, p. 340). In stark contrast, neo-Keynesians argued that the problem was not so much the power of large financial firms and their role in facilitating global capitalism but rather the fact that they received large bailouts that would subsequently commit governments to austerity programs to reduce state debt. "What the world needs now," commented American economist Paul Krugman (2012), "is for governments to step up their spending to get us out of this depression" (p. 39). Alternatively, in his now famous, *Capital in the Twenty-First Century*, French economist Thomas Piketty (2013/2014) claimed that the real solution to rising inequality was a progressive annual tax on capital; in his view, this "would make it possible to avoid an endless inegalitarian spiral while preserving competition and incentives for new instances of primitive accumulation" (p. 399).

Almost as quickly as these solutions were offered, however, their respective authors made clear to point out that they were unlikely to work. Leo Panitch and Sam Gindin (2012), for instance, made clear that any nationalization of the banks would have to rely on the "revival of a progressive economic nationalism" that has been all but "ruled out by the absence of anything like a national bourgeoisie for popular classes to ally with" (p. 340). Similarly, in the same breath that he suggested a progressive tax on capital, Piketty (2013/2014) warned his readers that such a tax would be almost impossible to achieve, since it would entail "a high level of international cooperation and regional political integration" that is not currently "within the reach of the nation-states in which earlier social compromises were hammered out" (p. 399). Joseph Stiglitz (2008), the American economist who famously repeated Milton Friedman's phrase in late 2008 that "we are all Keynesians now" (para. 1), put the matter plainly: "this global crisis requires a global response, but, unfortunately, responsibility for responding remains at the national level" (Stiglitz, 2009, para. 2).

That so many differently oriented scholars could point to the problem on one hand, and why their solution wouldn't work on the other, suggests that something else is going on – that there are larger forces at play that have made these solutions, some of which were once at least feasible during other historical periods, an utter impossibility today. In Canada, this was revealed in the lead up to the 2015 federal election. After the New Democratic Party (NDP) – Canada's once explicitly socialist, now kind of social-democratic party – was critiqued for telling voters that they would balance the budget, run no deficits, and were no danger to Canada's credit rating, Janice MacKinnon, the former NDP finance minister for Saskatchewan, admitted that it was not so much that the NDP did not want to tax the rich, but that the rules of the game had changed:

> The idea of taxing the rich is a critical 1960s NDP idea. What we had to come to grips with is, in a late twentieth, early twenty-first century economy, you can't do it ... It's a global economy, it's a competitive economy. We'd all love to tax the rich on the left, but on the ground, it no longer works. (as cited in C. Hall, 2015, paras. 17–19)

A similar event occurred during the 2019 federal election. When the Green Party proposed to implement a financial transactions tax, increase the corporate tax rate, and close the capital gains tax loophole, they were given a grade of "high uncertainty" by the Parliamentary Budget Office because of the ease at which tax evaders could escape the proposed measures (Green Party of Canada, 2019, p. 16). This reality is well supported by scholars who point out that capital today not only moves around the world with relative ease, but does so through a complicated network of tax havens that work to hide vast sums from national governments (Deneault, 2010/2011; St. Denis, 2022; Hoang, 2022; Murphy, 2017, Norfield, 2016; Trichur, 2022). One does not need an advanced degree in economics to understand why Canada's largest bank, the Royal Bank of Canada, registered 378 shell companies with Mossack Fonseca, the Panama-based law firm that was recently discovered to be helping tax evaders hide trillions from governments around the world (Kiladze & Marotte, 2016).[1]

That capital can so easily escape the nation state requires some explanation, however, since this has not always been the case. While some commentators thought that the 2008 financial crisis would lead to "a renewed assertion of the nation-state as the central locus of regulatory authority" (Germain, 2010, p. 12), or that it signalled the demise of globalization (Altman, 2009; O'Sullivan, 2019; Postelnicu et al., 2015; Summers, 2014; "Steam Has Gone Out," 2019), capital remains as global and footloose as ever, overseen by a growing network of transnational organizations and national regulatory agencies that put their recommendations into practice.[2] As political scientist Tony Porter (2014a) notes, "the

---

[1] A year later, in 2017, the Royal Bank of Canada was also implicated in the Paradise Papers, which further exposed the extent of these offshore networks (see https://offshoreleaks.icij.org).

[2] More recent statistics back up the case for ongoing, rather than declining, globalization. Citing DHL's Global Interconnectedness Index, the *Financial Times* notes that "although the [COVID-19] pandemic was a massive stress test for global

experience of transnational regulatory reform after the crisis indicates that the trends of the past three decades, which have involved a growth in transnational interdependence in financial transactions and governance, is continuing rather than reversing" (p. 5).

What reforms have emerged have been heavily impacted by industry lobbying, leading to relatively toothless policies that do little to fundamentally constrain the global reach of capital and its impacts (Chon & Fleming, 2014; Courville, 2012; Helleiner, 2013, 2014; M. Wolf, 2010). The economic historian Catherine R. Schenk (2020) portrays these reforms as simply "another turn of the wheel" (p. 8), "from regulation to deregulation and then to reregulation" (p. 12). More critically oriented scholars make similar arguments, seeing the post-crisis financial environment as evidence of the resiliency of the neo-liberal project, postponing the crisis rather than resolving it (Crouch 2009; Gamble, 2019; Helleiner, 2014; Peters, 2022; Streeck 2014, 2016; Walby, 2013). Even the former president of the National Bank of Canada, Léon Courville (2012), admits that

> nothing has happened except new tinkering with securities, disclosure and governance legislation. The game is still being played, but perhaps it is being played with more rules. I doubt that additional rules will have any effect other than, perhaps, to reinforce the tight and closed structure of the industry. (p. 20)

As economist William K. Tabb (2012) notes, efforts to bracket the crisis as the Great Recession, "with a beginning and an end followed by an economic recovery, obscure the manner in which excess financialization continues to contribute to high unemployment, extreme inequality, and stagnant living standards" (pp. 1–2). How, then, should we understand our current age of globalization, a period in which the old strategies no longer work, and the new ones seem impossible to achieve? And more importantly, what is to be done?

Globalization and the State

When we leave normal times and deal with periods of rapid social change (whether revolutionary or retrogressive), we are bound to expect even greater dislocations between the changing socioeconomic base and the

---

connectivity, it seems that integration is now higher, not lower, than before" (Tett, 2021, para. 16).

political-ideological superstructure. It is virtually a defining characteristic of such periods that all social relations become upset, volatile, fluid. Formulas that worked "as a rule" in stable times now become more variable approximations; it is necessary to go *behind* the formulas to keep close watch on the concrete patterns of change.

– Hal Draper (1977, p. 321)

One group will say that we are in an age of globalization; therefore, nation states no longer matter. The other side recognizes states still matter, so they really see there is no globalization.

– Michael Hardt (as cited in Özselçuk, 2015, p. 1)

Following Saskia Sassen (2006), my main argument in this book is that we should understand globalization as a novel historical epoch constituted by a centrifugal organizing dynamic that is drawing elements of territory, authority, and rights (TAR) away from the nation state, despite still being coded as national or operating through national domains; and that this overall process severely limits the extent to which the nation state can absorb capitalist crises or be a site of successful social reform. While significant commentary suggests that events such as the 2008 financial crisis, Brexit, the US presidential election of Donald Trump, and the COVID-19 pandemic, among others, are indicators of the return to a more nation-centred politics, my goal in this book is to highlight a variety of changes to the property relations of capitalism that make that outcome unlikely.

Yet, as the above quote by Michael Hardt demonstrates, globalization scholarship remains starkly divided on the nature, meaning, and even reality of globalization and cognate phenomena like financialization.[3]

---

3 There continues to be little consensus as to the meaning of globalization, with the term being defined in a variety of ways. Christian Fuchs (2010) provides a useful list of definitions: "'an increasing number of social processes that are indifferent to national boundaries' (Beck, 2000, 80); the 'capacity to work as a unit on a planetary scale in real time or chosen time' (Castells, 2000, 10); the 'intensification of worldwide social relations which link distant localities in such a way that local happenings are shaped by events occurring many miles away and vice versa' (Giddens, 1990, 64); the 'widening, deepening and speeding up of worldwide interconnectedness in all aspects of contemporary social life' (Held et al., 1999, 2, 15; see also Held and McGrew, 2007, 2f); 'the compression of the world as a whole' (Robertson, 1995, 40); 'circumstances where territorial space is substantially transcended' (Scholte, 1999, 12); and 'the rapid developing and ever-densening network of interconnections and interdependencies that characterize modern life' (Tomlinson, 1999, 2)" (pp. 215–16).

For the sceptics, globalization is an overstated, or even illusory phenomena – a discursive cover for the neo-liberal project at home and abroad.[4] This is because they do not see the phenomenon as anything qualitatively new; since earlier periods of capitalism were also characterized by relatively open systems of trade and commerce, they see the post-1970s period of capitalism as more or less the same, but perhaps with slightly more globalization and financialization. The geographer David Harvey (2000), for instance, writes that "something akin to 'globalization' has a long presence within the history of capitalism" (p. 54). Tabb (2009) similarly claims that "the most significant features of what is called globalization have always been part of capitalist development, even if the forms are different in different periods (including our own)" (p. 1). Analogous statements can be found when scholars refer to "today's globalization" (Panitch, 1994, p. 63), or "the recent bout of

---

Suffice to say that globalization is an essentially contested concept (Gray, 1977). So too with financialization, which has no clear definition: "For some, financialization is about finance-as-industry growing larger in its share of GDP or profitability. For others, it is about the growing power of finance in corporate decision-making via shareholder value. Financialization is also invoked to explain the growing need not only for households to borrow for everyday living, especially housing, but also for university education and basic consumption" (Bryan et al., 2020, p. 261).

4 For instance, Calhoun (2002) writes that "globalization and the coming of postnational and transnational society are often presented as matters of necessity ... economic imaginary is deployed to suggest that globalization moves of itself, and governments and citizens have only the option of adapting" (p. 147). Harvey (2005) similarly notes that neo-liberalism is typically "subsumed under the term 'globalization'" (p. 2). In a more recent edited volume, Satgar (2020) writes: "For over three decades the main buzzword of development, international relations and policy making has been 'globalisation.' It is a descriptive concept used to characterise processes underway in the global political economy related to production, trade, finance, technology and labour. It has been an overworked term, sometimes evoking the metaphor of a happy 'global village' in which all countries are equal and in which there is smooth mobility not just of finance and goods, but also of labour and technology. The embrace of globalisation has also promised that all ships will rise as the tides of competition and winds of integration buttress the engines of national economies. Inequality and poverty will all be history in this global market utopia according to the promises and rhetoric of globalisation discourse. Or more poignantly, we would all be Americans and would all have been conscripted to the 'end of history' in which the US standard of liberal democracy was also our common standard" (p. 1). Similar accounts can be found in a number of texts: see Anievas, 2008; Boyer & Drache, 1996; Bromley, 2003; Callinicos, 2009; J.B. Foster, 2003; Desai, 2013; D. Gordon, 1988; Harvey, 2003, 2009; Helleiner, 1997; Hirst & Thompson, 1996/2015; Kapstein, 1994; Panitch, 1994; Panitch & Gindin, 2005, 2012; Sakellaropoulos, 2018; Satgar, 2020; J. Smith, 2016; Stokes, 2005; Tabb, 2009, 2012; Wallerstein, 2000; Weiss, 1997, 1999, 2003; Wood, 2002a, 2007.

globalization" (Harvey, 2009, p. 98). Immanuel Wallerstein (2000) sums up this view when he writes that "globalization is a misleading concept, since what is described as globalization has been happening for 500 years" (p. 251).

Whether borrowed from Marx's (1894/1993b) claim that "the world market itself forms the basis for this [capitalist] mode of production" (p. 451), or Wallerstein's (2010) own concept of a capitalist world-system, the general idea held by these scholars is that globalization does not represent a unique period within the history of capitalism but is instead simply the most recent iteration of capital's inherent need to expand. "They may call it globalization or postmodernity," Ellen Meiksins Wood (1998) writes, "but it is really just capitalism" (p. 8). In viewing globalization as the resurgence of a pre-existing tendency, these authors do not see the phenomenon as challenging or transforming the territorial nation states that continue make up the global political economy; as they frequently point out, nation states are not only the "authors and enforcers" (Panitch & Gindin, 2005, p. 101) of globalization, but "global capitalism is more than ever a global system of national states" (E.M. Wood, 2002a, p. 25). As a result, it is typical for these scholars to view our current period as a new version of the earlier "age of imperialism" that characterized the late nineteenth and early twentieth centuries (Bromley, 2003; Callinicos, 2009; J.B. Foster, 2003; Harvey, 2003; Norfield, 2016; Panitch & Gindin, 2012; Sakellaropoulos, 2018; Satgar, 2020; J. Smith, 2016; E.M. Wood, 2003). This is also the view taken in the field of Canadian political economy, in which globalization and financialization are used as evidence to reproduce a long-standing debate as to whether Canada is a dependency of the American empire, or a secondary imperialist power in its own right (Albo & Klassen, 2013; Burgess, 2000, 2002; Carroll & Klassen, 2010; T. Gordon, 2010; Hurtig, 2003; Ikeda, 2004; Kellogg, 2005, 2009, 2015; Klassen, 2008, 2009, 2014; McQuaig, 2007; Seccareccia, 2007; Stanford, 2008, 2014; Watkins, 2007).[5]

---

5 I review this debate in more detail elsewhere (Garrod, 2018), but the main debate is whether domestic or foreign capitalists dominate Canada's economy. The dependency interpretation views Canada's dependency as resulting from the country's long-standing domination by foreign capital, mainly British and American (e.g., Drache, 1977; Levitt, 1970; Lumsden, 1970; Naylor, 1975/1997; Teeple, 1972). Those who hold this view argue that the country's relative underdevelopment as compared to the United States is the result of a historically dominant mercantile-financial ruling class whose interest in short-term gains has ended up orienting the economy towards resource extraction and branch-plant manufacturing, thus leading to low productivity

While other scholars agree that the outward expansion of capital is a long-standing feature of capitalism, and that nation states are central to the legal construction of contemporary globalization and financialization, they see today's version as being fundamentally different, representative not of a resurgent tendency but as an epochal transformation of capitalism that involves the rise of a transnational capitalist class (TCC) and transnational state apparatus (TNS) composed of nation states, inter- and supranational organizations, and political/economic forums that function to reproduce the conditions for capital accumulation across the globe (Burbach & W.I. Robinson, 1999; Demirović, 2011; J. Harris, 2005; Liodakis, 2005, 2010, 2016; W.I. Robinson, 2001, 2003, 2004, 2012a, 2012b, 2014, 2017, 2018, 2020, 2022; W.I. Robinson & J. Harris, 2000; Sklair, 2001; Sklair & Robbins, 2002).[6] Where, in the previous

---

and technological imports. Canada is thus understood to be a "vanishing country" (Hurtig, 2003) that is increasingly being drawn into the American empire as a result of a ruling class who press "for policies – both domestic and foreign – that please the US elite" (McQuaig, 2007, p. 59). The solution, these scholars argue, is to push for greater economic self-reliance, which would enable Canada to realize its own destiny. In contrast, the imperialist interpretation takes issue with the idea that Canada continues to be dominated by foreign capital. Continuing the argument begun by earlier critics of the dependency approach (e.g., Carroll, 1986; Kaufman, 1985; S. Moore & Wells, 1975; McNally, 1981; Niosi, 1985; Resnick, 1982; Veltmeyer, 1987), scholars arguing the contemporary version note that a substantial majority of assets within Canada are now owned and controlled by Canadian capitalists and that this represents "a long term tendency, well entrenched now for more than 30 years" (Kellogg, 2005, p. 36). This dichotomous view of Canada as either a dominated or dominating power was problematized earlier by Wallace Clement (1975, 1977a) and Glen Williams (1988, 1994). They argued that while Canada sits "firmly within the economically developed centre of the international political economy" (G. Williams, 1988, p. 15; see also Clement, 1977a, p. 130), it also had a pattern of development that more closely resembled that of peripheral nations. As such, they argued that it is more accurate to treat Canada as a zone or subsystem of a "global capitalism divided along class lines" (Mertins-Kirkwood, 2014, p. 17), as opposed to a self-contained actor responding to external forces; while Canadian capital certainly has imperial ambitions, subordinate classes experience the effects of a dependent economy first-hand. The study presented here is an attempt to tread this more nuanced middle ground.

6 The most popular theorist of the TNS, sociologist William I. Robinson (2004), defines it as "an emerging network that comprises transformed and externally integrated national states, together with the supranational economic and political forums, and has not yet acquired any centralized institutional form" (p. 88). In more recent work, Robinson (2014) has added some key modifiers: "We can conceptualize a TNS apparatus as a loose network comprised of inter- and supranational political and economic institutions together with national state apparatuses that have been penetrated and transformed by transnational forces, and have not yet acquired and may never acquire any centralized form" (p. 67). George Liodakis (2010) is another

national epoch, capitalists might have turned to their own nation states to pursue their class interests, these scholars claim that in our current epoch of globalization, the transnational fraction of the capitalist class is attempting "to convert the entire world into a single unified field for global accumulation" (W.I. Robinson, 2014, p. 7). They argue that as a result of this process, the class relations of global capitalism are now "so deeply internalized within every nation-state that the classical image of imperialism as a relation of external domination is outdated" (W.I. Robinson, 2007, p. 23). The real phenomenon that requires explaining according to them is thus "the contradiction between the descending form of capitalism organized around the nation-state system and an arising form of accumulation organized in the transnational world order" (J. Harris, 2005, p. 329).

Subject to a number of valid critiques in various publications and symposia,[7] this side's emphasis on global phenomena and their use of arbitrary periodization schemas has often left them scrambling to

---

theorist who claims that the TNS is "constituted by international organizations (UN, IMF, World Bank, WTO, OECD, and so on), in close interconnection with the most powerful capitalist states and various international capitalist groupings (G7 or G20, World Economic Forum, the Trilateral, and so on), and plays a crucial and increasingly powerful role in forming the conditions for cooperation, the basic policies and the strategy for capital on a world level" (p. 63). Alex Demirović (2011) provides a similar definition of what he terms the "transnational network state," in which there is an emerging "apparatus that consists of an ensemble of state apparatuses on a local, national and international scale as well as formerly private organizations" (p. 56). Similar to other definitions, Demirović (2011) sees the transnational network state as having the specific function "of organizing the transnational element, developing policy and controlling the reproduction of the global accumulation process in the interest of this capital sector" (p. 53).

7 The most common critiques of the TNS are that transnational forms of accumulation are not particularly new (Carroll, 2012, 2013; Lacher, 2006; Macartney & Shields, 2011; McMichael, 2001; Tabb, 2009; Teschke & Lacher, 2007; E.M. Wood, 2002a, 2007); that TNS theory is based on a mechanical relationship with the rise of transnational capital (Bieler & Morton 2014; Block, 2001; Cammack, 2009; Carroll, 2012; Mann, 2001; McMichael, 2001; Tabb, 2009); that TNS theory makes a category error by including supranational forums as part of the TNS (Arrighi, 2001; Mann, 2001; Van der Pijl, 2001); that TNS theory is based on an arbitrary periodization schema (J. Moore, 2001; E.M. Wood, 2007); and that TNS theory makes the global into an abstract space, detached from the materiality of national forms of territorialization (Cammack, 2009; Carroll, 2012; McMichael, 2001; J. Moore, 2001). Critics also claim that the reality and extent of transnational capital is overstated (Anievas, 2008; Panitch & Gindin 2012; Prashad, 2012; Starrs, 2017; E.M. Wood, 2002a), and that nation states are not only the principal agents of globalization but remain powerful actors in the global economy (Barrow, 2005; Panitch & Gindin, 2012; Van der Pijl, 2001). Lastly, as Carroll and Sapinski (2016) accurately point out, "in practice, the distinction between 'national'

explain exactly why globalization represents an epochal shift – especially since, as their critics point out, capital has always been at least tendentially global (Harvey, 2000; Tabb, 2009; E.M. Wood, 2002b, 2007).[8] Furthermore, their research has often lacked the level of specificity needed to support their claims of an emerging TNS, leading many scholars to reject it on the basis that it "is not a state, transnational or otherwise" (Cammack, 2009, p. 89), and thus "an unnecessary theoretical construct" (p. 90). These issues are additionally compounded by claims that the TCC has directly instrumentalized the TNS,[9] despite significant evidence that capitalist networks remain predominantly national (Klassen & Carroll, 2011). As William K. Carroll (2012) points out, the hegemony of transnational capital "has been grounded less in the agency of a dominant class fraction imposing its will and more in the enhanced structural power that capital has attained" (p. 367).

---

capitalists and 'transnational' capitalists is blurry" (p. 46), making it difficult to determine which fraction of the capitalist class is responsible for these changes.

8 For example, W.I. Robinson's (2004) schema is split into four capitalist epochs, each denoted by a symbolic date: the first, running from 1492 to 1789, is the epoch of mercantilism and primitive accumulation; the second, running from 1789 to 1900, is the epoch of competitive or classical capitalism; the third, running from 1900 to 1970, is the epoch of corporate or monopoly capitalism; and the fourth, running from 1970 until today, is the epoch of globalization (pp. 4–5). In contrast, Liodakis (2005) distinguishes three epochs based on technology, the organizational subsumption of labour and resources under capital, the concentration of capital, and the varying forms of state authority and regulation: 1492–1900, the epoch of laissez-faire capitalism; 1900–1970s, the epoch of monopoly capitalism; and 1970s onwards, the epoch of globalization (p. 342). While both schemas are helpful for demonstrating the various historical forms of capitalist accumulation and their attendant social forms, they both fail to get at what is explicitly national or global about them. In other words, they fail to make the connections between these forms of accumulation and their attendant geographic political and economic expressions.

9 W.I. Robinson (2004) writes, for instance, that "the TCC has directly instrumentalized this TNS apparatus, exercising a form of TNS power through the multilayered configuration of the TNS" (p. 88). In response to criticism, W.I. Robinson (2014) has since tempered this view, referring to this class as an emergent TCC that "operates across borders in numerous countries and has attempted to convert the whole world into a single unified field for global accumulation" (p. 7). Liodakis (2005) similarly writes that "a merger is taking shape among fractions of the ruling classes beyond national frontiers, crystallized in an international oligarchy or transnational capitalist class" (p. 346). Likewise, Demirović (2011) writes that the capitalist state "no longer organizes power blocs on a national level but acquires the contours of a state that organizes a transnational fraction of the ruling classes" (pp. 52–3).

But I question whether we need to go so far in our critiques. Part of Marx's (1939/1971) method, as outlined in *Grundrisse*,[10] is to go behind the political and economic categories of our present in order to examine the historically specific social relationships that make them possible. As such, I want to entertain the notion that just because some aspects of globalization are not as global as they have been made out to be does not mean that they are necessarily national. While I very much share the view that globalization represents an epochal transformation of the global political economy, it is one taking place inside the nation state to a greater degree than most scholars realize, and in ways that obfuscate the nature and extent of transformation. As Sassen (2006) notes, for instance, many globalizing processes do not scale at the global level but are instead located deep within national domains and remain coded as such; all too commonly, however, these processes get "absorbed into conceptual frameworks that equate their location in a national setting with their being national, which obscures their global dimensions" (p. 4). This is particularly the case with capital, whose national elements (such as corporate board interlocks, corporate domicile, or the nationality of ownership) are frequently used to disprove the existence of the TNS by suggesting that the reality or extent of global capital is overstated (see, for example, Anievas, 2008; Panitch & Gindin, 2012; Prashad, 2012; Starrs, 2017; E.M. Wood, 2002a).

The effort, here, is thus double-sided. On the one hand, I want to distance myself from the idea that since the nation state is still here that it still works the same as it always has – that is, within a competitive interstate framework in which nation states act solely on behalf of their national capitals, which are typically taken to mean a country's largest firms.[11] This is partly because the extent and nature of transnational

---

10 See the section, "The Method of Political Economy" (Marx, 1939/1971, pp. 33–43). As Kain (1980) explains, "Each category is stamped and molded by the particular structure of the period. It will not be exactly the same category which appears in a later period. Thus the later categories and their structure cannot be deduced from the earlier; each category can only be fully understood in the context of the structure of categories to which it belongs. Categories and their structure thus have to be fundamentally reunderstood in each new epoch" (p. 296). See also Ollman's (2003) chapter, "Studying History Backward: A Neglected Feature of Marx's Materialist Conception of History."
11 Wallerstein (2000) provides a succinct version of this conceptualization: "States are by definition rivals, bearing responsibility to different sets of rival firms" (p. 56). But we could make the case with Marx (1894/1993b) as well: "The national character of the Mercantile System is therefore not a mere slogan in the mouths of its spokesmen. Under the pretext of only being concerned with the wealth of the nation and the

corporate activity today makes it extremely difficult to determine corporate nationality and what sorts of claims we can make on that basis. As Coleman and Porter (2003) note, for instance, the strength of Canada's banking sector has long been the basis on which Canadian political economists have staked at least part of their claims about Canadian development.[12] Since the 1980s, however, Canada's financial system has undergone significant changes that mirror a wider transformation of capitalism itself. The removal of capital controls and deregulation – i.e., the removal of the long-standing barriers separating banks and insurance, investment, and trust companies – has made possible a sort of placelessness of money that is not only reflected in ever-present financial crises but also in "onion-like layers of transnational ownership" (W.I. Robinson, 2014, p. 34) that continue to blur the lines of corporate nationality. Although most large Canadian corporations remain Canadian owned and controlled, and Canada exports more capital than it imports – a long-standing feature of imperial states, as many Canadian political economists tell us (Burgess, 2002; T. Gordon & Webber, 2018; Kellogg, 2015; Klassen, 2014) – these indicators do not actually tell us much about the changing character of the Canadian nation state in a period in which investment in all directions has risen starkly.[13] Not only is some of this renewed domestic ownership the result of foreign investment leaving Canada for greener pastures elsewhere, but it begs larger questions about the reorganization of capitalism itself.[14]

---

sources of assistance of the state, they actually declare that the interests of the capitalist class, and enrichment in general, are the final purpose of the state. At the same time, however, they show their awareness that the development of the interests of capital and the capitalist class, of capitalist production, has become the basis of a nation's power and predominance in modern society" (p. 921).

12 For dependency theorists, this strength signifies Canada's historical over-reliance on commerce relative to production and is thus indicative of the country's weakness; for imperialist theorists, this strength is reflective of the country's advanced industrial status by virtue of the "central role played by finance capital in coordinating the economy and extracting revenues from abroad that is characteristic of the largest and most developed capitalist countries" (Coleman & Porter, 2003, p. 243).

13 Canadian direct investment abroad was more than 19 times larger in 2020 than in 1987. Foreign direct investment in Canada was more than nine times larger in 2020 than in 1987. See Table 36–10–0008–01 in Statistics Canada (2024).

14 Regarding the character of post-1970s outward capital flows, see Baragar & Seccareccia (2008); Marchak (1985); Soederberg (2000); and Sweeny (1997). Snyder's (2018) article in the *Financial Post* highlights capital's recent exodus from Canada. Similar comments are found in recent speeches by the CEO of RBC, Dave McKay (2018a, 2018b, 2019).

The largest portion of Canadian outward investment, for example, is in finance and insurance, with the top destinations being the United States, the United Kingdom, and Luxembourg, a well-known tax haven.[15] Is Canada dominating these countries? It seems unlikely.

The essence of this question was brought up earlier by Patricia Marchak (1985). Although she did not use the term globalization, she was clear to point out that the inherent mobility of capital makes it difficult to locate Canada's relative position in the global political economy by virtue of the composition of Canadian capital. As she notes:

> Capital is mobile, Canadian capital no less than any other. It will flow into Canadian industry if there are higher margins of profit to be gained there than in Hong Kong or Alabama. It will flow into industry if there is more to be gained there than in loans on the international markets. This is true today, and must surely have been true in times past. (p. 683)

Noting that this mobility has only increased over time, Marchak points out that this means that some Canadian capital today is now "embedded in transnational corporations which have long ceased to have national domiciles; some in multinational corporations still operating to the advantage of one of the world's regions more than others" (p. 683). The point is that as Canadian firms globalize and financialize their activities, it becomes increasingly difficult to identify the significance of their nationality and, thus, what sorts of claims we can make on that basis.[16]

Take, for example, Canada's largest bank, the Royal Bank of Canada. Despite being headquartered in Canada, the Royal Bank of Canada (2021a) operates in 29 countries around the world, and half of its principal subsidiaries are incorporated in tax havens such as Luxembourg,

---

15 Statistics Canada (2021) notes that finance and insurance constituted a 37.7 per cent share of all outward Canadian investment in 2020.

16 Marchak (1985) gives an example of the complexity of post-1970 outward capital flows: "As the international portion, and capital originally tied to US parent firms, moves elsewhere for cheaper operating costs or new resources, the balance under Canadian control naturally increases in proportion. As well, the sales of Canadian properties in extractive industries (where most of the change has occurred) have permitted Canadian companies to expand within Canada; they have not pushed American companies away, but have rather picked up the pieces. In forestry they have picked up pieces that includes denuded lands and antiquated mills, facts not revealed in Statistics Canada data on ownership" (p. 683).

the Grand Cayman Islands, and Barbados.[17] Magna International (2021), the world's largest automotive supplier, operates in 28 countries and, despite being headquartered in Aurora, Ontario, similarly has almost half of its principal subsidiaries incorporated in tax havens, including Delaware, Luxembourg, and Hong Kong. Prior to selling Weston Foods in 2021, George Weston Limited (2020), the owner of Canada's largest food and drug retail companies (including Shoppers Drug Mart, Loblaw, and Joe Fresh) had 33 production facilities across North America, with subsidiaries incorporated in Ontario and Delaware, alongside global distribution networks. The Weston family also owns Holt Renfrew, luxury London department store Selfridges, and, through its Wittington Investments company, Associated British Foods (2021), which is one of the world's largest food, ingredients, and retail companies; it has operations in 53 countries "across Europe, Africa, the Americas, Asia and Australia" (p. 2), and it has repeatedly been implicated in tax evasion schemes.[18] Suncor (2021), initially an American branch plant, has subsidiaries in Canada, the United States (Delaware, again), and the United Kingdom, which represent their interests in the North Sea. Even Bell Canada (now BCE Inc.) had interests in 74 countries by 1976 (Wilson, 2000).

Deneault and Sacher (2012) similarly point out that 75 per cent of the world's mining firms are incorporated in Canada, with 60 per cent of them registered on the Toronto Stock Exchange, "even though their capital is not necessarily Canadian in origin" (p. 16). Many of these so-called Canadian firms do not possess a single claim in Canada and are incorporated here only for the various benefits provided to them by the Canadian state. In a report on how Canadian companies use trade agreements, Mertins-Kirkwood (2022) points out that some of these so-called Canadian firms using investor-dispute mechanisms against poorer countries are in fact "multinational compan[ies] treaty shopping in Canada" (p. 21). While a significant body of literature argues that the Canadian state is imperialist because it acts on behalf of Canadian mining firms around the world, nowhere does this research point out what, exactly, makes any of these firms explicitly Canadian except their location of incorporation (Deneault & Sacher, 2012; T. Gordon, 2010; T. Gordon & Webber, 2008, 2011, 2013, 2014, 2016; Veltmeyer, 2013a, 2013b).

---

17 See Deneault (2015) for more details on the relationship between Canada's chartered banks and tax havens. A *CBC News* article by Dubinsky (2016) outlines the typical process by which corporate actors use Barbados to avoid taxes.
18 For instance, see Boffey (2013).

With numerous foreign subsidiaries, links to transnational ownership groups, and listings on foreign exchanges, by most metrics, these firms ceased being explicitly Canadian a long time ago.[19] As Laura Macdonald and I point out elsewhere, "making the assumption that 'Canadian-based' mining capital is the same thing as 'Canadian' mining capital ignores the fact that regardless of ownership networks or 'home base,' all corporations have to deal with the fundamental nature of competition within an increasingly global system of capitalism" (Garrod & L. Macdonald, 2016, pp. 111–12). This is not to suggest that foreign capital now dominates the Canadian state, or that Canadian capital does not have imperial ambitions, but rather that the ongoing concentration and centralization of capital has led to the emergence of new property relations that enable corporations to organize in new ways, move more freely around the world, and limit the extent to which nation states can legally intervene in their accumulation activities. To argue that globalization is nothing new, then, is to ignore the ways in which these new property relations fundamentally problematize the accuracy of conceptual frameworks premised on traditional geographical markers rooted in different sets of property relations. As Harvey (2007) puts it, it no longer makes sense to say things like "'the specific rules of the world economy have been transformed, in keeping with the changing needs of US capital' because it is not entirely clear ... that the category of 'US capital' ... makes sense any more" (p. 67).[20]

On the other hand, I also want to escape from what Sassen (2006) refers to as the endogeneity trap: the tendency to confine the study of globalization to explicitly global processes and institutions. As she notes, simply pointing to the "features of the global amounts to a description but not an explanation of globalization" (p. 4). This is especially the case in the literature on the TNS, in which supranational institutions, global production relations, and a transnational fraction of the capitalist class are all used as evidence that a new state form is

---

19 A recent study by Statistics Canada breaks down the current reality (Schaffter & Fortier-Labonte, 2019). Only 0.8 per cent of all enterprises operating in Canada are considered multinational enterprises (MNEs), which they define as a group of two or more legal entities that are required to prepare consolidated financial statements, where one of the legal entities of the group resides outside Canada. Although these MNEs are less than 1 per cent of all enterprises, they hold 67 per cent of all assets in the Canadian economy, with Canadian majority-owned MNEs owning 49 per cent of the total, compared to 18 per cent for foreign majority-owned MNEs.

20 Similarly, as political scientist Kanishka Jayasuriya notes: "What is clear is that the idea of 'national capital,' or indeed, national developmentalism, is simply not viable in the current circumstances" (as cited in Sprague, 2010, p. 133).

in the making, without much attention given to the transformation of the nation state itself.[21] As Philip McMichael (2001) notes, "the concept of the 'transnational state' speaks to the metamorphosis of the national state as much as it speaks to the elaboration of multilateral institutions to regulate global circuits of capital and commodities" (p. 203). While the nation state remains a fundamental part of globalization and financialization, it is clear that "its sovereign powers have changed along with the range over which state effects are felt" (Harvey, 2007, p. 67). As Carroll and Sapinski (2016) point out, for example, globalization and financialization have radically altered the role of the nation-state in interstate competition:

> In international competition, the state's predominant role shifted from that of promoting "its" capitalists as leading agents of a national economy requiring robust effective demand (as in Keynesian and social-democratic industrial strategies), to that of promoting its territory as an attractive site for transnationally mobile investment intent on cutting its costs of production to the bone. (p. 40)

Similarly, as pointed out by Stephen Gill (1992) through his concept of "new constitutionalism," a significant part of what we refer to as globalization has been the emergence of a variety of different "efforts to insulate important economic agencies and agents from popular scrutiny and accountability, and thus to narrow democratic control of the economy" (p. 269). Whether expressed in the deregulation of national

---

21 Carroll (2012) notes, for example, that "an overemphasis on fractional struggle also underplays the importance of structure in the dynamics of capital accumulation and class formation. [William] Robinson's [2012b] assertion that transnational capital is the hegemonic fraction on a world scale, imposing its direction on the global economy and shaping 'the character of production and social life everywhere,' downplays the growing structural power of capital (Gill & Law, 1989) and the tendency for transnational accumulation to transform the field of decision-making even for local capitalists, states, and other actors ... For firms and even state actors, the fact that competitors function in a globalized field is enough to lead to the embrace of a standpoint of global capital ... one need not 'liaise' with the transnational capitalist class to develop this perspective. It is this structurally grounded shift in the general horizons of economic calculation – for various agents at various sites of the world system – that has marked the most recent era of globalization" (p. 367). The point was ultimately made much earlier by Poulantzas (1974/1975), who noted that "in reality it is the specific structure of each social formation that is reorganized with regard to the internationalization of capital" (p. 82).

financial systems, or the creation of private zones of autonomy that allow powerful economic actors to escape national-level regulations (and here, we can include things like free trade agreements, special processing zones, tax havens, dark pools, shadow banking, and temporary foreign-worker programs), each involves a highly specific reorientation of rights (i.e., nationally enforced property relations), the result of which demarcates a particular territory in which the nation state is restricted from constraining economic actions, thereby insulating them from potential democratic interventions.[22]

The ability to effectively escape national regulations not only restricts the policy options available to different levels of government but also forces them to borrow vast sums from large financial institutions to make up for lost tax revenue. Similarly, the investor–state dispute settlement (ISDS) mechanisms found in many trade agreements grant transnational corporations (TNCs) the right to sue national and subnational governments for policies that work to restrict their ability to accumulate capital. As Leo Panitch (1994) made clear many years ago, these agreements thus work to transform nation states into "authors of a regime which defines and guarantees, through international treaties with constitutional effect, the global and domestic rights of capital" (p. 64). Taken together, these changes not only work to pervert the competitive party system that sits at the heart of liberal democracy, making it "into a sham of competition between political parties with more or less the same agenda" (Teeple, 2007, p. 141), but also raise larger questions about the transformation of the nation state and the novelty of globalization as a historical period. As such, my goal is not to defend the theory of the TNS as it currently stands, nor is it yet another attempt to prove which group of capitalists now dominates Canada's domestic market. Instead, I want to use a more nuanced interpretive lens to highlight how the property relations of capitalism are changing, and how, in the process, "particular components of the national state begin to function as the institutional home for the operation of powerful dynamics constitutive or critical for 'global capital'" (Sassen, 2006, p. 223). It is my contention that this process fundamentally constrains the extent to which the nation state can be a site of successful social reform.

---

22 There are numerous examples analyzed in the literature on global political economy; see, for example, Clarkson & Wood (2010); Deneault (2011); Gill & Cutler (2014); McBride (2011); Pistor (2019); Neveling (2015); Nichols (2018); Sassen (2014a).

Historical Property Regimes as Assemblages of Territory, Authority, and Rights

All property relations in the past have continually been subject to historical change consequent upon the change in historical conditions.
– Karl Marx & Friedrich Engels (1848/1978b, p. 484)

Political economy is the study of power derived from or contingent on a system of property rights; the historical development of power relationships; and the cultural and social embodiments of them.
– Patricia Marchak (1985, p. 673)

The position of those who see globalization as nothing new is typically based on one of two periodization schemas that are then used to disprove the notion that there is anything qualitatively different about today's version: (1) that there have long been transnational trade networks (e.g., Arrighi, 1994/2010; Harvey, 2000; Tabb, 2009; Wallerstein, 2000); or (2) that there is nothing in globalization that disrupts the private property relations that have long defined the capitalist mode of production (e.g., Lacher, 2006; Teschke & Lacher, 2007; E.M. Wood, 2002a, 2007). In both schemas, the nation state is essentially understood to act as it always has, on behalf of its national capitals, which are typically represented by the country's most dominant firms. E.M. Wood (2007) provides a good critique of the first version by noting that it neglects the specific character of the very property relations that brought capitalism into being. Her own alternative, however, fails to register how the property relations of capitalism today are changing or the ways in which those changes are subsequently transforming the role of the nation state.[23] As such, I want to make a slightly different

---

23 In my view, E.M. Wood's (2007) critique overlooks the many changes to property over the history of capitalism that have significantly altered how that mode of production functions and is organized over time. A great example is the coming of the modern corporation, which fundamentally transformed "the nature of the rights, entitlements, and obligations bundled with the ownership of productive enterprises" (Roy, 1997, p. 11). As Henwood (1998) notes, the shift from direct ownership to the ownership of shares "enabled a whole class to own an economy's productive assets, rather than being bound to a specific property as they once were" (p. 13). The emergence of the modern corporation thus made possible a "tremendous expansion in the scale of production and enterprises which would be impossible for individual capitals" (Marx, 1894/1993b, p. 567). Only in the most general, abstract sense is capitalism the same thing down through the ages. Differentiating modes

argument: rather than focusing on whether the capitalist mode of production (and thus, capital) is still organized on national lines, or in the process of becoming global, I want to instead put forth the proposition that the national and the global are better understood as different property regimes. Doing so should make clearer how, by virtue of the movement of the rights of capital and the authority over those rights to the transnational level, the nation state is being transformed into a transnational state; that is, a state that acts as a capability for globalizing capitals, no matter where they reside.

To do this, I want to start like Marx (1939/1971) and blow up the category of the state to examine what it consists of and how we can track this entity over time.[24] Despite long-standing debates on the nature, role, and even existence of the state, a few general points should help elicit a clearer understanding of the transformation at hand (Barrow, 1993; Jessop, 2016). The first is that "the" state does not exist.[25] The

---

of production at such a high level of abstraction thus fails to address the need to distinguish changes within them – especially those that have a significant impact on how people are able to reproduce their lives.

24 Kain (1980) provides a good overview of Marx's approach: "The new method which Marx elaborates in the *Grundrisse* and employs in *Capital* he calls the 'dialectic method.' It begins by considering general characteristics common to different historical periods of production so that by comparison it will be able to identify elements which are not general but specific to the historical period in question. It follows from this that we cannot simply and straightaway begin to study a historical period. The method does not begin with the actual empirically given economic reality, the real and the concrete, just as it presents itself to us. Economists of the seventeenth century, Marx tells us, began this way, and their first task was to subject this actual living whole to analysis in order to establish a set of simple abstract concepts, such as division of labor, value, money, and so forth. Only at this point was it possible to begin to distinguish specific from common characteristics, and only at this point could the real construction of economic systems begin.

Capital, for example, begins with an analysis of such a concept, the commodity, the main category, 'the economic cell-form,' of capitalism. One then seeks to discover the relations which hold between abstract categories and to trace out their interconnection in the epoch being studied. One ascends from simple categories toward a conceptual grasp of the whole as a 'rich totality of many determinations and relations.' Only in this way does an adequate scientific grasp of the concrete replace the vague chaotic impression one had at the start. The concrete, for Marx, is the organized and articulated concentration of many determinations and relations. It is not given at the start for thought but is the outcome of a process of analysis and investigation" (pp. 294–5).

25 As Miliband (1969) notes, "There is one preliminary problem about the state which is very seldom considered, yet which requires attention if the discussion of its nature and role is to be properly focused. This is the fact that 'the state' is not a thing, that it does not, as such, exist. What 'the state' stands for is a number of particular

state is not a unitary entity or object but rather a complex assemblage of "institutions, agencies, and practices that is more or less extensive, more or less connected with economic and other social relations, and at best, only ever relatively unified" (Jessop, 2016, pp. 17–18). The second is that this assemblage plays an important role in enforcing the property relations of a social formation; that is, the historically specific rights, claims, entitlements, and obligations that define and structure the relationships between people and things.[26] As Teeple (2000) notes, "these are the rights that comprise the main principles that inform the legal framework institutionalized by the state" and, as such, "define the fundamental basis on which relations between real, material contending interests are played out" (p. 83).[27] The third point is that the state does not have any content of its own other than that determined by the

---

institutions which, together, constitute its reality, and which interact as parts of what may be called the state system" (p. 49). The point is also made lucidly by Abrams (1988): "The internal and external relations of political and governmental institutions (the state-system) can be studied effectively without postulating the reality of the state. So in particular can their involvements with economic interests in an overall complex of domination and subjection" (p. 75).

26 The legal scholar Joseph W. Singer (2000) provides a useful description of property as a social relationship: "Property law defines entitlements and obligations that shape the contours of social relations. Property is something we must collectively define and construct. It is not given to us whole; it does not emerge fully formed like Athena from Zeus's head. It is closer to a piece of music that unfolds over time. Like music, property gets its sense of stability from the ongoing creation and resolution of various forms of tension. The tensions that inform property are the tensions inherent in social relations. The solutions to the problems of property conflicts lie in understanding the connection between property and human relationships. Relationships sometimes form stable patterns, but they are also ongoing and constantly renegotiated. They may even end. Their beginnings and endings, their shape and character over time, are topics of intense human interest. And perhaps surprisingly, it turns out that the law of property is intimately connected with them. Judging whether a property right is justified requires us to consider the ways in which the recognition of legal rights in property structures social relations" (pp. 13–14).

27 This point is shared by both neo-Marxists (e.g., Poulantzas, 1968/2018) and neo-Weberians alike. Mann (1984) writes, for instance, that "the state is an arena, the condensation, the crystallization, the summation of social relations within its territory" (p. 208). In this sense, as Wallace Clement (1977b) points out, the primary role of the state in capitalist societies is to enforce and defend the rights of private property: "to change the economic functions of private property would be to alter radically the fundamental role of the state" (p. 226). Wendy Brown (1992) similarly notes that "however deeply and variously involved the state may be with capitalist accumulation and legitimation, the state's capitalist *basis* remains its guarantee of private ownership as private property rights" (p. 15).

rights it enforces and defends. In other words, the state does not possess its own logic or interests, but is part of a wider social totality defined by the specific property relations that organize how a society reproduces itself.[28] As Marx (1844) once put it, "the state and the organization of society are not two different things. The state is the organization of society" (para. 52). The fourth is that in changing the pre-existing system of rights to benefit certain organized groups, the struggle between these groups will end up transforming the role and nature of the state; on this basis, the history of rights should thus be understood as "the history of changing modes of production and their respective social relations" (Teeple, 2007, p. 137).[29] From this it follows methodologically that if we want to understand how the nation state is transforming, then we need to understand how the system of rights that sustains capitalism is changing.

To do this, I suggest blending the above insights into the organizing role of property with the analytical framework developed by Saskia Sassen (2006) in *Territory, Authority, Rights*. Her primary claim is that many globalizing processes do not scale at the global level but are instead often located within national domains and remain coded as such; this means that we should not rely on labels such as "national" and "global" to indicate the specific level of operation. She suggests instead that we treat the national and global as different assemblages of territory, authority, and rights (TAR). By disaggregating these categories into their constitutive elements, we are thus able to avoid comparing them as "complex wholes" (p. 5), treating them instead as complex

---

28 This is not to suggest that state managers or military officials, for instance, do not have their own interests, but rather that the state does not, as such, possess its own interests because it is merely an institutional ensemble through which real people act.

29 This approach is one suggested, but not often taken, by Marx and Engels (1932/1978a) in *The German Ideology* (see, for example, Balakrishnan, 2015). The concept of a mode of production was used to explain the emergence of capitalism and distinguish it qualitatively from other historical forms of the division of labour, mainly feudalism. Empirically, it refers to the combination of the productive forces (raw materials and labour power) and associated property relations of an age. The concept came out of Marx's critiques of Hegel, Bauer, and the classical political economists (among others) for their failure to explain civil society, the sphere of private interests that would later become known as the capitalist economy. Where other writers sought to explain the emergence of this type of society on the basis of human nature or the development of the human mind, Marx (1859/1978b) argued that it was instead the result of a transformation in "the material conditions of life" (p. 4) – that is, the result of the long process by which mobile private property came to dominate feudal landed property.

relation systems whose capabilities (defined as institutionalizations of TAR) eventually reach tipping points, leading them to support a new organizing logic.[30] Through this nuanced macroscopic view, we are thus better able to highlight the "foundational differences between the world scale of several earlier phases of the world economy and today's global economy" (p. 14). More importantly, we avoid having to posit that the "ascendance of a new order necessarily means the end of the old order" (p. 9), as is often done in the globalization debates.

Although Sassen has been criticized for not explicitly analyzing class (W.I. Robinson, 2009), her framework can easily incorporate the above insights into the relationship between class and the state with a slight tweak that orients it more directly towards property. This is possible because all property regimes imply a territory over which rights apply, an authority to enforce them, and specific rights, entitlements, or claims. As many scholars make clear, historical forms of territory, authority, and rights are all constituted by those very property relations that give them substance and meaning. In his book *Oligarchy*, for example, Jeffrey Winters (2011) notes that all historical states are, in essence, a form of wealth defence that work to defend pre-existing property (and thus, class) relations. As these relations are transformed, however, they typically bring forth new ruling classes and changes to the state, as is often the case in the aftermath of a revolution (see also Carruthers & Ariovich, 2004). Similarly, Scott Prudham and William Coleman (2011) point out that all forms of territory represent the "spatial expression of power relations in general and the more specific expression of property rights and their administration in the delineation of particular spaces" (p. 13). This is because all property regimes "lead to the geographic extension of social relations and institutions and to geographic integration via the articulation of disparate places under more or less common (though by no means homogenous) modes of governance" (p. 14). As the geographer Nicholas Blomley (2011) puts it, property, at its core, "involves

---

30 In Sassen's (2006) framework, tipping points refer to events, defined "by their significance as markers of transition" (Abrams, 1982, p. 195). Sewell (1996) describes them as "sequences of occurrences that result in transformations of structures" (p. 843). Organizing logics are defined as the prevailing dynamic through which capabilities are institutionalized. Sassen (2006) identifies three: the centrifugal logic of the medieval epoch, consisting of several encompassing normative orders; the centripetal logic of the national epoch, consisting of one master normativity; and the centrifugal logic of the global that is currently in the process of separating that master normativity "into multiple partial normative orders, thereby leaving open the question as to its sustainability" (p. 10).

boundary-work, in which both bounded and relational spaces are at work" (p. 205). Property thus not only links the "spatial dynamics of what goes on between states with what goes on within states" (Prudham & Coleman, 2011, p. 13), but it is also "critical in the demarcation of coherent periods (*longues dureés*) of global integration, disintegration, and hegemony" (p. 15).

Sassen's (2006) main claim – that "each mode of politico-economic organization embodies specific features when it comes to territory, authority, and rights" (p. 32) – highlights the centrality of property to all forms of social organization and, therefore, the structured and organized ways in which the accumulation of capital has taken place historically. As political theorist Andrew Reeve (1986) notes, it is property that "provides the links between an economic system, a legal system, and a political system" (p. 7). According to anthropologist C.M. Hann (1998), this is why property works especially well to "facilitate comparative analysis in the fields of social organization where economic, politics, and law intersect" (p. 5). This intersection is certainly the case for capital since, as legal scholar Katharina Pistor (2019) points out, "capital is made from two ingredients: an asset and the legal code" (p. 2).[31] As such, "how assets are selected to be legally coded as capital, by whom, and for whose benefit are questions that cut to the core of capital and the political economy of capitalism" (pp. 3–4). Against the idea that capitalism is a mode of production constituted by surplus extraction through the market, Sassen's (2006) framework allows us to be far more specific by zooming in on the specific configurations of rights (and their relevant enforcement mechanisms and territorial reach) that have constituted different ways of organizing the accumulation of capital over time. As she notes, this approach not only "produces an analytics that can be used by others to examine different countries in the context of globalization," but also "different types of assemblages across time and space" (p. 5).

This consideration of both time and space corresponds well with the overlapping nature of historical change that Massimiliano Tomba (2013) has identified in Marx's historiography. Using a geological metaphor, Marx (1881) makes clear that the long transition from common to private property does not exist in distinct stages (as it does when the mode

---

31 Similarly, as Adkins et al. (2020) note, "The ability to define and enforce property rights in order to secure income flows from assets is an issue that prominently involves legal, political and other institutions, and the contestations that take place inside them" (p. 26).

of production is used to periodize), but rather, "as in geological formations, these historical forms contain a whole series of primary, secondary, tertiary types" (para. 41); in other words, they always overlap.[32] Sassen (2006) makes a similar point: first when she criticizes world-system theorists for assuming that competition and market forces have been in existence prior to the emergence of capitalism (p. 75); and again when she highlights how the elements of the new order emerge out of the old: as she points out, during the early days of capitalism, "kings, nobility and the church were the dominant actors, obscuring the fact that capitalism was in the making" (p. 85). Similarly, she notes that "even as industrial capitalism was becoming the dominant dynamic, most people, most firms, and most political debates were not centred on it. Objectively the prevalent condition remained agriculture and trade" (p. 420). By disaggregating the national and the global into their component parts, we are able to register those elements that although still labelled national, might instead be supporting a global organizing dynamic. The emphasis, here, is thus on getting away from the view that is so common in the globalization debates: "that the sum of a given set of parts inevitably produces the same key assemblage" (p. 15). While the organizing logics of both the national and global epochs of capitalism involve states and world political economies, they are each aligned in different ways, and with different outcomes. As such, I want to follow Sassen's (2006) approach to demonstrate how "key capabilities developed in an earlier phase can become foundational to a subsequent phase but only as part of a new organizational logic that in fact also foundationally repositions those capabilities" (p. 15).

For our purposes, this means focusing on the nation state as a capability for the development of capital. This is because, as economic sociologist Richard Swedberg (2003) notes, "the state helps to construct markets in a variety of ways: by introducing general rules for competition and cooperation, by setting the parameters for the way that corporations view the market, and by designing the rules of exchange" (p. 173). Coleman and Porter (2003) similarly point out that "all markets are institutions whose boundaries and modes of operations are anchored in rules, norms, and the protection of private property rights" (p. 252; see also North, 1990). Where other approaches point to the continuing

---

32 The same point is made by Barrow (1993): "Historical social formations usually consist of a dominant mode of production that is hierarchically linked to a periphery of subordinate modes of production and to previous historical stages of the dominant mode of production. This results in a historical class structure and in patterns of political conflict that are actually far more complex than the analytic two-class model that Marx considers typical of 'pure' capitalism" (p. 53).

presence of the nation state as evidence that globalization is nothing new, my argument here is that specific elements of TAR are shifting in ways that are significantly transforming the role of the nation state and the general shape of the global political economy in different ways than in the past. States have not retreated, as one popular line of thinking goes, but are instead becoming "reconfigured in terms of both their scale and in terms of what they do" (Major, 2013, p. 31). Pistor (2019) captures the emphasis of what I am trying to get at when she notes the following:

> The fact that capital has become global does not refute the argument that state power is central for capitalism. For capital's global mobility is a function of a legal support structure that is ultimately backed by states. Many states have committed themselves under their own domestic law, or in international treaties, to recognize the priority rights that were created under foreign law. They regularly enforce foreign law in their own courts and lend their coercive powers to executing the rulings of foreign courts or arbitration tribunals. This legal infrastructure is the backbone for global capitalism and explains why today's merchants no longer have to venture home to protect their spoils. (p. 18)[33]

To demonstrate the extent of this reconfiguration, I want to highlight the movement of the rights of capital and the authority over those rights to transnational spaces over the last 50 years. My argument is that this process should be understood as an epoch-level shift that is transforming nation states from a capability to develop and grow national capitals into a capability for globalizing capitals; that is, those corporations who long ago conquered their domestic markets and are now rapidly expanding abroad.[34]

---

33 Furthermore, as Porter (2005) notes, "In the case of FDI, the property rights in the host country that are conferred on the MNC by its ownership of investment are not at all self-evident and unchanging. On the contrary, these rights have been constituted not just by the act of investing, but simultaneously by the frequently contested domestic and international legal context in which the relationship between these rights and other rights, such as those of sovereign states or employees, are adjudicated … The MNC is not a fixed autonomous organizational form, but rather a contested and changing organizational arrangement that is heavily shaped not just by its internal structure, but by the intersecting legal, political, technical, scientific, and financial institutions and practices in which it is engaged and on which it is dependent" (p. 99).

34 My argument is somewhat similar to that outlined by Scott Lash and John Urry (1987) in their book, *The End of Organized Capitalism* – that is, that there has been a shift from national corporate economies regulated by nation states to a more

The Neglect of Banking in Canadian Political Economy

> There are few economic issues in the life of a country that do not involve the banks in one way or another. And if they involve the banks, they also touch on politics.
> – Robert MacIntosh (1991, p. 1)

In studying the contemporary transformation of the nation state, I have tried to follow Swedberg's (2003) advice that "one should first locate the interests of the actors, and then empirically explore and follow up on the hypotheses generated by this focus on interests. In brief, follow the interests!" (p. xii). As such, this book tracks the interests generated by the endless drive to accumulate capital that sits at the heart of capitalism, and the impacts of the resulting centralization and concentration of capital that occurs in the process. To track these interests, I trace the transformation of the assemblage of TAR that has sustained the Royal Bank of Canada over time – in particular, the struggles over its rights at different points in history, what those rights allowed it to do and where, and what the implications were of having the right to do so. As the most dominant bank in Canada since 1925, and one that has long been a central institution "in the business life of the nation's bourgeoisie" (Nerbas, 2013, p. 20), there is no better marker of this transformation than the Royal Bank of Canada.

But there are other reasons why studying a bank in particular can help to reveal the novelties of our age. The first is that banking is an ancient economic activity. In ancient Babylon, for instance,

> palace and temple officials loaned their own funds and, in time, deposits that were entrusted to them. In medieval Italy and Spain, institutions were established for the purpose of funneling private savings toward public use, in particular to fund the government's debt. (Grossman, 2010, p. 1)

---

globalized form of capitalism that is more effective at undermining or escaping these regulations. As Carroll (2002) notes, however, "the end of nationally organized capitalism is, of course, only one side of a reorganization of capital into a more globalized field of accumulation, within which the policies of particular states are disciplined both by the threat of capital strikes and by neoliberal norms enforced by institutions such as the World Trade Organization" (p. 340). As such, this book attempts to empirically track the transformation of property relations that are bound up with this reorganization, and how they ultimately work to reorient the character and role of the nation state in ways that are beginning to problematize existing national labels and categories.

Similarly, as Marx (1867/1991) points out in the first volume of *Capital*, money capital was the first form of capital to appear historically and the "final purpose of the whole devilish undertaking" (Mandel, as cited in Marx, 1885/1993a, p. 18) of the capitalist mode of production. As such,

> banks are a rich site for tracking the movement of imperial power and capitalism. After all, they do more than simply accept deposits and grant loans. Banks finance wars, increase the money supply, and enable the construction of public works. (Bridges, 2021, p. 931)

An analysis of the history of banking can thus provide us with a means of distinguishing between the earlier national economy centred on international trade and capital flows governed by nation states, and today's global economy, which, as Sassen (2014b) notes, is "centred on powerful firms using national governments to make private global space for their operations" (p. 2). While both periods involve various forms of outward expansion and accumulation by dispossession (that is, the often violent transformation of non-commodities into commodities), the earlier period involved a capitalist core dominating a non-capitalist periphery (E.M. Wood, 2003). Today, however, "it is the very advanced sectors of the economy that are appropriating the resources of what was till recently the 'advanced' capitalist economy" (Sassen, 2014b, p. 2).[35] As Sassen (2014b) further notes, no sector illustrates this quite "as well and as dramatically as high finance, the most complex and also most predatory advanced sector" (p. 2). What used to be the study of boring bankers who followed the 3–6–3 rule – "take in deposits at 3%, lend the money at 6%, and be on the golf course by 3PM" (Carruthers & Kim, 2011, p. 240) – has since become the study of an incredibly dynamic, complex, interdependent, and ultimately unstable sector of the global economy by virtue of the breakdown of the legal barriers dividing banks, trust companies, investment dealers, and insurance companies: in other words, the transformation of banking into finance, or what many have come to call "financialization."[36]

---

35 E.W. Wood (2003) raises a similar problematic: "We have no theory of imperialism that adequately comprehends a world that consists not of imperial masters and colonial subjects but of an international system in which both imperial and subordinate powers are more or less sovereign states" (p. 152).

36 There is now an immense body of literature on financialization that is too broad to cover here. For a comprehensive review of this literature, see the 2015 special issue of the *Socio-Economic Review* (Kornrich & Hicks, 2015). Other important reviews include Borch & Wosnitzer (2020); Carruthers & Kim (2011); G.F. Davis & Kim (2015);

The second reason is the extent to which globalization and financialization are linked. Tabb (2012) points out:

> Financialization has occurred in a context of globalization, and there has been growth in the importance of finance within countries. Between 1990 and 2006 the number of countries whose financial assets exceeded the value of their GDP more than doubled (from thirty-three to seventy-two). By 2006 all the industrial economies and the largest emerging market countries had financial markets at least twice the size of their GDP ... At the peak of the financial bubble (2006), the value of the world's equities was rising by $9 trillion or 20 percent a year (at constant exchange rates). (p. 24)

As a result, the global financial system is now "the cutting edge of global class relations insofar as property/ownership relations are structured on a global scale through the circuits of financial capital" (W.I. Robinson, 2014, p. 140).[37] Considering the extent to which the globalization of banking and finance is commonly treated as the "quintessential case or driving force of globalization" (Porter, 2005, p. 13), I claim that we can better understand the constitution of our age by focusing on the historical transformation of a small regional bank-cum-global financial institution – in this case, the Royal Bank of Canada. In this sense, I very much agree with the economist Richard Grossman (2010) when he suggests that "identifying the forces that historically have been responsible for banking evolution may provide some insight into understanding those at work today" (p. 2).

A third reason is the lack of research on the chartered banks in the field of Canadian political economy. There are, of course, works about the banks from other fields, although these too are relatively thin

---

K. Hart & Ortiz (2014); Keister (2002); Mader et al. (2020); and Samman et al. (2015). Like "globalization," there is no accepted definition of the term. As Lapavitsas (2013b) notes, "the term 'financialization' has been widely deployed in political economy, sociology, geography, political science, and increasingly in popular debate, since the late 1990s. Its prominence evidently reflects the ascendancy of finance for more than three decades. And yet, there is no universally accepted notion of financialization within social science; the term might be increasingly used, but its meaning remains elusive" (p. 13).

37 Similarly, as Adkins et al. (2020) note in their recent book, *The Asset Economy*, "this new logic of inequality has mixed 'hypercapitalist' logics of financialization with 'feudal' logics of inheritance to reshape the social class structure as a whole. The generational dimension interacts with the speculative logic of the contemporary financial system to shape asset-based lifetimes" (pp. 6–7). See also, Woodman (2022).

considering the outsize importance of the banks in the Canadian economy. There are texts of business history that involve the banks (e.g., Bal, 2017; Bliss, 1987/2018; Darroch 1994; Deneault, 2018; Denison, 1967; Ferland 1989; P.J. Hudson, 2010; Nerbas, 2013; Newman, 1979, 1989, 1999; Quigley, 1986, 1989; G.D. Taylor, 2008; G.D. Taylor & Baskerville, 1994; Turley-Ewart, 2000; Whittington, 1999); and more specialized texts on the place of the banks within the financial system (e.g., Binhammer, 1968/1988; Buckley, 1974; R.E. Cameron et al., 1991; Carr et al., 1995; Creighton, 1933; Eckardt, 1914/2016; Jamieson, 1953; McIvor, 1958; Neufeld, 1958, 1967, 1972; Paterson, 1976; E.L.S. Patterson, 1932; F.W. Taylor, 1911); and more recent works that focus on deregulation, the impacts of globalization, and the 2008 financial crisis (Halpern et al., 2016; Iacobucci et al., 2006; Kobrak & Martin, 2018; Martin, 2010; Meredith & Darroch, 2017; Neufeld, 2001; Puri, 2012; Puri & Nichol, 2014). There are also some works examining the governance and regulation of transnational finance (Helleiner, 1995, 1999, 2013, 2014; Helleiner et al., 2010; McKeen-Edwards & Porter, 2013; Porter, 2005, 2014b). Despite the resurgence of literature on banking and finance related to the overall trend of financialization, however, there have been almost no works of political economy focusing exclusively on the chartered banks. Indeed, as economists Mario Seccareccia and David Pringle (2020) note, "compared to scholarship on other sectors of the Canadian economy – namely, the primary resource (staples) and manufacturing sectors – the existing political economy literature on Canadian finance is relatively thin and indistinct" (p. 321). As such, this study attempts to rectify this lack, as well as answer economic historian Neil Rollings's (2021) call for a renewed analysis of the history of business power and its arrangement.

As Fligstein (2021) points out, this lack is not limited to Canada. In referring to the literature surrounding the 2008 financial crisis, he notes that

> the banks had oddly not been a significant part of the story. Instead, the causal story has tended to focus on regulators, the individuals who bought mortgages, financial instruments, CEOs and traders, and capital flows. The firms that created modern finance and the many markets that made up the industry at its demise have rarely received sustained analysis. (p. xiii)

So too in Canada. This is somewhat surprising, however, given that the strength of Canada's banking sector has long been the basis on which many political economists have staked at least part of their claims about

Canadian development. And this sector is nothing if not strong. Business scholars Patricia Meredith and James Darroch (2017) note:

> Banking in Canada is a protected oligopoly. No one can buy more than 20 per cent of a Canadian bank without approval from the minister of finance. Only regulated financial institutions – in other words, banks and credit unions – have direct access to the payments system and to deposit insurance. The not-so-surprising result is that the industry earns unusually juicy returns. The return on equity for Canadian retail banking averages about 40 per cent, far in excess of their cost of capital and much higher than other countries ... This is true even though Canada has twice as many bankers as the average G20 country, and even though our bankers earn twice as much on average as other Canadian workers. (p. 149)

Regardless of whether one sees the chartered banks as indicating either the country's strength or weakness relative to other imperial powers, the fact of the matter is, as Gustavus Myers (1914/1972) put it in his landmark study, *A History of Canadian Wealth*, "nowhere in the world can be found so intensive a degree of close organization as among the bank interests of Canada" (p. 2). As each other's largest shareholders (Tencer, 2016), the chartered banks are Canada's most powerful corporate actors, past and present. Their founders were not only prominent members of Canada's early merchant establishment but were also "well represented in the legislative assembly or, better still, in the legislative council, which was the appointed executive before the days of full responsible government" (MacIntosh, 1991, p. 7). The chartered banks were also central actors in the creation of the idea of a Canadian nation. As Bal (2017) notes, they crafted a particularly "Canadian" staff to overcome local regionalisms, and their statistics were used to "see" the country in ways that were previously unimaginable.[38] As such, the economist John Chant (1979) rightly notes that "any

---

[38] As Bal (2017) notes, the government of bank staff went far beyond overcoming regionalism: "With regards to staff, banks restricted employees from having debt and taking part in gambling, but also from engaging in stock or real estate speculation ... Managers even tracked employee relationships outside of work to ensure quality of company. Being seen studying the 'Rule Book' was deemed to be a mechanism for advancement" (p. 9). In terms of "seeing" the country, Bal (2017) writes: "Banks often operated as an agent for the government domestically and abroad ... this capacity very arguably reflected the centralized ability of banks, through branching system [sic], to see trends before the government (the census for example only provided a snap-shot after the fact). As a result, Canadian banks, though operating independently of the Government of Canada, were nevertheless

examination of 'major concentrations of corporate power' in Canada would be incomplete without a close scrutiny of the role of the chartered banks" (p. 191).

That such scrutiny has not yet occurred in Canadian political economy is partly a result of a significant weakness in Marx's analysis of the transition to capitalism that has been carried through more recent studies of the world economy and, thus, the Canadian experience. Although Marx (1867/1991) was interested in the unique nature of the social relations that constituted the capitalist mode of production, he was particularly interested in industrial capital, the form of wealth involved in the production process (e.g., factories, mines, railroads). Consequently, he had much less to say about those other forms of capital involved in circulation and exchange, such as commercial or financial capital (both emerged from merchant capital).[39] This selective focus reflects one of the main precepts of historical materialism: that history moves forward through the development of the productive forces and that industrial capitalists (along with their counterpart, the industrial proletariat) are agents of this type of economic change. Noting in *Theories of Surplus Value* that "commercial and interest-bearing forms of capital are older than industrial capital" ("Addenda," sec. 2, para. 1), Marx (1863) pointed out that they did not necessarily lead to the development of capitalism in and of themselves. For instance, Marx (1867/1991) notes that merchant's capital remains stuck in the sphere of circulation and thus does not have a significant effect on the productive forces of society.[40] According to Marx's labour theory of value, only the expenditure

---

uniquely situated to centrally influence national economic policy and shape national economic trends, more so than banks in other banking systems" (p. 14).

39 As Sewell (2010) notes, Marx "tended to be dismissive of mercantile activity, which he saw as parasitic on other modes of production – feudalism, slavery, simple commodity production and industrial capital alike" (pp. 85–6).

40 Marx (1867/1991) writes: "It can be understood, therefore, why, in our analysis of the primary form of capital, the form in which it determines the economic organization of modern society, we have entirely left out of consideration its well-known and so to speak antediluvian forms, the merchants' capital and usurers' capital. The form M–C–M', buying in order to sell dearer, is at its purest in genuine merchants' capital. But the whole of this movement takes place within the sphere of circulation. Since, however, it is impossible, by circulation alone, to explain this transformation of money into capital, and the formation of surplus-value, merchants' capital appears to be an impossibility, as long as equivalents are exchanged; therefore, that it can only be derived from the twofold advantage gained, over both the selling and buying producers, by the merchant who parasitically inserts himself between them. It is in this sense that Franklin says 'war is robbery, commerce is cheating.' If the valourization of merchants' capital is not to be explained merely by frauds practised

of living labour in the production process of a commodity can create new value; as such, only industrial capital includes a process that creates new wealth rather than just siphoning it off from other sectors of society. Since commercial and financial capital play no significant role in the production process according to Marx, they are relatively unimportant for his schematic analysis of a pure capitalist system as it exists in *Capital*.

The neglect of circulatory capital in the schematics of *Capital* is contradicted by Marx's (1867/1991) more accurate, albeit sometimes confusing, historical writings on the "so-called primitive accumulation" (p. 874). For Marx (1894/1993b), the development of merchant capital was a historical precondition for the development of the capitalist mode of production because it enabled the concentration of monetary wealth and production for trade, which subsequently transformed "products more and more into commodities" (p. 444). Since this form of capital existed in a variety of older social formations, however, Marx was reluctant to give it a revolutionary role in the emergence of capitalism. As he notes, merchant capital, "taken by itself, is insufficient to explain the transition from one mode of production to the other" (p. 444). That statement seems contradictory when we place it beside Marx's (1867/1991) historical analysis of primitive accumulation, which was the process that first gave money the magical power of capital: the ability to self-expand. Arguing against the classical political economists who portrayed the prehistory of capital in terms of thrift and hard work, Marx argued instead that capital emerged through state power via colonialism and the development of the credit system (pp. 915–19). Through the creation of the national debt – what Marx referred to as the "alienation by sale of the state" (p. 919) – and the tax system, Marx argued that the transition from feudalism to capitalism was sped up "as in a hothouse" (p. 915). As he points out, it was the emergence of the national debt that "marked the capitalist era with its stamp" (p. 919).

As the economist Anthony Brewer (1980/2002) notes, however, the exact role of all these factors in the transition is not very clear (p. 41). All Marx (1867/1991) offers on the subject is a brief exegesis on the role of public debt, which allows, with "the stroke of an enchanter's wand" (p. 919), the creation of public bonds that make sure that creditors are

---

on the producers of commodities, a long series of intermediate steps would be necessary, which are as yet entirely absent, since here our only assumption is the circulation of commodities and its simple elements" (pp. 266–7).

never exposed "to the troubles and risks inseparable from [capital's] employment in industry or even usury" (p. 919). The logical presumption is that the riches captured from the colonies by looting, enslavement, and murder flowed back to Europe to be transformed into capital via "a turnover in the actual personnel of the landowning class, with *nouveau riches* buying out declining and indebted feudal magnates" (Brewer, 1980/2002, p. 41). In any case, Marx (1867/1991) was not so much interested in the process but the result, writing: "the national debt has given rise to joint-stock companies, to dealings in negotiable effects of all kinds, and to speculation: in a word, it has given rise to stock-exchange gambling and the modern bankocracy" (p. 919). Despite being decorated in national titles, the great banks were, in his view, simply groups of private speculators: "the agents and beneficiaries of economic violence" (Dodd, 2014, p. 60). This is why Marx (1867/1991) remarked that capital comes into the world "dripping from head to toe, from every pore, with blood and dirt" (p. 926). It is also why banks figure so prominently within the classical theories of imperialism. Through the credit system, Marx (1894/1993b) saw the emergence of "a new financial aristocracy, a new kind of parasite in the guise of company promoters, speculators and merely nominal directors" (p. 569). The Canadian political economist R.T. Naylor (1972) sums up this view when he writes: "The rentier, a pure parasite – living off interest and dividends on past investments or rents on past property accumulations without performing any socially necessary role in the capitalistic productive process itself" (p. 3).

This parasitic view of banking has since led to a tendency to view the emergence of capitalism as a fractional struggle between a developing industrial capitalist class and those older social groups tied to interest-bearing and commercial capital, forms which are "found in the most diverse socio-economic formations" (Marx 1867/1991, p. 728). As a result, banking has often been treated as a subordinate form of accumulation that operates solely "in accordance with a specific logic determined by the dominant social-property relations and the prevailing conditions of social reproduction" (E.M. Wood, 2007, pp. 162–3). While this is true to a certain extent given the dependent nature of financial capital, it neglects the reality that all social actors have the agency to influence the property relations of their respective social formations; that is, they have the ability to change the rules and rights relating to what it is they do to sustain their livelihood. Treating production as primary and circulation as secondary neglects the important role of merchants and financiers in the transformation of feudal property relations and the eventual transition to capitalism (see, for example, Ingham, 1999). As anthropologist Eric Wolf (1982) notes,

> By dint of its very success, mercantile wealth began to multiply the channels of commodity exchange, rendering tribute takers increasingly dependent upon it. It generated ever larger amounts of money-begetting money and invested that wealth so as to increase the flow of commodities to the market. In the process it drew producers in different parts of the world into a common web of exchanges, adjusting existing relations of production to embrace commodity exchange, or subsidizing coercive arrangements for the production of commodities. (p. 86)

If one is to look back on European history from the sixteenth century onwards, merchants (and the banks that resulted from their accumulation activities) played a key role in the establishment of a world trading system, actively facilitating the race for the colonies by the European powers, and often playing a quasi-military role in suppressing resistance from local populations (e.g., the Hudson's Bay Company). In their analysis of the English merchant class, for instance, Robert Brenner (2003) and Bruce Carruthers (1996) have both demonstrated just how much of England's early modern politics were influenced by the demands of the commercial sector. Similarly, Jairus Banaji (2007) has argued that the great mercantile companies of the seventeenth and eighteenth centuries were clearly "involved in production in ways that contradict the concept of merchant capital as a mere mediation between extremes" (p. 65). Since "it was merchant capitalism which innovated the unlimited partnership and the whole spectrum of forms of association that flowed from it" (p. 55), Banaji argues that it is "unreal to suppose that the self-expansion of commercial capital was simply grounded in some simplistic formula like 'buying cheap and selling dear'" (p. 65). In discussing the case of eighteenth-century France, the historian, William Sewell Jr. (2010), similarly points out that

> the largest and most dynamic industries were usually based primarily on circulating capital and were organized under mercantile forms. It was above all by means of mercantile techniques – through mechanisms of purchase and sale, lubricated by credit – that the subsumption of labour by capital progressed most spectacularly in eighteenth-century France. (p. 86)

Taken together, these accounts suggest that circulatory forms of capital not only played a central role in the creation of modern capitalism and the consolidation of the national state (see also, Banaji, 2020; Brewer, 1980/2002; Sewell, 2021) but are also active drivers of transformation today.

Although Marx (1894/1993b) was wary to give merchant capital a revolutionary role in the development of capitalism, even he did not completely discount it from being able to; he simply gave the caveat that it would depend "entirely on the historical level of development and the conditions this provides" (p. 729). In pointing to the primacy of industrial capital or the labour theory of value, many scholars have thus neglected the actual lived history in which capitalism came into being and the relevant property relations that had to be transformed in the process. This is especially important in the Canadian case where it was a landed class of "gentlemanly capitalists" (Cain & Hopkins, 1986, 1993) who, in concert with the colonial administration, first utilized the corporate form to implement government functions without parliamentary accountability, provide the money supply for the colonies, constrain democratic pressures in urban centres, and administer the construction of Canada's early transportation infrastructure (Schrauwers, 2008, 2010). While Canadian dependency theories were correct to stress the mercantile-financial character of this early ruling class, they were misguided in claiming that Canada's dependent status follows from the fact that this class was involved in accumulation relating to circulation and not production. As many economic historians have since pointed out, many colonial merchants were clearly involved in manufacturing, and the many difficulties relating to Canada's early industrial ventures had more to do with the small size of the population and lack of infrastructure rather than the specifically mercantile-financial orientation of Canada's early ruling class (Acheson, 1972; L.R. MacDonald, 1975; Pentland, 1981; Richardson, 1982).[41] Similarly, as Neil Quigley (1986) notes in the case of banking, there is no evidence before 1914 that Canadian banks "actively 'sought out' American investors;

---

41 As L.R. MacDonald (1975) notes, evidence from England and the United States "makes it impossible to argue that, as a general rule, merchant capital has historically discouraged the growth of industry. Just the opposite. Adherents of the theory are forced, then, into the unenviable position of asserting that Canadian merchants were different than merchants elsewhere. Unenviable because very little Canadian evidence has been collected on the matter, and what there is suggests they were not. Moreover, even if anything at all can be proven, it will not be characteristic of 'mercantile capital' at all, but merely a predisposition of Canadian merchants, a much less exciting prospect. There are various indications that in Canada, as elsewhere, merchants were the strongest supporters of, and got deeply involved in, the growth of manufacturing" (pp. 273–4).

or that bankers clearly identified their own interests, and those of the financial institutions for which they worked, as complimentary to those of American industrialists" (pp. 52–3). As put simply by the political scientist Glen Williams (1979), "there is substantial evidence to suggest that Canada's merchants and bankers either financed or directly participated in the establishment of many of the new post-1879 industries" (pp. 336–7).

These historical issues are compounded by theoretical ones relating to an overly schematic view of the fractional nature of the capitalist class that rests on the primacy of production. The various processes of production and exchange are not separate in real life; they are both integral parts of production as a social process.[42] As Brewer (1980/2002) notes, "capitalist production as a whole includes many separate production processes and the processes of exchange that link them" (p. 29). Since interest-bearing capital is simply the reallocated spare money capital of the capitalist class, it "does not constitute the revenue foundation of a separate social group – of the 'monied' capitalists" (Lapavitsas, 2013b, p. 118).[43] Making claims based off the strength of different fractions of capital also neglects the fact that "all big capitalists tend to become money-capitalists" (Norfield, 2016, p. 55) and that "finance is not a parasitical entity but an integral element of the capitalist economy" (Lapavitsas, 2013b, p. 122).[44]

---

42 As W.I. Robinson (2014) notes, this is because "the capitalists' class power is asserted over corporations and states as well as over the popular classes via these institutions – through financial mechanisms. The generalization of exchange value that is a defining characteristic of capitalism presupposes that money embodies the whole set of capitalist relations, including social power relations and the exercise of social power through institutions, especially through the state. Under capitalism, production is always for profit, and the realization of profit is always through exchange for money. Production and money are therefore in unity unless that unity is broken by crisis" (p. 140).

43 Sassen (2006) points out more generally: "The emerging bourgeois propertied class included a mix of social groups, both old and new: members of the nobility involved in commercial enterprises, farming, or mines; great merchants and financiers who displayed their success by purchasing estates; merchants who became manufacturers and then established mills; and manufacturers and traders who became bankers. Together they handled the country's economy, and the state helped enable this" (pp. 104–5).

44 Lapavitsas (2013b) provides further explanation: "Marx's theoretical emphasis on 'monied' capitalists reflects the influence of classical political economy and should be treated with caution. Relative remoteness from productive activities and a potentially predatory outlook are important features of the lender, but the relationship of lender to borrower is considerably deeper ... The accrual of interest, furthermore, is hardly limited to a distinct section of the capitalist class that owns capital available for lending. In mature capitalism the typical lending agent is a

As Doug Henwood (1998) notes, "ownership is represented through monetary claims, and the exchange of those claims in the financial markets amounts to the social construction of ownership" (p. 11). The development of capitalism, whether in Canada or elsewhere, was not the result of a fractional battle between different embodied representatives of capital's circuitry, but a much more complex transformation of land, labour, and money into commodities (Myers, 1914/1972; Polanyi, 1944/2002; Sewell, 2021). As Robert Brenner (2003) notes in the English case, the development of capitalism was not in contradiction to the landed class, but rather something that "took place within the shell of landed property and thus ... to the benefit of the landed aristocracy" (p. 649).[45] As such, we should avoid using the mercantile-financial character of Canada's early ruling class to explain Canadian development and instead look at the various struggles by which the chartered banks – Canada's most dominant corporate sector – have attempted to transform those property relations that have constrained their accumulation activities. In other words, rather than taking for granted the institutions of capitalist banking, we should actually examine how they have been arranged over time. Doing so, I argue, will allow us to comprehend just how much the assemblage of TAR, on which capitalist activity depends, has changed, as well as the implications for anticapitalist struggles.

A Note on Sources

It is important to provide a brief note on the sources used in this book. Readers will observe that I rely heavily on Duncan McDowall's (1993) official history of the Royal Bank, *Quick to the Frontier*. I do so because there is so little publicly available information on the bank. As banking

---

financial institution that lends money capital collected across the capitalist class, and even across other classes. The concept of the 'monied' capitalist has limited explanatory power over the lending phenomena of financialized capitalism" (p. 115).

45 There is significant evidence that early capitalists tried to incorporate both their activities and social status within the feudal system (by purchasing noble titles, for example) rather than in opposition to it (see Tigar & Levy, 1977/2000). Sassen (2006) makes a similar point about the class nature of this transformation: "The principal agent was the bourgeoisie that had come from the merchant and banking sectors, from dealers and manufacturers, and, in England, from a portion of the nobility. This emergent new class articulated its economic and political project around the notion of freedom, something that held across the major powers of the time. In England this class was involved with affairs of the state through Parliament: it sought and secured freedom of trade and production, freedom to pay labor at its lowest level, and freedom to defend against workers' alliances and revolts" (p. 99).

historian John Turley-Ewart (2000) notes, Canada's banking history is relatively underexplored when compared to countries like the United States, France, and Britain, because the chartered banks "unnecessarily restrict access to primary materials," a reality that makes the creation of any "banking history an arduous exercise for scholars" (p. vi). Sociologists, historians, and business scholars alike have all noted this difficulty in their own attempts to shed light on the activities of the chartered banks (Darroch, 1994; Deneault, 2015; P.J. Hudson, 2010), and this book is no different. Ultimately, the Royal Bank's archives are private, and my own attempt to get access to them was unsuccessful. In personal correspondence with P.J. Hudson, I was pointed back towards McDowall's book. While I have done my best to supplement my use of that text with corporate documents, newspaper articles, and the findings of official reports and commissions, there is no doubt a wealth of material that remains hidden to public eyes.

Despite this lack of primary materials, however, I still feel that it is important to highlight the activities of such a powerful financial institution. As scholar-activist Susan George notes, while those with "wealth and power are in a better position to hide their activities and are therefore more difficult to study, any knowledge about them will be valuable to movements for social justice ... Better a sociology of the Pentagon or the Houston country club than of single mothers or LA gangs" (as cited in W.I. Robinson, 2014, p. 215). While I have done my best to examine the materials at hand, I should note that this book is not an attempt to uncover a secret history of the bank, but rather that which can be plainly seen in their own corporate documents and the business press. I do not need to make my argument on the basis of such material and would – very much, in fact – argue the opposite: that much of today's epoch-level change is happening right before our very eyes. The constant fascination with that which is secret (something oft-suggested to me by my colleagues during the writing of the dissertation on which this book is based) reminds me of an earlier quote by Jane Jenson (1989), who, in promoting a regulation approach to the study of Canada, argued that by the application of useful categories, "there is no need to force Canadian history, to find [in] a single wartime public opinion poll or an entry in Mackenzie King's diary the evidence for class mobilization which resulted in a postwar settlement" (p. 88). In similar fashion, this book takes the position that the conceptual and analytical framework used reduces the need to uncover such secret activities, as helpful as they may be to the overall argument. In other words, what I attempt to provide in this book is a new interpretation of those events that can plainly be seen by everyone.

I should note, however, that during the research process there were a variety of sources examined that were not cited in the main text for various reasons. For the reader interested in such sources, I will mention them here. Some of the more significant works include those on Canadian finance and banking (C. Armstrong & Nelles, 1988; F.H. Armstrong, 1967; Binhammer, 1968/1988; Buckley, 1974; R.E. Cameron et al., 1991; Carr et al., 1995; Creighton, 1933; Crow & Fischer, 2002; F. Daniel, 2002; Denison, 1967; Eckardt, 1914/2016; Freedman, 1998; Iacobucci et al., 2006; Jamieson, 1953; McIvor, 1958; Neufeld, 1958; Paterson, 1976; E.L.S. Patterson, 1932; F.W. Taylor, 1911; Tax Justice Network, n.d.); those on the history of the Royal Bank of Canada (J. Heron, 1969; Ince, 1970); and primary sources from the Royal Bank itself, such as the bank's *Monthly Letter* from 1943 to 2008, its *Newsletter and Interim Report* from 1976 to 1983, and its annual reports from 1966 to 2022. I also examined every mention of the Royal Bank of Canada in the following newspapers: the *Globe and Mail* from 1844; the *Financial Times* from 1888; and the *New York Times* from 1851.

Another note is required on naming conventions. Like many old corporations, the name of the Royal Bank of Canada has changed over time. It began as the Merchants Bank before turning into the Merchants Bank of Halifax. It was then changed to the Royal Bank of Canada before finally turning into simply RBC (or, depending on the unit, the suitably redundant RBC Royal Bank). In the text, I refer to whatever name the bank was using during the time I am referring to it. I do note, however, when a name change has taken place, as they are almost always significant to the changing contexts in which the bank has found itself.

Lastly, after much deliberation, I have decided to remove scare quotes around the terms *national* and *global* throughout the text. These quotes were initially used to signify that I was referring to something that was nominally national or global (or commonly referred to as such) but was not necessarily supporting national or global processes. In the end, however, I felt that this was too confusing for the reader and only ended up complicating matters. That said, this book is an attempt to get us to stop thinking about the national and the global as different scales, and rather to think of them as different configurations of territory, authority, and rights. As such, the reader is warned in advance that my use of these terms is not simply indicative of the scale of operation.

Chapter Outline

The book proceeds as follows. Chapters 2 and 3 explore the history of the Royal Bank of Canada and can be understood as an attempt to see how what we refer to as national capital was constructed. In chapter 2, "Making National Capital: The Origin of the Royal Bank of Canada, 1864–1944," I argue that the late nineteenth and early twentieth century can be distinguished from our own by virtue of the creation of a national system of property relations – that is, by a centripetal organizing dynamic of TAR towards the national level. I identify four shifts in TAR – Confederation and the *Bank Act*; implementation of the National Policy; the *Finance Act*; and the creation of the Bank of Canada – to represent this drawing in as it relates to the chartered banks. I claim that the overall effect of this organizing logic was to provide the chartered banks with the capability to grow through both expansion and protection. As such, I conclude that we should understand this period of capitalism as the making of what is commonly called national capital.

In chapter 3, "The Expansion of National Capital: The Growth of the Royal Bank of Canada, 1945–1974," I continue this exploration of the history of the bank from 1945 to 1974. I argue that this period represents the interregnum between the national and global epochs of capitalism. I make this argument on the basis that the period begins with a continuation of the centripetal organizing logic that characterized the earlier period of capitalism – that is, a continued drawing in of TAR to the national level. Despite increasing levels of global economic activity, the rights of capital and the authority over those rights remained primarily at the level of the nation state, giving governments a number of different policy options to regulate and control capital. I identify the Bretton Woods system as one indicator of this intensification. The relative success of this system in protecting national capitals would have the subsequent effect, however, of increasing competition among domestic financial institutions, leading many banks to escape national regulatory control via the Eurodollar markets, whose foreign currency flows would eventually overwhelm the Bretton Woods system. I conclude by arguing that the collapse of Bretton Woods represents the tipping point into our present global epoch by unleashing the power of financial capital.

Chapter 4, "Making Global Capital: RBC in the Digital Age, 1975–2008," represents an attempt to understand where we are today by continuing the exploration of the bank's history from 1975 to 2008. I highlight an emerging centrifugal dynamic of TAR that stands in stark contrast to the organizing logic of the national epoch of capitalism. I argue that this emerging logic gives us a small glimpse into a much larger transformation: the construction of a truly global system of rights for capital outside the grasp of national politics. I identify three shifts in TAR – the movement of authority over banking to supranational institutions; financial deregulation; and so-called free trade agreements – to represent this centrifugal dynamic as it relates to the chartered banks. I claim that the overall effect of this organizing logic is to provide globalizing capitals (including what were formerly national capitals) with the capability to grow and expand by constraining the power of the nation state to enact policies that negatively impact the accumulation of capital. As such, I conclude that we should understand our present period as a new historical epoch that consists of the making of global capital.

Chapter 5, "Emerging Tendencies and Trajectories: 2009–2022," is an attempt to understand where we are going by extending my analysis of the Royal Bank of Canada into the present to explore some emergent shifts in TAR and their potential implications. In particular, I focus on new forms of escape from the nation state, such as dark pools and Canada's Temporary Foreign Worker Program (TFWP); new free trade agreements, such as the Comprehensive Economic and Trade Agreement (CETA), and the Comprehensive and Progressive Agreement for Trans-Pacific Partnership (CPTPP); and new, so-called institutional technologies, such as blockchain. I argue that while the full effect of these shifts in TAR is still unknown, they all contribute to the development of a global property regime in which the nation state is increasingly limited in the actions it can take against corporate interests.

Chapter Two

Making National Capital: The Origin of the Royal Bank of Canada, 1864–1944

What is in the interest of the country is in the interest of the banks.
  – Charlie Neill, general manager of the Royal Bank of
  Canada, 1924 (as cited in McDowall, 1993, p. 206)

Introduction

One of the central claims that runs throughout this book is that significant changes to the property relations of capitalism over the last 50 years have fundamentally altered the structure of the global political economy in terms of the relationship between capital and the nation state. In this chapter, I set up a historical foil by which to compare the national and global epochs of capitalism. Rather than asking the long-standing question of whether Canada is dominated by local or foreign capitalists, I instead ask how this earlier period in Canadian history differs in its fundamental configuration of territory, authority, and rights (TAR) in respect to capital today. How were the property relations that sustained capitalism during this period organized, and how did they contribute to the making of what is typically referred to as national capital?

The reason for asking these questions is because, as Sassen (2006) notes, there has been "a sort of capture by the nation-state frame of much of the post-sixteenth century history in the West" (p. 7). What she means is that since "the ascendence of the nation-state and its capture of all major components of social, economic, political, and subjective life" (p. 9), there has been a tendency to treat the nation state as if it has played the same role historically – that is, as if simply because it is still here, it somehow provides the basis for the same sort of organizing dynamic that characterized this earlier period of imperialism and capitalist nation building. What I seek to demonstrate throughout the rest of the book is that this is not the case, and that the assemblage of TAR that sustains global capitalism today is indeed changing in epoch-defining ways that increasingly reduces the meaning and efficacy of Canadian liberal democracy.

In this chapter, I explore how this earlier period of TAR was configured in Canada. I do this using the framework I set up in the introduction for the analysis of globalization vis-à-vis a case study of the transformation of the Merchants Bank (later, the Royal Bank of Canada). That framework can be summarized by saying that the history of TAR reflects the history of changing modes of production and their respective social relations, such as the role, character, and type of state that persists, as well as its shape and fundamental dynamics. I argue that the late nineteenth and early twentieth century can be distinguished by virtue of the creation of a *national* system of property relations – that is, by a clear centripetal organizing dynamic of TAR towards the national level. In stating this, I do not wish to suggest that capital was the primary actor in this process; as others accurately note, the territorial state existed long before capitalism proper (Elias, 1939/2000; Lacher, 2006; Teschke, 2003; E.M. Wood, 2002b). Rather, what I wish to highlight is that this earlier period can be distinguished from our own by the movement of the rights of capital, and the authority over those rights, to the national level; more specifically, in the case of banking, this meant that "the principal foundations of financial governance ... were organized around national institutions" (Germain, 2010, p. 25). I identify four shifts in TAR – Confederation and the *Bank Act*; the introduction of the National Policy; passing of the *Finance Act*; and creation of the Bank of Canada – that represent this drawing in as it relates to the chartered banks. What was the overall result of this organizing logic? To provide the chartered banks with the capability to grow via both expansion and protection. As I demonstrate in later chapters, the development of this capability is a crucial factor in the transition to our global epoch.

The chapter proceeds as follows. First, I introduce the Merchants Bank and give a brief overview of the character of pre-Confederation banking. Next, I focus on each of the shifts in TAR noted above and explore their effects on the Merchants' structure, operations, and activities. Special attention is paid to the specific nature of the conflicts between the Merchants Bank, the other chartered banks, and the provincial and federal governments. I argue that these shifts in TAR represent the growth of capital during a particular stage in its historical development; as such, I conclude that we should understand this period of capitalism as the making of what is commonly referred to as national capital.

Pre-Confederation Banking and the Merchants Bank

Any arrangement of property relations is constituted by a system of enforceable rights or claims within a given space; these relationships subsequently give a social formation its specific shape and dynamic. The constitution of these rights is not the outcome of some efficient process or well-laid plan but rather the result of continuous social and political struggle in which organized groups (whether from business, labour, or government, to give a few modern examples) try to affect the outcome (Fligstein, 2002, p. 33). In this sense, state building is the historical process by which certain groups are able to get the state to make rules that benefit their interests. These rules include not only what can be owned and exchanged (e.g., land, labour power, money) but also the right to pool individual capitals together into corporations that are legally treated as fictitious individuals (Cerri, 2018; Roy, 1997).[1] As Clement (1979) notes, "corporations are legal fictions, the creatures of property relations endowed with the rights of capital" (p. 232). Policies that function to regulate corporations also fall under the ambit of property relations since they are rules that regulate what can be done with what is owned. Given the specific nature of the property relations of the early Canadian colonies and their respective social dynamics, a centripetal logic of TAR was already well underway by the time the Merchants Bank was founded in 1864. Briefly describing the nature of these property relations and how they shaped the character and dynamics of pre-Confederation banking should help us reflect on the making of the national assemblage of TAR and the wider significance of this shift.

From the Treaty of Paris until Canadian Confederation, the British territories in North America were independent colonies. They were almost completely separate and communicated directly with the British government rather than with each other.[2] They were ruled by an oligarchy of colonial officials and merchants (sometimes referred to as "gentlemanly capitalists") whose wealth was rooted in office, trade,

---

1 *Mozley and Whiteley's Law Dictionary* (1977) defines the corporation as "a number of persons united and consolidated together so as to be considered as one person in law, possessing the character of perpetuity, its existence being constantly maintained by the succession of new individuals in the place of those who die, or are removed" (p. 82).
2 Until the completion of the Canadian Pacific Railway in 1885, for example, the quickest route from England to the colonies of Vancouver Island and British Columbia, "was by ship to Panama, overland to the Pacific, and then up the coast to Victoria" (MacIntosh, 1991, p. 31).

and land.[3] Where the newly independent American colonies had been oriented towards settlement, the remaining colonies of British North America were "basically a source of raw materials" (Clement, 1977a, p. 35). As such, their legal and regulatory framework was one "conceived, planned, and developed to suit the great extractive monopolies belonging to the financial oligarchy" (Deneault & Sacher, 2012, p. 184). The ability of this oligarchy to gain such wealth was the result of the so-called rights of Englishmen that constituted the basis for the emergence of capitalism in both England and its various colonies, as well as the transformation of the absolutist state (Blackstone, 1753/1893; Macpherson, 1962; Wood, 2002b). These rights were essentially the hard rights of private property – "the concrete rights of ownership, control and conduct, earned by struggle and competition" (Lower, 1946, p. 111) – that allowed these gentlemanly capitalists to justify their appropriation of most of the arable land in the colonies and the subsequent exploitation of their resources for the purpose of making money by trade, especially via the early merchant corporations like the Hudson's Bay Company.[4] As Deneault and Sacher (2012) note, these gentlemanly capitalists did not come to Canada "to create a specific nation, even less to establish

---

[3] The label "gentlemanly capitalists" is a reference to P.J. Cain and A.G. Hopkins (1986, 1993), who argue that the role of industry in the emergence of British imperialism is overstated. They instead point to the importance of the British gentry and their shift from rentier capitalism to commercial agriculture, and from there, to the domination of the financial service sector. They claim that these gentlemanly capitalists retained a leading role in the military, Parliament, House of Lords, and cabinet until late into the nineteenth century. Numerous historical studies demonstrate that this group of merchants and colonial officials was particularly significant to the creation of capitalism in Canada, including its investment in early industrialization efforts (e.g., L.R. MacDonald, 1975; Myers, 1914/1972; Quigley, 1986; Richardson, 1982; Schrauwers, 2008, 2010; Teeple, 1972; Woodcock, 1989). As Pentland (1950) notes, "merchants played the leading part in banking; they provided much of the financing for the local railroads of the sixties [1860s]; and they dabbled even in manufacturing" (p. 466). They also tended to see themselves not as Canadian, but as part of a Britain's imperial ruling class. Andrew Smith (2012) notes, for instance, that "in studying this period of Canadian history, one is struck by the sheer anglophilia of Canada's elite, who sought knighthoods and closely identified with all things British" (p. 459). Deneault (2015) similarly points out that "London, far more than Canada, was the horizon to which members of the Canadian propertied classes looked" (p. 17); it is thus "impossible to say whether they were Canadian or British" (p. 18). For details of this pertaining to the Royal Bank of Canada, see McDowall (1993, pp. 11–50).
[4] It is important to note that property rights have been left out of the *Canadian Charter of Rights and Freedoms* (1982) and are administered provincially, owing to Canada's history as a collection of separate colonies. For an overview of debates over whether to include property rights in the *Charter*, see Johansen (1991).

a sovereign republic: they came to strip a territory of its resources" (p. 180).[5]

These private property rights – and the state violence that enforced them – were not only central in allowing the colonial ruling class to exploit Canada's various staples but were also a central part of British financing to its various colonies, since "investment ultimately transferred property overseas and nothing was more fundamental to investors' interests than the security of that property" (Dilley, 2012, p. 71). More than 100 years later, the president of the Canadian Bankers Association, S.H. Logan (1937), would put the matter similarly, writing, "without confidence neither international capital nor international trade can be expected to flow freely" (p. 149). As such, the role of both the early colonial states and the post-Confederation Canadian nation state was the protection of these rights and, thus, the classes that benefitted from them.[6] As Heller (2012) notes, "capitalism in Canada grew under the protection of the Canadian state through the establishment of a legal system protecting private property, the privatization of land and natural resources" (p. 227). As the British Empire continued its expansion, these private property rights were stretched across other territories (such as the Caribbean), thus providing Canada's ruling class with numerous opportunities for protected accumulation activities.[7]

---

5 As Jenkins (1996) notes, "when they took over management of new land in their rash of colonization, the British exported the doctrine of enclosure" (p. 101). Teeple (1972) provides a brief description of the period: "The genesis of the mercantile capitalist in Canada is found in the British merchants at the time of the Conquest. Like so many vultures, they 'were first at Quebec at its fall' and then followed the troops to Montreal, where they established their colonial headquarters for the fur trade. The position of this merchant class was central in the new colony as a result of its 'alignment' with the military government. A unity of interests was to be expected, for one motive of the military conquest was to seize the profitable fur trade. This oligarchy of colonial officialdom and merchants soon appropriated the land by way of gifts and grants. Thus, the wealth and power of the ruling class in the British North American colonies came to be founded in office, trade, and land" (p. 61). As such, both colonial administrators and merchants had no particular concern for the welfare of the colonies: they were valuable only insofar as they "magnified imperial wealth and power" (Pentland, 1981, p. 151).
6 Naylor (1975/1997) notes: "Many of the most critical political decisions taken by the ruling class in the colony were conditioned by the state of Canada's relations with the British capital market. British capital built most of the major works of commercial infrastructure in the provinces; public finance depended upon the pleasure of the imperial government and the London private 'merchant' banks; and Canadian development policies and the structure of its capital markets and financial institutions were moulded to ensure the greatest facility of entry of British capital" (p. 20).
7 As Pistor (2019) notes, "Exporting law has a long history. English settlers and colonizers applied the common law throughout the growing empire and sent judges

Having begun the process of colonization during the transition from mercantilism to capitalism, however, the colonies were still governed by a variety of legislative orders that applied to different phenomena in an uneven manner.[8] This system of differential rights and duties was, as Sassen (2006) notes, a holdover from feudalism that was only beginning to change in earnest by the late eighteenth century (pp. 25–73). The right to issue promissory notes payable on demand for circulation as money, for instance, was not originally the exclusive right of the government or Crown in either Great Britain or the colonies; rather, it was the common right of those who chose to exercise it. As a result, the early colonial banks were typically made up of groups of merchants who simply organized themselves into co-partnerships to facilitate "the movement of staples from Canada to external markets" (Naylor, 1975/1997, p. 67). As sociologist Richard Swedberg (2003) notes, this is because part of the mercantilist project was the creation of colonies such as Canada, whose independent economic development "was effectively stifled ... since manufacture was allowed to develop only in the home country" (p. 143). It is for this reason that the historians of early Canadian banking are quick to point out that during this period, "Canadian trade with Britain was still greatly hampered by the remnants of her late colonial system and the navigation laws" (Shortt, 1897, p. 14), leading many of early Canada's gentlemanly capitalists to necessarily be transnational investors, investing some of their money in the United States: "in the case of Lower Canada, the money which left the Upper Province went

---

to far-off places to implement it. Napoleon Bonaparte's troops brought the French legal codes with them wherever they went, extending the reach of French law to Poland in the East, and to Spain, Portugal, and Egypt in the South. Imperialism was not only about military conquest, but also about spreading the legal system of the European states to the colonies they created in Africa, Asia, and the Americas" (p. 133).

8 Pentland (1981) provides a description of its general effect on class in the Canadian context: "In the eighteenth century, and in the first half of the nineteenth century in most parts of the provinces, there was a general acceptance of a class structure derived from, though no less clear cut than, European ones, that involved differential rights and duties, and criteria of loyalty and 'respectability' rather than of merit by some objective test or success in the marketplace. Until about 1840, the privileged and educated and their supporters were quick to emphasize that Canada was substantially free of the democratic practices of the barbarous Americans and, therefore, of the mob rule and thoughtless measures which they produced. The determination of policy by those born and trained to rule implied the denial of role not only for the masses but for 'natural' laws and forces" (pp. 159–60).

largely to the United States; from Kingston it passed chiefly to Sackelt's Harbor and Oswego" (p. 15).[9]

As the general scale of capital accumulation grew over the latter part of the eighteenth century, these merchants began to petition the Crown for charters of incorporation – in other words, new rights – that would allow them to overcome the limits of the partnership form.[10] It is thus no surprise that one of the earliest references to banking came from Lower Canada, the dominant commercial colony in what is now Canada, in 1792, when "some gentlemen of Montreal decided to establish a bank under the name of the Canada Banking Company. Only a private bank of deposit, however, resulted from this effort" (Curtiss, 1948, p. 151). In 1808, there was another attempt to establish a bank in Lower Canada after a charter was requested from the legislature, but it was not granted by the Crown. With lack of currency being a significant issue in Lower Canada, the Bank of Montreal was eventually organized under articles of association in 1817. A charter was requested in 1818, "but reserved by the governor for the significance of the royal pleasure. The royal assent was withheld and the Bank of Montreal continued as a private partnership" (Breckenridge, 1894, p. 25). In 1818, the Quebec Bank was also started, along with the Bank of Canada (not to be confused with the central bank created in 1934), but both were similarly denied charters.

In the winter of 1820, the shareholders of each of the three banks "again petitioned the legislature to be erected into bodies corporate and politic" (as cited in Breckenridge, 1894, p. 21). They argued that "without the benefit of incorporation, the beneficial purpose contemplated by the establishment of the banks would be imperfectly attained, and

---

9 As J. Evans (2019) notes, "For the emerging financial and merchant classes, the problems of imperial rule were generally linked to trade regulations which restrained the local elite's accumulation of wealth. The Navigation Acts, for example, restricted the shipment of goods to or from the colony on non-British ships, while further colonial regulations restricted the manufacture of clothing (1768) in Canada, and trade with the US and West Indies (1784). These conditions, when combined with the effects of the British Corn Laws on trade with Britain itself, effectively denied growth opportunities for Canadian merchants" (p. 200).

10 As Teeple (2005) notes, "the corporate form emerged with the growing accumulation of capital and the consequent need to have a structure that reflected this accumulation and its continuous expansion" (p. 93). He continues: "The absolutist state was responding to and promoting a logical growth in the nature of private property, its aggregation; this socialized capital was the only way of overcoming the serious limits to the development of the productive forces presented by pre-capitalist petty commodity production" (p. 95).

great inconveniences would be incurred in the conduct of their business" (p. 21). The benefits were then, as now, fairly obvious. Private partnerships had no public shareholders; any partners were thus personally responsible for the company's debts. They also could not hold any property, and without a separate legal personality, could not sue or be sued.[11] Receiving incorporation was thus a necessary precondition for the investment needed to expand. The banks "prayed, therefore, to be incorporated under regulations and provisions as nearly corresponding with the terms of their original association as it might be, and under such other regulations and provisions as the legislature might prescribe" (Breckenridge, 1894, p. 21). On 17 March 1821, "the prayers of the petitioners were granted" (p. 22). Three charters incorporating the banks were presented by the legislature for royal assent. They were reserved by the governor for over a year and became law in 1822.[12]

---

11 In its modern form, the corporation is a legal entity that is effectively recognized as a fictitious person under the law, possessing certain civil rights. Modern incorporation thus provides many benefits, including: (1) the protection of personal assets against the claims of creditors and lawsuits; (2) the ability to easily transfer ownership; (3) the ease at which retirement funds can be established; (4) lower rates of taxation; (5) the ability to raise funds through the sale of stock; (6) durability over time; and (7) the ability to secure a credit rating independent of the status of shareholders and directors (Berle & Means, 1932/1968; Chandler, 1977; Monks & Minow, 2011). Like earlier corporate entities, the modern corporation has been utilized for several different purposes, including the provision of large, public infrastructure projects (Roy, 1997; Schrauwers, 2008, 2010; Soederberg, 2010). Since the late nineteenth century, however, it has mainly become a legal-institutional vehicle for the accumulation of capital (Fligstein, 2002; Henwood, 1998; Veblen, 1904/2005).

12 Sweeny (1997) provides a useful overview of the Bank of Montreal's early activities: "The Bank of Montreal was formed in 1817, as a joint venture between the principal Montreal-based branches of imperial mercantile houses and a limited number of New England and New York merchants. The Americans accounted for 47% of the initial stock subscription and in the early years, through their influential Boston committee of shareholders, directed the Bank's highly lucrative export trade in hard currency. In the first five years of its existence the Bank of Montreal exported to the United States well in excess of half a million Spanish dollars and at least £37,000 sterling in gold. Thereafter, having drained the colonial economy of a not insignificant part of its specie reserves, the Bank carried on a large export trade to New York in sterling Bills of Exchange drawn by the Commissariat General and the colonial government, in excess of £670,000 worth by 1830. This was the very best paper in the world and accordingly received a substantial premium on the New York market. The Bank of Montreal monopolized this trade by 1822. It was a classic example of buying cheap and selling dear: the colonial authorities, by accepting the Bank's own notes in payment, substantially increased both circulation and general acceptance of the Bank's currency; while the Bank pocketed the bulk of the premium in New York" (pp. 318–19).

In Upper Canada, the first bank charter was granted in 1819 to the Bank of Kingston, and the second in 1821 to the Bank of Upper Canada. The Bank of Upper Canada was a quarter owned by the colonial government and largely controlled by the Family Compact, a small group of gentlemanly capitalists who dominated political and economic life in Upper Canada. Schrauwers (2008) explains:

> The Bank of Upper Canada, the Clergy Corporation, and the Canada Company served as the financial backbone of the colonial state and of the small group – the Family Compact – that directed these closed institutions. The Canada Company provided the executive branch of government – the lieutenant governor and his executive council – with revenues independent of elective control. The Bank of Upper Canada, as the largest creditor in the province, effectively controlled the colony's money supply and through its note issues enabled mercantile domination of trade and the land speculations of the Family Compact. These three chartered corporations represent a delegation of state control to non-elective bodies that shielded their directors with separate identity and limited liability. (p. 236)

The Bank of Upper Canada quickly gained a monopoly in the province after the collapse of the private Bank of Upper Canada at Kingston and the inability of the Bank of Kingston to start within the period of its charter. With control of the legislative council, the Family Compact was also able to restrict efforts by others to obtain new charters. A financial crisis in 1821 and 1822, however, gave the assembly the opportunity to protest the Compact's monopoly, and in 1832 another charter for the Commercial Bank of the Midland District was granted to the earlier interests associated with the Bank of Kingston. In 1830, the British government would attempt to issue instructions to the colonies as to what was desirable in a bank charter for the purpose of protecting British shareholders, but these instructions were not initially followed. Later amendments were found to be more agreeable.[13]

---

13 Curtiss (1948) notes: "Some dispute arose over these Acts [charters] in which the British government threatened to disallow them. Strong representations were made from Canada, however, and the Acts were finally allowed. But the British government stated that they would allow no further Acts (a resolution not strictly adhered to), unless they conformed to the set of instructions sent out in 1833, which contained the following provisions: (1) suspension of cash payments for sixty days in the forfeiture of the charter; (2) notes issued at any branch to be redeemable at the head office but not at other branches; (3) one-half the capital to be paid in immediately; (4) loans to directors or officers (or on paper bearing their names) to

Each bank required a separate act of incorporation. Since there was no general banking code, the charter functioned as "the source of the bank's legal capacities" (Curtiss, 1948, p. 151). At the time, these corporate banking charters were "essentially a gift of the state" (Henwood, 1998, p. 253).[14] They were basically "a licensed monopoly to which the Crown delegated specific aspects of its sovereignty" (Schrauwers, 2008, p. 254). While they all gave the banks a separate legal personality, and thus the right to hold property, to sue and be sued, and, most importantly, limited liability for shareholders, the specifics of each were slightly different, and they were limited to operating within their respective colonies. In actual fact, most of the earliest charters "recycled entire paragraphs from charters and articles of association Hamilton drafted for American banks" (A. Smith, 2012, p. 458) in an effort to entice American investment.[15] Having copied its charter almost directly

---

be limited to one-third of the total advances; (5) no bank to hold its own stock or to lend on it; (6) a weekly statement of the bank's affairs to be made and a semi-annual statement to be sent out to the legislature; (7) shareholders to be liable for the amount of their shares – the 'double liability'; [and] (8) compliance with certain conditions in making loans – in general, to see that the bank remained a creditor and did not become a partner. These provisions have been set out in some detail to show the influence of the British government on Canadian banking development. The third, fourth, and eight provisions were already in operation, and the first practically so; the others were gradually inserted in the charters after this time, although it was not until after 1841 that all were included. Thus, while there was a local tendency towards better banking laws, the influence of the British government hastened and secured these sound developments" (p. 153).

14 As Teschke (2003) notes, "mercantilism meant essentially the private ownership and accumulation of state-sponsored titles to wealth for the mutual benefit of king and privileged traders and manufacturers" (p. 209). The early European chartered companies were thus "largely ways of rewarding court favourites, sycophants, and nobility, or as a way of raising revenues or advancing other private interests" (Teeple, 2005, p. 95). They effectively functioned as extension of state sovereignty by virtue of the rights, powers, and privileges granted to them by their respective monarchs. Charles II of England, for instance, granted the Hudson's Bay Company in 1670 an exclusive and perpetual monopoly of trade and commerce; possession of the lands, mines, minerals, timber, and fisheries; full power to make laws, ordinances, regulations, penalties, and punishments; and the right to employ an armed force, appoint commanders, erect forts, and any other measures necessary for the protection of its trade and territory (Myers, 1914/1972, pp. 38–47). As Naylor (1972) notes, the success of these early chartered companies led to new class relations: "the *nouveau riche* merchants began congregating in the City of London where they soon became the chief lenders and funders of government debt" (p. 4).

15 As former president of the Canadian Bankers Association, Robert MacIntosh (1991), points out, "It was not only American ideas, but American capital which influenced the first Canadian bank charters. One of the biggest problems in getting new banks

from the First Bank of the United States, founded in 1791, we can take the Bank of Montreal's as somewhat typical of the period:

(1) The directors were to be British subjects and, under certain conditions, were individually and jointly liable for some actions of the bank;
(2) Shares were to be of £50 denomination each, with graduated voting so that no shareholder had more than 20 votes;
(3) The corporation was empowered to sue and be sued in the corporate name; to issue bank notes payable on demand in legal coin; to receive deposits and to deal in bills of exchange, to discount notes, to deal in gold or silver bullion, and to sell stock pledged, but not redeemed; to have and to hold mortgages on real property for debts contracted to it in the ordinary course of its dealings, but not to lend on mortgages or to purchase them; to hold real estate to the value of £1,000 annually and no more;
(4) An annual return was to be made to the shareholders. (Curtiss, 1948, p. 152)

As Breckenridge (1894) notes, these types of government limitations were readily accepted by the colonies' merchant class in return for "the concessions of incorporation, the currency of their notes in revenue, assured protection against forgery, the power easily to enforce stock subscriptions and the like" (p. 152).

The proliferation of orders that characterized the early colonial period would start to reverse with the unification of Upper and Lower Canada in 1841 and the move away from mercantilist policies by the British, as represented by the Reform Bill of 1832, the repeal of the Corn Laws in 1846, and the repeal of the Navigation Acts in 1849. The 1840 *Act of Union* was itself the result of the rebellions of 1837 and 1838 and the subsequent collapse of the provinces' commercial credit in Britain. The idea was that "spreading the burden of repayment of the bankrupt

---

started was the lack of capital. Even the Montreal community did not have sufficient local resources to found the Bank of Montreal. A substantial number of the first shares were held by wealthy families in Boston, New York, and Philadelphia" (p. 9). As he rightly points out many pages later, however, "the founders of the Canadian banks wanted American capital but not their votes. The earliest bank charters were intended to keep control in the hands of the local establishment in Saint John and Montreal, and later in Halifax, Kingston, and York. The ruling oligarchies were conservative and British and not at all anxious to introduce republican ideas from south of the border" (p. 158).

upper province's debts over the population of the almost debtless lower province would both reassure existing British debenture holders and widen the revenue base for future issues" (Naylor, 1975/1997, p. 22). As part of unification, there thus began a process of standardizing existing bank charters, as well as extending "the corporate powers of each bank to the whole province" (Breckenridge, 1894, p. 90). Combined with the state-sponsored shift towards the building of railways (A. Smith, 2012, p. 474), unification not only opened up new territory in which the banks could operate but also preserved "the monopoly held by the few chartered banks in Canada" (Myers, 1914/1972, p. 100).

The *Act of Union* also signalled the start of a long struggle to transfer the chartered banks' right to issue notes to the state. The *Act to Establish Freedom of Banking* of 1850, which was a failed attempt to replicate the United States unit-banking system, was similar in this respect; however, it was also the first act that applied to *all the banks equally*, a feature that would come to characterize the post-Confederation banking order. Changes to the Bank of Montreal's charter in 1854 were also extended to the other chartered banks, further indicating a shift towards a standardized system (Curtiss, 1948, p. 154). The note issue problem would arise again in 1866 after the failure of the Bank of Upper Canada and the Bank of Montreal's subsequent refusal to loan the government more money.[16] In response, the government passed the *Provincial Notes Act* in an attempt to link the note issue to the needs of the British administration by granting the province a monopoly on the issue of one- and

---

16 MacIntosh (1991) notes that when the Bank of Upper Canada "failed a few months before Confederation, the new Dominion of Canada took a heavy loss, because most of its deposits handed down from the Province of Canada were at the Bank of Upper Canada. Rather than pursue the shareholders for the double liability, Sir John A. Macdonald buried the whole issue as quickly as possible, probably because most of the shareholders were Tory party supporters. To prevent questions being asked about the failure, the government saw to it that all the books and records of the bank were sold to a waste paper dealer for $20 a ton, thus providing the earliest known instance of waste recycling in Canada" (p. 17). This situation puts the Bank of Montreal's refusal to lend to the Province in greater context: "The government in which the Honourable (afterwards Sir) A.T. Galt acted as Minister of Finance, was obliged, in 1866, to raise some $5,000,000 to discharge the floating debt. The credit of the province had suffered in the English market on account of the renewal, from time to time, of the balances in arrears. The Minister averred that the Canadian banks were unwilling to extend to the government a loan amounting to 15 per cent of their capital. The Bank of Montreal was already a creditor for $2,250,000, and was pressing for payment. The government would not trust to the chance of meeting the engagements of the country by large loans at high rates of interest" (Breckenridge, 1894, p. 177).

two-dollar notes; there was also another attempt to create a central bank for the same purpose, but it too would fail.

In Nova Scotia, the situation was slightly different. Nova Scotia was a relatively self-contained colony run by merchants for merchants; as such, there wasn't the constant tension between the colony's merchant class and the imperial government as compared to Upper and Lower Canada, where the interests of the Family Compact and Château Clique were occasionally in conflict with the desires of the Colonial Office.[17] The Bank of Nova Scotia was first chartered in 1832 and was the first bank to include the double liability provision in its charter (MacIntosh, 1991, p. 12). The trend soon caught on, and, with only slight adjustments in 1847 and 1856, later charters incorporating a number of other Nova Scotia banks were almost identical. All were merchant banks, "offering to discount bills, to handle foreign exchange, and to take deposits at 3 per cent per annum" (McDowall, 1993, p. 21). Interestingly, none of the Nova Scotia merchant banks failed prior to Confederation; as Breckenridge (1894) notes, "the banking system as originally worked out caused so few difficulties and promoted so much the convenience and prosperity of the colonies, that they felt very little temptation to change it" (p. 162). The private banks carried on all branches of banking, including note issue, in competition with the chartered banks. In both cases, "their proprietors were men of wealth; they enjoyed the confidence of the community, and conducted their business according to recognized banking principles" (p. 162). "The banking history of Nova Scotia," as Breckenridge (1894) notes, is thus "not eventful" (pp. 162–3).

The Merchants Bank was one of these private banks. Formed in 1864 by a group of wealthy Haligonian merchants – J.W. Merkel, Edward Kenny, Thomas Kinnear, John Duffus, William Cunard, John Tobin, George P. Mitchel, and Jeremiah Northup – the bank was a response to Halifax's growing prosperity resulting from the outbreak of the American Civil War. Like all the colonial banks, the Merchants Bank was mainly involved with the financing of trade; being a Nova Scotian bank, however, they were more closely oriented towards the sea, existing as they did "on the margins of a vast imperial trading system" (McDowall, 1993, p. 16). Their initial role was to connect the vast mercantile flows of wealth connecting London to Canada and the West Indies under the

---

17 Similar to the Family Compact in Upper Canada, the Château Clique was a small group of gentlemanly capitalists who held significant power in Lower Canada. They controlled the executive and legislative councils, dominated the judiciary, and occupied senior bureaucratic positions until the 1830s.

protection of the British Empire, acting chiefly as an agent for larger banks involved in the staples trade, such as the Imperial Bank in London, the Union in Newfoundland, the Union in Prince Edward Island, and the New Brunswick Bank.[18] By late April of 1864, the Merchants Bank had put advertisements in the local press announcing their services: the discounting of promissory notes and acceptances, advances on approved securities, the purchase and sale of bills of exchange, and the depositing of money (p. 23). With a capital base of only $200,000, the Merchants rented out the old Bank of Nova Scotia offices on Bedford Row; as of 2 May 1864, the Merchants Bank was open for business.

Unlike incorporated entities, a co-partnership like the Merchants' "had no public shareholders nor any obligation to explain itself to the mercantile community it served" (McDowall, 1993, p. 24). It had no separate legal personality, and thus could not hold property, could neither sue nor be sued, and all shareholders were personally responsible for all debts of the company. "Anchored in law in only the flimsiest of ways" (p. 16), and with little to no commercial information to rely on, the members of a co-partnership "had no option but to proceed on the basis that a man's word was his bond" (p. 18). As a result, partnerships "formed and broke apart with great regularity" (p. 16). This older style of banking would all change, however, with Confederation and the creation of the Canadian nation state, which would set off a number of shifts in TAR that would greatly enhance the Merchants' capabilities to accumulate capital – albeit, at the expense of their home region.[19]

---

18 MacIntosh (1991) notes: "For a time in the nineteenth century, Nova Scotia enjoyed a booming triangular trade: wooden sailing ships built on the Atlantic seaboard carried lumber and salt cod to the Caribbean, where the cargo was off-loaded and replaced with sugar and molasses bound for Britain. The ships then returned with manufactured goods to Halifax and the seacoast ports" (p. 25).

19 Sweeny (1997) explains the eventual impact on the region: "Local control of nine Maritime banks was lost prior to the Great War, while in Western Canada consolidation took place primarily in the 1920s. This timing was important. The effective elimination of locally-based banks in the Maritimes compromised the already problematic competitive position of Maritime-based industrial firms. For the future of many of these firms, faced with increasing corporate concentration in English Montreal and southern Ontario, the loss of an embryonic regional capital market was significant. In the 1920s manufacturing employment was devastated, with job losses of 50% in industrial centres and 15% of Maritimers took the difficult decision to migrate elsewhere" (p. 326).

Confederation and the *Bank Act*

While a centripetal organizing dynamic of TAR was already in the works before Confederation, it was greatly accelerated by the creation of the new Canadian nation state, the Dominion of Canada, which would come to absorb many of these elements. The collapse of the Reciprocity Treaty with the United States in 1865 meant that the Canadian colonies no longer benefitted from free trade in staples (Dilley, 2012; L.E. Davis & Gallman, 2001). Teetering on the brink of bankruptcy due to fraud, financial mismanagement, and railway speculation (Myers, 1914/1972), the Province of Canada attempted to extend its credit on the London markets by way of a union with the similarly indebted Maritime colonies.[20] Although they were initially dismissive of the idea, the Confederation of the colonies came in 1867 after Nova Scotia and New Brunswick were blocked from their own financing by British investors, leaving them with no choice but to amalgamate if they wanted to receive more loans (Naylor, 1975/1997, pp. 30-1). The name of the new nation state, the Dominion of Canada, was chosen by the imperial government over the Kingdom of Canada in order "to avoid possible offence to anti-monarchical sentiment in the United States" (Corbett, 1938, p. 156).

Confederation was a reflection of the more general process of nation building in the nineteenth century, to which the earlier *Act of Union* was a part.[21] The practice ultimately meant the creation and

---

20 Van Houten (1991) provides more detail: "By 1867, both Canada and the provinces of New Brunswick and Nova Scotia as well as a larger number of municipalities were deeply in debt at a time when the railway companies they had lent or given money to were either on the verge of bankruptcy or had actually gone bankrupt. These companies demanded even more financial support. In all $145,795,853 were spent in Canada on the construction of just over 3,000 kilometres of rail. Nova Scotia and New Brunswick together spent $8.9 million on 437 kilometres of rail. On the eve of Confederation, Canada, Nova Scotia and New Brunswick had a total net debt of $96.2 million, $50.2 million of which were the result of investments in and loans and other financial commitments to the railways. The Province of Canada had an additional $18.7 million in debt because of canal construction. In short, three-quarters of the debt was incurred for transportation. In 1866, the service of this debt absorbed 21%, 28% and 30% of the revenues of Nova Scotia, New Brunswick and Canada respectively" (p. 49).

21 This is not to suggest that there were not practical reasons for Confederation – there were. Confederation solved three immediate problems for the colonial ruling classes: (1) it expanded the taxation base by pooling together provincial tax revenue, thus enabling the federal state to provide more funds to private railway companies; (2) it removed interprovincial trade barriers, thus providing at least some remedy for

consolidation of a coherent domestic market within a certain territory.[22] It thus involved "the abolition of 'internal' tariffs, tolls, customs duties, and the destruction of precapitalist property relations, among other barriers to a 'regional' free-trade system" (Teeple, 2000, p. 156). As Swedberg (2003) notes, this process was "anything but automatic; it could only be done, with the help of political actors, especially the state" (p. 140).

In Canada, we can see this in respect to the 1854 decision to abolish the seigneurial system in the Province of Canada (although it continued on for a short period afterwards) and the *Rupert's Land Act* of 1868, which formally transferred the remaining territory and rights held by the Hudson's Bay Company to the newly created Dominion (Myers, 1914/1972). Nation building also involved the creation of a single legal jurisdiction, a corresponding political system, and, typically, a common national identity, although this has long been problematic in Canada for a number of reasons (see Bliss, 2006; Lipset, 1990; Raney, 2009; Rao, 2010; Resnick, 2005). During this period, once an integral market over a certain territory had been created, it became an economic necessity to secure those borders and to expand them to include other territories – especially so if those territories were still defined by precapitalist relations. These various processes formed the substance of colonialism and imperialism during the so-called age of empire (Hobsbawm, 1987). As Shaw (2000) notes, "the classic national-international system was a world of rival empires ... The dominant form of the state was not, therefore, simply a nation-state, but the *nation-state-empire within an interimperial system*" (p. 104). Since Canada itself was a colony – or rather, a series of British and French colonies – its existence was necessarily part

---

those markets lost as a result of the abrogation of the Reciprocity Treaty with the US; and (3) it provided a slight measure of protection against the rising power of that country. That said, my purpose here is to highlight that the solution of the colonial ruling classes to these problems – the creation of a territorially defined nation state – followed a similar world-historical pattern to that of other capitalist countries. It is in this sense that we can understand this period as the making of national capital.

22 McNally (1981) notes: "Every national capitalist class is concerned ... to protect and expand that section of the world market which it is privileged to treat as its national market. As a result, the consolidation of capitalist nation states is bound up intimately with the extension of the home market. As Marx points out in his discussion of primitive accumulation, the use of state power is a central feature of the transition to the capitalist mode of production. State power, 'the concentrated and organized force of society,' is the 'midwife' of the birth of the new society. Political force, expressed in the form of state power, 'is itself an economic power.' This is especially clear in the case of Canadian Confederation" (p. 54).

of this outward expansion. Yet, we can also see a sort of internal imperialism of the West during this period, as well as the expansion of Canadian corporations to English and French colonies in the Caribbean, a process that ultimately relied on the extension of the rights of private property to those territories under the protection of their colonial masters.[23] I discuss both in greater detail later on.

In respect to the chartered banks more specifically, Confederation continued the centralization of TAR started in 1841 by requiring all the existing banks to be chartered in order to protect their shareholders, and through the opening up of the territory in which they were legally allowed to operate. In this sense, Confederation represents the beginning of the creation of what would later become a national system of private property relations. It was by virtue of the strength of the chartered banks at Confederation, their dominant role in the colonial economy, and their ownership and control by the ruling classes of the former colonies that the *British North America Act, 1867* gave the federal government exclusive authority over all matters pertaining to currency and banking. As Neufeld (1972) notes, the chartered banks "accounted for three quarters of financial intermediary assets; they handled the foreign exchange business; and their stock was by far the most important security traded on the embryonic stock exchanges" (p. 88). As such, "there was no doubt in the minds of Canadians that the scattered banks of their new Dominion were the engine of financial growth in their nascent economy" (McDowall, 1993, p. 27).

The task of integrating the various colonial currency and banking regimes was initially put aside, however, due to "the demands of political nation-building" (McDowall, 1993, p. 27). A temporary act set to expire in 1870 was rushed through Parliament making the existing provincial charters into Dominion charters that immediately gave all the banks the legal right to operate in any part of the new territory that

---

23 Pentland (1950) provides a useful description of the overall transformation: "About the middle of the nineteenth century, the Province of Canada was transformed from a raw, staple-producing area to a rounded, integrated economy that might be called metropolitan. Signs of the change were visible in 1830, unmistakable in 1840. By 1850 change had gone too far to be turned back, and 1860 and 1870 can denote only the filling out of the home-market exchange economy already implicit. Purely extractive industry was overlaid with a secondary development involving an elaborate transportation system, a capitalistic agriculture, an extensive list of manufactures that appear to have been efficient in their day, and a creditable financial structure. Probably the most telling evidence of the transformation was the fact that this colony, so recently at the mercy of the fluctuations of imperial markets for one or two commodities, could undertake successfully to swallow an empire of its own in the years after 1867" (p. 457).

now constituted the Dominion of Canada; similarly, in 1868, the earlier provincial notes put into circulation were transformed into Dominion notes, indicating that the government was likely to introduce a national currency at some point. The Maritime banks also became subject to the same taxation regime of the more dominant central provinces: "to the tax of one per cent, upon excess of their average circulation, above the average weekly amount of coin and bullion kept in their vaults" (Breckenridge, 1894, p. 219). As Manitoba, British Columbia, and Prince Edward Island joined Confederation, "the scope of the *Dominion Bank Act* was extended to these territories, and such banks as existed came under it" (Curtiss, 1948, p. 155). It is in this sense that Breckenridge (1894) notes that in respect to banking, "the creation of the Confederation and the establishment of a united Parliament marked the close of one period of Canadian history" (p. 224). From that point on, the assemblage of TAR that formed the basis of the banking business in Canada would become increasingly national despite the extent and continuation of their foreign, mercantile dealings.

Confederation initially divided Halifax's mercantile elite, with some seeing "danger in the scheme, an abandonment of the colony's oceanic heritage" (McDowall, 1993, p. 14). Jeremiah Northup and Thomas Kinnear of the Merchants Bank, for instance, originally joined with anti-Confederate Joseph Howe in calling the move a "reckless gamble" (p. 28), and they affixed "their signatures to anti-union petitions that were sent to London" (p. 15). Their fear – which was quickly borne out – was that Confederation would allow the more powerful central banks, led by the Bank of Montreal with assets of $6 million, to enter their territory with a hungry eye; by contrast, the largest Halifax bank was the Bank of Nova Scotia with assets of only $560,000. Other directors of the Merchants were not so sure that Confederation was an altogether bad thing, considering Nova Scotia's economic status. With the fisheries failing in 1867 and 1868, trade with the West Indies drying up, and the abrogation of the Reciprocity Treaty with the United States in 1865, the Merchants' own publications highlight the fact that Halifax had become deprived "of a paying trade in many commodities" (Royal Bank of Canada, 1920, p. 11). It was also obvious to many of the Merchants' directors that Nova Scotia's traditional mercantile economy was at odds with the nature of the emerging coal, steel, and railway industries.[24] They thus hoped that Confederation could help save

---

24 While some of Nova Scotia's merchants hoped that Confederation might help the province's fledgling industrial sector, it instead destroyed it by enabling externally owned capital into the region: "The coal mines had been expected to form the basis

the bank by providing protected banking opportunities in the West. Despite knowing that Confederation would inevitably bring the more powerful Montreal banks to Nova Scotia, the directors of the Merchants eventually made their peace with it.

With the temporary banking legislation set to expire in 1870, Halifax's merchant elite knew that a federal charter was likely "the minimum price of admission into the new world of Canadian banking" (McDowall, 1993, p. 28). Without one, banks would not be permitted to expand nationally. Getting one was thus necessary to compete against the existing chartered banks, which could now legally operate in any part of the Dominion's territory. Furthermore, as Breckenridge (1894) notes, without the protection of limited liability, it would be impossible for private banks to secure the capital necessary to expand their operations – although by this time liability had already been extended "to twice the amount of subscribed shares, in compliance with imperial regulations respecting colonial banks" (pp. 361–2). Anticipating these changes, the directors of the Merchants applied for and received a federal charter. On 22 June 1869, an act incorporating the Merchants Bank of Halifax (so named to avoid confusion with the already existing Merchants Bank of Canada) received royal assent. With an authorized capital of $1 million, the "competent though not very wealthy institution" (McDowall, 1993, p. 24) was legally transformed into a national corporation. This would be the first step on the way to making the Merchants Bank a form of national capital.

The next step was the creation of a standardized system of national banking via the 1871 *Bank Act*.[25] As Andrew Smith (2012) notes, the *Bank Act* was a crucial part "of the project of making the Canadian nation-state" by virtue of integrating "the financial systems of the previously separate colonies" (p. 456). Conservative Finance Minister Sir John

---

of industrialization: instead the coal was shipped to Ontario to feed branch plant manufactories there" (Naylor, 1972, p. 28). Veltmeyer (1979) similarly notes that "in the late 1880s and early 1890s, and then again in the early twentieth century, industry after industry and bank after bank, largely based on local capital, fell to this consolidation. In fact, by 1914 the Maritimes had become a branch-plant economy with most of its capital controlled from Montreal or Toronto" (p. 21). As a result of these economic developments, "at least 300,000 Maritimers abandoned the region over the first three decades of the twentieth century" (p. 21).

25 The *Bank Act* of 1871 technically consisted of several pieces of legislation passed between 1870 and 1871: "'An Act to Establish One Uniform Currency for the Dominion of Canada,' 34 Victoria (1871), chap. 4; 'An Act Relating to Banks and Banking,' ibid., chap. 5; 'An Act Respecting Certain Savings Banks in the Provinces of Ontario and Quebec'" (A. Smith, 2012, p. 457, n. 12).

Rose would make this same point in the House of Commons, where he presented his banking scheme on 14 May 1869. Emphasizing "the need for financial uniformity in all provinces" (A. Smith, 2012, p. 486), he noted that "few of the forty-two banks in the Dominion operated under precisely the same regulations" (p. 486). The role of the *Bank Act* was thus to standardize the rights of the chartered banks at the national level, essentially acting as their shared charter, and to protect them by restricting their competition.[26] As "the political dynamic in Canada involved a contest among different groups of bankers and other non-landed elites" (A. Smith, 2012, p. 464), it is not surprising that the more powerful Bank of Montreal took the opportunity to suggest to Rose that a reorganization of banking was needed to better suit the requirements of a rapidly changing Canadian economy. Their plan was to reorganize the system into three tiers of banks: the first would naturally consist of the Bank of Montreal, which would become the government's bank along the lines of the Bank of England; the second would consist of the chartered banks, which would serve the more general interests of commerce; and the third would, similar to the United States model of banking, consist of small, local, unit banks, which would look after farming and regional manufacturing interests. As if not to be too lopsided towards the Bank of Montreal, Rose's scheme also involved stripping all the banks of their right to issue notes alongside the creation of a national currency issued by the banks on the condition that they purchased government debt. To make his case, Rose reminded the House of Commons that up to now

> all merchants had been required to keep a directory of banknotes as thick as a "Family Bible" on their tills so they could evaluate the current market worth of such notes as the "shinplasters" of Michigan, the despicable "red-dogs" of Indiana and Nebraska, and the miserable "stump-tails" of Illinois and Wisconsin. (A. Smith, 2012, p. 487)

In actual fact, Rose's plan reflected the Bank of Montreal's own needs: profits in the foreign exchange markets had declined significantly; corporate debentures were growing as a portion of collateral against their loans; and they had increased their involvement with the ailing Grand Trunk Railway. It is thus no surprise that "to the largest bank

---

26 As Baum (1974) notes, "With purpose, Canada through its federal government caused financial control to reside in the banking industry, which is subject to exclusive federal jurisdiction. Indeed, a bank's charter is the *Bank Act*" (p. 5).

in North America, the Bank of Montreal," Rose's scheme "affirmed its dominance and found hearty support" (Turley-Ewart, 2000, p. 5). Had the plan been successful, it would have relegated all but the Bank of Montreal "to the status of local currency-dispensers" (McDowall, 1993, p. 29). As a result, the rest of the chartered banks "acted in virtual unanimity to condemn the proposal" (p. 29). With Rose retiring back to London amidst the firestorm to pursue "a successful career selling North American railway securities" (A. Smith, 2012, p. 488), it would take the newly knighted finance minister, Sir Francis Hincks, to come up with a solution. In what would eventually become the government's preferred strategy of dealing with the banks, Hincks simply got them all together and asked them what they wanted. The making of the act was thus described by George Hague, the general manager of the Bank of Toronto, as "a joint committee of Parliament and banks" (as cited in Naylor, 1975/1997, p. 74).

While most of the population would surely "have favoured legislation to restrict the concentration of financial power" (A. Smith, 2012, p. 471), the event demonstrated the facts of the matter: that "Canada's banking and currency laws reflected the ideas of a small elite of political and business leaders rather than those of the uneducated masses" (p. 460). With the chartered banks relatively free to craft their own regulations, the first *Bank Act* represented a compromise between the Montreal, Toronto, and Maritime banks that ultimately re-established the pre-Confederation order of things. In this sense, it reflected the shared belief among Canada's ruling class that Canada "needed to align its financial laws with those of the mother country if the colony was to have access to British capital" (A. Smith, 2012, p. 457). The Bank of Montreal would lose its formal position as the government's bank, and no provision was made for the introduction of local unit banks; the federal government would continue to issue one- and two-dollar notes, with the rest issued by the chartered banks, secured by a cash reserve of one-third Dominion notes. While the new, cash-strapped Dominion government "preferred to monopolize the whole note issue" for purposes of domestic development, Helleiner (2003) notes that they "encountered enormous opposition" (p. 94) from the chartered banks.

Once completed, the *Bank Act* gave the chartered banks the right "to take deposits and to deal in, discount, and lend money on commercial paper, stocks, bonds, and debentures of municipal and other corporations, and on federal, provincial, British or foreign public securities" (Royal Bank of Canada, 1953, p. 2). It also forbade them from dealing in goods, wares, and merchandise, or engaging in any trade or business (Galbraith, 1970, p. 16). While the *Bank Act* did permit the banks to "engage in and carry on such business generally as appertains to the business of banking" (p. 16), it did not clearly specify what this business might be. The banks have since interpreted this to mean that they should not have a controlling interest in non-financial corporations, in contrast to the form that finance capital (the blending of financial and industrial capital) took in some countries.[27] Like the earlier colonial charters, the *Bank Act* was also set to be reviewed every 10 years. The bank's official historian, Duncan McDowall (1993), claims that this was in order "to keep the system vital and open to shifts in economic opportunity" (p. 30). In contrast, the former president of the Canadian Bankers Association, Robert MacIntosh (1991), claims that the decennial review was designed "to provide further [government] control, not for competitive advantage against other financial institutions" (p. 11), having originally been used by the legislature of Lower Canada "to keep its hand on the collar of the Bank of Montreal, so that it could have a second look at its offspring and at the proposals of other candidates for bank charters" (pp. 10–11). As we will see more clearly later, regardless of its makers' original intentions, the frequent retooling of the *Bank Act* would ultimately work to reinforce the chartered banks' power by giving them the capability to quickly respond to internal and external threats. As Andrew Smith (2012) puts it, "this bundle of statutes laid the foundations for oligopoly, branch banking, and relative stability" (p. 457).

While the rights contained in the first *Bank Act* mainly dealt with the practicalities of banking – in other words, what the banks were and were not allowed to do – their ultimate effect was to give the chartered banks the legal right to expand over the entirety of the new Dominion's

---

[27] Sweeny (1997) notes: "The most important change in banking during this period was the emergence of three distinct groups of finance capital each centred on a chartered bank, the Montreal, the Royal and the Commerce. Each group included older industrial concerns, major new corporations and financial intermediaries in brokerage, insurance and trust operations. Furthermore, all three groups developed important interests abroad: the Royal in the Caribbean, Central and South America, the Montreal in Mexico and the Commerce in Brazil. The structure of power within these groups was unusual. With the exception of their trust company subsidiaries, the banks did not control associated companies in manufacturing, transportation, finance or utilities. Control remained with the leading shareholders, who were most frequently particular families. These bourgeois held equity interests in their respective banks, but their holdings were never large enough to constitute outright control. This diffuse structure of power did not mean these groups lacked coherency, for the bank boards were loci of power administered collectively by these prominent families" (p. 325).

territory; in this sense, we can understand them as a crucial part of making a national market for banking. As Lower (1946) notes, this "extension of financial control was marked by the action of the chartered banks of the central region, which rushed to establish branches everywhere, without much competition from the outlying banks" (p. 347). As the Bank of Montreal rushed to the Maritimes, the Merchants Bank of Halifax was forced to adopt a two-part strategy to survive.

The first part of its strategy involved building up its commercial accounts in Halifax, which included firms related to its directors' other business activities (of which there were many, including industrial ventures), such as T. & E. Kenny & Co. and S. Cunard & Co. The second part of the strategy involved outward expansion. Moving "along the arteries of trade that bound innumerable Nova Scotia towns to their metropolis" (McDowall, 1993, p. 34), the Merchants opened branches in Pictou, Antigonish, Bridgewater, Lunenburg, Truro, Weymouth, and Sydney, with many of them being merely "formalizations of old trading relationships" (p. 38). From 1871 to 1886, the Merchants established a total of 25 branches and sub-agencies in Nova Scotia, New Brunswick, and Prince Edward Island, including correspondence arrangements with banks in London and New York. They also moved swiftly to areas under common British rule, such as the West Indies.[28]

The Merchants' quick expansion is the clearest explanation as to why it remains one of Canada's largest banks. To put the scale of this expansion in context, the Bank of Nova Scotia (today, Scotiabank) opened only 15 branches over the same period. In this sense, the *Bank Act* provided the chartered banks with the capability (if they chose to use it) to expand into the new regions opened up by Confederation, a process we see with the Merchants after the National Policy and the construction of the Canadian Pacific Railway (CPR). As McDowall (1993) notes, "the Merchants' ability to pay its dividend without interruption throughout the years 1869 to 1887 suggests that, despite the uneasiness induced by

---

28 Baum (1974) notes: "In 1871 in the new nation of Canada, banks as the dominant financial institution were competing among themselves for position, for areas each could control. It was not unexpected for the maritime banks, that is, the Bank of Nova Scotia and the Royal Bank of Canada, to move with significant force into the West Indies" (p. 18). Baum goes on to explain the strategy: "It must be said that trade merely provided an opportunity for the maritime banks to occupy an area not taken by the then well-established central Canadian banks. After Confederation in 1867, the maritime banks had to find a place for themselves; they were at a competitive disadvantage with the more centrally located banks. Thus it was that the maritime banks had to seek out opportunities that were marginal to their central competitors" (p. 19).

its steady expansion, growth brought an element of protection from the economic woes of the [Maritimes]" (p. 41). Andrew Smith (2012) similarly points out that, in a more general sense, "the Canadian system of transcontinental branch banking helped protect depositors by ensuring that the viability of a bank was not tied to the fate of any single community" (p. 456). In providing the chartered banks with the capability to grow and expand, the *Bank Act* was therefore a necessary part of the construction of the entity we refer to as national capital. The establishment of a truly national market would not be complete until much later, when the "various means of communication – such as the telegraph, the telephone, and the railroad – would tie together even the most distant localities" (Swedberg, 2003, p. 142) of the new Dominion. For the chartered banks, these developments would enable them to move across the country and sweep up the remains of failed banks, getting much larger in the process (see MacIntosh, 1991, pp. 25–35).

The National Policy

The next significant shift in TAR in respect to banking was the National Policy, which was ultimately a means of extending the territory of the nation state and laying down the communicative foundations for national economic activity. As Teeple (2000) notes, this is why "the construction of roads and canals and later railways and the telegraph became synonymous with nation building; it was but the building of the infrastructure for a territorially defined regime of accumulation" (p. 162). The spirit of the age was thus "build a new state, and BUILD! Build the state, shove out its boundaries as far as possible, build railways, build industries and cities!" (Lower, 1958, pp. 25–6). This type of centripetal organizing dynamic was a common feature of the latter half of the nineteenth century, with most polities seeking "safety from the gales of global market competition behind ever higher tariff walls, buttressed with government subsidies to domestic industries and imperial expansion" (Palen, 2016, p. ix), and the Dominion of Canada was no different. First introduced by Sir John A. Macdonald's Conservative Party in 1876 and put into action in 1879, the National Policy consisted of three parts: (1) the building of a transcontinental railway (the CPR); (2) a strong immigration policy to fill out the West; and (3) higher tariffs and patents, a key protection of property rights.[29]

---

29 Sir John A. Macdonald described the need for the National Policy as such: "We have no manufacturers here. We have no work-people; our work-people have gone off

Duties on manufactured goods, for instance, were raised from 17.5 per cent to 30 per cent, 35 per cent, and in some cases 45 per cent, with textiles, iron, and steel especially favoured (Beaulieu & Cherniwchan, 2014, p. 150). As historian Arthur Lower (1946) notes, the National Policy simply took the basic sketch of the Canadian nation state designed at Confederation and "put up a fiscal fence around it" (p. 373).

The National Policy was the result of a variety of factors, not least of which was British Columbia's entry into Confederation in 1871 on the promise of a transcontinental railway and the more general state of the global political economy in the 1870s. With foreign demands on timber increasing as a result of the global railway boom, the Dominion's economy up to this point had been doing rather well, and "the banks, it may be expected, shared in this expansion" (Breckenridge, 1894, p. 204). But a world depression in the late 1870s would reverse this trend. Economic growth fell to less than 5 per cent per year, while imports grew more than 13 per cent (p. 218).[30] This disparity in trade was a significant problem for Canada. While Britain could settle its balance of payments by extending new loans to the colonies, Canada's federal government had no such means at its disposal, a reality which led to the collapse of a number of overextended banks.[31] Alongside the failure to negotiate another

---

to the United States ... These Canadian artisans are adding to the strength, to the power of a foreign nation instead of adding to our own. Our work-people in this country on the other hand are suffering from want of employment. If these men cannot find an opportunity in their own country to develop the skill and genius with which God has gifted them, they will go to the country where their abilities can be employed, as they have gone from Canada to the United States ... If Canada had a judicious system of taxation they would be toiling and doing well in their own country" (as cited in Naylor, 1975/1997, p. 7).

30 Breckenridge (1894) provides some context: "Building operations in Canada and the United States, and the rapid additions to the railway system in either country, raised the price of lumber. With the increase of other foreign demands, they stimulated the timber trade, and caused abnormal inflation. The speculation extended to timbered lands and timber limits. All sorts of manufacture were pushed to the bounds, which, in 1875, were acknowledged to have been unreasonable. Municipalities of every grade caught the infection and adopted the pernicious system of granting bonuses to manufacturing companies proposing to establish themselves in the district of the grantors ... The time is best described as one of increased activity in manufacture, transportation and exchange" (p. 204).

31 On the collapse of overextended banks, see Naylor (1975/1997, pp. 118–50). Eichengreen (1996/2008) provides a succinct description of the problem: "In the case of Britain, and to a lesser extent other European creditors, an increase in foreign lending might provoke an offsetting shift in the balance of merchandise trade. Increasingly after 1870 – coincident with the advent of the international gold standard – British lending financed overseas investment spending. Borrowing by

Reciprocity Treaty with the United States, and the rise of protectionism more generally due to Britain's inability to incorporate Germany, Japan, and the United States into a free trade empire (Panitch & Gindin, 2012; Sassen, 2006), the Canadian government was forced to adopt similar nation building measures that would ultimately work to extend and strengthen the national political economy, and thus the country's most powerful corporate actors: the chartered banks. As Polanyi (1944/2002) notes, this sort of protectionism "helped to transform competitive markets into monopolistic ones" (p. 227). The specific effect of the National Policy on banking was therefore less to do with the legislation itself and more to do with the opening of the territory on which the banks could operate. Where the earlier *Bank Act* had given the chartered banks the legal right to operate across the entirety of the new Dominion's territory, the National Policy provided the physical infrastructure, in the form of the railway, to make this a reality, a feature captured by the title of Duncan McDowall's (1993) official history of the Royal Bank, *Quick to the Frontier*. The National Policy would thus give the banks the capability to follow the staples trade across those territories that had previously been the exclusive property of the Hudson's Bay Company.[32] This

---

Canada or Australia to finance railway construction created a demand for steel rail and locomotives. Borrowing to finance port construction engendered a demand for ships and cranes. The fact that Britain was a leading source of capital goods imports to the countries it lent money to thus helped to stabilize its balance of payments. A decline in the volume of capital flows toward primary-producing regions, in contrast, gave rise to no stabilizing increase in demand for their commodity exports elsewhere in the world. And similarly, a decline in commodity export receipts would render a capital-importing country a less attractive market in which to invest. Financial inflows dried up as doubts arose about the adequacy of export revenues for servicing foreign debts. And as capital inflows dried up, exports suffered from the scarcity of credit. Shocks to the current and capital accounts thus reinforced each other" (pp. 38–9).

32 Pentland (1981) explains the matter clearly: "The National Policy of 1879 was one weapon of Canadian imperialism. Its purpose was not to make Western Canada also a participant in a self-contained economy; for the West was fully expected to sell its staple product in world markets, as it did, and there appears to have been no regret that the new Canadian structure was made more vulnerable and dependent than its predecessor. The task of the National Policy of 1879 was rather to ensure that unprotected Western wheat was carried by protected Canadian railroads and handled by protected Canadian traders, and that the supplies of the West should come from protected manufacturers, in order that as much as possible of the gains to be made would be drawn to old Canada, and not to Britain or the United States. It was this imperial prospect that brought merchants and railroads suddenly around in the 1870s, so that Eastern Canada spoke with an undivided protectionist voice" (p. 173).

internal imperialism would subsequently enable them to attract new portfolio capital from foreign, mainly British, sources. In the case of the Merchants more specifically, it would also enable them to move into Montreal in 1887 and win significant industrial accounts.[33]

The timing of the National Policy also coincided with the decennial review of the *Bank Act*, reigniting calls to create a national currency as a means of "discouraging imports, promoting domestic industry, and reducing the country's dependence on foreign loans" (Helleiner, 2003, p. 75). Supporters of the plan, such as merchant and politician Isaac Buchanan, claimed that a national currency was needed to guarantee "the full employment of the people and the development of the productive resources of the country" (p. 88).[34] He and his supporters argued that "the state, rather than private banks, should be the institution issuing notes in Canada because money was linked to sovereignty" (p. 117).

---

33 In the wake of bad loans to Nova Scotian steel producers and sugar refiners in the 1880s, alongside an internal case of embezzlement in 1882, Edson Pease, an accountant for the Merchants, led the move to Montreal in 1887 to secure new corporate clients in order to avoid regional stagnation. Pease would eventually become the bank's CEO and managing director. McDowall (1993) relates the following: "At the fulcrum of Pease's assault on Montreal was his concerted attempt to win corporate clients. Since the 1840s, Montreal had been the seat of Canada's 'industrial revolution.' Ease of transportation and British North America's most concentrated market had fostered industrial growth along the banks of the Lachine Canal, growth now accelerating under the impetus of the protectionist National Policy. Within weeks of arriving in the city, Pease had subscribed to the Bradstreet credit-rating service and was soon knocking on business doors. He could not hope to dominate any one company's financial needs, but he could aim for a portion. Two early conquests were Lyman Sons & Co., a wholesale chemical and drug producer, and the Pillow Hersey Manufacturing Co., a metal-working enterprise. On August 22, 1887, for instance, the board approved a $25,000 loan at 5 ½ per cent to cover part of Pillow Hersey's payroll. Other accounts followed: St. Lawrence Sugar Refining, Montreal Blanket, Frothingham & Workman, Drummond McCall, Dominion Cotton, Bell Telephone, and Belding Paul & Co." (pp. 57–8).

34 In many ways, Isaac Buchanan represents a typical member of Canada's ruling class of the day. He was a Scottish-born Protestant, merchant, and eventually politician, who arrived in Montreal from Glasgow in 1830 as a junior partner of the trading firm William Guild and Company. In fear of being outflanked by rival Montreal firms, and optimistic about western expansion, Buchanan moved Guild and Company's operations to York (Toronto) before eventually buying out Guild's share of the firm with his brother Peter. After making a name for himself in Toronto, founding the city's Board of Trade, the St. Andrew's Society, and the Toronto Club, Buchanan eventually settled in Hamilton. Upset with the repeal of the British Corn Laws, Buchanan would spend his later life promoting economic protectionism and the development of the railways to spur on Canada's nascent industrial sector (McCalla, 2003).

Making National Capital: 1864–1944   71

Although their attempt failed, it would represent another stage in the ongoing struggle to transfer the chartered banks' right of note issue to the nation state for the purpose of building up the national political economy.[35] Unsurprisingly, the chartered banks would also exert "an energetic opposition" (Breckenridge, 1894, p. 290) to calls to remake their charters after the National Banking System of the United States. They also rejected a proposal to establish government inspection of the banks on the basis that it was "far better to rely on the careful organization of the banks, the vigilance of the directors, and the inspection by trained men of its own staff" (p. 291).[36] Once again, the minister of finance simply asked the chartered banks to create their own "Bank Act": "some plan mutually advantageous to the government and the banks" (as cited in McDowall, 1993, p. 60). The result was, unsurprisingly, a provision that raised the capital-stock requirements of new banks, making it harder for them to form. The revised *Bank Act* of 1871 also made it a misdemeanour for any enterprise to assume "the title 'bank' without authority under the general banking laws of the Dominion" (Breckenridge, 1894, p. 293). Later revisions to the *Bank Act* would further raise capital requirements and require all the banks to make their notes redeemable at offices across the territory of the new Dominion, ensuring "that all notes circulated across the whole country without discount" (Helleiner, 2003, p. 126). National prudential regulation also emerged in the form of the Bank Note Circulation Redemption Fund, which required the banks to deposit five years of their average yearly note circulation with the minister of finance to "redeem the notes of a failed institution if the liquidators failed to do so" (Estey, 1986, p. 351). With their shared interests coming together as they got larger, the chartered banks created the Canadian Bankers Association (CBA)

---

35 As Turley-Ewart (2000) notes, "A concurrent circulation shared by the banks and the federal government added new funds to the Dominion's treasury but not as much as a total monopoly would have. Hincks subsequently sought monies lost to this concession by turning to the Post Office Savings Banks launched in 1867 and Government Savings Banks which Ottawa took over from the provinces and began expanding in 1871. Bankers could still issue their own notes, but would face stiff competition for deposits from the government, especially in the Maritimes" (p. 9).

36 Years later, the president of the Canadian Bankers Association, B.E. Walker (1893), would remark: "When the audit system was proposed we resisted because we felt that it pretended to protect the shareholders and creditors, but did not really do so, and if the audit did not really protect it seemed better that shareholders and creditors should not be lulled into imaginary safeguards, but be kept alert by the constant exercise of their own judgement" (p. 23).

in 1891.[37] Parliament would later grant the CBA the legal right to block new banks from receiving charters, thus allowing the chartered banks to grow relatively unimpeded in the national market (Morck et al., 2007, p. 115).

The cumulative effect of all of these policies can be seen in the transformation of the Merchants Bank, in particular, its rapid expansion and growth. While the Merchants' directors had initially seen the National Policy as a means of "nationalizing Halifax" (McDowall, 1993, p. 43) via the transportation of Maritime sugar and steel to central Canadian markets, reality would be far less kind. The United States would win the battle of the ports, and Montreal would win the battle over the location of Canadian sugar production. With the Maritimes stuck in a depression in the 1880s, the Merchants were forced to respond by moving "south to Britain's warmer colonies or to other centres in the Atlantic fishery" (p. 45), negotiating entry into Bermuda in 1882, St. Pierre and Miquelon in 1886, and Cuba in 1899.[38] Further moves would come

---

[37] Darroch (1992) explains the role of the CBA in creating orderly markets: "The same spirit which encouraged industry concentration further encouraged banks to seek complementary rather than direct competitive positions because competition does not promote stability. A stable oligopolistic market structure demanded that different competitors seek differentiated positions in order to avoid direct competition and its inevitable consequence of price competition. The creation of Canadian Bankers' Association in 1891 was a key event in cementing and promoting the maintenance of orderly markets" (p. 154). Naylor (1975/1997) explains the general effect: "After the Canadian Bankers' Association was formalized in 1890, interest rate competition was minimized. Competition thereafter took the wasteful form of proliferation of branches to secure both savings deposits and new clients for loans. It was standard big business behaviour, excess capacity coexisting with a restricted number of units operating behind barriers to the entry of new firms, and refraining from price competition" (p. 96).

[38] It is important to note that there is a certain amount of contingency in these movements that defies any logic of capital. The Merchants' entry to Bermuda, for instance, was the result of their accountant, David Duncan, being ordered to travel there after getting sick. Within a month, Duncan "had struck a deal with the mayor of Hamilton, Nathaniel Butterfield, to act as the Merchants' agent 'as an experiment' for a year" (McDowall, 1993, p. 163). The event is recorded in the Merchants' minutes dated 30 March 1882: "Mr. Duncan, the Accountant, having been confined in his house through a severe attack of rheumatism, the President being of opinion that his (Mr. D's) health was not fully re-established, suggested a visit to Bermuda, to which the Board assented. Mr. Duncan was accordingly advised by his physicians to avail himself of the opportunity, as calculated to do him much good, and he was also authorized by the Board in the event of his finding a suitable opening to establish an agency of the bank at Hamilton" (Royal Bank of Canada, 1920, p. 16).

Butterfield's son was also sent back to Canada, to learn from the Merchants Bank, but this would end in disaster. After suspecting that Butterfield was using

in 1890 after the collapse of the English merchant bank Baring Brothers, which created suspicions in England as to the "soundness of all foreign investments" (Royal Bank of Canada, 1920, p. 18). With the flow of English capital to Canada temporarily restricted, the Merchants negotiated a correspondent agreement with Chase National Bank in New York, giving them access to foreign exchange and credit facilities, as well as the opportunity to invest their surplus abroad.

Like the rest of the chartered banks, the Merchants' rapid growth in the 1890s made them acutely aware that Canada's economic development was not happening fast enough. Writing on behalf of all the banks, the Bank of Nova Scotia's cashier (general manager), Thomas Fyshe, complained in 1895 that "the population and business of the country are both growing very slowly, so much as to suggest the gravest doubts whether we have been using the best means to make the most of our resources" (as cited in Quigley, 1986, p. 34). The Merchants would respond to this in three ways. The first was similar to all the chartered banks, which started building up solid portfolios of American railway and utilities bonds (Deneault, 2015, p. 16). Quigley (1986) notes, for instance, that "between 1881 and 1900, the securities held by all Canadian banks increased from 1.6 per cent of total assets to 9.3 per cent; with 51 per cent of the latter figure being railway and other corporate securities" (p. 35). The second was to create a trust company that would link them to the larger Bank of Montreal.[39] The third was to expand the geographical scope of their operations.[40] They would do

---

his affiliation with the Merchants to further his own commercial ambitions, his son was sent back to Bermuda in 1886. For the next three years, the Merchants would attempt to maintain their own agency on Front Street, but without the help of local Bermudians to assist in penetrating the local market, the operation failed. After 1890, Bermudian merchants would pass legislation insulating their banks from foreign competition, and, in 1904, the Butterfields would incorporate their own bank, using the lessons they learned from the Merchants. This experience would lead the Merchants to closely guard future foreign agencies, treating them as an extension of the national branch system. The Butterfields remain one of Bermuda's prominent families today.

39 The directors of the Merchants would form the Eastern Trust Company in 1893. The Merchants would then align with Montreal Trust, created by the Bank of Montreal, which would later link up with Royal Trust, completing the circle.

40 As Turley-Ewart (2000) notes, this was a strategy shared by all the banks: "At the *fin de siècle* Canada was in motion, its banks in transition. Speeding trains carried tens of thousands to the prairies. The 'Laurier Boom' drove an economy that led the industrial world. Growth spurred ambition and its corollary – competition. By 1900 the race was on. The Merchants Bank of Halifax marched west as 'The Royal Bank of Canada.' The Bank of Nova Scotia's focus and head office moved to

this by moving further into those areas of the Caribbean under British rule and by taking advantage of the National Policy to move further west with the opening of the frontier (P.J. Hudson, 2010). Branches were opened in Atlin, Grand Forks, Bennet Lake, Ymir, and Vancouver's East End, as well as in Republic, Washington, "where Montreal mining interests had investments and where the Merchants saw an opportunity to profit from foreign exchange" (McDowall, 1993, p. 69).[41] Having begun the process of staking their claim to the Canadian West, the Merchants would also push into Ontario in 1899 after purchasing an ailing branch of the Banque Jacques-Cartier in Ottawa. McDowall (1993) notes that it was this expansionary strategy that made the Merchants "a national bank" (p. 124).

With a network of branches that now extended from Victoria to Havana, the Merchants' name seemed increasingly anachronistic to its directors. The Merchants Bank of Halifax thus became the Royal Bank of Canada in 1901, a name with "imperial and national pretensions" (P.J. Hudson, 2010, p. 37). Then-president of the Royal Bank, Thomas Kenny, claimed that the change was needed since "the bank's 'changed circumstances' demanded 'a title distinctive and comprehensive'" (as cited in McDowall, 1993, p. 76). The name change was also followed by a head office move to Montreal in 1907, further cementing the bank's status as a national bank.

Toronto; Walker's Commerce reached out to the Pacific and Atlantic and the Bank of Montreal followed. Others, like the Union Bank of Canada, Merchant's Bank of Canada, Quebec Bank, and the Imperial Bank launched expansion plans as well. The Sovereign Bank, Metropolitan Bank, Crown Bank, Northern Bank, Home Bank, Sterling Bank, Farmers Bank and the Bank of Vancouver opened their doors and joined the fray. In 1899, 663 bank branches served 5.3 million Canadians, roughly one for every 8,000 Canadians. Nineteen hundred and twenty-seven branches dropped the ratio to about one for every 3,200 by 1908" (p. 118).

41 Lest the reader imagine these western offices as typical, well-built, urban or suburban branches (thus implying some sense of attendant development), it is useful to remember that they were essentially wooden shacks. Letters from staff recall the branch at Bennet Lake as being "so full of cracks you can hear the wind whistling through them" (McDowall, 1993, p. 88). A similar style of branch in Gowganda, Ontario, whose waterfront is now called Banker's Bay, is described in "The Birth of a New Mining Town" (1909) in the *Globe and Mail:* "Away further to the left a big Canadian flag flapped before the door of the Royal Bank of Canada's tent. Beside it to the left the log structure of the Canadian Bank of Commerce was beginning to show its stately lines, and, to complete the row, stood a surveyor's log shanty, a contractor's big log camp and a huge tent on the ice just off the shore, labelled 'Baxter's Hotel'" (p. 5).

As we have seen, this new status was the result of the capabilities provided to them by the Canadian state: that is, their right to operate throughout the Dominion (as well as through those other protected colonies over which British private property rights extended), their right to restrict newcomers from impinging on that right, as well as their ability to move across the country via the railroads. The bank's official historian makes mention of this when he writes that the Royal's branches typically sprung "up at the 'end of steel'" (McDowall, 1993, p. 72). These capabilities thus made it possible for the Royal to create an extensive branch network that moved capital from areas that saved to areas that borrowed: "surplus capital from savings on which the bank paid 3 per cent could be transferred to regions hungry for capital and lent for 6 to 7 per cent, not only enhancing profits, but more importantly, building up clientele" (p. 70). Sir Byron Edmund Walker (1893), the first president of the Canadian Bankers Association and president of the Canadian Bank of Commerce, would put a more positive spin on the general nature of these changes:

> The banks in Canada, with thirty, forty, or fifty branches, with interests which it is no exaggeration to describe as national, cannot be idle or indifferent in times of trouble, cannot turn a deaf ear to the legitimate wants of the farmer in the prairie provinces, any more than to the wealthy merchant or manufacturer in the East. Their business is to gather up the wealth of a nation, not a town or a city, and to supply the borrowing wants of a nation (p. 19).

As Bal (2017) notes, these national branch networks, complete with employees practising an explicitly Canadian (as opposed to local) identity, and head offices that recorded branch-specific data about reserves, loans, and deposits were not only crucial in enabling the chartered banks to see the national economy "far before economists imagined it even to exist" (p. 14) but were in fact central actors in this process, constructing "the very nature of the national space it sought to manage" (p. 1).

The creation of national branch networks was greatly accelerated by another revision to the *Bank Act* in 1900 that allowed the chartered banks to merge without obtaining a special act from Parliament. While the Royal was still a relatively small bank at this time, "with only 162 of the nation's 2367 branches" (McDowall, 1993, p. 124), it used this revision to spread out across the country and absorb local and government savings banks. Moving west, the Royal would possess 21 branches in British Columbia and 25 in Ontario, including a branch in every provincial capital by 1908; moving east, it would absorb most of the Maritime banks by 1910.[42] As noted in the *New York Times*, for instance, the takeover of the Union Bank of Halifax added "some $16,000,000" to the Royal's assets and increased their "capital and reserve to nearly $13,000,000" ("Canadian Banks to Merge," 1910, p. 8). With the Royal having absorbed one of its rivals, the *Times* would note that the merger was part of a more general "tendency toward consolidation among Canadian banks" (p. 8). The takeover of government savings banks was especially significant in this process because it not only increased the Royal's deposits, and thus, the strength of their lending position, but it also redirected the public's savings from bonds (state, municipal, railroad) and public buildings towards commercial banking.[43] As McDowall (1993) notes, "more than anything else, mergers vaulted the Royal into the leadership of Canadian banking" (p. 125).

The Royal's domination of the national market was not without struggle, however, and it often required exerting federal authority over provincial governments. As the regional character of banking disappeared, it was sometimes unclear which level of the state (municipal, provincial, federal) had rights over certain aspects of the chartered banks' activities. An example of this can be seen in 1909 when a guarantee was given to the Alberta and Great Waterways Railway by the Alberta government. When the $7.4 million in bonds were floated in London, the Royal, along with two other banks, the Union Bank of Canada and the Dominion Bank, "agreed to create construction accounts in New York for the proceeds" (McDowall, 1993, p. 208). After the project was derailed by scandal, the Alberta government demanded that the Royal divert the funds back into the province's general revenue. When the Royal refused, the Alberta government took them to court. The *New York Times* noted that the sum was "the largest amount ever sought to be recovered in an action in [Alberta]" ("Sues Banks," 1910, p. 11). When the Alberta government won, receiving $6.5 million in damages, the Royal appealed the decision, taking it all the way to the Judicial Committee of the Privy Council in London. As McDowall (1993) notes, the result could have been a disaster for the Royal, as any hint that their capital "was subject to the whims of provincial governments could

---

42 For expansion in British Columbia and Ontario, see McDowall (1993, pp. 70–3), and for expansion in the Maritimes, see McDowall (1993, pp. 133–4).

43 When asked in the House of Commons in 1913 whether his savings department differs from the government savings banks as a whole, Sir Edmund Walker, president of the Canadian Bank of Commerce, replied, "Oh yes, we take the savings money and use it in commercial banking" (as cited in Naylor, 1975/1997, p. 93).

spoil investor confidence" (p. 208). In 1913, the Royal's solicitor, future prime minister and Royal director R.B. Bennett, argued that Alberta had acted *ultra vires* (beyond one's legal powers or authority) when they denied bondholders their civil rights as set out in Section 91 of the *British North America Act*. The *Edmonton Bulletin* reacted to the decision by noting that it was "a particularly flagrant case of protection of private or corporate interests against public right. The province is being ground between the upper and nether millstone of the Privy Council and the Royal Bank" (as cited in Hanson et al., 2003, p. 41). For the chartered banks, however, the ruling meant that the power of the Canadian state was now their "ultimate guarantee in the face of a regional challenge" (McDowall, 1993, p. 208).

The *Finance Act*

While Confederation, the *Bank Act*, and the National Policy functioned as capabilities enabling the chartered banks to grow and expand, the banks' growth was fraught with the contradictions of capital accumulation – that is, the self-destructive tendency of capital to eat away at the very conditions that sustain it. The government would thus be forced to transfer some of the rights of the chartered banks to the nation state in exchange for a variety of protective services that would enable them to continue their expansion.[44] The first transfer was the 1914 *Finance Act*, and the second was the 1934 *Bank of Canada Act*. Both would put the expansion of credit in the hands of the national government, as opposed to the banks; in doing so, they would protect the chartered banks from the contradictions of their own accumulation activities by providing them with more capabilities to aid in the development of the national political economy. In this sense, we can understand these two Acts as a reflection of a more general nationalization of state capabilities that would ultimately reach their apex with the emergence of the welfare state.

The origins of both Acts can be found in the growing power of the chartered banks and their effect on national economic development. The annual fall sale of crops in the West – remember, at this time,

---

44 Polanyi (1944/2002) notes: "Modern central banking, in effect, was essentially a device developed for the purpose of offering protection without which the market would have destroyed its own children, the business enterprises of all kinds" (p. 201). Fred Block and Margaret Somers (2014) have expanded on this idea recently, noting that "the growth and elaboration of central banking created a variety of means by which the impact of international forces was lessened" (p. 55).

Canada was mainly a country of farmers – brought with it a demand for ready cash; since the banks could only circulate notes to the extent of their paid-up capital, however, there was always a cash drought each fall that "tended to choke national development" (McDowall, 1993, p. 74). After consultation with the CBA, the finance minister revised the *Bank Act* in 1908 to allow the chartered banks to increase their "note circulation during 'crop-moving' season to 115 per cent of their capital base" (p. 74). This revision was significant because for the first time it gave the federal government a direct mechanism to affect the volume of credit. The 1913 *Bank Act* revision would expand this mechanism by creating a Central Gold Reserve that would allow the banks to obtain excess circulation upon the deposit of gold or Dominion notes: in other words, a sort of rudimentary central bank, a taste of what was to come.

The 1913 revision also required the chartered banks to secure ministerial approval for mergers before they were approved by their shareholders. Because of this requirement, the finance minister was "put in a better position to ensure that the public interest was served by a proposed merger" (McDowall, 1993, p. 144). As McDowall (1993) notes, the revised *Bank Act* was a clear response "to the public mood of reform" (p. 144), as the growing size and power of the chartered banks had, by this time, become a fetter on the economic development of the West.[45] The chartered banks defended their size on the basis that it was a requirement of the increasing scale of economic development.

---

45 Naylor (1975/1997) provides some historical context: "As early as 1883, Manitoba businessmen complained of a financial squeeze imposed upon them at the instigation of central Canadian financial magnates. This agitation contributed a great deal to the creation of the Commercial Bank of Manitoba in 1885 to service the local community. By 1907, agitation was widespread in BC for a system of provincial banks. The existing banks were accused of draining surplus funds from the province for the benefit of eastern enterprise while BC firms were starved for credit. The Bank of Vancouver was established in 1911 in response to these local needs. In Alberta, the farmers' organizations long advocated a Provincial Bank of Issue and a system of provincially chartered local unit banks on the American state bank model. In Saskatchewan, a Royal Commission investigating agricultural credit called for increased control of financial institutions within the province and denounced the chartered banks, who conspicuously lacked directors from the western provinces. The little Weyburn Security Bank was held up as a model before the 1913 Committee on Banking. And a western member of the House of Commons that year denounced the *Bank Act* for facilitating the creation of a 'money trust' by encouraging mergers and inhibiting new entrants. What was needed, he claimed, was 'more banks, and a scattered management of banks, rather than concentration.' These sentiments were repeated by the Grain Growers Association" (pp. 101–2). Further details are given by McDowall (1993) from the Royal's perspective (p. 141).

The Royal's then-president, Herbert Holt, would tell shareholders in 1912 that when Canada was "a country of small affairs, small banks sufficed, but that we must have banks to handle the large operations of the present day" (as cited in McDowall, 1993, p. 124).[46] A similar sentiment was expressed by Nathaniel Curry, a Nova Scotia industrialist, who wrote to the finance minister in 1913 to argue that the current scale of economic development made it "absolutely necessary to have large banks" (as cited in McDowall, 1993, p. 452, n. 5). Later, in 1919, the general manager of the Bank of Nova Scotia, H.A. Richardson, would remind the same finance minister that "only large and strong banks can expand" (as cited in McDowall, 1993, p. 124).

While the outbreak of the First World War in 1914 would put a slight halt on the expansion of the chartered banks, the *Finance Act* would allow it to continue apace by putting the expansion of credit in the hands of the Canadian government. The start of this process began with the end of the "Laurier boom" and the start of the First World War.[47] With investment from Europe slowing down, panicky savers began to raid their deposits to purchase gold. The significance of the event is explained by McDowall (1993):

> The backbone of the Canadian banking system was the gold standard. The ultimate guarantee for anyone holding a Canadian banknote was that it was backed by gold or gold in the form of Dominion notes. While

---

46 It is important to stress the extent of corporate control enjoyed by capitalists like Holt. As Peter C. Newman (2004) notes, "Sir Herbert Holt ... came closer than any tycoon before or since to wielding power on a scale that determined Canada's fiscal direction. During his ascendancy in the first three decades of the twentieth century, he gained control of three hundred companies on four continents, including Holt Renfrew (named after its founding furrier, John H. Holt, who died in 1915). He also controlled shipyards, international utilities, a forest empire that produced 10 per cent of the world's newsprint, hotels, streetcar systems, railways, and, although he seldom saw a movie, he founded the Famous Players theatre chain. He controlled the Royal Bank of Canada, headed what was then the world's largest corporation, Hydro-Electric Securities Ltd., and in 1928, when Canada's total paper currency in circulation was worth $300 million, directed assets worth $3 billion" (pp. 113–14). For more on Holt, see Nerbas (2013).

47 McDowall (1993) describes the situation: "In the spring of 1913 this felicitous relationship of eastern banker and western grower suddenly became strained. The Laurier boom finally faltered in the face of a sharp slump in the North Atlantic trading economies; grain demand slackened, and credit contracted in London. Drought accelerated the collapse: wheat yield per acre in 1914 was only 74 percent of its 1913 level. The downturn soon reverberated throughout the banking industry" (p. 210).

this ensured confidence and stability in the national currency, the reserves backing a bank's circulation were essentially non-earning and tended to crimp a bank's ability to expand credit in a buoyant economy. When Ottawa partially alleviated this strain by creating the Central Gold Reserve, [Edson] Pease [the Royal's general manager] was strongly in favour of it as a means of expanding the Royal's credit. Extra circulation, made possible by the deposit of gold or Dominion notes in the central reserve, gave the bank added reach in the national economy. (p. 151)

The outbreak of war, however, unsettled this system, as wealthier Canadians began to hoard gold as a financial hedge against disruptions in the market. The federal government responded by suspending the gold standard in August of 1914, instead letting the chartered banks create credit up to 15 per cent of their paid-up capital by borrowing Dominion notes. Secured with "collateral of high-quality securities, such as municipal, utility, and railway bonds" (McDowall, 1993, p. 211), the banks were allowed "'excess circulation' beyond the traditional crop-moving period of the year" (p. 211). While the banks were now backed by the confidence of the federal government and their solvency ensured, the agreement was also illegal, running counter to the *Bank Act*. In response, Prime Minister Borden quickly called a cabinet meeting to ratify the changes, and "when Parliament convened later in August, 'An Act to Conserve the Commercial and Financial Interests of Canada' – the *Finance Act* – made the whole exercise legal" (p. 212).

The *Finance Act* signalled an important shift in the relationship between the chartered banks and the Canadian nation state. Prior to the First World War, the chartered banks were only loosely constrained by regulatory legislation and usury laws, with the CBA functioning "as a legally sanctioned cartel, fixing interest rates, delineating spheres of influence, and regulating entry into the business" (Naylor, 1985, p. 65). With the introduction of the *Finance Act*, however, not only did the nation state became the lender of last resort, but the suspension of the convertibility of Dominion notes into gold meant that the federal government could "resort to the printing press to finance part of Canada's war effort" (p. 67); as such, it now had a mechanism to alter "the level of bank cash and therefore the credit base of the chartered banking system without reference to the net movement of monetary gold" (p. 68).

The federal government was forced to use this tool due to the failure of Britain to finance the cost of Canada's military operations overseas. While the British government initially promised to finance this cost through a $60-million advance from the treasury, by March 1915 their generosity was exhausted, forcing Ottawa to resort to the printing press and to impose new user taxes "on financial, railway, and telegraph companies" (McDowall, 1993, p. 213). As McDowall (1993) notes, the significance of this nationalization of authority is that it "put the power of expanding credit in the hands of the government, not private bankers" (p. 153). Similarly, the Treasury Board of Canada would also acquire the power to fix interest rates, a power that was previously under the control of the CBA within the limits set by the usury laws. As Naylor (1985) notes, "the change was symbolic of the political forces at work during the war and continuing just after it" (p. 91). Authority that had previously been exercised by a private sector business association by virtue of the delegation of power to it by the federal government was now "ceded to a politically appointed, civil service organization" (p. 91).

By the end of the war, most of the chartered banks had become accustomed to their new relationship with the state. The general manager of the Royal, Edson Pease, felt differently, however; elected to the head of the CBA in 1916, Pease argued that it was "not a good principle for the government to engage permanently in the banking business" (as cited in McDowall, 1993, p. 212). He suggested instead that it would be more prudent to have an independent bank of rediscount similar to the US Federal Reserve – in other words, an independent central bank:

> If we had a bank of rediscount patterned somewhat after the Federal Reserve Bank in the United States, it would render legitimately available millions of assets in the form of high grade commercial paper, now lying dormant in the portfolios of the banks, and thereby greatly increase our financial resources. (as cited in McDowall, 1993, p. 154)

The suggestion was immediately rejected by the Bank of Montreal, which tended to refuse any policy that threatened its position as the government's banker.[48] Having overseen the federal government's financial affairs in London since Confederation, the Bank of Montreal still managed the government's loans and departmental accounts. Unsure whether to divide the government's accounts among all the chartered banks or allow the Bank of Montreal to continue as the government bank, the finance minister would simply extend the *Finance*

---

48 As Turley-Ewart (2000) notes, "Edson Pease's appeal for a central bank was as much about managing Canada's credit as wrestling the government's account from the Bank of Montreal. Pease and Sir Vincent Meredith 'were not on speaking terms.' Sir Frederick Williams-Taylor and the Royal Bank's general manager, Charlie Neill, 'barely tolerated each other'" (p. 305).

Act until the normally scheduled 1923 revision; as McDowall (1993) notes, "the *status quo* prevailed" (p. 156).

By protecting Canada's financial system – and thus, the chartered banks – the *Finance Act* enabled the Royal to continue expanding. Although they were already well established in the territories of the Caribbean over which British private property rights extended, the postwar period would see a massive expansion of both their foreign and domestic banking business.[49] In part, this was due to the US Federal Reserve Act of 1913, which freed American banks from their territorial confines. Where the Royal previously played an important role in mediating capital flows between New York and London through self-made tax havens in those areas of the Caribbean under British rule, it was now forced to adapt to competition from American banks rushing abroad. This inevitably meant that it would have to expand further to survive. From 1918 to 1925 the Royal doubled the number of its international branches, becoming Canada's leading international bank with 121 branches in 28 countries (Darroch, 1994, p. 127). It also purchased a 15-storey office building on the northeast corner of William and Cedar Streets for their New York agency. As noted in the *New York Times*, the purchase was the "result of the recent expansion of banking activity in New York" and was "in line with the tendency of banks to buy property for permanent occupancy, because of the rapidly narrowing area in the financial section available for their use" ("Canadian Bank Buys," 1919, p. 6).

This expansion continued at home as well. As McDowall (1993) notes, "the Royal's pre-eminence as Canada's leading international banker was in large measure rooted in its ability to muster sufficient manpower at home to realize its ambitions abroad" (pp. 158–60). As part of Mackenzie King's push to break the Bank of Montreal's monopoly on government banking, the Royal gained several important government

---

49 P.J. Hudson (2010) provides some detail on their Caribbean expansion: "Substituting political ties for economic tethers, the Royal Bank embarked on a major push in the Anglophone Caribbean through a strategy that combined mergers and acquisitions of existing institutions with branch expansion. In some case, it gained near-total control of the commercial financing of the colonies in which it set up shop. In 1910, it absorbed the Union Bank of Halifax, which in addition to its thirty branches in the Canadian Maritimes had agencies in Trinidad and Puerto Rico that largely served the financial needs of the Canadian utility and rail companies operating in the two islands. The Bank of British Honduras in Belize, which financed Belize's hide and mahogany exports, was taken over in 1912 and soon thereafter, according to its manager F.R. Beattie, it was 'conduct[ing] the entire banking business of the colony'" (p. 39).

accounts, such as Canadian National Telegraph. They also expanded through government-assisted mergers with failed banks.[50] The spectacular failure of the Home Bank of Canada on 18 August 1923, however, forced the federal government to revise the *Bank Act* to include an Inspector General of Banks "to police the system by making an annual inspection of each chartered bank" (McDowall, 1993, p. 148), as recommended by a royal commission (see McKeown, 1924).[51] Having previously operated without any inspection system due to "concerns about cost, efficiency and duplication of work being performed by internal and external auditors" (Office of the Superintendent of Financial Institutions [OSFI], n.d., para. 5), the new Office of the Inspector General of Banks (OIGB), created in 1925, would naturally follow the British model, "which did not include on-site examinations and placed a great deal of reliance on self-regulation" (para. 5). To influence this shift in authority, the Royal lent the government one of their own bankers, Charles S. Tomkins.

With "bankers' fears of political interference" (McDowall, 1993, p. 232) minimized, the Royal's national expansion could continue apace: branches were opened in Quebec mining towns, the grain port of Churchill, Manitoba, and Fort St. John in the BC interior. By 1929, the

---

50 The Royal took over the Union Bank of Halifax in 1910, the Traders Bank of Canada in 1912, Quebec Bank in 1917, Northern Crown Bank in 1918, and the Union Bank of Canada in 1925 (Dominion Bureau of Statistics, 1927). Morck et al. (2007) provide more details as to how the conditions of the Great Depression led to the rise of the widely held firm: "Canada's banking system underwent a profound crisis in the 1920s and another in the 1930s. World War I inflation ushered in several years of deflation, bankruptcies, and bank failures. Much merger activity in the early and mid-1920s involves government orchestrated consolidations of healthy banks with distressed ones in the early 1920s. By 1928, Canada had only ten chartered banks, down from thirty in 1910. The last narrowly held family bank, Molson's Bank, was taken over by the Bank of Montreal. The downturn wiped out several of the professional managers running former Aitkin group firms and several old family fortunes, contributing to the decline in importance of family groups" (p. 112).
51 Originally founded in 1854, the failure of the Home Bank was the result of poor loans and fraud alongside a recession created by the chartered banks raising interest rates in 1920 in an attempt to control rising prices. As the demand for credit fell, the resulting recession drove prices down dramatically, making many assets worth less than the money initially loaned to acquire them. In this case, Home Bank was simply the one left holding the bag. In the aftermath, 10 officials from the Home Bank were arrested on charges, including fraud, and 60,000 prairie farmers lost their life savings, prompting Prime Minister Mackenzie King to launch a royal commission into the cause of the failure in 1924. For more on the failure of the Home Bank, and banking without deposit insurance, see Carr et al. (1995); Kyer (2017); Lew & Richardson (1992).

Royal would possess 44 branches in Montreal, 37 in Toronto, and 20 in Vancouver. The process was similar with the other large, chartered banks. In 1927, for example,

> The Bank of Montreal held 25.98% of the resources of all banks. The Royal Bank, the Canadian Bank of Commerce and the Bank of Nova Scotia accounted for 26.09%, 16.54% and a little more than 8% respectively. Together these four banks accounted for 77% of banking assets. (Van Houten, 1991, p. 71)

Taking over smaller banks as they moved across the country, the three largest chartered banks – the Royal Bank, the Bank of Montreal, and the Bank of Commerce – would also start to represent "centres of integrated financial groups" (Carroll, 1986, p. 53), possessing three or more directors on each other's boards (Piédalue, 1976; Sweeny, 1997). The Royal was thus not only Canada's largest bank, but it had also become, as historian Don Nerbas (2013) notes, a central institution "in the business life of the nation's bourgeoisie" (p. 20), a point reflected in the addition of the provincial crests of all the provinces to their new building on Montreal's St. James Street.[52] As Nerbas (2013) remarks, it was the "tallest building in Montreal ... a testament to the bank's rising stature in business and finance" (p. 3).

Having already taken over most of the country's smaller banks, the Royal's own publications note that by the 1920s there "were now no cities but a few towns in Canada in which the bank was not represented" (Royal Bank of Canada, 1920, p. 25). As such, the Royal began to set up foreign trade departments in Montreal and New York, with the New York office overseeing the newly created "New Business Department," which was meant to "get in touch with American firms established or proposing to establish branches outside of the United States" (Quigley, 1986, p. 36). The Royal's plan was less about American imperialism and more to do with a combination of factors, such as Canada's low population and industrial capacity, its geographical proximity to the United States, the general scale of capitalist production, technological change, and "the passing of the American frontier, [which] created a larger number of US firms possessing the capability

---

52 As McDowall (1993) recounts, "When the directors commissioned the New York architects York and Sawyer to design a new head office – taller than the Bank of Montreal's – on St. James Street in 1926, they instructed them to decorate the gilded ceiling of the main banking hall with the provincial crests of all the provinces, not just the coats of arms of Halifax and Montreal" (p. 162).

and will to expand overseas" (Quigley, 1986, p. 43).[53] It was also a reflection of the resources and personnel of the chartered banks, who were now finally large and specialized enough to design and operationalize their "industrialization by solicitation" strategy to develop Canada's economy.[54] They hoped that there would be increased trade as a result of the establishment of American branch plants, which would enable American corporations to "take advantage of the preferential tariffs applying to Canadian goods entering other British Dominions" (Quigley, 1986, p. 49). Through this strategy, Canada became one of the first modern outsourcers available to globalizing American capital. Entering via direct investment in the form of branch plants to jump the tariff wall, this investment profile would define Canada's industrial and resource sectors for the next 60 years, providing multiple opportunities for the chartered banks to profit (Clement, 1977a; L.E. Davis & Gallman, 2001; Naylor, 1975/1997). American companies paid special attention to Canada not only "because of its proximity but mainly because they wanted to partake in the profit to be made in a country with vast stores of natural wealth and a rapidly expanding market" (Van Houten, 1991, p. 127). S.H. Logan (1937), a supervisor in the foreign department of the Canadian Bank of Commerce, put it as follows: "It is largely the export markets that dictate the prosperity of the country, as the commodities we have to sell, such as wheat, fruit, fish, lumber, newsprint, metals, certain manufactures, find their principal markets abroad" (p. 149). Twenty years later, A.J. Knowles (1957), a retired superintendent of the Royal Bank of Canada, would remark on the strategy's success:

> Gross foreign capital invested in Canada is roughly $15 billion at date, and about $10 billion of this came from the USA. Very little foreign capital is

---

53 For more on the unique relationship between American branch plants and Canadian chartered banks, see Sweeny (1997, pp. 333–4).
54 Naylor (1985) provides more details: "As early as 1920 the Minister of Finance, Sir Thomas White, had recommenced the old game of publicly inviting American capital to partake of Canada's corporate fruits. With the foundations already in place in the pre-war boom through joint ventures, licensing arrangements, and cartel agreements, and with a legacy of wartime industrial cooperation to reinforce the ties, American capital responded quickly and favourably to America's new position as dominant world capital exporter by flowing freely into Canada. Mineral development, pulp and paper, automobile, electrical product, and chemical plants were the most favoured sectors" (p. 99). As Quigley (1986) notes, however, "the emergence of the 'industrialization by solicitation' strategy in Canadian banks accords with current interpretations of the process by which firms with multinational aspirations appeared in the US. It also coincides with important changes in the organization and management of industrial companies" (p. 43).

invested in bank shares, but it seems that US investors control about half the capital in Canada's mining smelting, petroleum and manufacturing industries. Most of the capital employed in the oil industry is reported to be foreign-owned. (p. 135)

He would also point to a further reality, one which has long been at the basis of competing accounts of Canadian development: that this "capital movement is not a one-way trend" (p. 135). He continues: "Gross Canadian investment abroad is almost half the amount of foreign capital invested here" (p. 135). As later authors have demonstrated, this investment profile would begin to transform in the 1970s (Burgess, 2002; Carroll, 1986; Kellogg, 2015; Klassen, 2009, 2014), a point to which we will return.

The Bank of Canada

The world stands upon the verge of a period of prosperity similar to that which is now being experienced in North America, and ... the volume of our trade will soon rise to new and unprecedented levels.
– Herbert Holt, president of the Royal Bank of Canada, 1929 (as cited in Nerbas, 2013, p. 3)

The Great Depression had a significant impact on the Royal, and with the creation of the Bank of Canada in 1934, the Royal's relationship to the Canadian state was fundamentally altered. The Great Depression was triggered by the collapse of share prices on the New York Stock Exchange on Black Tuesday, 29 October 1929, and quickly spread around the world.[55] As Struthers (2021) notes,

> In Canada, the changes were dramatic. Between 1929 and 1933, Canada's Gross National Expenditure (overall public and private spending) fell by 42 per cent. By 1933, 30 per cent of the labour force was out of work. One in five Canadians became dependent upon government relief for survival. The unemployment rate remained above 12 per cent until the start of the Second World War in 1939. (para. 3)

---

55 For an excellent overview of the conditions leading to Black Tuesday, see Gordon Thomas and Max Morgan-Witts's (1979) *The Day the Bubble Burst: A Social History of the Wall Street Crash*.

Farming communities in Western Canada were hit especially hard by the collapse of wheat prices. One of the more significant effects, however, was the freezing of credit, which had a knock-on effect on all other areas of the economy.

The Bank of Canada was initially set up as a private institution empowered to regulate internal credit and foreign exchange, give the government impartial financial advice, and use monetary action to avoid national economic crises.[56] In return for these services, the chartered banks surrendered their right to issue notes, thus ending Canada's distinctive medley of banknotes, as well as their gold reserves.[57] Four years later, Prime Minister Mackenzie King nationalized the entire operation; in doing so, he brought a central element of the chartered banks' activities – credit creation – under the authority of the nation state for the protection and development of the national political economy.[58] The federal government was now the guarantor of the Dominion's note circulation, assuming the risks of being the lender of last resort. Given the strength of the chartered banks, their long-standing desire to retain their right to issue notes, and their wish to keep the government at arm's length from their operations, the creation, and subsequent nationalization, of the Bank of Canada can be seen as a sort of last-ditch effort to stabilize Canada's national political economy during the Great Depression – albeit one that was supported by the Royal Bank as early as 1918 for the purpose of ending "the suzerainty of the Bank of Montreal as the government's banker" (McDowall, 1993, p. 156).

Having already earned full legislative powers over internal and external affairs in 1931 because of the Statute of Westminster, Canada's Prime Minister, R.B. Bennett, asked the CBA to consider a form of central bank in 1931 "because he hoped it would lessen the country's

---

56 The Bank of Canada provides this function by way of the chartered banks: "by changing the total amount of cash reserves available to the chartered banks, it can oblige them to adjust their portfolios of liquid assets and their willingness to compete for deposit liabilities" (Van Houten, 1991, p. 175). The Bank of Canada is also able to influence interest rates through the buying and selling of government securities, and "can affect short-term interest rates by manipulating the prime bank rate" (p. 175).
57 See E. Gilbert (2002) and Helleiner (2003) for more on the creation of Canada's national currency.
58 Van Houten (1991) notes: "In 1938, the government nationalized the Bank of Canada. Four years earlier, the *Bank of Canada Act* had empowered the bank to determine the total amount of cash reserves available to the chartered banks and therefore gave it control over the rate of expansion of the total assets and liabilities of the banking system as a whole. Nationalization transferred that power to the state" (p. 83).

dependence on New York banks that he believed controlled the value of the Canadian dollar" (Helleiner, 2003, p. 153). Bennett was not just influenced by nationalist concerns, however, but also "by pressure from more left-wing forces who gained strength during the Depression and demanded more activist monetary policies" (p. 153). Public sentiment had shifted strongly against big capital since the 1920s, and the chartered banks were no exception. Writing in *Canadian Banker*, B.C. Gardner (1938), an assistant general manager for the Bank of Montreal, remarked that "during and since the depression banks have been attacked on all sides and even the individuals engaged in the banking business have been assailed personally" (p. 187). The banks' increased usage of Section 88 of the *Bank Act*, which allowed them to seize cattle, tractors, and other farm implements to settle debts, had made them increasingly unpopular in the Prairies. After a Saskatchewan MP told Bennett that the Royal Bank manager in Borden was "'simply taking the shirts off the backs of the people' by exercising his Section 88 prerogatives, Bennett warned the bank's head office that such incidents fed political radicalism – 'the nourishment upon which the Woodsworth faction [i.e., the Co-operative Commonwealth Federation] feeds'" (McDowall, 1993, p. 248).[59]

Since the chartered banks were concerned that a central bank could "fall under the thrall of politicians" (McDowall, 1993, p. 27), they instead joined Canada's other large corporations in calling for a merger of the Liberal and Conservative Parties in order to create the political conditions to avoid national insolvency by amalgamating the publicly owned but debt-burdened Canadian National Railway (CNR) with the privately owned CPR. Warned by Montagu Norman, the governor of the Bank of England, that if nothing was done "about the railway problem it would break the country" (as cited in Nerbas, 2013, p. 141), the plan was, as Nerbas (2013) notes, little more than an attempt to "shore up the old political economy and restore the power of capital" (p. 147). Accurately sensing the public's reaction, Mackenzie King argued that the plan would end up sacrificing "democracy to serve the ends of plutocracy" (as cited in Nerbas, 2013, p. 146) and elevate the Co-operative Commonwealth Federation (CCF) – whose platform included the nationalization of the chartered banks – to the status of

---

59 Bennett also told the president of the CBA that "it is idle to expect any member of Parliament or Canadian citizen for that matter to justify some of the acts of the banks in driving customers to the wall who are unable to liquidate their liabilities under existing circumstances" (as cited in McDowall, 1993, p. 248).

official opposition.[60] Instead, the Royal "took a $12.2 million share of a $60 million dollar loan to Canadian Pacific to rescue it from defaulting on a series of short-term obligations that could not be financed on troubled Wall Street" (McDowall, 1993, p. 269). While the original plan of the chartered banks was unsuccessful, it demonstrates the extent to which they were willing to go to retain their rights and privileges. Despite the existence of a later essay in *Canadian Banker* claiming that "social injustices will not be corrected by submergence of all classes in an autarchic state run by labourers or by capitalists" (Womersley, 1937, p. 202), it must be admitted that capital's solution to the crisis in Canada was disturbingly similar to the forms of authoritarianism that were emerging in other, formerly liberal-democratic, countries.[61]

In any case, this attempt to solve the issue was eventually thwarted by the results of the 1933 Royal Commission on Banking and Currency, which asked a number of basic questions about the operation of the banking system:

To what extent and through what organizations should the volume of credit and the currency be regulated? On what body should lie the primary responsibility for maintaining the external stability of the country's currency? To what institution may the Government of the day be most

---

60 McDowall (1993) relates how "the leader of the CCF, M.J. Coldwell, pushed for bank nationalization, arguing that the creation of national credit should not be left in the hands of 'irresponsible boards of directors'" (p. 304).
61 There are a number of essays in *Canadian Banker* that are disparaging to communism and labour in general, but perhaps the best example is that by Wilfrid Womersley (1937), a senior employee of the Royal Bank's Winnipeg branch, who writes the following: "Widespread propaganda makes the utmost use of the fact that recent upheavals have taken a Communism-versus-Fascism complexion and urges the claims of Communism as the only real protection 'the masses' have against Fascism. Communism masquerades under the name 'Workers' Democracy' (as if there could be a workers' democracy any more than there could be an aristocrats' democracy or a farmers' democracy)" (p. 201); "labour in Canada realizes now, more than ever, that it is not the sole heir to all the benefits of material progress but that it is a partner – and often, an actual co-owner – with capital. Labour with capital spells progress; labour against capital means, eventually, dictatorship" (p. 202). He also expressed paternalistic fears that Canada's youth, "in its anxiety to be 'up and doing' some-times takes short cuts to its objective without waiting to appraise the indirect consequences; that there are diseases in our political and economic structure to be cured and that youth may be led to consider amputation a less troublesome remedy than a lengthy administration of the medication of conciliation and the serum of education" (p. 202).

suitably turn for informed and impartial advice on matters of financial policy? (p. 62)

The report noted that "in the great, and an increasing, majority of countries the answers to these questions has been found in the existence or the creation of a central bank" (p. 62). As Germain (2010) points out, the 1920s marked the first great wave of central bank expansion as countries around the world attempted to deal with new problems relating to the development of their respective financial systems, with the final national level of innovation coming in the 1930s "as a consequence of the collapse of stock markets and the onset of the Depression" (p. 32). Putting it plainly, the Royal Commission on Banking and Currency (1933) argued that "as an instrument [the central bank] is the means by which the state – which must necessarily retain ultimate sovereignty in matters affecting the currency – can give effect to the national policy" (p. 63). The stage was therefore set for a shift in authority away from the chartered banks and towards the institutions of the nation state.

For the Royal specifically, their activities over this period make clear just how necessary the Bank of Canada was to reproducing Canadian capitalism in the context of the Great Depression. Profits made during the First World War had enabled all the chartered banks to export capital to Britain, the United States, and various British Caribbean colonies. Their profits during this period were mainly derived from their new relationship with the nation state as a result of the *Finance Act* and the creation of war bonds, which the banks underwrote.[62] In an attempt to establish itself in Germany, the Royal had provided loans to German banks through its New York, London, and Paris offices.[63] The Royal

---

62 McDowall (1993) notes: "The 1918 target of $300 million was overshadowed by a $690 million result from over a million subscribers. 'That we are able to handle these gigantic sums is amazing,' Pease confided to a friend. 'It is proof of the great increase in the wealth of the country since the war began. It is hard to believe that in addition to taking care of the government requirements and the flotation in Canada of $350,000,000 of domestic loans, the deposits of the banks today are $500,000,000 greater than they were before the war began'" (p. 216).

63 A manager for the Royal Bank in Paris reveals how the nature of TAR during this period operated, as compared with today: "Under French laws then in force, we had the option of establishing a branch of the bank or of taking out a charter for a separate French company, with the capital in French francs, all the shares to be owned by the head office of our bank, thus giving it full control. Each plan had been adopted by English and United States banks in France, and each had certain features to recommend it. We chose the latter, and in actual practice it gave us complete liberty of action to handle all classes of banking business normally engaged in by French banks" (N.G. Hart, 1951, p. 103).

was already owed $9.4 million by 1930 when the conditions of post-war Germany (hyper-inflation and social instability) caused the Weimar Republic to sign a Standstill Agreement in 1931, halting all their foreign debt obligations. In combination with the earlier collapse of the Cuban sugar industry, the collapse of wheat prices, and the general financial conditions of the Great Depression, the Royal was out roughly $33 million. In 1932, the Canadian government would attempt to extend some credit to the chartered banks by allowing them to borrow $35 million at 3 per cent, which was subsequently loaned back to the government at 4 per cent. As McDowall (1993) notes, "it had little or no impact on credit conditions" (p. 269).

To avoid immediate collapse, the Royal first attempted to take over its debtors' stock, but it was blocked from doing so by the *Bank Act*. The Royal was admittedly in a difficult situation, since "among the $23 million in questionable domestic loans were the businesses of some of Canada's premier financiers: T.B. Macaulay, Harry Gundy, and, indirectly, [Royal President] Herbert Holt" (McDowall, 1993, p. 257). As McDowall (1993) notes, any attempt to force the liquidation of these accounts would necessarily provoke a major crisis of confidence in Canadian business: "who in the bank, after all, would have the temerity to demand repayment of a $2.9-million loan to the Consolidated Investment Corporation, a 1929 Holt holding-company creation?" (p. 257). The Royal's solution was simple: just break the law. Three of the Royal's directors – A.J. Brown, G.H. Duggan, and Herbert Holt – created the Islemont Securities Corporation, which, after taking a loan from the Royal for $7,992,780 secured with $8 million of its own 20-year collateral trust bonds, began to purchase large blocks of Royal shares from its debtors, thus easing the bank's overall debt load. As McDowall (1993) notes, "the tactic was quickly mimicked to relieve the pain of debt elsewhere in the portfolio" (p. 260).[64] An Order in Council from Prime Minister Bennett, the Royal's former lawyer, also allowed the bank to "value securities they then held at prices higher than the depressed market prices" (Park & Park, 1962, p. 55).[65] While some of the chartered banks still held to their earlier position that the *Finance Act* provided a more than adequate means of creating credit and that "the profits they garnered from circulating their own notes helped to

---

[64] McDowall (1993) also notes that it was "no coincidence that, in 1934, the *Bank Act* was revised to prohibit a bank director from voting approval for any loan to a concern in which he held an interest" (p. 261).

[65] It is no surprise that after his retirement from politics in 1938, Bennett was promptly made a director of the Royal Bank.

pay the costs of running a national branch system" (McDowall, 1993, p. 273), it was becoming increasingly clear that having a central bank would help avoid such crises in the future, especially in the context of the more general wave of central bank creation in the 1920s (Germain, 2010, p. 31). To offset the loss of some of its rights and privileges, the Royal would, once again, get one of its own, assistant manager Graham Towers, appointed as the first governor of the Bank of Canada. As reported in the *New York Times*, the choice of Towers over a Bank of England man was due to "fear[s] that Canada's finances might be controlled by London" ("Canada Picks Head," 1934, p. 37).

While the creation of the Bank of Canada allowed the chartered banks to "entertain ideas of credit expansion at the end of the decade" (McDowall, 1993, p. 283), it also fundamentally changed their relationship with the state. Having lost significant rights in return for their security, the banks were now subject to political pressures like never before. Despite this reality, many bankers argued that it had to be done to ensure their continued growth. Writing in *Canadian Banker*, H.T. Jaffray (1941), the general manager of the Imperial Bank of Canada, scolded those who claimed that the central bank restricted their freedom: "I would only say to them that nothing has been done which is not in the best interests of the country and of the freedom of the world, and that their individual inconveniences are a minor matter" (p. 150). Similarly, D.M. Marvin (1937), an economist with the Royal Bank, astutely pointed out that "the quality and the management of the Bank of Canada is and will remain a large factor in the welfare of business in every part of the country" (p. 33). While true, the creation of the central bank also meant that the chartered banks "could no longer count on their informal confabs with the finance minister to make sure their views were understood" (McDowall, 1993, p. 276). Instead, they would increasingly rely on "paid lobbyists, radio 'propaganda,' and advocacy programs to preserve their stake in Canadian society" (p. 276). Much of this propaganda was targeted at those political parties, such as Social Credit and the CCF, that directly challenged their power, especially in the West.[66] Put simply, the creation of the Bank of Canada meant that "Canadian banking would never be the same again" (p. 272).

---

66 For instance, there was a CBA-promoted speaking tour by famous writer and former Royal employee Stephen Leacock: "'I spoke,' Leacock reported, 'on literary, humours and college stuff, and on Social Credit'" (McDowall, 1993, p. 282). For more on the class context of Alberta during this period, see Macpherson (1953/2013).

Conclusion

In this chapter, I argued that the mid-nineteenth to early twentieth century can be distinguished from our present epoch by the creation of a *national* system of property relations: that is, a centripetal organizing dynamic of TAR towards the national level. My main claim is that as a result of this drawing in, this period should be understood as the making of what we have come to call national capital. This form of capital rested on the construction of a nation state, that is, a domestic market within a certain territory.[67] The main role of the state during this period was to protect the rights of private property necessary for the capitalist market to function and to extend the territory on which this market operated, thus making the national epoch of capitalism one characterized by various forms of imperialism and nationalism. By virtue of this drawing in of TAR, I argue that the institutions of the state were transformed into a capability for the growth of domestic capital both via the extension of territory and by means of providing protection against the contradictions of the accumulation process. In colonies like Canada, this process took place later than other European states, but it took place nonetheless. As Sassen (2006) notes, "the various colonizing efforts took place within the frame of the domestic and imperial expansion of national capitalisms" (p. 140).

To demonstrate the empirical reality of this transformation, I provided an analysis of the transformation of Canadian banking via the history of the Royal Bank of Canada from 1864 to 1944. I identified four shifts in TAR – Confederation and the *Bank Act*; the National Policy; the *Finance Act*; and the Bank of Canada – to represent this drawing in as it relates to the chartered banks. Through Confederation and the *Bank Act*, the rights of banking were standardized and brought to the national level where they were enforced by the institutions of the new nation state, the Dominion of Canada. The territory on which the banks could operate was also extended across the continent by virtue of the National Policy. As articulated by P.E. Corbett (1938) in *Canadian Banker*, "at various times since 1867 the Dominion government has attempted to regulate in a uniform way for the whole country matters of business

---

[67] Although speaking about the United States, Sassen (2006) captures the spirit of the age: "This period saw the establishment of basic governing institutions, the acquisition and distribution of new territory, the promotion of national and international commerce, the development of a powerful national defence and a formalized yet flexible national legal system, and the growth of aggressive policies of regulation, administration, and redistribution" (p. 124).

life concerning all of our people" (p. 161). The main struggle during this period in respect to the banks was in the form of capitalist competition between the chartered banks themselves (in particular, the Bank of Montreal versus the other chartered banks) as well as between the chartered banks and the federal government over the rights of banking. As these dynamics of accumulation played themselves out, the nation state was forced to take increasing control over the creation of credit in the form of the *Finance Act* and, eventually, the currency itself via the creation of the Bank of Canada. I claim that these shifts in TAR transformed the state into a capability for the growth of the chartered banks by enabling them to expand and by protecting them against external competition, as well as against the contradictions of their own accumulation activities. As we will see in the next chapter, while these shifts in TAR made the nation state into a capability for the growth of national capital, it would soon become a fetter on this growth, leading capital to seek out new, unregulated, international activities.

Chapter Three

The Expansion of National Capital: The Growth of the Royal Bank of Canada, 1945–1974

Towards the end of his presidency, Earle McLaughlin reflected that the Eurodollar was "a pretty good invention. I don't know what we would do without it."

– Duncan McDowall (1993, p. 407)

In the early 1970s, when the chairmen of the Big Five banks threw up their opulent skyscraper head offices on Bay Street, each one higher than its competitor's, the only exception was Royal Bank chairman Earle McLaughlin. His building didn't try to compete for number of floors, but became the most appropriate symbol of Bay Street in that its windows were coated with real gold.

– Peter C. Newman (2004, p. 7)

Introduction

In the last chapter, I explored how the mid-nineteenth century through the early twentieth century was constituted in its configuration of territory, authority, and rights (TAR) in respect to banking in Canada. I was mainly concerned with exploring the wider questions of how the property relations that sustained capitalism over that period were organized and how they contributed to the making of what we typically call national capital. I argued that this period of capitalism can be distinguished by virtue of the creation of a *national* system of property relations – that is, by a centripetal organizing dynamic that drew elements of TAR to the national level – which made the state into a capability for the growth of national capital, embodied by the country's largest firms.

In this chapter, I extend this analysis into the mid-twentieth century. The reason for doing this is, like before, to more clearly define the differences in TAR that mark the boundaries of our global age. As such,

I am not concerned here with the divergent interpretations of the facts of this period as provided by theories of Canadian development, which are rooted in the character and nature of Canada's capitalist class in relation to other national capitalist classes.[1] Instead, I am concerned with the specific configuration of TAR that sustained capital over this period and what it enabled capital to do so that we can better appreciate the differences between the national epoch of capitalism and our emerging global epoch. Put simply, my argument in this chapter is that the period from 1945 to 1974 represents a transition between the national and global epochs of capitalism; on the one hand, there is the emergence of increasing levels of global economic activity, but still within the context of a world economy constituted by national systems of property relations. In other words, the post-1945 world order was one that was still national-international, not global.

I make this argument on the basis that the period begins with a continuation of the centripetal organizing logic that characterized the earlier period of capitalism, that is, a continued drawing in of TAR to the national level. Despite increasing levels of global economic activity, the rights of capital and the authority over those rights remained primarily at the nation-state level, giving national governments a variety of options to regulate and control capital flows. I identify the Bretton Woods system as one indicator of this intensification. While there is little doubt that Bretton Woods made possible an "unrelenting capitalist internationalization" (Carroll, 1986, p. 188) within the context of a larger "boom in the world economy under American hegemony" (Watkins, 1989, p. 30), I argue that it is wrong to treat this period as an extension of our present global epoch since Bretton Woods did all this without requiring nation states to relinquish their authority to manage or participate in the national economy, as is the case today under neoliberal globalization.

---

1 Canadian theories of imperialism, for instance, tend to see the period as characterized by a more general internationalization of capital, in which there is an "enlarged presence of US-controlled monopoly capital in Canada, together with an intermingling of powerful US financial groups within Canadian finance capital" (Carroll, 1985, p. 45). In contrast, theories of dependency see the vast increase in American investment in Canada over this period as further evidence of the subordinate status of Canada's capitalist class. While there is a recognition that this period was one "of prosperity for both the United States and Canada" (Watkins, 1989, p. 30), the overall view of dependency theories is that Canada remains "the most important colony of the US" (Teeple, 1972, p. xii).

For the most part, the period was characterized by nation states protecting their domestic capitals from external forces. As put by political scientist Robert Cox (1981), "welfare nationalism took the form of economic planning at the national level and the attempt to control external economic impacts upon the national economy" (p. 146). The relative success of this sort of protection would have the result, however, of increasing competition among domestic financial institutions, leading many national banks to find new ways of escaping national regulatory control in the form of the Eurodollar markets. While these events took place within the more general centripetal organizing dynamic of the period, I claim that the collapse of the Bretton Woods system under the weight of the Eurodollar markets should be understood as the tipping point that ushered in the global organizing dynamic of TAR that remains with us today. In chapter 4, I argue that we should understand this shift as the emergence of a global system of property relations and, thus, the making of global capital.

The current chapter begins with an exploration of why the Bretton Woods system should be understood as part of the national epoch of capitalism, especially as it relates to banking and finance. Then, I focus on the more general effects of Bretton Woods on the Royal Bank of Canada. I argue that the sort of financially restricted national political economy engendered by this system – characterized as it was by relatively strict capital controls when compared to our present epoch – led to increased domestic competition from the so-called near banks, and that this, in turn, led the Royal, as well as the rest of the chartered banks, to expand via the Eurodollar markets. While these markets allowed the chartered banks to grow extremely large, the massive flows of foreign currency that they generated eventually overwhelmed the Bretton Woods system. I conclude by highlighting some of the reasons why we should understand the collapse of this system as the tipping point into our current global epoch, as well as some of the larger consequences for banking and finance.

The Bretton Woods System

The end of the Second World War brought significant shifts to TAR in respect to banking. One of these shifts was the Bretton Woods system, which was the result of the 1944 United Nations Monetary and Financial Conference held in Bretton Woods, New Hampshire. The conference set out a system of fixed exchange rates pegged to the US dollar, which was subsequently pegged to gold, allowing the United States to run a trade deficit without devaluing its currency. Doug Henwood (1998) provides a concise explanation of the system:

> Unlike the classic gold standard, in which all countries expressed their national currency in terms of gold, the Bretton Woods system used the dollar as the central value, and the dollar in turn was fixed to gold. Countries could hold dollar reserves in their central bank for the settlement of international trade and finance on the knowledge that they could cash those dollars in for a fixed amount of gold. The dollar, as was said, was as good as gold. (p. 43)

The Bretton Woods system also included the creation of the International Monetary Fund (IMF) to provide short-term loans to countries having balance of payments problems to give them time to make the proper adjustments without the deflationary consequences of an automatic gold standard, as well as the creation of the World Bank (WB), which was, as Cox (1981) notes, "a vehicle for longer term financial assistance" (p. 145). The general view of the system as set out in the pages of *Canadian Banker* was that

> for a trading nation like Canada there should be significant benefits, since the Bank helps to strengthen the economies of less developed countries, making it possible for them to engage in a more active trade, and the Fund aids in strengthening currencies, making more orderly trade possible. (C. Kilpatrick, 1959, p. 116)

Years earlier, however, the editor of *Canadian Banker*, F.A. Knox (1945), highlighted what would become one of the main problems with these institutions and their eventual role in ushering in global neo-liberal reforms: "they would impose upon sovereign states as borrowers the necessity of conforming to the monetary ideas of the lenders no matter what the purpose of the loan" (p. 32).

This reality has since led many scholars to argue that Bretton Woods was either an indicator of the beginning of the global epoch (Burbach & W.I. Robinson, 1999; Hardt & Negri, 2000; W.I. Robinson, 2004; Teeple, 2000), or that there hasn't really been any significant qualitative change to the global political economy since the system's demise (Arrighi, 1994/2010; Eichengreen, 1996/2008; Panitch & Gindin, 2012; Wood, 2003). As Sassen (2006) notes, this is because many elements of our contemporary period mirror aspects of the Bretton Woods era:

> These include micro trends such as the rise of the transnational banks ... and the establishment of various multilateral systems for economic

operations, including the IMF and the World Bank, which continue to be central organizations in the current global era. Further, key demands by the United States in the framing of the Bretton Woods system were akin to the later neoliberal policies of the 1980s and 1990s, making it easy to argue that the current global phase had already begun then or, alternatively, that there is nothing distinct about the global phase of the 1980s onward. (p. 159)

We should be wary, however, of treating Bretton Woods as either evidence of American imperialism in the Canadian context, or as the beginning of our global epoch.

Although the new institutions of the Bretton Woods system can certainly be understood to be part of the economic imperialism of the United States, they were not simply imposed on Canada's ruling class.[2] As noted by one of the 1944 conference participants, Canadian economist A.W.F. Plumptre (1977),

> It is true, and it was true at the time, that the new international institutions, largely fashioned in Washington, were designed to serve the international interests of the United States. The charge that they could in many respects be considered as the creatures of American "capitalist imperialism" can in a sense be accepted. It does not follow, however, that their establishment and operation were contrary to Canadian interests as perceived at the time or subsequently by Canadian governments or Canadians generally. The kind of postwar world the Americans, in collaboration with the British, were attempting to build was one that was in large measure well adapted to Canadian requirements, and as a result of Canadian efforts the adaptation was improved. (p. 31)

Furthermore, once Bretton Woods was not well adapted to Canadian requirements, the government was simply able to operate differently, a good example being the decision to float the Canadian currency in 1950

---

2 A similar point is made more generally by Shaw (2000): "The strongest new internationalism was, in reality, that of the West itself. At the core of the post-war order was the victorious wartime Western alliance of the United States, Britain and France. Democracy was partly a spontaneous demand of people and parties in countries formerly occupied by the Axis powers. But it was also an order imposed by the victors, in Germany and Japan to pre-empt a resurgence of military aggression, elsewhere in Europe to tie nations into the Western bloc, and reinforced by the Marshall Plan. The goal was to co-opt German and Japanese power by demonstrating to local elites that their national aspirations could be met within a US-led orbit. At the heart of the new phase of national-international world order was a form of Western unity in which interstate alliance was linked to democratic political forms" (p. 115).

to continue the flows of American capital into Canada. As Kobrak and Martin (2018) explain, Canada's special relationship with Britain and the United States

> made its own adherence to the rate constraints particularly difficult. Canada's ability to convert its foreign currency receipts earned by trade surpluses with other nations into US dollars to fund its chronic US trade deficit was undermined by the devaluations of the 1930s and by the strong dollar established under Bretton Woods. (p. 193)

While Canada would eventually re-peg their currency to the US dollar in 1962 with "the help of a rescue package of just over USD$1 billion from the IMF, the United States, and the United Kingdom" (p. 194), the earlier decision to unpeg belies the characterization of a Canadian ruling class dominated by American interests. Despite the decision to unpeg, Canada, like many countries, "profited from the economic growth and stability produced by the Bretton Woods system" (p. 195).

Another way that the Bretton Woods epoch differs from our own is that unlike today's so-called free trade agreements, the Bretton Woods system did not reduce the ability of nation states to regulate capital but rather strengthened it. Where the international monetary order had previously been in the hands of private bankers and financiers, Bretton Woods gave control of this system to a series of government regulatory bodies. As such, the multilateralism of the Bretton Woods system did not prevent state economic coordination or national protectionism (as is the case today) and instead enhanced the ability of the nation state to be used in such a way. As Helleiner (1995) notes, Bretton Woods granted nation states "the explicit 'right' to use capital controls" (p. 317), which are rules regulating the cross-border movement of money. In other words, "the capital account was understood to be a legitimate subject of control for governments" (Germain, 2010, p. 50). By granting nation states the right to use capital controls, the Bretton Woods system not only enabled nation states to develop capabilities to protect national economies from external shocks, but it did so without restricting the ability of national "governments to manage their economies and function as significant economic actors" (Sassen, 2006, p. 161).[3] As Germain

---

[3] Shaw (2000) similarly notes that most nation states during this period "retained considerable autonomy in their internal economic, social, and political relations. Indeed, while shorn of their empires and their classic independent military functions, nation-states were in other senses *more* powerful institutions, and more embedded in national society. Common national experiences of war, the expansion of state

(2010) notes, "the central innovation of the Bretton Woods agreements concerned the acceptability of these controls in the name of enhancing and preserving monetary stability" (p. 51). The editor of *Canadian Banker*, F.A. Knox (1945), put the matter similarly:

> Banks themselves have no hesitation in risking money to smother a run on a weaker bank to prevent the contagion spreading. Why should the nations be reluctant to do the same? If such aid is promptly extended and a reduction of foreign trade thereby avoided, there will exist the most favourable environment for the success of such an anti-depression policy. (p. 34)

Even the General Agreement on Tariffs and Trade (GATT), which is sometimes identified as the beginning of the global epoch by those who see it as the "institutional means for a negotiated removal of all national barriers to world trade" (Teeple, 2000, p. 54), was never meant to eliminate all trade barriers between countries, as is the case with today's so-called free trade agreements.[4] The GATT was merely a provisional agreement that "aimed at dismantling some of the protectionist measures that had built up over the previous two decades" (Brummer, 2014, p. 43) to deal with the Great Depression and the ravages of the Second World War. Not only were both the Bretton Woods system and the GATT far "more tolerant of politically diverse choices at the national level" (McBride, 2005, p. 144), but they both also allowed for "the liberalization of trading rules with a considerable degree of state autonomy in policy making" (p. 145). As legal scholar Chris Brummer (2014) notes, the GATT was also relatively limited in scope, leaving a wide range of sectors untouched, "from financial services to construction to, perhaps most importantly, agriculture" (p. 43). It also had weak enforcement powers: GATT panels only had "limited disciplinary power beyond stigmatizing countries as non-compliant with their treaty obligations" (p. 43).

Such an arrangement is in great contrast to today's free trade agreements, which sometimes go as far as legally restricting nation states from legislating against transnational corporate interests. As such,

---

socio-economic functions due to war and the consolidation of democracy all meant that state apparatuses and their leaders were stronger at the national level" (p. 127).

4 As I discuss in chapter 4, the North American Free Trade Agreement (NAFTA) was crafted in such a way as to be extended to other countries over time; it has since provided the model for other free trade agreements, such as the Canada–European Union Trade Agreement and the CPTPP, among others.

we should understand the extent and content of government control during the Bretton Woods era as making for a "substantively different international financial system from what gets launched in the 1980s" (Sassen, 2006, p. 160). Regardless of the international and multilateral character of the Bretton Woods system and the role of American dominance in shaping that system, it was still fundamentally "aimed at building the national economy and polity ... [and] governing the international system in order to protect the national interest, no matter the definition of the latter" (p. 161). We should therefore understand the Bretton Woods era as part of the national epoch of capitalism; it was an institutional framework to govern national systems of capitalist property relations. In other words, the rights of capital continued to be located at the national level and were still enforced and protected by nation states that had a considerable amount of autonomy – especially when compared with today – as to how they went about doing that. It seems more accurate, then, to understand this period as a continuation and intensification of the earlier centripetal organizing dynamic that had been building over the previous decades, a dynamic that was geared towards developing and building up national capitals.

The reality of this can be seen more clearly by reflecting on the specific results of Bretton Woods on Canadian banking as well as the changing activities of the Royal Bank during this period. It is important to note that the Bretton Woods system emerged in response to a number of ad hoc exchange controls created to protect national political economies from the vagaries of the Great Depression and the Second World War.[5] As Christophers (2013) notes, during this period, "the world of

---

5 For instance, in Canada, exchange controls were introduced through an Order in Council passed on 15 September 1939 as part of the *War Measures Act*, which, through the Foreign Exchange Control Order, established a legal framework for the control of foreign exchange transactions via the Foreign Exchange Control Board (FECB). On 30 April 1940, these controls were stiffened even further, requiring all Canadian residents (including the Bank of Canada) to sell all foreign currency that they owned to the FECB. Powell (2005) provides more detail: "To conserve Canada's foreign exchange and effectively support the value of the Canadian dollar, the Board introduced extensive controls. These controls allowed the Board to regulate both current and capital account transactions, although most current account transactions, other than travel, were treated fairly leniently. Permits were required for all payments by residents to non-residents for imports of goods and services. Permits were also required for the purchase of foreign currencies and foreign securities, the export of funds by travellers, and to change one's status from resident to non-resident. Residents were also required to sell all foreign exchange receipts to an authorized dealer. Interbank trading in Canadian dollars ceased" (p. 54).

international money and banking shrunk back from its previously open and integrated configuration to become, in short order, a collection of largely self-contained financial islands" (p. 103). This meant that banking began to occur more *within* borders than across them as various forms of exchange were restricted; as such, there was an increase in the significance of foreign branches that could capture the business of multinational corporations (MNCs) operating in new territories to avoid tariff walls.[6] Quigley (1986) notes, for instance, that the Royal used its head office in Montreal and its New York agency for exactly this purpose: "as centres for co-ordinating the bank's pursuit of multinational corporations" (p. 37). Although American law restricted the Royal from taking direct deposits, its location on the doorstep of the New York money market made this a non-issue. Literally well positioned to access international trade and corporate accounts, the Royal established a trust-company affiliate in New York – the Royal Bank of Canada Trust Company – that allowed it to act as "registrar and paying agent for corporate and government clients issuing bonds on the New York market" (McDowall, 1993, p. 289).

The move to New York was one that was simple enough in banking terms, but was also representative of much larger shifts in the world economy. Although the Royal had made significant profits off its London operation (conveniently located across the street from Canadian Army Headquarters), it was clear that New York was quickly becoming the centre for what remained of international finance: "with London trapped under a blanket of war regulation, New York prospered" (McDowall, 1993, p. 289). Despite the Royal noting publicly in its June 1949 *Monthly Letter* "the degree to which [Britain's] economic recovery is bound up with Canada's own economic future" (p. 3), the Royal's general manager, James Muir, gave a much different interpretation nine years earlier, stating, "I have lost neither love nor loyalty for the old kingdom but I do think I see its plight rather more clearly than those who live too close to the forest" (as cited in McDowall, 1993, p. 290).

The shift from London to New York occurred at the same time that the rest of the world was beginning to shake off the vestiges of colonial

---

6 As Norfield (2016) notes, this had the effect of privileging national financial institutions by virtue of their ability to lean on their home currency: "As capitalism expands to create a world market, the operations of financial companies expands alongside those of commerce and industry. In this, too, they receive support from their national base – if only in the national currency to which they have privileged access via the home central bank. Access to the home currency is commonly their area of advantage over banks and financial institutions in other countries" (p. 67).

rule, itself evincing a larger centripetal shift in TAR at the world scale: the proliferation of the nation state form.[7] Within a single decade of the end of the Second World War, national liberation movements had arisen in most of the colonial world: in Vietnam, Malaysia, Dutch East Indies, Korea, the Philippines, and India; in Algeria, Egypt, and Kenya; and in the Middle East. These movements were typically accompanied by the desire for financial sovereignty. For the Royal, this was most explicit in the Caribbean and Latin America. In 1939, for instance, the Royal was forced to leave Panama "after the republic passed legislation requiring the banks to make compulsory purchases of state bonds" (McDowall, 1993, p. 315). Similarly, in 1946, the nationalization of Argentina's central bank forced "all banks in the country to act as its agent" (p. 315).[8]

While banking was still international in the sense that foreign branches continued to exist, there was less cross-border banking activity, and what activity remained in foreign countries was increasingly subject to the decisions of domestic governments, a point I discuss in greater detail below. Even in Canada, there were growing calls for various forms of protectionism that led the Royal to take to the media to argue that the country did not have to choose between industrial development and free trade. Jeffees (1952) writes in the *Globe and Mail*, for instance, that Muir "believes that tariff protection tends both to retard and to conceal the true efficiency of a nation's industry" (p. 20), and that "there is little doubt in his mind that 'Canada can achieve both industrial development and free trade' and he thinks that the Canadian problem is to hasten the process" (p. 20).[9] All this to say, that with international capital flows constrained, the national economy began to

---

[7] Wimmer and Feinstein (2010) note that this period constitutes the largest growth of nation states by virtue of anti-colonial movements in British Asia, the Middle East, and French and British Africa. Other significant periods of nation-state creation include the fall of the Hapsburg and Romanov Empires after the First World War and the fall of the Soviet Union.

[8] Lest the reader start to feel sorry for the Royal, things at this time were not all bad. In 1950, Cuba created its own central bank and refused to accept American dollars as legal tender. The Royal gladly accepted the change by providing technical advice as part owner of the Banco Nacional de Cuba; as such, "by the decade's end, the Royal Bank was still Cuba's largest bank, with annual deposits averaging over $100 million" (McDowall, 1993, p. 315).

[9] In 1948, the Royal posed a rhetorical question to the readers of the June edition of its *Monthly Letter*: "One of the perplexing questions for a country wealthy in natural resources is: how far should I forego a nationalistic economy in the interest of international good?" (p. 1). As should be clear, the bank's answer to this question has always been the same: pretty far.

take on a greater importance than it had previously, and this meant an increase in domestic competition that would ultimately lead to the globalization of financial capital that characterizes our present period.

Domestic Competition

The financially restricted national political economy of the Bretton Woods era brought with it new configurations of TAR that are still evident to different degrees among the various liberal democracies today. While these new configurations would help protect capital from external forces (thereby enabling corporations to grow extremely large), they would also cause an increase in domestic competition and, thus, new ways of escaping national regulatory control. For the most part, these configurations were initiated under the auspices of the so-called Keynesian welfare state (KWS), the name deriving in part from the work of economist John Maynard Keynes, and so-called because, as sociologist Janet Siltanen (2002) points out, in Canada, like elsewhere, the emergence of Keynesian social reforms tended to be ad hoc rather than part of a larger strategy of social citizenship.[10] In this sense, as Göran Therborn (1984) notes, "parliamentary democracy and the welfare state forms seem to be institutional state traditions – of law, state structures and state-society relations – and class perspectives" (p. 17). As such,

> the timing of new applications and elaborations of institutional traditions, and the extent of the assertion of a particular class perspective should be seen as being determined, for the most part, by the balance of sociopolitical forces and by the conjunctures of capital accumulation. (p. 17)

The actual and varied expressions of the welfare state across the capitalist world were thus far from the stated mark, with each being "contingent on labour mobilizing a sufficient amount of political and economic

---

10 Siltanen (2002) further notes: "While I recognize that there has been a profound deterioration in the range and level of social support and services available to Canadian citizens, I do question whether it is correct to see this deterioration as also a shift away from social citizenship. The question is whether these services and supports ever rested on accepted claims of the social rights of citizenship. Talk of equality and rights may have been more tolerated, even welcomed, in the 'golden age,' but the proof of principle, especially on the part of governments, must be in actions and results. On these latter criteria, there does seem sufficient grounds to question whether the establishment of the social rights of citizenship ever grounded the welfare policy regime of the immediate post-World War II decades in Canada" (p. 402).

power, which it could do in the more or less closed national economies of the post-war era" (Streeck, 2016, p. 21). One aspect of Keynes's thinking, however, would come to predominate in almost all of them: "above all, let finance primarily be national" (as cited in Christophers, 2013, p. 109). As Teeple (2000) points out, "the principal assumption in [Keynes's] work was the existence of a national economy in which, he argued, the state could intervene to influence levels of investment and domestic income and thereby partially regulate unemployment through national 'demand management' policies" (p. 17). The actual form of this state intervention came in a variety of degrees depending on the balance of socio-political forces in each country, but it typically included some level of socialization of the costs of production through state credits, guarantees, grants, and concessions, as well as the reproduction of the working class through public works and various forms of income support.[11] Unemployment insurance and family allowances were in place in Canada by 1945, for instance, and hospital insurance would arrive in 1957. Other interventions came in the form of the

---

11 There was even a certain amount of support for these initiatives among government and corporate elites, who saw them as a way to create a golden age of capitalism. We should thus be wary of seeing their emergence too simply as either a begrudgingly given compromise from ruling classes or a hard-fought battle won by labour. McDowall (1993) gives an example from the Royal Bank in which assistant manager Randolph Noble expresses his support for these policies to a friend: "In 1942, Principal James of McGill had given Ottawa its first glimpse of a planned and prosperous future in a report that advocated government support of key national industries like housing and agriculture. A year later, another McGill academic, Leonard Marsh, presented an even broader blueprint for peacetime 'social security.' The central thread of both reports was the avoidance of unemployment through the deliberate stimulation of prosperity. Government fiscal and monetary policy should be used to craft prosperity and to prevent any return to the social calamity of the thirties. 'I profoundly disagree with your theory that the rehabilitation of the world can be left to the haggling of the market,' Noble wrote to an American friend in 1944, 'in other words, to free enterprise'" (pp. 301–2). As McDowall (1993) earlier notes, Canada's chartered banks were "willing participants in the system of controls that Ottawa stretched over the economy" (p. 291).

A similar point of view was expressed by the first prize winner in the Canadian Bankers Association junior essay competition, Thomas G. Beynon (1959), a teller with the Toronto-Dominion Bank: "In conclusion it may be stressed that there are reasonable arguments for and against the welfare state. However, the economic arguments against increasing social welfare are purely theoretical and lack empirical support, and from the moral point of view any suffering and unsatisfied basic needs are a black mark against any country as wealthy as Canada. On these grounds I should like to endorse the progress made in the welfare direction and even urge that we take the extra steps necessary to become the complete welfare state defined earlier in the essay" (p. 52). How times change.

Industrial Development Bank (forerunner to the Business Development Bank of Canada) in 1944, and the Central Mortgage and Housing Corporation (forerunner to the Canada Mortgage and Housing Corporation) in 1946, foregrounding "the pervasive role of government in driving post-war economic growth" (Puri, 2012, p. 160). As Teeple (2000) notes, no matter the form, all of these interventions relied on the "delimited national labour market and relative immobility of national capital in the relatively closed national economy, prior to the 1970s" (p. 13).[12]

For Canada's chartered banks, the emergence of the welfare state also meant "a monthly surge of cash passing from the government to the citizenry, most of which worked its way into the economy through the banks" (McDowall, 1993, p. 308). As Puri (2012) notes, "It was during [this] initial period of rapid economic growth that the current Big-Five national banks dramatically expanded their asset base and national reach" (p. 161). Government securities, for instance, quickly became the largest component of the Royal's asset base (even more than its loan portfolio) and the surge in cash from the government to the citizenry was so sizable that the Royal was forced to set up their own government department at the Ottawa branch to batch process government cheques. This change was highlighted as early as 1938 by J. Douglas Gibson, an economist with the Bank of Nova Scotia:

> From the standpoint of the banker, the most significant development of recent years has been the radical change in the character of bank assets. Short-term loans to industry, trade and agriculture, i.e., current or commercial loans, are now a much smaller proportion of bank assets than formerly, while securities, representing in the main loans to governments, are a much larger proportion. (p. 145)

Furthermore, as a result of the Second World War, many of the Royal's traditional clients in power, food, raw metals, transportation, chemicals,

---

12 Streeck (2016) similarly notes that "the structure of the post-war settlement between labour and capital was fundamentally the same across the otherwise widely different countries where democratic capitalism had come to be instituted. It included an expanding welfare state, the right of workers to free collective bargaining and a political guarantee of full employment, underwritten by governments making extensive use of the Keynesian economic toolkit" (p. 78). Within the relatively closed national economies of the Bretton Woods system, "capital had to content itself with low profits and confinement in a strictly delimited economic sphere, a condition it accepted in exchange for economic stability and social peace as long as it saw no way out of the national containers within which its hunting license had been conditionally renewed after 1945" (pp. 21–2).

and construction were reinvigorated: "familiar accounts – Acadia Sugar, National Drug & Chemical, Price Brothers, Shawinigan Water & Power – dramatically increased their borrowing" (McDowall, 1993, p. 309).[13] As a result, the Royal Bank would become the first Canadian bank to post assets of $2 billion by 1945; by 1950, their assets topped $2.5 billion ("Royal Bank Report," 1951, p. 18).

Changes to the *Bank Act* in 1944 similarly reflected the growing importance of a national consumption-based economy as the chartered banks were granted new rights allowing them to move into the realm of consumer loans. With Canada quickly transitioning from a country of farmers to a country of city-dwelling workers, "the government proposed that the Act be amended to allow the making of hitherto risky small loans under $500" (McDowall, 1993, p. 304).[14] In order to boost domestic consumption, the federal government lowered the interest rate to 6 per cent, thus bringing the chartered banks into the consumer loan business. As McDowall (1993) notes, "these were the years in which Canadians learned to indulge their dreams on the 'never-never' plan" (p. 310).

Here though, the chartered banks were outmanoeuvred by the smaller finance and trust companies – the so-called near banks – that were not regulated by the *Bank Act* but instead incorporated provincially. Supported by a federal government that wanted to increase domestic competition, alongside frustrated Western provincial governments that believed that the chartered banking system had "not been adequately responsive to Western needs" (as cited in Estey, 1986, p. 365), most of the near banks came from the West.[15] As reported in the *Globe and Mail*, the Royal publicly complained that this

> so-called "easy consumer credit" can be costly both to the consumer and to the economy as a whole. The effect on sales is immediate and gratifying

---

13 During this period the Royal would also make inroads into Quebec via the pulp and paper, aluminum, and hydro power sectors. Quebec's premier at the time, Maurice Duplessis, saw the Royal as a means of "integrating the province's resource base into the continental economy" (McDowall, 1993, p. 328).

14 McDowall (1993) notes: "The cities would be the crucial post-war frontier for banking; the war put wages in people's pockets, and it was relatively easy to capture their business" (p. 308). This was because, as C. Heron and Storey (1986) observe, "the traditionally large, flexible pool of underemployed, 'semi-proletarianized' Canadian farm dwellers declined drastically after World War II as farmers' children left for the city in unprecedented numbers" (p. 20). See also L. Johnson (1979) and Radforth (1986).

15 Estey's (1986) *Report of the Inquiry into the Collapse of the CCB and Northland Bank* provides a list of these Western banks: "The Bank of British Columbia was

to business; but repayment of the debt by the public in the future may well result in an enforced reduction in consumer spending. ("The Royal Bank of Canada," 1953, p. 8)[16]

While this might seem like a pragmatic approach to the expansion of consumer debt, a more likely interpretation is that the chartered banks were simply upset that they were not getting their cut of these new lending profits. They were still able to get a piece of the action, however, since "it was to the banks that the finance companies turned for their initial float of capital" (McDowall, 1993, p. 311). For their part, the Royal secured the "steady patronage of Household Finance and General Motors Acceptance" (p. 311). A retired superintendent of the Royal Bank would describe the nature of this new world of banking simply, noting that "banking is a competitive business between bank and bank, and also, to some extent, between banks and finance companies, trust companies, insurance companies and every other business that extends credit in any shape or form" (Knowles, 1957, p. 134). He would also offer, with prescient foresight, a taste of things to come: "whatever changes may be brought about in our monetary and credit policies, it is practically certain that new and additional responsibilities will be given to the chartered banks" (p. 135).

The main factor in the chartered banks' distaste for the near banks was their freedom from the constraints of the *Bank Act*. Where the chartered banks were constrained by the *Bank Act*'s 6 per cent interest ceiling, the near banks could lend at whatever interest rate they wanted. As such, when the prime rate rose to levels that denied the chartered banks a sufficient spread between the cost of lending and the ceiling, they

---

established in 1967, along with the Bank of Western Canada which never came into operation. The Unity Bank of Canada was established in 1972 ... The Canadian Commercial Bank (initially the Canadian Commercial and Industrial Bank) and the Northland Bank were created in 1975 ... The Continental Bank of Canada came into existence in 1977. All of these banks were established by act of Parliament. Two more small western banks were granted letters patent in 1983 and 1984" (pp. 365–6).

16 This message was merely a repeat of that given to the Royal by the governor of the central bank three years earlier: "In November 1950, Ted Atkinson of the Royal Bank came to Ottawa to tell [Graham] Towers that 'the wave of optimism' sweeping the Canadian economy was 'still fairly high.' The governor of the central bank responded that the banks had better cool consumer and commercial demand for credit. Towers would habitually urge the general managers to 'weed out some of the less urgent demands on our resources.' When James Coyne succeeded Towers as governor in 1955, the message remained unchanged: 'a remedy must not be sought in monetary expansion or deficit financing'" (McDowall, 1993, pp. 324–5).

were forced to stop providing loans. The near banks, on the other hand, simply moved their rate up. Furthermore, since the chartered banks were subject to different reserve ratios, the near banks had more flexibility to manoeuvre. The 1954 *Bank Act*, for instance, obliged the chartered banks to "to keep at least 8 per cent, and if requested, as much as 12 per cent, of their deposits with the Bank of Canada as a cash reserve" (McDowall, 1993, p. 332). By offering small instalment loans to consumers, or credit towards the purchase of automobiles, the near banks were able to capture an increasing proportion of the total assets of the financial sector: "by 1954 ... the [chartered] banks supplied only 15.6 per cent of Canadian consumer credit; the 'near banks,' led by the finance companies with 26.1 per cent, and various 'point of sale' retail dispensers of credit, such as department stores, purveyed the rest" (p. 332). The chartered banks responded by convincing the government to amend the *Bank Act* in 1954 so that they could provide mortgage loans, chattel (e.g., car or household) loans, and loans made against the security of hydrocarbons in the ground.[17] While mortgages were only around 5 per cent of the Royal's outstanding debt in 1945, this had ballooned to 20 per cent by 1962.[18] The Royal's president defended this growth by

---

17 The right to lend on the basis of hydrocarbons in the ground was a reflection of the discovery of oil in Leduc, Alberta, in 1947. As the largest bank in the Alberta oil fields, the Royal quickly came to be referred to as the "'R-oil' Bank" (McDowall, 1993, p. 384). By 1953, the Royal had accounts of 47 per cent of the companies listed in the Alberta oil directory; by 1967, this would rise to 53 per cent, with the bank capturing 75 per cent of new business in the oil patch, a trend later reinforced by the soaring energy prices of the 1970s. Recent research by Carroll (2017) and the Corporate Mapping Project (Carroll & Daub, 2018) confirms that the Royal remains the largest financer of the oil industry in Canada.

18 Interestingly, the federal government had been trying to get the chartered banks to provide mortgage loans since the late 1940s. The Canada Mortgage and Housing Corporation (CMHC) was a Crown corporation created in 1946 (originally called the Central Mortgage and Housing Corporation) to regulate *National Housing Act* loans, but since trust and insurance companies were only permitted to loan up to the extent of their paid-in capital, the housing industry soon found itself in crisis. With the postwar baby boom in full swing, the federal government stepped in and tried to convince the chartered banks to provide housing loans. As MacIntosh (1991) notes, "as far as the banks were concerned, the proposal to bring them into residential mortgage finance came out of the blue" (p. 115). The Royal initially balked at the suggestion but would end up sending its future president, W. Earle McLaughlin, to Ottawa to study whether mortgage lending would leave the bank short of liquidity (McDowall, 1993, p. 334). The major change came from allowing the banks to have mortgages insured through the Canadian Housing Corporation. As Puri (2012) notes, "changing the mandate of the Canadian Housing Corporation from a mortgage company to an insurer helped the government privatize the mortgage

stating that the bank merely wanted to put "greater purchasing power in the hands of the individual" (G. Hudson, 1959, p. 3). This lending trajectory would change, however, after the federally sanctioned mortgage rate crossed the 6 per cent limit in 1959:

> James Muir, chairman and president of the Royal Bank of Canada, says curtailment of credit has been forced on chartered banks by tight money coupled with the 6 per cent legal ceiling on the lending rates of chartered banks. ("Canadian Explains Bank," 1959, p. 45)

As a result, the Royal quickly dropped from a 33 per cent share of the mortgage market in 1958 to 0.2 per cent in 1961.[19] Without the flexible interest rates enjoyed by the near banks, the chartered banks were unable to realize satisfactory profits in mortgage lending. A more interventionist governor of the Bank of Canada, Jim Coyne, would also ask the chartered banks to halt "their headlong competition for corporate accounts, which had led them, he believed, to make excessive long-term loans and purchases of corporate securities" (MacIntosh, 1991, p. 127).[20] In this context of increased domestic competition, the chartered banks

---

market in a controlled manner" (p. 161). See MacIntosh (1991) for more on the creation of the CMHC and the *National Housing Act*.

19 MacIntosh (1991) notes that "there is little doubt that the 6 percent ceiling on bank lending rates was the key factor in fast growth of the trust companies and mortgage and loan companies, starting about 1955. The Porter Commission report noted that the assets of the trust companies went from 6.8 percent of bank assets in 1955 to 12.6 percent in 1962" (p. 206). From 1959 to 1964, "the number of provincially supervised companies went from thirty-three to forty-seven. The number of trust company branches exploded from 137 in 1956 to 470 in 1967" (p. 207).

20 Coyne would also attempt to get the chartered banks to separate "their savings deposits from the rest of their deposit business, and to invest all savings deposits in housing mortgages and longer-term securities of provinces and municipalities" (MacIntosh, 1991, p. 128), the idea being that "if the balance sheets of the banks were segregated in this way, there would be a steadier flow of money for housing and other long-term purposes" (p. 128). As MacIntosh (1991) notes, "there was a huge outcry in the press" (p. 128), with the financial writer of the *Globe and Mail*, Fraser Robertson, writing in response, "One! Two! Three! Four! Hup! Fall into line there, comrades ... You will learn the fatality of bourgeois attempts to sabotage the Bank of Canada" (as cited on p. 128). Canadian economist E.P. Neufeld would also respond, noting that "to require the banks to hold specific types of assets against their two kinds of deposits implies a preconceived notion as to what constitutes a desirable distribution of money capital" (as cited on p. 128). One might also point out that *not* having a preconceived notion of such a distribution is a political position, as well.

responded by moving "aggressively into the short-term money market" (McDowall, 1993, p. 333), and by expanding internationally.[21]

Since international banking was unregulated by the *Bank Act*, it offered the chartered banks a chance to escape the new constraints of domestic banking. The 6 per cent ceiling on loan interest, for example, did not exist abroad. As a result, the Royal's foreign assets started to grow at a pace that "far outstripped growth of [its] domestic assets" (McDowall, 1993, p. 343). The Royal's first major expansion during this period was, like before, into the Caribbean and Latin America. Branches in the region grew from 61 in 1950 to 101 by the end of the decade; and by 1960, the Royal's 27 South American branches made the Royal Bank dominant over all other Canadian banks on that continent. As it reached deeper and deeper into Latin America, the Royal used its corporate power to transform the laws of the countries in which it operated, making them more beneficial for foreign capitalists. As McDowall (1993) notes, the Royal cared little whether dictators in Haiti, the Dominican Republic, or Cuba "treated their local economies as fiefdoms" (p. 343). It, like the other Canadian banks, saw the region as one made up not of individual countries, but as "a single area where they do business" (Baum, 1974, p. 53).

A good example is Jamaica. After finishing his tenure as the governor of the Bank of Canada (1934–54) and as the alternate governor of the IMF (1946–54), former Royal executive Graham Towers was asked by the Jamaican government to review the role of Jamaica's financial institutions and consider whether the country should create a central bank (Fullerton, 1986, p. 286). Officially appointed by the United Nations Technical Assistance Administration and in consult with the Bank of Canada and the Canadian Ministry of Finance, Towers's report made

---

21 As Lapavitsas (2013b) notes, short-term money markets came to exist due to the demand for liquidity in the normal course of banking: "supply of loanable capital in the money market emerges as banks find it expensive to hold spare liquidity; demand comes from banks seeking to borrow liquidity to fund assets" (p. 131). Competition from the near banks led the chartered banks to start pressuring the Bank of Canada for such a market as early as 1954. The Royal's president, James Muir, would make his case for a Canadian money market on the grounds that such markets were "a symbol of economic maturity and strength," as well as a prerequisite for progress, especially for a "country like Canada whose economic future depends on the expansion of world trade and investment" ("Greater Money Market," 1954, p. 22). In reality, they are simply a means of growth in the absence of other profitable investments. As MacIntosh (1991) shows, the shift into the short-term money market "was a major factor in the development of the wholesale market for commercial 'paper' in Canada" (p. 127).

several suggestions that would ultimately restrict "the range and action of political authorities while giving (foreign) bankers more freedom" (Deneault, 2015, p. 36). The creation of a central bank in Jamaica, for instance, was rejected by Towers on the basis that monetary independence might lead to "inflation, instability, and retardation of development" (as cited in Deneault, 2015, p. 36). This is despite the fact that Canada had created its own central bank 15 years earlier with no ill effects. Towers also argued that the creation of a central bank was unnecessary since Jamaica had the "wholehearted co-operation of existing banks" (p. 36), of which, three out of four were Canadian, including the Royal. Further offshore-style legislation came with the creation of an international business company (IBC) in 1956. As Deneault (2015) explains, the IBC allowed companies or shareholders registered in Jamaica to receive funds from abroad without paying any taxes; it was thus "the first step in a process that has led to the transformation of almost every territory in the British Caribbean into an offshore jurisdiction" (p. 37). Similarly, Sir Stafford Sands, the finance minister of the Bahamas, became a director for the Royal in 1966. Two years earlier, he had written a book detailing how Americans could avoid taxes by setting up shop in the Bahamas. He is often credited as the principal architect of the Bahamian tax haven (Chodos, 1977).

As a reaction to these policies and the devastating economic conditions that resulted from their implementation, Jamaica achieved self-government in 1959. Other colonies would soon follow, spurred on by a more general anti-colonial movement against the power of foreign banks. In Trinidad, for example, C.L.R. James would lament that "Independence Square is surrounded by some of the most magnificent buildings in the territory and all of them are foreign banks. That's how we live. They rule the place" (as cited in P.J. Hudson, 2010, p. 35). James was right, of course. Canadian banks controlled 60 per cent of Trinidad's commercial and retail banking. Similarly, after six decades in Cuba, the Cuban Revolution forced the Royal to sell their Cuban assets. While they continued to finance Cuban trade, Fidel Castro nationalized all but two foreign banks in 1965, effectively ending the Royal's dominance of Cuban banking; although the bank was nationalized, it was still "permitted to withdraw its capital stock," which was, as reported in the *New York Times*, "the first time that a foreign bank has been permitted by the Cuban Government to withdraw its capital stock. All other banks were nationalized without any compensation to their stockholders" (Philips, 1960, p. 34).

As McDowall (1993) notes, the Bay of Pigs "provided a kind of symbolic swan song for the bank's retail system in the Caribbean and Latin

America" (p. 365). Despite attempts to localize its branches by dropping "Canada" from the name, the overall trend in the 1960s was a gradual disinvestment from the region, punctuated by the occupation of the Royal's Trinidadian branch by the National Joint Action Committee on 26 February 1970. As Peter Hudson (2010) notes, the Royal was not seen as "an innocent agent of a goodly and innocuous developmentalism, but a symbol of a rapacious imperialism" (p. 35), a point made clear by the fact that the Royal had already been bombed in Cuba as early as 1931, as reported in the *New York Times*: "The authorities are redoubling their efforts to apprehend the bomb throwers, who have been carrying on a campaign of terror since the beginning of the recent revolutionary movement" ("Havana Bank," 1931, p. 8).

The Royal grew elsewhere, however, through its links to large MNCs.[22] As a by-product of its earlier industrialization by solicitation strategy, the Royal was already well connected to American MNCs and, as such, "prominent American accounts – First Boston, US Steel, and Merrill Lynch – began appearing in the loan approvals. In 1957, for instance, the bank provided financial support for Aristotle Onassis' shipping activities and the Gulbenkian Middle-Eastern oil empire" (McDowall, 1993, p. 341). The Royal also moved, like it had earlier in Canada, into regions of the world where industrialization was just emerging, such as in Dallas, Texas, where a representative was posted in 1958 to capture American oil interests, or in China, which was rapidly trying to "surpass the productive powers of the Western world," according to the Royal's president, James Muir (as cited in McDowall, 1993, p. 346). Such moves were aided by the WB, which provided the world's largest banks with assorted benefits, such as the ability to profit from third-world development projects. In 1957, for example, the WB provided a $40-million loan to the government of the Belgian Congo (now the Democratic Republic of the Congo) for a highway building program. As Park and Park (1962) note, the loan was not so much a do-good operation but rather a means to enrich the Belgian firms

---

22 As Teeple (2000) notes, the growth of international banking was not just restricted to the Royal but reflected larger shifts in the development of global capitalism: "Just as these financial markets grew in accord with the rapid expansion of foreign trade, growing competition at the international level, and the internationalization of productive capital, so too did an international banking system. Between 1950 and 1974, the number of international branches of the large national banks grew from a handful of US and Commonwealth banks with small assets and representing a small percentage of the parent's earnings to a far-flung international branch system with assets and earnings often approaching or exceeding the domestic operations" (p. 60).

connected with the Royal. These international efforts were so successful that by 1960, the Royal, the Bank of Montreal, and the Canadian Imperial Bank of Commerce (CIBC) ranked among the 12 largest banks in the world, with the Bank of Nova Scotia and the Toronto-Dominion Bank (TD) trailing close behind; "combined these five banks held 15 per cent of the international market" (Darroch, 1992, p. 153).

That Canada's chartered banks could be so successful during this period demonstrates the extent to which the restrictions of Bretton Woods helped to protect national capitals from external forces. It did not help them from internal forces, however, since this system also helped foster an increase in domestic competition that eventually forced the banks to escape national regulation by increasing their level of international activity. The problem, however, was that much of this business was still subject to and limited by the regulations of the host country. Further still, their domestic banking activities remained highly regulated. To grow large enough to vanquish their domestic competitors, the chartered banks would require a territory absent of regulations that would allow them to overcome the existing limits to accumulation. They would find this territory with the creation of the Eurodollar markets.[23]

The Eurodollar Markets

The Eurodollar markets were relatively unregulated territories for accumulation that were formed in 1957 after the Bank of England decided not to regulate any "transactions taking place in dollars if they were carried out by two non-residents" (Deneault, 2015, p. 32). As Deneault (2015) observes, it was the first time in modern financial history that "banks could deal with very large amounts of money in currency not supervised by their government" (p. 32). While the creation of the Eurodollar markets was in some sense a means of helping the City of London regain some of its former glory as the centre of international finance, it was also a reflection of the success of the Bretton Woods system in restricting transnational flows of capital. As Porter (2005) notes,

---

23 Sassen (2006) speaks to the same phenomenon in the American context: "Some of the problematic outcomes in the 1970s for the United States were a result of the economic growth in the 1950s and 1960s. That growth led US banks and financial investors to search for ways to get around the walls built into the banking and financial sectors to protect them from the types of reverberations that had characterized the 1929 stock market crash. This search contributed to the formation of the offshore markets" (p. 167).

the Eurodollar markets provided a way for "the most internationally active firms to circumvent these restrictions without requiring governments to dismantle them" (p. 18). As corporations extended their reach around the world, they were able to evade domestic capital controls by "depositing their capital in foreign currency markets" (W.I. Robinson, 2004, p. 111). In other words, they did not send their dollars back home but deposited them instead as Eurodollars in third-country banks. Teeple (2000) notes that this effectively created a supranational financial system "that was and remains largely beyond the control of national central bank regulation" (p. 60). Archival documents from the Bank for International Settlements (BIS) similarly point out that "what was new about the Eurocurrency markets was 'the scale on which it is now taking place, the extent to which operations are conducted across national frontiers and, perhaps, the degree of competition among banks for foreign currency deposits'" (as cited in Yago, 2013, p. 158). The end result was the global spread of unregulated American dollars and other core-country currencies that large banks subsequently used to provide short- and medium-term loans to other large corporations and governments. The significance of this shift is noted by Porter (2005), who writes that "the present period of financial globalization ... began with the Eurodollar markets" (p. 51).

Interestingly, in its competition with the near banks, the Royal helped pioneer the Eurodollar market in Canada "by taking US dollar deposits from the Moscow Narodny Bank in Toronto" (McDowall, 1993, p. 407). After returning from a trip to Russia to promote trade in the mid-1950s, the Royal's president, James Muir, noted that the Russians were "anxious to trade with any country, and that 'it is in Canada's interest to promote trade wherever she can'" (as cited in "Russia Sells Banker," 1956, p. 12). Regulation Q of the US Federal Reserve Act had put an artificially low ceiling on interest gained in New York on offshore deposits, meaning that the Russians required somewhere to invest their US dollars. Offshore deposits made in Eurodollars in Toronto offered a much higher rate of return. As the deposits of these Eurodollars grew larger and larger, the Royal saw the potential profits to be made by using them to provide loans to expanding MNCs and national governments. As the international market for short- and medium-term loans began to grow, so too did the size of the chartered banks.

The Eurodollar markets were a huge boost for capital during this period because they were unconstrained by national regulations or political pressures. Hayes and Hubbard (1990) have described them as "the first marketplace without a home base" (p. 27). As Deneault (2015) notes, the sums involved were so large that they embarrassed the world's largest banks, who were forced to use an offshore discretion to keep them hidden from the public (p. 32). Internationally, Eurodollar deposits ballooned from just USD$3 billion in 1960 to USD$75 billion in 1970. Here again, Canada's chartered banks played a crucial role, transforming "the Caribbean into a vector for Eurodollars and illicit transactions, thus launching the great project of moving the entire world offshore" (p. 33). Later, near the end of his term, the Royal's president, W. Earle McLaughlin, remarked that the Eurodollar was "a pretty good invention. I don't know what we would do without it" (as cited in McDowall, 1993, p. 407). By the end of the 1950s alone, the Royal's $4.3 billion in assets represented "a quarter of the whole industry's assets" (p. 326).

With Eurodollar profits booming, the chartered banks were finally able to wipe out their domestic competition. Given the changing nature of finance, as well as a public disagreement between Bank of Canada president James Coyne and Prime Minister Diefenbaker over "the government's decision to renew the interest rate caps on bank loans" (Puri, 2012, p. 162), Diefenbaker asked Dana Porter, Chief Justice of Ontario, to lead a Royal Commission on Banking and Finance (the Porter Report) in 1961. Using the language of justice and fairness, the chartered banks argued that the near banks should be left alone, and that instead, similar rights and freedoms should be extended to the chartered banks. When the Porter Report suggested that trust companies should have all the freedoms and responsibilities of the chartered banks, the Royal's McLaughlin responded by arguing the opposite: "that the area of competition should be widened by allowing the chartered banks to do trust company business" (as cited in "Better Late," 1964, p. 6). Similarly, when it was proposed that the chartered banks be prohibited from owning more than 10 per cent of the stock of another company (Royal Commission on Banking and Finance, 1964, p. 563), McLaughlin responded by asking whether "non-banking financial institutions or non-financial institutions be completely free to invest in, own, or control any banking institutions" (as cited in "Better Late," 1964, p. 6). A simpler statement of the Royal's position is found in their 1966 *Annual Report*:

> Competitive balance and the efficiency of monetary policy can best be achieved by leaving the near-banks alone, and extending to the banks the freedom now enjoyed by the near-banks. This is far superior to the alternative of shackling the near-banks with legal cash-ratio requirements and interest ceilings. It is better to extend freedom than to proliferate controls. (p. 15)

When the dust finally settled in 1967, the revisions to the *Bank Act* were effectively a coup for the chartered banks, albeit with some slight concessions. While they were now prohibited from owning trust companies – thus ending the Royal's affiliation with Montreal Trust – the Act also removed the 6 per cent ceiling on loans, lowered cash reserve requirements, and eliminated restrictions on the banks' involvement in mortgage financing (Freedman, 1998). The chartered banks were also required to finally accept deposit insurance as part of a separate act, a scheme long bemoaned by them, as well as by previous federal governments who "feared becoming too deeply involved in the world of private banking" (Kyer, 2017, p. viii).[24] With the Federal Deposit Insurance Corporation (FDIC) already operating successfully in the United States, the major push for deposit insurance in Canada came after the failure of several near banks almost immediately after the release of the Porter Report.[25] With no legal justification for extending federal jurisdiction over the provincially regulated near banks as the Porter Report suggested, and with Ontario introducing their own deposit insurance system in 1965, the Pearson government took a different route, and instead enticed "provincial regulators and near-banks into voluntarily accepting federal oversight" (p. 6) by offering deposit insurance through a newly created Crown corporation, the Canadian Deposit Insurance Corporation (CDIC). Created via the *Canada Deposit Insurance Corporation Act* of 1967, federally regulated financial institutions, such as the chartered banks and federally incorporated deposit-taking trust companies, were now required "to insure their deposits (initially $20,000 for each depositor) through premium payments to the CDIC" (Estey, 1986, p. 357). Provincially regulated deposit-taking institutions were also allowed to participate in the scheme, subject to provincial government approval.

While the chartered banks rejected deposit insurance as being unfair and unnecessary,[26] the revised *Bank Act* was generally "praised by

---

24 When the plan was announced by Finance Minister Mitchell Sharp in the House of Commons, the main criticism, according to the *Toronto Star*, was "that it didn't go far enough in protecting small investors" (Hazlitt, 1967, p. 11).
25 As Kyer (2017) notes, "In 1965 the Atlantic Acceptance Corporation, Canada's sixth largest finance company, failed. This was followed by the near collapse of Stratford, Ontario's British Mortgage and Trust Company. The Ontario government established a public inquiry into the Atlantic Acceptance affair and the adequacy of provincial regulation [the Kimber Report]. Then in 1966, a federal investment company, Prudential Finance, failed. Concern about the state of Canada's financial institutions was widespread. People questioned the stability of the system" (pp. 39–40).
26 The president of the Toronto-Dominion Bank, Allen Thomas "AT" Lambert, characterized deposit insurance as "a terrible burden and a little frightening" (as

bankers as being 'market-freeing'" (McDowall, 1993, p. 357), quickly transforming them into producers of consumer credit: "diversified retail financial services for the man of ordinary means" (Neufeld, 1972, p. 134).[27] With Chargex (now Visa) cards, mutual funds, consumer loans, and electronic banking beginning to figure into the long-term financial calculations of the average Canadian, the chartered banks began to see the spread between their bank deposits and loan rates widen. Whittington (1999) reports that "in just one year, the Royal Bank recorded $50 million in credit-card transactions" (p. 28). Similarly, as noted later in the Royal Commission on Corporate Concentration (1978),

> after the 1967 revision of the *Bank Act* the profitability of the chartered banks increased quite substantially as of course was expected. The 1976 Economic Council of Canada study shows an increase in the after-tax rate of return on equity of the seven largest banks from an average of 8.1% in the 1963–67 period to 12.9% in 1968–73. The study notes that this latter figure is higher than that for all U.S. insured banks in the same period. (p. 226)

As their profits increased, the chartered banks' profit rate would start to run consistently above those of their main rival institutions, the near banks, allowing them to double "their rate of asset expansion within a single decade" (Newman, 1979, p. 136). As such, the near banks were no longer a competitive threat to the big banks – a reality that is still the case today. A few years later in an industry brief, the Canadian Bankers Association (1975) would reflect on the whole process, arguing that while "the competitive conditions that have prevailed in recent years

---

cited in Kyer, 2017, p. 55). The Royal's W. Earle McLaughlin argued that deposit insurance was not only unnecessary, since "the safety of the chartered banks is unquestioned," but that it would also force the chartered banks to subsidize their competitors: "the federally and provincially chartered near-banks" ("Royal Bank Boss," 1967, p. 11).

27 This is not to suggest, however, that the chartered banks were happy with the entirety of the Act. In an industry brief published by the Canadian Bankers Association (1975), they continued to point out that: "there are important restrictions on the chartered banks from which the non-banks are free. One of these, for example, is the requirement that the banks maintain substantial deposits with the Bank of Canada free of interest. These funds are available only for settlement of transfers between banks and for establishing the cash base of the money supply through central bank operations. They represent a proportion of chartered bank deposits amounting to above 6% which brings no return. While other deposit-receiving institutions are required by their governing statutes and regulations to hold reserves for liquidity purposes these can be in income-yielding assets and do not completely sterilize the reserve for earning purposes" (p. 15).

has on the whole been constructive," there continues to be "an increasing lack of clarity in lines of jurisdiction and regulation over the banking function in Canada" (p. 14).

From the perspective of the chartered banks, this lack of clarity did not only apply to the near banks but to foreign banks as well. With Citibank's purchase of the Mercantile Bank of Canada (a decade-old, Dutch-owned trading bank) in 1963, the federal government had become increasingly concerned about the possibility of an American takeover of the chartered banks.[28] In the Royal Commission on Canada's Economic Prospects (1957), otherwise known as the Gordon Report, the government had already recommended that "appropriate action be taken to prevent any substantial measure of control of these institutions [the chartered banks and life insurance companies] from coming into the possession of non-residents," given that such institutions, "form the very core of our financial and business system and together they control a considerable portion of the personal savings of Canadians" (p. 397). As such, when Citibank arrived in Canada it prompted the

---

28 Despite no constraints on foreign banking until 1964, the history of foreign banks in Canada is a short and unsuccessful one, likely owing to the size and power of the chartered banks. The first was the Bank of British North America, created by a Royal Charter issued in 1836. Based in London, with offices in Toronto, Montreal, Quebec City, Saint John, Halifax, and St. John's, it was also the first bank to operate in British Columbia. It would become a casualty of the early twentieth-century merger and acquisition wave, as the Bank of Montreal bought it from its shareholders in 1917. The second was the Bank of British Columbia, which received a Royal Charter in 1862. Created in response to the gold rush of 1858, the bank, which was also based in London, found it hard to run its various colonial offices, with management noting that "it is very difficult to control people who are 6,000 miles away from the office" (as cited in MacIntosh, 1991, p. 156). After the US recession of 1893, the owners decided to sell the bank to the Bank of Commerce in 1901.

The third was Barclays Bank of Canada, which was chartered in 1928. With a distinguished board including former Prime Minister Sir Robert Borden, as well as long-time Quebec Premier Louis-Alexandre Tashereau, the bank's timing was unfortunate, opening a month before Black Tuesday. The subsequent play of events would lead to further bank mergers to avoid a foreign takeover: "With no dividends coming in, and with British foreign exchange controls preventing the parent bank from putting more capital into its Canadian subsidiary, the British parent initiated a proposal in 1955 to do a share exchange with the Imperial Bank of Canada. The share exchange gave Barclays 10 percent of the Imperial; it appears that Barclays then proceeded to acquire a further 10 percent of the Imperial in the market. This alarmed the board of the Imperial, which sought refuge in a merger with the Commerce in 1961" (MacIntosh, 1991, p. 157), creating the CIBC. While Britain's banks had been unsuccessful, government and bankers alike were far more worried about the American banks during the 1960s, given their growing size and power.

minister of finance to take immediate action, imposing limits on foreign ownership, forbidding any single shareholder from holding more than a 10 per cent stake, with aggregate foreign ownership capped at 25 per cent (Morck et al., 2007, p. 134).[29] There was, of course, a certain irony to the fact that while the government was fast-acting in protecting the chartered banks from foreign takeover, they were still advertising their services as brokers in Canadian firms:

> Not just where insolvency necessitated bank participation in the process of finding a purchaser and reorganizing debt; but anywhere where the security of the banking business to be done might be increased by a larger (multinational) firm taking over a smaller one. (Quigley, 1986, p. 37)

Furthermore, despite the government's concerns over the operation of foreign banks in Canada, it "never took much interest in the foreign operations of Canadian banks, even though they were the equivalent of export industries" (MacIntosh, 1991, p. 168). Former Liberal Finance Minister Walter Gordon would notably remark that the New York agencies of the chartered banks were "inconsequential" (p. 168).

Like the near bank issue, debate over the matter of foreign ownership consumed the late 1960s, with the Royal's president, W. Earle McLaughlin, arguing, like before, for openness and freedom, a reflection of things to come: "Is it reasonable," he asked, "for Canadian institutions to expect to participate in world markets while we deny foreign institutions access to ours?" (as cited in Royal Bank of Canada, 1966, p. 16). McLaughlin's position was one based on the rising strength of the chartered banks, which, if left alone to freely compete against domestic competitors, would easily be able to crush them: "I find it difficult to accept the premise that no new offices of foreign banks can be tolerated or that further growth of the one very small foreign-owned bank already here would be a threat to the 'Canadian context' of our banking system" (as cited on p. 16). Despite

---

29 The Chase Manhattan Bank of New York was also in discussion with the Toronto-Dominion Bank of Canada during this period about the feasibility of acquiring a controlling interest (MacIntosh, 1991, p. 162). Later, after the passing of the 1967 *Bank Act*, the Trudeau government would work out a way to "Canadianize" the Mercantile Bank: "The Minister of Finance, Edgar Benson, authorized a series of six issues of $5 million in the capital stock of the Mercantile, all of which had to be sold to Canadian residents. Citibank's share of the ownership in Mercantile was reduced to 25 percent by 1975 ... Not surprisingly, the parent bank's enthusiasm for its Canadian subsidiary waned" (MacIntosh, 1991, p. 170).

McLaughlin's argument that "banking legislation should substitute free competition for regulation wherever possible" (as cited on p. 11), the restrictions on foreign ownership did little to stop foreign banks from operating in Canada. "By securing provincial incorporation and posing as non-bank intermediaries" (Naylor, 1985, p. 138), foreign banks could still operate in Canada without reserve requirements and within many of those fields that the chartered banks were still barred from entering.[30] "Disenchanted with the government's poli-

---

30 Puri (2012) notes: "The Porter Commission's proposed limits on foreign investment were originally designed to promote the development of a strong domestic financial services sector and enable the Bank of Canada to more readily implement its monetary policies. However, these restraints had the unintended consequence of funnelling foreign investment into provincially regulated, 'near-bank' institutions such as trust companies and credit unions. Although these 'near-banks' were intended to service smaller, more localized interests, the influx of foreign investment created a shadow banking industry capable of competing directly with the chartered banks on a national scale" (p. 167).

MacIntosh (1991) points out that by not having to keep reserves with the Bank of Canada, the foreign near banks "actually had a cost advantage over the Canadian banks," (p. 171). As a result, "a flood of institutions – less regulated than the banks – poured into the country to compete with the banks. Slowly, painfully, the federal government came to the realization that it had not dealt with the foreign banking problem at all" (p. 171).

The Canadian Bankers Association (1975) would later recommend several changes similar to McLaughlin's initial proposal:

1. That the operation of foreign banks and their related companies in Canada be clearly brought under federal jurisdiction, and that there be a procedure for licensing their activities.
2. That the rights of foreign banks to own, directly or indirectly, subsidiary companies in Canada or make investments should not be any greater than the corresponding rights of Canadian banks to own subsidiaries or make investments in Canada.
3. That the business of a foreign bank may conduct in Canada through a subsidiary or affiliate be no more extensive in scope than the business a Canadian bank may carry on in Canada.
4. That a foreign bank be restricted in the number and location of offices it may open in Canada – most banks would favour a limitation to one office per foreign bank.
5. That the number of foreign banks (or their subsidiaries) that may operate in Canada should not be greater than the number of Canadian banks (or their subsidiaries) operating in the country of the foreign bank.
6. That a foreign bank must accept all the responsibilities as to the keeping of reserves with the Bank of Canada and complying with the general federal laws governing banking in Canada, including the maintenance of adequate capital in Canada.
7. The foregoing recommendations should apply only to foreign banks from a jurisdiction which grants at least equal status to Canadian banks. A similar requirement is in effect as a condition of entry into most other countries of the world and there is evidence that the United States will shortly move in this direction. (p. 27)

cies discouraging foreign investment and the inability to control the deficit," the chartered banks complained that Canada was "not being run in a very business-like fashion" (Darroch, 1992, p. 164). As such, the Royal would increasingly focus its business abroad where it was unregulated by the *Bank Act* and did not "have to hold cash or liquidity reserves against foreign-currency deposits" (Royal Commission on Corporate Concentration, 1978, p. 232).

The Royal's increasing focus on the international side of its business was not merely a reflection of the vast sums being made. By the 1970s, as McDowall (1993) notes, "the actual concept of most head offices in an age of electronic communication and jet travel was being steadily eroded in strategic terms" (p. 363). For its part, the Royal now possessed departments in 14 cities around the world that canvassed for regional business (Quigley, 1986, p. 37), and further expansion to the United States saw offices spring up in San Francisco, Denver, Houston, Pittsburgh, Miami, Dallas, Los Angeles, and Chicago. The Royal also opened offices in Beirut, Cairo, Dubai, Athens, and Bahrain. From 1965 to 1980, Canada's chartered banks acquired "in whole or in part more than 160 primary foreign banks and companies" (Darroch, 1992, p. 162). The end result of their international expansion was that by 1966, both the Royal and the Commerce were counted among the world's top 20 banks ("Canadian Banks Hold," 1966, p. B1). It is thus no surprise that later, in 1972, the Federal Report on Foreign Direct Investment referred to the chartered banks as "global corporations" (Baum, 1974, p. 5). This growth would come at a cost, however. The vast flows of money capital created by the Eurodollar markets began to overwhelm the capacities of the Bretton Woods system, not only causing its collapse, calling forth neo-liberal reforms still with us, but also acting as the tipping point into the global epoch of capitalism.

The Collapse of Bretton Woods

Kobrak and Martin (2018) suggest that "Bretton Woods collapsed because it worked too well ... An extraordinary increase in the movement of goods, services, and capital led to a corresponding reduction in the ability of the government to control financial actors" (p. 196). The Royal's growth during this period was thus a reflection of the circumstances of the day. There was a dialectical relationship between the rise of the Eurodollar markets on the one hand, and the growth of multinational corporate activity on the other. As Henwood (1998) notes, "production must be financed, and if all goes well, it throws off profits in money form, and globalized production is no exception, meaning that MNCs inevitably create financial flows alongside their productive activities" (p. 112).[31] The chartered banks' part in the process is described in the Royal Commission on Corporate Concentration (1978):

> During the past 10 years the nature of [the chartered banks'] international operations has changed dramatically. In the late 1960s, Canadian banks began a major expansion of their international activities, largely as a result of the rise of the Eurodollar market and multinational corporations. Banks have expanded from overseas branches and agencies to include representative offices, foreign affiliates and subsidiaries. (p. 232)

As multinational corporate activity required ever-greater sums of capital to expand, it meant that financial institutions were increasingly in possession of ever-greater sums of foreign currency. As a result, Eurodollar deposits around the world ballooned from just USD$3 billion in 1960 to USD$75 billion in 1970 before climbing to well over USD$1 trillion by 1984 (W.I. Robinson, 2004, p. 111). The foreign currency assets of Canada's chartered banks had amounted to only 25.1 per cent of their Canadian assets in 1966, whereas by 1976, they were up to 42.4 per cent (Royal Commission on Corporate Concentration, 1978, p. 232). These immense flows of money capital were fundamentally in contradiction with the fixed exchange rates and capital controls of the Bretton Woods system, making "it all but impossible to carry out orderly adjustments of currency pegs" (Eichengreen, 1996/2008, p. 2).[32] This situation was

---

31 As Canadian economist Stephen Hymer (1979) put it at the time, "the multinational corporation's need for short-term loans and investment arising from the continuous inflow and outflow of money from all nations, never quite in balance, has encouraged international banking and has helped integrate short-term money markets; its long-term financial requirements ... have broadened the demand for international bond and equity capital" (p. 82).

32 Major (2013) explains some of the major tensions of the 1960s: "In the United States, short-term capital began to pour out of the country, as American investors were attracted to higher European interest rates and newly stable currencies. By 1964 over $2.5 billion worth of short-term liabilities were held abroad. The French and Italians also began to show substantial short-term capital outflows after 1959. For other countries – the United Kingdom, Canada, the Netherlands, and Germany – the relaxation of capital controls brought a massive inflow of short-term capital. These figures, while small by today's standards, swamped the IMF's capacity to provide balance of payments financing. The national governments and international organizations charged with managing the postwar international monetary order faced, by the late 1950s, a real dilemma. On the one hand, no one was willing to go back to a time when transnational capital flows were more closely restricted; on the other hand, the current system of international monetary management was not designed to handle the scale and scope of these kinds of global capital flows."

further frustrated in Canada by a 1963 agreement with the United States that put a ceiling of USD$2.55 billion on reserves of foreign currencies. Finding it difficult to carry out currency adjustments in such a context, the Canadian government followed the advice of the chartered banks and unpegged the currency in 1970.[33] Amid their own dollar crisis, the United States would follow in 1971.[34] While there were a few attempts to patch the system together, most currencies began floating in 1973, with their value now set by trading on a vast international marketplace. Cleaver (2017) reflects on the period: "Suddenly changes in exchange rates were front-page news, and more of us were paying attention than just those who were travelling abroad" (p. 222).

The collapse of Bretton Woods had both immediate and long-term consequences for the global political economy. The first was the decline of the welfare state. While many welfare programs would remain (and

---

From this tension emerged a near decade-long process of institutional innovation to buttress the original Bretton Woods institutions with new forms of credit provision and facilities to finance balance of payments deficits" (pp. 37–8).

33 Having only pegged the currency to the US dollar in 1962, the Royal suggested unpegging it as early as 1968: "Mr. McLaughlin told the bank's 99th annual shareholders' meeting that unprecedented arrangements concluded with the United States in recent years have placed Canadian monetary policy in an intolerable squeeze. On one hand, the growth of Canada's vital reserves of foreign currencies was blocked by a ceiling of $2.55-billion imposed by Finance Minister Mitchell Sharp last May under a 1963 agreement with the United States. On the other hand, the Canadian dollar's value abroad could not grow because the exchange rate was pegged at 92.5 cents in US currency in 1962. The ideal solution to combat Canada's dangerous inflation would be to restore the floating dollar exchange rate that prevailed before 1962" (Lebel, 1968, p. B3). For more on Canada's general experience with the collapse of the Bretton Woods system, see Soederberg (2000).

34 Henwood (1998) provides more detail: "From soon after the war was over until today, the US has acted as the final source of world demand. There was the Marshall Plan, global military expansion, investment abroad by newly globalizing US multinationals, and always more and more imports – all of which scattered dollars around the world. That cascade of greenbacks, plus rising domestic inflation, meant that the dollar was no longer worth as much as it was supposed to be – that is, the gold price was artificially low – and that cashing in dollars for gold at posted prices was a marvelous deal. (No one took more pleasure in pointing this out than Charles de Gaulle.) Strains began appearing in the system in the late 1960s; the outflow of gold from the US to London was so great during the week of the Tet Offensive in Vietnam (March 1968) that the floor of the Bank of England's weighing room collapsed. The German mark broke free and appreciated in 1969, and repeated the break out in 1971. The French cashed in dollars for gold, and there were rumours that Britain was next. So in August 1971, Nixon closed the Treasury's gold window, ending the sale of cheap gold" (pp. 43–4). For more on the American context, see Konings (2011); Panitch & Gindin (2012).

are still with us today, albeit in altered or reduced form), the flows of international currency initiated by the Eurodollar markets and the subsequent collapse of the Bretton Woods system meant that capitalist nation states could no longer be managed as self-contained units. As such, nation states became increasingly reoriented towards the integration of their domestic economy with the global economy through neo-liberal reforms that claimed to increase the domestic economy's competitiveness. These reforms typically included the privatization or reduction of social programs, the driving down of domestic wages, and, crucially, the reduction of inflation (Bienefeld, 1992; Harvey, 2005; Teeple, 2000).[35] While these reforms took place in a variegated manner across the capitalist nation states of the world (N. Brenner et al., 2010), the emergence of neo-liberal policy was itself a reflection of the growing power of financial capital, since the existence of "very diverse inflation levels across the world was extremely problematic for the growth of a global financial market" (Sassen, 2014b, p. 3). Furthermore, as money capital gained the capability to move more freely around the world, the ability of the nation state to control and tax it declined substantially. The period after the collapse of the Bretton Woods system has thus seen a massive growth in household and state indebtedness (a process discussed in the next chapter) that is presently reaching crisis levels (Adkins et al., 2020; Graeber, 2011; Lapavitsas, 2013b; Lazzarato, 2012; Marazzi, 2010; Seccareccia & Pringle, 2020; Streeck, 2016).

The dismantling of Bretton Woods also produced a number of effects related to banking and finance more specifically. As Germain (2010) notes, the collapse

> can account for turbulent foreign exchange fluctuations, a deep international debt crisis involving developing countries, spectacular growth of financial markets, the internationalization of banking networks from many countries, dramatic reversals in the international accounts of major debtor and creditor countries, the emergence among these countries of

---

35 Cleaver (2017) provides a good description from the viewpoint of the working class: "As exchange rates among major currencies devolved into volatile fluctuations – both in response to our struggles and aimed at countering them – we became much more aware of how those fluctuations affected us. For example, if our struggles provoked capitalists to move their money into other countries, the resulting depreciation of our money – or an explicit decision by central banks to devalue it – increased the cost of imports and undermined our real wages. Associated appreciations, or revaluations, elsewhere increased the cost of exports, and by so doing tended to decrease them, costing lost jobs and wages" (pp. 222–3).

significant balance of payments imbalances, and several currency and banking crises. (p. 56)

As a partial result of these various events, nation states began to coordinate more closely in respect to monetary cooperation, a process that would ultimately lead to the construction of the European Union (EU) and the Euro, as well as the Group of Seven (G7), an intergovernmental forum that attempts to foster similar macroeconomic policies among the world's wealthiest countries.[36] While the G7 does not involve any new governing rights or powers, it is in a certain sense an embryonic transnational authority that works to determine the "proper" means for national governments to manage their national economies (i.e., national systems of property relations) within an emerging system of global capitalism.

In the years following the collapse of Bretton Woods, many other similar institutions have emerged for roughly the same purpose: to coordinate national political responses to what are, essentially, global economic problems. This has also included the reorientation of pre-existing international institutions such as the IMF, the WB, and the BIS, which have all taken on new roles. What is especially significant about these institutions is that many of the rules generated by them are eventually made into law by governments, meaning that unlike the national epoch, there has been a slow shift in authority away from the nation state and towards what are essentially private transnational institutions (Cutler, 2011; McBride, 2011). To put it simply, public authority "is no longer exclusively state-led. It is now involved in a compact with private authority, where a balance between competing institutional forms anchors authority" (Germain, 2010, p. 76). As Sassen (2006) notes, the primary aim of these new private authorities "is to set up a global system for governing trade, capital, services, and information flows through intergovernmental agreements on critical requirements such as financial reporting standards, the private property rights regime, or the global trading agreement" (p. 195).

The third and perhaps most significant consequence of the collapse of Bretton Woods has been "the liberation of embryonic transnational

---

[36] The G7's precursor, the G5, was created in 1974 and consisted of an informal meeting of the finance ministers and central bank governors of France, West Germany, Japan, the United Kingdom, and the United States. A year later, the G6 was created with the inclusion of Italy. Canada became the seventh member country to join the meetings in 1976. The criteria for membership is a high net national wealth and a very high human development index.

capital from the institutional constraints of the nation-state system" (W.I. Robinson, 2004, p. 111). The collapse set off what many have come to call financial globalization, the freedom of money capital to fly around the world at breakneck speeds looking for profitable avenues for investment. As Germain (2010) notes, "since 1974, when Richard Nixon began the process of reversing controls on the freedom of movement of capital, country after country has followed suit, and now we live in a world of almost full capital mobility" (p. 54).

As we have seen, the collapse of Bretton Woods was caused, in part, by growing national banks attempting to evade the regulatory powers of the nation state by accumulating liquid capital in offshore markets. In the following chapter, I discuss a number of the consequences of this shift in more detail, but for now, we can note two significant transformations: (1) the deregulation of the banking and finance sectors in capitalist countries around the world, a process that involves the removal of national constraints to their accumulation activities – mainly the removal of the legislated divisions between the various domains of finance (banking, trust, insurance, investment, and so on); and (2) so-called free trade agreements that involve the creation of large regional markets that not only reorient the role of the nation state towards the protection of the rights of the world's largest corporations, but also grant them new rights to sue national governments in private courts for policy decisions that impact their accumulation activities. I claim that this reorientation is transforming the role of the nation state into a capability for globalizing capitals and should be understood more broadly as part of the construction of a global system of property relations – that is, an emerging system of global rights for capital enforced by nation states. To me, this process not only provides empirical substance to claims that a transnational state is emerging but also demonstrates the extent to which we should understand globalization as a novel epoch within the history of capitalism. The details of these transformations will be provided in the next chapter, while many of their implications – of which there are many – will be dealt with in the final chapter.

Conclusion

Against the view that this period represents the beginnings of globalization, this chapter set out to explain why we should see it instead as an interregnum between the national and the global epochs of capitalism. I made this argument on the basis that despite an increase in international economic activity and multilateralism, the period was still primarily constituted by national systems of property relations, that is, by national assemblages of TAR. As such, the capitalist nation state continued to function as a capability for the growth of domestic capitals, despite an increase in international economic activity and coordination. It did this by not only protecting the basic rights of private property necessary for the domestic market to function but also by restricting the rights of foreign capitals within that territory, and by participating to a much larger degree within the national economy. While these measures were extremely successful in growing national capitals, this growth would also force the transformation of those elements of TAR that restricted capital's more general expansion.

To demonstrate the empirical reality of this characterization, I provided an analysis of the transformation of Canadian banking via the history of the Royal Bank of Canada from 1945 to 1974. I identified the Bretton Woods system as a continuation of the centripetal organizing dynamic of TAR on the basis that it did not require nation states to relinquish their authority to manage or participate within the national economy but strengthened their ability to do so. I argued that through the construction of a financially restricted national economy by virtue of foreign exchange and capital controls limiting the capacity of financial capital to flow unimpeded around the world, the Bretton Woods system led to an increase in domestic competition among the chartered banks from smaller finance and trust companies that were unconstrained by the restrictions of the *Bank Act*. This struggle, in turn, led the Royal, along with the other chartered banks, to expand via the Eurodollar markets to escape national regulatory control. While this enabled them to grow extremely large, crushing their near-bank rivals in the process, the massive flows of foreign currency generated by the Eurodollar markets eventually overturned the Bretton Woods system.

I concluded by highlighting some of the reasons why we should understand the collapse of this system as the tipping point into our current global epoch, as well as some of the consequences for banking and finance. As I discuss in the next chapter, if the earlier period of capitalist development can be understood as the making of national capital, then we should consider the period from roughly the mid-1970s to our present as the making of global capital – that is, as the construction of a *global* system of property relations, despite the persistence and importance of the nation state to this system as well as struggles against this overall trajectory.

Chapter Four

Making Global Capital: RBC in the Digital Age, 1975–2008

The proprietor of stock is properly a citizen of the world, and is not necessarily attached to any particular country.
– Adam Smith (1766/2000, para. 6)

An international capitalist class is emerging whose interests lie in the world economy as a whole and a system of international private property which allows free movement of capital between countries ... There is a strong tendency for the most powerful segments of the capitalist class increasingly to see their future in the further growth of the world market rather than its curtailment.
– Stephen Hymer (1979, p. 262)

We used to be a large Canadian bank with international interests. But now we are a large international bank with a strong Canadian base. There's a difference.
– Rowland Frazee, CEO of the Royal Bank
of Canada (as cited in Malcolm, 1980, p. D1)

Introduction

In the last chapter, I explored how the period from 1945 until 1974 was constituted in its configuration of territory, authority, and rights (TAR) in respect to Canada's chartered banks. I argued that we should understand that period as the interregnum between the national and global epochs of capitalism on the basis that it began with a continuation of the centripetal dynamic of TAR that characterized the earlier period of capitalism, as examined in chapter 2. I made that argument on the basis that despite increasing international economic activity and new forms of multilateral governance, the period was still constituted by national systems of property relations, that is, by a predominantly national assemblage of TAR. Under the national assemblage, the institutional structure of the capitalist nation state operated primarily as a capability for its own capitals by protecting the basic rights of private property necessary for the domestic market to function and by restricting the rights of foreign capitals within that territory. In other words, since the rights of capital remained an object of governance at the national level, governments were able to restrict these rights if they significantly impeded the development of the national political economy. In that context, the ability to do so rested primarily on the strength and character of the domestic ruling class. As such, the world of that period was made up of nation states that acted to protect the interests of their largest capitals, with domestic policy reflecting the balance of power between capital and labour.

In this chapter, I continue our analysis by focusing on those shifting elements of TAR that now problematize that interpretation of the global political economy. In particular, I explore an emerging centrifugal dynamic that stands in stark contrast to the organizing logic of the national epoch of capitalism. Instead of asking whether Canada is a secondary imperialist power or a rich dependency, I ask how these shifts fundamentally restructure the shape and character of the global political economy, in particular, the various ways in which these shifts reflect an "incipient, highly specialized and partial denationalization of specific components of national states" (Sassen, 2003, p. 4). The goal is to highlight the emergence of this new organizing dynamic, which remains coated in a historical residue that frequently leads to a misinterpretation of its character, recalling Marx's (1871/1978a) comment that "it is generally the fate of completely new historical creations to be mistaken for the counterpart of older and even defunct forms of social life, to which they may bear a certain likeness" (p. 633). As Bob Jessop (2018) notes, "while mercantilist and imperialist features remain, neo-liberalism and finance-dominated accumulation have radically changed how the world market operates" (p. 207).

As mentioned in chapter 1, my aim here is double-sided. On the one hand, I want to dispense with the idea that since the nation state is still here that it still works the same as it always has, that is, within a competitive interstate framework in which nation states act on behalf of their national capitals. On the other hand, I also want to escape from what Sassen (2006) refers to as the endogeneity trap: the tendency to confine the study of globalization to explicitly global processes and institutions. By focusing on the denationalization of specific elements of TAR that may still be located at the national level, the effort is to understand how and why an existing assemblage of TAR is able to become reoriented towards an altogether different organizing logic – that is, how capabilities, such as the nation state, are able to jump tracks and become a key site for the support and development of globalizing forms of capital. While both the national and global epochs of capitalism involved the outward expansion of capital, they are constituted by different assemblages of TAR, and different outcomes. In my view, the emerging centrifugal dynamic of TAR gives us a small glimpse of a much larger world historical transformation: the slow construction of a global system of rights for capital outside the grasp of national politics.[1]

The chapter proceeds as follows. First, I provide a brief discussion on how much of what falls under the label "globalization" refers to the reorientation of pre-existing national and international institutions and processes. Next, I focus on the impacts of these reorientations on the Royal's operations and activities. Specific attention is paid to the nature of conflicts between the Royal, the other chartered banks, and federal and provincial governments. I argue that these shifts in TAR are representative of the growth of capital past the institutional confines of a national system of property relations. As such, I conclude that we should understand our present period as a new historical epoch that consists of the making of global capital(ism).

Reorienting International Institutions

Up to this point, I have been concerned with demonstrating that, in respect to capital, Canada's earlier epoch of capitalism was characterized by a centripetal organizing dynamic in which TAR was continuously drawn in towards the nation state; in other words, the period was predominantly, insofar as capital was concerned, about constructing a national system of property relations (i.e., national systems of rights for capital governed by nation states). In contrast, since the collapse

---

1 The general argument here comes from Teeple (2000): "Politics in the form of liberal democracy in the national sphere enabled a citizenry to modify – and made it both necessary and advantageous for capital to compromise on – the exercise of the property rights attached to capital. But at the global level there is no comparable political structure or jurisdiction, and there the accumulation of capitalist private property can be pursued without political interference – though not without certain regulation or restrictions emanating from such organizations as the WTO, IMF, WB, and BIS. These constraints, however, are not political, but rather are the formalization of the rules of global competition between capitals. From this level and with the advantages of global self-generation, capital has little need to compromise with national political policy, and indeed it is positioned to demand broad policies reflecting its own needs – hence, neo-liberalism" (p. 129).

of the Bretton Woods system, much of the global political economy, including Canada, has been characterized by a centrifugal dynamic in which the rights of capital and the authority over those rights have either drifted towards remade international institutions or been reconfigured at the nation state level to accommodate the interests of globalizing capitals.

The reorientation of pre-existing international institutions is an important indicator of the organizing dynamic of our epoch. Major (2013) notes:

> Unlike the process of crafting Bretton Woods, which was characterized by deep conflicts between monetary authorities' interests in financial stability and national governments' interests in domestic economic growth, the "new international financial architecture" is the design of the transnational monetary authority that converges in intergovernmental forums like the G7 and the Bank for International Settlements. No longer framed in terms of whether international or domestic concerns should be privileged by the new system, the primary concern has been to find ways to ensure that national economic policy is sufficiently attentive to the needs of the international monetary system. (pp. 40–1)

As I argue in this chapter, this movement constitutes an important first step towards the construction of a global system of property relations, the characteristic feature of our age. My argument is that after the collapse of the Bretton Woods system, many new and pre-existing international institutions not only began to take on increased responsibilities relating to the regulation and reproduction of globalizing capital but, in doing so, also started to limit the capabilities of nation states to legislate against corporate interests in specific areas. In my view, this overall process is more significant than many existing accounts recognize, since it reduces the meaning of political rights within liberal democracies by reconfiguring laws, rules, and regulations in a variety of ways that limit the extent to which national or subnational governments can restrain the accumulation activities of globalizing capital. As Sassen (2006) notes, while "political nationalism may still prevail rhetorically," there are deep "structural tendencies that make international competition today function primarily as a mechanism for denationalizing capital" (p. 140). In other words, as nation states compete for capital to be invested in their own territories – competition that involves not only trying to attract the investment of foreign firms but domestic ones as well – they often do so by changing or making regulations and rules or by adopting so-called best practices that ultimately work to denationalize the social relations that constitute capital itself.

Some of these shifts are more legible than others, such as the structural adjustment policies pushed on developing countries by the International Monetary Fund (IMF) and the World Bank (WB) from the 1980s onwards.[2] While those two institutions have the power to directly provide loans to states in financial distress, thereby making their role in this process more legible, others work in less legible ways through the development of "regulatory practices (ideas, standards, rules, guidelines) within the context of how financial institutions operate across different markets and among fungible classes of assets" (Germain, 2010, p. 135). In the world of banking and finance, for instance, "behaviour can be heavily shaped by the best practices that are developed in technical reports produced by private-sector think tanks and research institutes" (Porter, 2005, p. 107). Multilateral institutions such as the Organisation for Economic Co-operation and Development (OECD), the World Trade Organization (WTO), the Bank for International Settlements (BIS), the Basel Committee on Banking Supervision (BCBS), and the Financial Stability Board (FSB), as well as sector-oriented associations such as the Institute of International Finance (IIF), the International Investment Funds Association (IIFA), and the Global Financial Markets Association (GFMA), all work to manage the risks of global capital accumulation and organize the shared interests of a variety of different financial actors (Major, 2013; McKeen-Edwards & Porter, 2013; Rude, 2005; Soederberg, 2004). As McBride (2011) remarks, however, the globalization of capital was not furthered in the post-Bretton

---

2 Harvey (2005) provides a brief description of the reorientation of the IMF and WB: "The Reagan administration, which had seriously thought of withdrawing support for the IMF in its first year in office, found a way to put together the powers of the US Treasury and the IMF to resolve the difficulty by rolling over the debt, but did so in return for neoliberal reforms. This treatment became standard after what Stiglitz refers to as a 'purge' of all Keynesian influences from the IMF in 1982. The IMF and the World Bank thereafter became centres for the propagation and enforcement of 'free market fundamentalism' and neoliberal orthodoxy. In return for debt rescheduling, indebted countries were required to implement institutional reforms, such as cuts in welfare expenditures, more flexible labour market laws, and privatization. Thus was 'structural adjustment' invented" (p. 29).

F.A. Knox (1945), editor of *Canadian Banker*, identified the possibility of such a shift earlier, noting that if loans were treated on a case-by-case basis, subject to "the familiar criteria of credit-worthiness," that such institutions "would impose upon sovereign states as borrowers the necessity of conforming to the monetary ideas of the lenders no matter what the purpose of the loan" (p. 32).

Woods era by creating "a corresponding set of institutions to match the new accumulation regime. Instead, older multilateral institutions created during an era of embedded liberalism were reformed on an ad hoc basis" (p. 26). This has led to the creation of what some have referred to as a multilevel state, in which specific governmental functions have been redistributed "upward to international institutions, downward to sub-national states, and laterally to the private sector" (Clarkson, 2001, p. 501).[3] And it is through this larger process that the "apolitical discipline of money" (Drainville, 1995, p. 8) has been permitted to reign.

---

3 Sassen (2006) provides more detail on some of the different ways in which national political rule has drifted to the transnational level: "Another aspect of this participation by the state in the implementation of a global economic system can be found in the new types of cross-border collaborations among specialized government agencies concerned with a growing range of issues emerging from the globalization of capital markets and the new trade order. These often build on long-standing networks ... Slaughter (2004) identifies three types of such government networks. One functions within international organizations in terms of issue areas. It involves the national ministries or agencies charged with the particular issue area: trade ministers in GATT, finance ministries in the IMF; defense and foreign ministers in NATO; central bankers in the Bank for International Settlements. A second type consists of government networks within the framework of an executive agreement. These are transgovernmental networks that emerge outside a formal international institution, even though members operate within a framework agreed on at least by the heads of their respective governments. Examples are transatlantic governmental interactions specifically authorized and encouraged by executive agreement. A third type consists of spontaneous government networks, a development of the current era. These networks arise outside formal intergovernmental agreements, whether treaties or executive agreements: the Basel Committee of the Bank for International Settlements (BIS) is a leading example. They are networks that lack a foundational treaty and nothing they do purports to be legally binding on the members. Another example is agreements among domestic regulatory agencies of two or more countries. The last few decades have seen a vast increase in these, with agreements that can be implemented by the regulators themselves, without further approval by national legislators. These have grown far more than traditional treaty negotiations.

There are multiple instances of this highly specialized type of convergence in regulatory issues concerning telecommunications, finance, the Internet, and so on. In some of these sectors there has long been an often elementary convergence, or at least coordination, of standards. What we see today is a sharp increase in the work of establishing convergence. For instance, we see an intensification of transactions among central bankers, necessary in the context of the global capital market. While central bankers have long interacted with each other across borders, we can clearly identify a new phase in the last ten years. The world of cross-border trade has brought with it a sharpened need for convergence in standards, as is evident in the vast proliferation of ISO [International Organization for Standardization] items. Another example would be the institutional and legal framework necessary for the operation of cross-border commodity chains and value-adding chains" (pp. 235–6).

The reorientation of the BIS is a good example of this more general phenomenon and a relevant choice for analysis, since, as Drainville (1995) notes, the BIS "was perhaps the most important to Canadian central bankers" (p. 17).[4] Despite having "much more limited powers than its sister organizations, the IMF and the World Bank," K. Alexander (2009) notes that it "has provided the backdrop for some of the seminal negotiations on financial policy and regulations since the early 1970s" (p. 307). Established in 1930 by the governments of Belgium, France, Germany, Italy, Japan, Switzerland, and the UK to facilitate reparation payments after the First World War, the BIS would lose its purpose almost immediately after starting, with the Hoover Moratorium of July 1931 leading to a one-year suspension of reparation payments, and the Lausanne Agreement of July 1932 cancelling them altogether (BIS, n.d.-c). While the creators of the BIS had hoped that it would grow into an international central bank, the editor of *Canadian Banker*, F.A. Knox (1943), pointed out at the time that "the tide of economic nationalism was running too strongly for it to make much headway against it" (p. 24). Instead, the BIS reoriented its activities towards facilitating "technical cooperation between central banks (including reserve management, foreign exchange transactions, international postal payments, gold deposit and swap facilities) and [towards] providing a forum for regular meeting of central bank Governors and officials" (BIS, n.d.-c, para. 6). With the monetary and economic department led by Per Jacobsson, a prominent neo-liberal economist within the Friedrich Hayek-led Mont Pelerin Society (Mirowski & Plehwe, 2009), the BIS would also begin to collect financial and banking statistics, with this research making "its way into the Bank's *Annual Report*, which soon established itself as a leading publication in its field" (BIS, n.d.-c, para. 8).

Having survived a liquidation resolution at Bretton Woods due to the lobbying efforts of European central bankers,[5] Jacobsson "used his position at the BIS to try to ensure that Marshall Plan aid was used not

---

4 For a comprehensive overview of the BIS, see Borio et al. (2020).
5 The BIS (n.d.-a) provides more details of how central bankers kept it alive: "In July 1944, a United Nations conference met at Bretton Woods in the United States to discuss the postwar international monetary system. The Bretton Woods Conference adopted a resolution calling for the abolition of the BIS 'at the earliest possible moment,' because it considered that the BIS would have no useful role to play once the newly created World Bank and International Monetary Fund were operational. European central bankers held a different opinion, and successfully lobbied for maintaining the BIS. By early 1948, the BIS liquidation resolution had been put aside. It was understood that henceforth the BIS would focus foremost on European monetary and financial matters" (para. 6).

to perpetuate inflationary conditions but to facilitate a return to more orthodox policies" (Helleiner, 1994, p. 66). Both US officials and European central bank governors, as Helleiner (1994) notes, were heavily influenced by Jacobsson's "constant insistence on the need to enforce discipline in monetary policy and move toward early free market convertibility" (p. 67), the latter of which the BIS would achieve by the end of 1958 as the technical agent of the European Payments Union (EPU) (Kaplan & Schleiminger, 1989). While neo-liberalism remained "on the margins of both policy and academic influence" (Harvey, 2005, p. 22) at this time, the networks created by the BIS between contemporary economists and financial practitioners meant that it was a central point of mixing between different strains of thinking about currency and credit in the twentieth century.[6] And although no documentation exists that can definitively prove the contribution of neo-liberalism to BIS policy and decision-making, banking historian Kazuhiko Yago (2013) argues that although the impact of neo-liberalism was less direct, it was nevertheless important:

> Even if indirect, the impact of the theorists respected by top BIS management, such as Roger Auboin, van Zeeland, or Jacobsson, should not be underestimated. Jacobsson in particular cited Hayek and Robbins in his journal articles and speeches, and after World War II he spoke of their neo-liberal theories frequently to counter Keynes and Keynesians. The actual

---

[6] Yago (2013) notes: "Per Jacobsson, the first head of its monetary and economic department, was one of the central theorists in international finance through the 1960s and he was the starting point of a network linking others including Knut Wicksell and John Maynard Keynes. In addition, the talent that each country sent to the BIS as representatives or staff included theorists and practitioners in their prime at that time or in the near future. Examples included Henry Strakosch from Great Britain, Charles Kindleberger of the United States and Karl Blessing of Germany. In the documents left behind from their day-to-day duties can be read points of dispute surpassing discussions of policy narrowly defined, covering currency and credit theory and further spreading to the broader subjects of capitalism and contemporary society. In this way, the BIS had a presence as a major crossroads at which various economic ideas representative of the twentieth century blended together and diverged" (p. xx). Despite this intermingling, Yago (2013) concludes that the dominant ideas that "impacted the BIS are neoliberalism and Wicksellian economic thought" (p. xx). Furthermore, there is a high degree of overlap at the BIS with either high-level bankers or the heads of central banks. Many BIS reports, for instance, are written by individuals that have a vested interest in specific regulatory matters. As such, it is very difficult to view the BIS as the neutral institution it makes itself out to be. For more on elite networks and the institutional infiltration of neo-liberal thought, see Carroll & Sapinski (2016); MacLean (2017); Slobodian (2018).

policies adopted by the BIS too show the impact of neoliberalism – in complex ways. (p. 46)

No doubt, the operations and reproduction of institutions like the BIS and the technical committees located there are not a direct result of the structural interests of banks but rather involve the sort of day-to-day enrollment described by McKeen-Edwards and Porter (2013) in their case study of transnational financial associations. As many scholars (e.g., Baker, 2006; Kastner, 2014; McKeen-Edwards & Porter, 2013; Porter, 2005; Walter & Wanslaben, 2020; D.R. Wood, 2005; Young, 2012) point out, these institutions were the sites of significant debates over monetary and financial policy, and they did not always involve globalizing forms of capital or dominant nation states getting their way – capture, no; influence, yes.

But acknowledging how these institutions work on a day-to-day basis does not deny the significant transformation of the international financial architecture that began to take place in the 1970s due to the globalization of capital in the form of the Eurodollar markets in the preceding decades. As Chris Rogers (2018) notes, despite the various disagreements and on-the-ground processes that eventually culminate in strategic policy choices, the sort of prudential regulation pushed by these sorts of institutions has ultimately worked "to recreate capitalist social relations in their neoliberal form" (p. 67). In highlighting the shift between a much more closely linked relationship between transnational financial authorities and central banks, the increasing autonomy of central banks, and the ways that these transformations reduce the meaning of nationally located political rights, we can better highlight the differences between the national and global epochs of capitalism. Where, in the previous epoch, national governments were "determined not to let their exercise of this new weapon in the armoury of economic nationalism [central banking] be limited in any way by any international authority" (Knox, 1943, p. 24), they now look to such authorities to coordinate the financial management of their economies.

Despite long being a meeting place for central bankers (especially European ones) in the postwar decades, the BIS really only became linked to the management of global banking through the establishment of the Standing Committee on Banking Supervision in 1974.[7] The

---

[7] Rost (2009) describes the nature of the relationship between the BIS and the Committee: "The Bank for International Settlements (BIS) provides the Secretariat for the Committee, and it is at the BIS headquarters in Basel that the Committee meets on a regular basis (usually four times a year). The Secretariat is mainly staffed

Committee, which was later renamed the Basel Committee on Banking Supervision (BCBS) in 1990, was established by the G10 as a "response to the globalization of financial institutions and markets" (Rost, 2009, p. 319) more generally, and to the failure of two-high profile banks – the Bankhaus Herstatt (Germany) and the Franklin National Bank (New York) – more specifically.[8] Located at the BIS, the stated purpose of the BCBS, as expressed in their 1975 Concordat, was "to ensure that no foreign banking establishment escapes supervision" (BCBS, 1975, p. 1). As Porter (2005) notes, the major concern of the G10 at the time was that globalizing banks would "play one jurisdiction off against another, or move from one jurisdiction to another, in order to escape regulation" (p. 35). As part of its quest to maintain monetary and financial stability in the new world of floating exchange rates, the Concordat suggested that a bank's home regulator should be responsible for their worldwide activities, and that there should be information-sharing between supervisory authorities. Helleiner (1994) describes the content of the Concordat simply: "encouragement of central bank cooperation for the purpose of maintaining global financial stability" (p. 174).

One of the major principles to come out of the larger process of reorienting the international financial architecture was that national governments should maintain the stability of their exchange rates by keeping

---

by professional supervisors on temporary secondment from member institutions. In addition to undertaking the secretarial work for the Committee and its many expert sub-committees, it stands ready to give advice to supervisory authorities in all countries" (p. 322). Despite not being an explicit part of the BIS, the Committee's location there is "necessarily strengthened through the facilities available at the BIS and national levels" (p. 322).

8 For more on the history of the BCBS, see Goodhart (2011); D.R. Wood (2005). Although previously discussed in chapter 3, Porter (2005) also provides a good summary of what led to the emergence of such transnational forms of regulation: "The globalization of finance that we are experiencing today can be traced back to the weakening of restrictions on cross-border financial flows that had been put in place in the mid-twentieth century. The political factors that encouraged the emergence of the Euromarkets, together with technological and organizational creativity of market actors, had, by the late 1960s, created a large enough quantity of lightly regulated financial assets outside the jurisdiction of the US and other governments responsible for the currency in which these assets were denominated, that some public-sector officials began to consider the implications of these cross-border financial activities for the stability of the system as a whole" (p. 32). Goodhart (2011) agrees: "The primary reason for the foundation of the BCBS was the implications for the monetary authorities of the growing globalisation of financial intermediation" (p. 10). While the BCBC does not possess any formal supervisory authority, countries generally observe the standards "because they participate in making the rules in order to strengthen the hegemony and integrity of the international banking system" (Clarkson, 2008, p. 317).

domestic prices stable (Baker, 2006). As Major (2013) notes, this represented a sharp reversal from the ideas that informed Bretton Woods: "Rather than shielding domestic policy from international monetary concerns, national governments were now responsible for conducting domestic monetary operations with an eye toward maintaining the value of their currency on foreign exchange markets" (p. 41). It is not difficult to understand why, since inflation erodes the value of money, thereby reducing the rate of return of financial assets. As Teeple (2011) explains, "price stability becomes an overriding goal in a financially dominated economy; the constancy of the value of money takes on an importance that it did not previously have" (p. 242).[9] With the decade's policies reflecting the rising dominance of denationalized financial capital, the inflation of the 1970s was ultimately a monetary reflection of the larger conflict between "a working class, demanding both employment security and a higher share in their country's income, and a capitalist class striving to maximize the return on its capital" (Streeck, 2016, p. 79). Both groups were acting on "mutually incompatible ideas of what is theirs by right," Streeck (2016) points out, with labour "emphasizing the entitlements of citizenship," and capital emphasizing the entitlements of private "property and market power" (p. 79). Despite being framed in terms of financial stability, the increased focus on inflation targeting during this period should be understood as a wider response to what was perceived – especially by neo-conservatives and neo-liberals (Finkel, 2006; Slobodian, 2018) – as irresponsible political demands by the working classes.[10] Moreover, as Sassen (2014b) notes,

---

[9] These trends were already well at work within international institutions prior to the collapse of Bretton Woods. As the managing director of the IMF before becoming the chief economic advisor to the BIS, Per Jacobbsen had hoped that "private business, and especially private banking, [would] reap some of the chief rewards of successful work by the Fund in fighting inflation and stabilizing currencies" (C. Kilpatrick, 1959, p. 117). As he put it himself, "orderly monetary conditions will give new chances to business ... especially as sound money is invariably followed by trade liberalization; i.e., by the elimination of quantitative restrictions affecting imports and exports" (as cited in C. Kilpatrick, 1959, p. 117).

[10] Finkel (2006) notes: "The origins of the neo-liberal assault lie in the economic stagnation of the 1970s. As both inflation and unemployment rose in tandem throughout the decade, conservatives questioned the efficacy of the Keynesian approach to economic policy that supposedly had been utilized by governments since the war to keep both inflation and unemployment in check. They argued that government attempts to reduce unemployment were causing inflation without affecting joblessness. The funds required for stimulative expenditures were being financed by government deficits, which, in turn, were financed by loans from financial institutions both at home and abroad. The loans by these institutions to

the existence of varying levels of inflation among different countries was also "extremely problematic for the growth of a global financial market" (p. 3).

One way this overall reorientation took place was through groups like the BCBS, who listed regulatory independence as one of their key best practices for national financial regulation, the most prominent of which has been central bank independence (Canova, 2000; Teeple, 2011; D.R. Wood, 2005). As Major (2013) notes,

> autonomy, from the central bankers' perspective, is a necessary barrier against the forces of democracy that have often stood in the way of the monetary authorities' ability to structure economic policy around the needs of international credit markets and price stability. (p. 42)

This autonomy, as Jacqueline Best (2018) points out, means that central banks end up operating "in political spaces exempt from many of the norms of liberal democratic politics and yet have the power to define and constrain liberal rights" (p. 328). As such, this process represents "the endogenization of the global agendas of financial markets in domestic institutional orders in an effective denationalization of macroeconomic policy" (Baker, 2006, p. 76). In other words, a transnational reorientation of a specific element of the nation state.

With all of this in mind, it is little surprise to find that as early as 1960, the Canadian Bankers Association (1960) was writing to the Senate Finance Committee to tell them that "good banking depends on

---

government allegedly 'crowded out' loans to the private sector, forcing interest rates up to record levels. In turn, this fuelled inflation. With companies unable to make loans, jobs in the private sector were disappearing at a faster rate than those that could be created in the public sector. Such viewpoints were joined to the more traditional conservative ones that argued the provision of state aid to those without incomes encouraged them to refuse the jobs that were on offer" (p. 286).

Vernengo (2022) makes a similar observation: "If fears of unemployment and the possible return of the Great Depression shaped the postwar period of growth and stability known as the Golden Age of Capitalism, it is inflation paranoia that has been dubbed analogously the Great Inflation. In this view, inflation is caused by government overspending, financed by money printing. State power and the excesses of democracy, defined simply as the rule of the majority, along with the inevitable demands for higher welfare spending, would bring down Western civilization, or at least American hegemonic power. The great priests of neoliberalism thought the problem should be dealt with at the root. Milton Friedman wanted an independent central bank that followed monetary rules, taming monetary expansion, while Friedrich Hayek wanted to privatize money. Adherents believe markets should impose limits on the demands of the masses" (pp. 91–2).

the confidence of the public in their banks. And confidence in banks is directly related to confidence in the purchasing power of money. Inflation destroys the environment in which such confidence flourishes" (p. 27). That organization would later describe the period leading up to the mid-1970s worryingly, as one typified by "an increasingly deep-seated inflation" (Canadian Bankers' Association, 1975, p. 4). With the BCBS promoting central bank independence, alongside the Bank of Canada's shift towards monetarist policy (Drainville, 1991, 1995; Seccareccia & Pringle, 2020), the message clearly being sent was "that inflation was the most pressing social problem and 'tight money' the most efficacious solution" (Naylor, 1982, p. 1). A few years later in 1980, the Royal's former CEO, Rowland Frazee, would keep the offensive going, taking to the press to publicly complain (in an article aptly titled "Royal Bank Outgrows Canada") that "Canada's greatest current problem is inflation" (as cited in Malcolm, 1980, p. B1).

It is important to remember that in the capitalist core, the directionality of this process was not strictly top-down, with directives coming from international institutions; as Drainville (1991) notes, "the task of the BIS was not to initiate new studies, nor did it act as the investigator of the international monetary system, [but rather] it sought to offer technical support for central bankers' meetings" (p. 114). As such, it was only after "central banks came to favour monetary targeting [that] the BIS became preoccupied with techniques of monetarist practices" (p. 114). That said, it is also important to note that BIS economists,

> drew attention very early on to the promises, and in the long term to the necessity, of monetary control and that in the decade of monetarism in the world economy, their empirical work is one of the focal points of central bankers discussions about the techniques, and political hazards, of monetary control. (p. 114)

As such, the relationship between central bankers and institutions like the BIS should be understood as dialectical, summed up by Milton Friedman's response to Governor Gerald Bouey's 1975 so-called Saskatoon Manifesto, a speech that introduced the Bank of Canada's newfound faith in monetary targeting: "It is a marvellous speech. It is the best speech I have ever heard a central banker give ... I could have written it myself" (as cited in Courchene, 1976, p. 111). Taken together, then, "global monetarism was not about imposing a uniform path for money growth the world over; it was about coordinating and arranging different national monetarisms and fashioning a coherent international regime out of this varied patchwork" (Drainville, 1995, p. 16). Contra

Keynesianism, which focuses on increasing demand via full employment, monetarism uses the money supply as the primary means of stabilizing national political economies.[11] As Naylor (1982) notes, however, despite the oft-repeated rhetoric of keeping one's house in order, these policies actually end up causing a rise in government debt, "for tight money drives up the unemployment rate and slows the growth of national income – causing federal disbursements to rise and tax receipts to fall. And tight money imposes an astronomical increase in the cost of servicing the federal debt" (p. 8).[12] Furthermore, when combined with trade liberalization and fiscal austerity – two other common features of neo-liberal regimes – monetarist policy helps contribute to the "decoupling of real wages and productivity" (Seccareccia & Pringle, 2020, p. 343) that has been characteristic of the post-Bretton Woods

---

11 Seccareccia & Pringle (2020) explain: "The intellectual cover for the Bank's singular focus on fighting inflation, rather than reducing unemployment, was provided by monetarist theory developed by Milton Friedman and later by the New Classical Macroeconomics pioneered by fellow Chicago School economist Robert Lucas. These schools of macroeconomic thought emphasized that both the monetary and fiscal authorities had but one principle objective: to combat inflation. If not perturbed by discretionary activist Keynesian policies, the private economy naturally would tend towards some long-term non-accelerating inflation rate of unemployment" (p. 341).

12 Streeck (2016) provides further explanation: "A central topic of current anti-democratic rhetoric is the fiscal crisis of the contemporary state, as reflected in the astonishing increase in public debt since the 1970s. Growing public indebtedness is put down to electoral majorities living beyond their means by exploiting their societies' 'common pool,' and to opportunistic politicians buying the support of myopic voters with money they do not have. However, that the fiscal crisis was unlikely to have been caused by an excess of redistributive democracy can be seen from the fact that the build-up of government debt coincided with a decline in electoral participation, especially at the lower end of the income scale, and marched in lockstep with shrinking unionization, the disappearance of strikes, welfare-state cutbacks and exploding income inequality. What the deterioration of public finances *was* related to was declining overall levels of taxation and the increasingly regressive character of tax systems, as a result of 'reforms' of top income and corporate tax rates. Moreover, by replacing tax revenue with debt, governments contributed further to inequality, in that they offered secure investment opportunities to those whose money they would or could no longer confiscate and had to borrow instead. Unlike taxpayers, buyers of government bonds continue to own what they pay to the state, and in fact collect interest on it, typically paid out of ever less progressive taxation; they can also pass it on to their children. Moreover, rising public debt can be and is being utilized politically to argue for cutbacks in state spending and for privatization of public services, further constraining redistributive democratic intervention in the capitalist economy" (p. 53).

period.[13] This why Harvey (2005) makes a distinction between the neo-liberal state in theory and the neo-liberal state in practice; despite raging against government debt, in reality, neo-liberal policies actually increase it.

One can simply look at the results: the combination of neo-liberal and monetarist policy in Canada has led to an explosion of public debt. As Statistics Canada (2009, 2017) records, from 1867 to 1975, Canada's accumulated federal debt was only $21.6 billion, a period that covered two world wars, numerous infrastructure projects, and decades' worth of hospitals, universities, and other public building projects. From 1975 to 2008, however, that same debt ballooned to over $490 billion, a significant part of which is simply interest on the original loans.[14] Despite the ongoing claims of those on the right that increasing state indebtedness is simply the result of "electoral majorities living beyond their means" (Streeck, 2016, p. 53), a study by Statistics Canada makes clear that this is not the case: "It was not explosive growth in program spending that caused the increase in deficits after 1975, but a drop in federal revenues relative to the growth of GDP and rising debt charges" (Mimoto & Cross, 1991, p. 3.17). As Deneault (2018) notes, this pattern creates a spiral effect:

> From a strictly logical point of view, it can be deduced that this shortfall for the treasury, which translates into recurring budget deficits, generates additional debt service costs for government. Every year, to make ends

---

13 Some authors argue for a strict distinction between neo-liberalism and monetarism, since "monetarism is not – nor did it appear to policy makers in the 1970s – a laissez-faire program. Rather it is a program for government control of economic volatility" (Clune, 2013, para. 22). Despite significant disputes as to what falls under the heading of neo-liberalism (Birch & Springer, 2019), and whether its impact is uniform or variegated (N. Brenner et al., 2010), the main project, as expressed by historian Quinn Slobodian (2018), is definitively not a laissez-faire approach to markets or the economy in general: "What neoliberals seek is not a partial but a complete protection of private capital rights, and the ability of supranational judiciary bodies like the European Court of Justice and the WTO to override national legislation that might disrupt the global rights of capital" (pp. 12–13). And as he notes, this is "a project in which states play an indispensable role" (p. 13). This is backed up by Nancy MacLean (2017) in her well-titled book, *Democracy in Chains*, which explores the intellectual history of the neo-liberal economist James M. Buchanan. The overall project of neo-liberal theorists thus goes some way towards explaining the affinity between neo-liberalism and monetarism in the context of the various economic crises in the 1970s.

14 For a visual representation of the extent of this transformation, see "Canada's Debt in Inflation-Adjusted Dollars 1961–2010" in "WTF" (2011).

meet, governments must borrow from the financial institutions that they now [tax] at a lower rate than before or not at all. (p. 40)

As the Statistics Canada study demonstrates, "higher debt charges accounted for the bulk (70%) of the increase in spending" (Mimoto & Cross, 1991, p. 3.9), and "the drop in the ratio of total revenues to GDP can be traced to tax measures introduced beginning in the 1970s" (p. 3.12) that included "the transfer of tax revenues to the provinces, indexation of the tax system, and three income tax cuts" (p. 3.12).[15] The study also points out that "since 1986, the ratio for personal income taxes has risen sharply," while corporate taxes "have remained at a relatively low level," reflecting the fact that neo-liberal tax reform has simply "shifted the tax burden from corporations to persons, and from income taxes to consumption taxes" (p. 3.15).[16]

By raising interest rates to combat inflation, the Bank of Canada was therefore initiating "a massive redistribution of income towards the rentier class" (Naylor, 1982, p. 17). To maintain their ability to borrow, federal and provincial governments are increasingly subject to the confidence of global investors "in the management of Canadian financial and economic affairs" (Naylor, 1985, p. 118), a shift that ultimately reduces the meaning and impact of national political rights.[17] As Streeck

---

15 In terms of the debt charges more specifically, the study notes that "interest payments on the debt have soared from about 2% GDP in the first half of the 1970s to 6% [in 1991]. In absolute terms, the debt charges have jumped more than ten-fold from $3.3 billion in 1974–75 to $41 billion. Put another way, interest payments are equivalent to 32% of all revenues [in 1991] compared to 11% in 1974–75" (Mimoto & Cross, 1991, p. 3.8).

16 Deneault (2018) describes the long-term impact of these shifts: "Year after year, the federal government's budget report shows that less than 15 percent of its revenues come from business and approximately 50 percent from individuals. In other words, individuals are being asked to pay three-and-a-half times as much. In 1979–80, the ratio was approximately two to one. (That is without counting sales tax, which weighs more heavily on households and now accounts for 11 percent of the tax base.) If we add up all the income tax paid by Canadian individuals at the federal and provincial levels, and compare it with what corporations pay, we find the latter accounted for 13.7 percent of government revenues in 1965 and only about 8 percent today (7.9 percent in 2007 and 8.3 percent in 2013). Meanwhile, the share borne by individuals has surged from 20 percent in the mid-1960s to over 30 percent in 2013" (p. 41).

17 There are numerous examples that capital had a clear role to play in disciplining national governments during this period. Teeple (2000) notes, for instance, that "in both England and New York, financial markets stopped buying long-term debt in order to impose their views that government borrowing and expenditures were too high" (p. 217; see also Young et al., 2017). Similarly, Streeck (2016) observes that "the

(2013) notes, however, this "rapid rise in public indebtedness was a general, not a national phenomenon" (p. 1), with public debt increasing in almost all of the OECD countries from the 1970s onwards. If we recall Henwood's (1998) earlier comment, borrowed from Marx, that "the public debt is a powerful means of ensuring that the state remains in capital's hand" (p. 23), then it should be clear how the reorientation of international institutions represents the means by which some of those interests are met: in this case, by promoting the autonomy of central banks in such a way that the manipulation of interest rates can undermine "the policy objectives of the elected government" (Naylor, 1982, p. 33). Furthermore, as William Robinson (2014) notes, these shifts in policy, have greatly contributed to the overall growth and globalization of capital as "governments from First and Third World alike turn to investors worldwide to finance deficits" (p. 144).

Hager (2015) has explored this phenomenon in the United States, exploring how the holdings of public debt have rapidly become concentrated within the financial sector, subsequently reinforcing "patterns of social inequality" and proceeding "in tandem with a shift in government policy, one that prioritizes the interests of government bondholders over the general citizenry" (p. 505). While the shift in government policy towards the satisfaction of bondholders is clearest in respect to the Greek financial crisis (Varoufakis, 2011), it is one felt among all capitalist countries, to different degrees.[18] In expanding state debt, the shift towards the reduction of inflation and the

---

same Manhattan-based ratings agencies that were instrumental in bringing about the disaster of the global money industry are now threatening to downgrade the bonds of states that accepted a previously unimaginable level of new debt to rescue that industry and the capitalist economy as a whole" (p. 91). Moody's, for instance, has recently downgraded Ontario's credit rating due to its deficit (Canadian Press, 2018). Similarly, in Newfoundland and Labrador, the Premier's Economic Recovery Team has recently recommended a massive austerity program in order to avoid having changes "forced on us by bond rating agencies" (as cited in Roberts, 2021, para. 42).

18 Teeple (2000) notes: "This indebtedness contains much of the secret of capital's control over the state, as creditor over debtor. Since banks and other financial institutions finance government borrowing, these institutions gain, through the public debt, a powerful lever over state policy. The financial markets can refrain from purchasing government debt, the IMF can and does withhold credit facilities, and bond-rating agencies (such as Standard and Poor in the United States) can set higher interest rates, all by way of reflecting the confidence of capital in government programs and policies. In short, the last thing that the corporations want or can afford is a debt-free state. As present or future tax revenues become insufficient to manage the debt, however, the repayment will be squeezed from reduced expenditures in health, education, and social security, or higher taxes on the working

management of the national currency has enabled governments to rationalize cuts to health care, welfare, pensions, education, and so on, all in order to serve the immense debt loads (Bienefeld, 1992; Teeple, 2000). William Robinson (2014) puts it simply: "the more government debt, the more states must adopt policies that satisfy the holders of bonds and other creditors" (p. 144). Sassen (2006) notes that it is this shift in particular that is "critical to the particular process of economic globalization that took off in the 1980s" (p. 3). It was also during this period, as Streeck (2016) explains, that our current era of "'post-democracy' was born" (p. 22).

It is important to recall, however, that the reason for this shift was the immense growth and expansion of capital via the Eurodollar markets over the preceding decades. As Soederberg (2004) notes, transnational forms of authority like the BCBS

> emerged as a response to financial capitals to establish a regulatory regime to assist in the continued centralization and concentration of wealth in an interstate system characterized by increasing forms of competition for and dependency on private, short-term financial flows. (p. 75)

To put this growth into perspective, by 1974 the Royal Bank of Canada "owned five times more assets than the largest non-bank financial institution, then the Sun Life Assurance Co., and 3.5 times more than the assets of Bell Canada, the largest privately owned industrial corporation" (Van Houten, 1991, p. 95). In the context of growing public concerns over the increasing size and power of the corporate sector,[19] Canada's federal government created the Royal Commission on Corporate Concentration in 1975 after a rumoured attempt by the Power Corporation of Canada to take over Argus, a large holding company. The Commission was to report on

> the nature and role of major concentrations of corporate power in Canada; the economic and social implications for the public interest of such concentrations; and whether safeguards exist or may be required to protect the public interest in the presence of such concentrations. (Royal Commission on Corporate Concentration, 1978, p. xix)

---

class. The lowering of personal income taxes simply increases the pressure to retrench or privatize the welfare state" (p. 105).

19 As Carroll (1989) notes, during this period "corporate capital became more concentrated within the 100 leading enterprises, which by 1985 controlled 52 per cent of all non-financial assets" (p. 90).

The government's official position was that corporate concentration reduces competition and that competition was a necessary means of directing "productive activity in such a way as to maximize national income" (p. 2).[20] But the government's concerns were also likely related to significant redirections in capital flow. As Sweeny (1997) notes, the "exceptional nature of the Canadian situation" had long been rooted in the middling range of American-owned industrial firms, which "accounted for 40% of all industrials" (p. 333). With American transnational corporations (TNCs) moving their manufacturing plants to cheaper developing countries, Canadian "capitalists repatriated control of many foreign-held firms, decreasing the foreign control of nonfinancial corporate assets from 37.0 per cent in 1971 to 23.4 per cent in 1985" (Carroll, 1989, p. 91). During this period, Canada would also become a net exporter of foreign direct investment, most notably to the United States: "between 1975 and 1984 total Canadian direct investment in the US expanded 438%" (Carroll, 1989, p. 91). In response, Canadian-based corporations began a massive global expansion, "transforming themselves into transnationals" (Van Houten, 1991, p. 153). For many scholars, this shift in capital flow represents evidence of Canada's transformation from a rich dependency to a secondary imperialist power (Carroll, 1982, 1986; Kellogg, 2009, 2015; Klassen, 2009; Niosi, 1981, 1985). But it also highlights the extent to which this process was fundamentally constrained by the existing juridical and territorial boundaries imposed by a national system of property relations.

Globalizing Canadian capitalists responded to the Royal Commission on Corporate Concentration by creating the Business Council on National Issues (BCNI),[21] which was essentially a lobby group for globalizing capitals operating in Canada. Led by the chartered banks, along with companies active in resource extraction and manufacturing, the BCNI was comprised of the CEOs of 150 leading Canadian-based corporations, which administered over $700 billion in assets, $250 billion in annual revenue, and employed over 1.5 million Canadians (Langille, 1987, p. 42). The list of members originally included the presidents of eight chartered banks, 10 insurance companies, 18 oil and

---

20 For a critical perspective on the outcome of the Commission, see Gorecki and Stanbury's (1979) edited volume, *Perspectives on the Royal Commission on Corporate Concentration*.
21 The group is now referred to as the Business Council of Canada (BCC). As Carroll (2012) accurately notes, in Canada, "there was no pitched fractional battle for state power, but rather, a developing global vision among major capitalists, both 'national' and 'transnational'" (p. 366).

pipeline companies, including Imperial, Shell, Gulf, and Texaco, as well as manufacturers such as Kodak, Ford, and Canadian Industries Limited (CIL). As Langille (1987) notes, within this lobby group, there was little distinction between American and Canadian corporations, with firms "like Inco, Stelco, and Trizec co-exist[ing] with Xerox, IBM, and ITT" (p. 42). This was made explicitly clear with the later rebranding of the BCNI into "the more cosmopolitan Canadian Council of Chief Executives, signifying its project to blend the 'national interest' with an appreciation of 'regional' North American and 'global' interests, all of them defined from a capitalist standpoint" (Carroll, 2012, p. 366). To be sure, by the mid-1970s the concentration and centralization of capital had led capitalists in all core countries to have "little respect for national boundaries that threaten the flow of capital or hinder their access to new markets" (Langille, 1987, p. 43). The BCNI was thus one means by which globalizing capital could lobby against public concerns about corporate concentration, and the oft-suggested solution of economic nationalism. To do this, the BCNI would simply reverse the language of the Commission, suggesting that if the government wanted competition, it should simply remove all existing barriers to capital accumulation and allow Canadian corporations to expand abroad unabated.

As one of the most dominant Canadian members of the BCNI, it is not surprising to find the Royal making similar arguments in its own documents. In its *Newsletter and Interim Report* (Royal Bank of Canada, 1976a), for instance, the bank patronizingly dismisses concerns over corporate concentration as the petty complaints of a spoiled society:

> In a society such as ours, where material needs receive high priority, people were prepared to accept some discomforts that have sometimes accompanied increased industrialization. But society's expectations, like the connotation of words, are changing significantly. We reached the stage in Canada where corporate business has, in the course of solving certain problems, been charged with the creation of social problems. And the larger corporate business is perceived to be, then the more vulnerable it becomes to these charges because its actions affect a large number of people and institutions. And it is more visible. This had led to increasing demands by the general public for exercise of more direct control of influence over the activities of corporate business. (p. 4)

The Royal goes on to argue that any attempt to restrict the activities of corporations by way of economic nationalism is to neglect the realities of globalization: "in these days of instant communication across international boundaries, credit can flow from Zurich to Vancouver in the wink of an eye" (Royal Bank of Canada, 1976b, p. 4). The Royal also claimed that any attempt "to build a barricade around the Canadian market" would be "doomed to failure" since Canadian corporations "operate on a world-wide basis, and ... can fund their operations in the financial markets of the world" (p. 4). "The key," the bank claimed, was in controlling "access to the Canadian market so that we can bargain for the best possible access to markets abroad" (p. 4).

The Royal's concern about its access to foreign markets was due to the growing size of its foreign earnings. The Royal admits as much in its own publications, noting that 30 per cent of its total profit after tax "is now earned from non-Canadian sources" (Royal Bank of Canada, 1976a, p. 4). In fact, since the beginning of the 1970's, the bank's net domestic earnings had only increased by an average of 14.6 per cent annually, compared to its international operations, which were growing by an average of 24.3 per cent annually. The Royal also mentions that its size was the only thing allowing it "to compete successfully with other world-scale banks" (Royal Bank of Canada, 1976c, p. 21), forcing it to reject anything that would constrain its size, dominance of the domestic market, or ability to expand abroad. Such claims vindicate Marx's (1867/1991) comments about capital's inherent tendency towards centralization and concentration – and it is this basic dynamic that continues to force the transformation of nation-state institutions today.

The Royal's growth concerns were augmented by the continued existence of foreign and near banks, which, in the eyes of the Royal, had been given unfair advantages despite engaging in banking business. Beginning from the premise that "open competition under equal rules benefits the public" (Royal Bank of Canada, 1976b, p. 1), the Royal argued publicly "that all those institutions carrying on banking business *no matter how they are chartered and no matter what other business they do*, should have their banking activities subject to the federal law" (p. 2).[22] In doing so, the bank would often elicit a subtle

---

22 This was the position of the CBA as well: "In response to Turner's invitation, the CBA submitted a brief to the Minister of Finance in October of 1975. The brief noted that Canada already had about thirty-five to forty affiliates of foreign banks from Germany, Italy, France, Holland, Belgium, Spain, Portugal, the United Kingdom, Greece, and Switzerland as well as the United States, Japan, and Hong Kong. It noted that these offices were considerably larger operations than the traditional 'suitcase' bank – an expression which described the sort of travelling-salesman type of banking operation, whereby a foreign banker sets up an office in a hotel room and tries to market large commercial loans to Canadian borrowing corporations. The CBA brief noted that there were about 130 Canadian corporations wholly or partly owned by foreign banks and corporations which were doing some sort of banking business. It said: 'There are today no laws or regulations or even guidelines

nationalist sentiment by reminding the public that "one of the proposals put forward by the Fathers of Confederation when they met for Canada's first Parliament in 1867 was that banking should be a national responsibility" (p. 1). There is obviously a significant amount of irony to these statements given that, as the bank was making them, it was also pushing for further reforms that would remove restrictions on its activities. But the strategy of the chartered banks in this context was clear; as Naylor (1985) notes, they wanted to force "competing financial institutions to come under federal jurisdiction and to hold reserves with the Bank of Canada" (p. 139). Doing so would significantly limit the finances of foreign and near banks in such a way that the larger chartered banks would be able to simply push them out of the market by sheer size alone. The Royal's own publications even note that its competitors' desires to hedge the Royal in was based on "fears that chartered banks are growing too rapidly" (Royal Bank of Canada, 1976c, p. 1).

When the Royal Commission on Corporate Concentration (1978) wrapped up, it concluded with the suggestion "that no radical changes in the laws governing corporate activity are necessary at this time to protect the public interest" (p. 413). The basis for the conclusion was linked to the growing size of international markets:

> If, as seems to be true in many industries, large size is necessary for efficient operations and to compete in international markets, efforts in Canada to reduce corporate concentration by limiting the size of firms will further reduce the competitiveness of Canadian firms in world markets. (p. 405)

The Commission was clear, however, that as Canadian firms "expand to world size, there may well be a significant increase in corporate concentration in Canada" (p. 405). In particular, the Commission singled out the chartered banks, which Parliament had already recognized as "major concentrations of corporate power" (p. 219). They were, as the Commission claimed, large by any standard:

> Large in Canada, large in terms of their international reputations and operations, large in the number of their branches throughout the country, and

---

for foreign banking operations in Canada. There are no specific provisions for the conditions under which a branch, agency or office may be established by a foreign bank in Canada ... Foreign banks, either directly or indirectly, exercise far broader powers in Canada than Canadian chartered banks.' It recommended that 'the operation of foreign banks and their related companies in Canada be clearly brought under federal jurisdiction'" (MacIntosh, 1991, pp. 172–3).

large in their physical presence in the buildings with which they are identified in major Canadian cities. (p. 221)

The banks were so big, in fact, that journalist Peter C. Newman (1979) pointed out that "if Canada had as many banks proportionately as the US, there would be approximately 1,400 banks in this country, instead of 11" (p. 101).

The Commission was also clear to note the significance of the Eurodollar markets to the banks' growth, stating that "foreign-currency operations have made a major contribution to the overall asset and liability growth of the Canadian banks over the last decade" (p. 232). The Commission also warned of the changing nature of international banking, pointing out that "the biggest and most powerful of the US banks have gone far beyond taking deposits and offering short- and medium-term loans" (p. 237).[23] The Commission recommended that it would not be "desirable in Canada to have the melding of commercial banking and underwriting functions that is occurring in the United States, because of the very real dangers in concentrating so much financial and economic power in one set of institutions" (p. 237). Despite the fact that the chartered banks "had expanded their market share to control over 90 percent of Canada's banking industry" (Puri, 2012, p. 166) by the end of the 1970s, the Commission concluded that there was "no conclusive evidence that the banks are earning monopoly profits," and it recommended that the government "encourage further entry into the industry," so long as those new entrants "operate under the *Bank Act*" (Royal Commission on Corporate Concentration, 1978, p. 408).

At the same time as the federal government was deciding what to do about foreign banks in Canada, the chartered banks were happy to continue their accumulation activities abroad. The unregulated nature of the Eurodollar markets meant that there were few limits as to what services financial institutions could provide to their clients; this meant that Canada's chartered banks could diversify beyond the constraints of the *Bank Act*, which maintained the traditional divisions between the four pillars of Canadian finance: the chartered banks, trust companies,

---

23 As explained by the Royal Commission on Corporate Concentration (1978), "If a company wants to expand its financial base, a bank like Citicorp, JP Morgan, Chase Manhattan, or First Chicago will undertake normal short- and medium-term commercial lending, advise the corporation on possible acquisition or divestiture (at a fee), help it structure and organize a new issue of equity or debt, and also arrange for private placements of these securities with institutional investors" (p. 237).

investment dealers, and insurance companies.[24] With Toronto acting as the second capital of the Eurodollar market, Canada's chartered banks were easily able to increase their hold on foreign assets. Chodos (1977) notes that by 1976 the banks held 30 per cent of their assets and 30 per cent of their liabilities in foreign currencies (p. 106). For the Royal more specifically, international banking activities made up 31 per cent of its assets and 51 per cent of its profits by the 1980s; in contrast, the bank's domestic operations only returned 50 cents on 100 dollars' worth of assets, while its international operations returned 84 cents on the same amount (McDowall, 1993, p. 412). The spirit of the age was thus expressed by the Royal's CEO, Rowland Frazee, when he remarked, "Everything we do now we think globally no matter what type of business we're dealing with" (as cited in McDowall, 1993, p. 412).

The veracity of Frazee's remarks can be seen in the Royal's participation in the Orion Bank, a consortium that consisted of Chase Manhattan Bank, National Westminster, Westdeutsche Landesbank, Credito Italiano, and the Mitsubishi Bank of Japan – or, "the six most powerful banks in the world" (W. Hall, 1982, p. 18) as reported in the *Financial Times*. Consortiums like Orion, which was formed in 1970 in the City of London, were a common feature of the day and were mainly used to spread risk among many large national banks who were not yet large enough to provide the scale of loans required by expanding corporations and infrastructure projects.[25] As one of the Royal's own publications notes, Orion played "a vital role in meeting the complex financing

---

24 As Puri (2012) explains, it was actually these divisions that helped the banks consolidate their corporate power over the Canadian market: "In the 1970s and early 1980s, the Big-Five banks began to assert their influence over financial markets, and as a result of the lack of effective domestic competition they were able to shift to a non-price based competition model and develop a conservative business model which emphasized high profit margins and risk aversion. The ability of the Big-Five to consolidate their near monopoly in the Canadian banking industry was largely driven by the rigid separation of the securities, trusts, and commercial finance companies from the chartered banks and the *Bank Act*'s outright exclusion of foreign banking institutions. These factors encouraged the development of a shadow banking industry, with foreign banks acquiring control over the more liberally regulated credit unions and trust companies, eventually forcing regulators to develop the substance-based approach to regulating banking activities under the *Bank Act* originally contemplated by the Porter Commission" (p. 166).
25 Puri (2012) notes that this was also due to traditional divisions of banking and finance that existed in Canada until the mid-1980s: "Although banks were permitted to own securities for their own portfolios they were not permitted to underwrite the distribution of securities or provide investment counselling to consumers ... However, as the global economy began to accelerate in the 1970s and 1980s,

needs of governments, corporations and major international development projects" (Royal Bank of Canada, 1976c, p. 4). Having financed over USD$7 billion in loans through Orion by 1976, the Royal would go on to join several other consortia in the 1970s related to large infrastructure projects in the North Sea, Mexico, Iran, and Brazil.[26] But as the various banks involved in Orion grew larger as a result of the Eurodollar markets, each started to draw the best business away from the consortium and back towards its parent bank. In response, the Royal bought out its partners in 1980, renaming it the Orion Royal Bank. By incorporating in the City of London, the move allowed the Royal to act less like a traditional bank and more like the sort of integrated financial institutions that would eventually come to characterize the global financial system that emerged in the 1980s.

Orion also allowed the Royal to expand by capturing more business than could be had in the domestic economy alone. As reported in the *New York Times*, by 30 April 1980, "the Royal's operations outside Canada for the first time produced more after-tax revenues than its operations at home – $38.1 million versus $37 million on total revenues of $1.8 billion" (Malcolm, 1980, p. D1). This trend was not restricted to the Royal alone, however. As pointed out in the article, the Royal's moves reflected the more general trend of "many major Canadian companies seeking growth beyond the confines of Canada's market of 23.7 million people, smaller even than South Korea" (Malcolm, 1980, p. B1). While the Royal's CEO claimed that this outward shift was because "world trade is growing faster than domestic economies" (as cited on p. B1), the reality had more to do with the dialectical relationship between the two that was causing unpredictable conditions of profitability. As William Robinson (2004) notes, "offshore capital markets grew from $315 billion in 1973 to more than $2 trillion in 1982, and by the end of the 1970s, trade in currencies was more than 11 times greater than world commodity trade" (p. 112). As such, corporations began to reduce "their risks by diversifying their operations around the world, thus accelerating the entire globalization process" (p. 112).

For the Royal, this meant expanding into the larger, and more lucrative, American market, a reality reflected by its $100 million investment

---

banks became increasingly involved in short-term financing and syndicated loan markets" (p. 172).

26 The Royal also became a shareholder in Equator Bank, a consortium catering to the financial needs of post-colonial Africa in 1975 (McDowall, 1993, pp. 410–12). It also joined the Polar Gas Project in 1979 to help provide syndicate financing for Petro-Canada.

in the New York Trust Company in 1979, "a move that rival bankers described as an important new element in the already keen competition for the banking business of medium-sized companies in the United States" (Bennett, 1979, p. D1). The acquisition immediately made the Royal North America's fourth-largest bank in assets, following the Bank of America, Citicorp, and Chase Manhattan. In 1980, Frazee would comment on what all these changes meant for the Royal: "We used to be a large Canadian bank with international interests. But now we are a large international bank with a strong Canadian base. There's a difference" (as cited in Malcolm, 1980, p. D1).

Back in Canada, the recommendations of the Royal Commission on Corporate Concentration were put into place through the 1980 revision to the *Bank Act*.[27] While the chartered banks were unsuccessful in getting the federal government to impose mandatory reserve requirements on their near-bank rivals, there were, as always, a number of juicy concessions in the form of new rights that reflected their growth and power. The chartered banks were permitted, for instance, "to encroach on the fiduciary activities of the trust companies" (Naylor, 1985, p. 140). They were also allowed to administer their own registered home ownership savings plan (RHOSP) and registered retirement savings plan (RRSP), providing the chartered banks with a cheap source of funds due to "the implicit tax subsidy on the interest rate offered to depositors and because of the exemption from the requirements of holding reserves against them" (p. 140). The chartered banks were also "granted the Orwellian privilege," as Naylor (1985) describes it, "of investing their position funds in their own shares" (p. 140), effectively allowing them to seize part of staff salaries by placing it into the bank's equity base.

The most significant concession, however, was that the revised *Bank Act* required foreign banks to incorporate federally, removing them from provincial jurisdiction (recall that this was an issue for the chartered banks in the last chapter). As a result, foreign banks operating in Canada were restricted from using the assets of their parent banks as the reserves on which they lent. Instead, they were forced to keep their reserves with the Bank of Canada, effectively subjecting them to the fiat of the minister of finance in respect to their number of branches. Their asset-to-capital ratios were also set "at a maximum level well

---

27 The Department of Finance published the *White Paper on the Revision of Canadian Banking Legislation* in August 1976 that provided the broad outlines of their thoughts on foreign banks leading up to the 1980 *Bank Act* revision (see D.S. Macdonald, 1976).

below those of the domestic banks" (Naylor, 1985, p. 140). With their share of total bank assets limited to 8 per cent of the domestic assets of all banks, the foreign banks were essentially restricted from competing against the chartered banks.[28] All foreign banks combined, for example, could account for no more than a quarter of the Royal's assets. Although some economists saw the 1980 *Bank Act* as enabling "foreign banks to operate in Canada on the same footing and with the same competitive opportunities as domestic banks" (Boreham, 1989, p. 192), the strict limitations imposed on foreign banks made it clear that it was instead, as Naylor (1985) claims, "a victory for financial centralization and chartered bank hegemony" (p. 140).[29] Furthermore, since there were technically more banks in Canada than before, the Act allowed the federal government to claim that there was more competition, thus fulfilling the recommendations of the Royal Commission on Corporate Concentration while also "deflecting public pressure to curb the monopoly power of the existing chartered banks" (p. 141).[30] More important, perhaps, is that the Act allowed the chartered banks

---

[28] American bank Citicorp (now Citigroup) was particularly displeased by the change: "Under legislation that took effect in Canada today, the size of any foreign-owned banking operation will be limited to 8% of the domestic assets of all banks. The biggest of the foreign banking operations in this financial center is Citicorp Canada, wholly owned by Citicorp. According to Citicorp Canada's president, Charles Young, his company – by law, not yet a bank – has assets that will reach $2 billion (Canadian) by the end of the year. Mr. Young said the Canadian move was part of a trend toward more protectionism, but suggested that Citicorp Canada, with its less than $2 billion assets, was hardly a threat to Canadian chartered banks. (Royal Bank of Canada listed assets at April 30 of $58.5 billion)" ("Canadian Law Limits," 1980, p. B1). For more on this overall development from the perspective of the CBA, see MacIntosh (1991, pp. 173–9). As he notes, Citicorp's claims above are suspect: "The foremost bank in the scramble to get in line for a license was Citicorp, which had created a small family of financial subsidiaries ... From the beginning, Citicorp was not only the largest of the foreign bank subsidiaries but one of the most profitable. By 1984 it was already rivalling in size its half-sister the Mercantile" (p. 178).

[29] Puri (2012) notes: "The 1970s helped to firmly establish the hallmark conservative tendencies of Canadian banks and regulators. The lack of meaningful competition in the banking industry enabled the Big-Five domestic banks to develop the conservative lending practices that facilitated their economic stability. By the time the federal government allowed foreign banks to compete with domestic institutions, the 'Big-Five' were already firmly established with consumers" (p. 168).

[30] The *Report of the Inquiry into the Collapse of the CCB and Northland Bank* notes the following: "From 35 active banks at the end of Confederation year, the Canadian banking system expanded to include 51 active banks in 1874, a nineteenth-century peak not exceeded until the introduction of Schedule B banks following the 1980 revisions" (Estey, 1986, p. 364).

to demand equal treatment abroad. As Minister of Finance Donald S. Macdonald (1976) noted in the *White Paper on the Revision of Canadian Banking Legislation*, "if we provide a basis in law for the operation of foreign banks in Canada we can expect our own banks to obtain the reciprocal recognition in other countries which is necessary if they are to extend their participation in international markets as we would like" (pp. 25–6).[31] This was significant, since the banks had been facing "declining profitability" at home, forcing them to "expand geographically and in product line to compete" (Darroch, 1992, p. 167). To this effect, the Royal opened an office in Beijing in 1981 to mediate China's access to Eurodollar loans, with later offices being opened in Shenzhen, Shanghai, Sydney, Bangkok, Taipei, Seoul, Tokyo, and Singapore for the same purpose.

Some of the Royal's loans would turn sour, however, due to what has been termed the less-developed country (LDC) debt crisis. As mentioned above, globalizing banks like the Royal had been making significant profits by recycling their Eurodollars – as well as their newly generated "Petrodollars" resulting from the oil shocks of the 1970s – through massive loans to governments in the Global South (D. Cameron, 1983).[32] As William Robinson (2004) notes, "international bank

---

31 MacIntosh (1991) makes a similar argument: "considerations of reciprocity were certainly a factor in issuing so many licenses [57 letters of patent for a license by the end of 1982]" (p. 179) to foreign bank subsidiaries in Canada. The 1976 *White Paper on the Revision of Canadian Banking Legislation* also outlines the reason why foreign banks were wanted at all; because of "the additional financial support which they with their world-wide connections can bring to the development of our resource industries and trade" (p. 25).

32 MacIntosh (1991) provides more context: "The LDC debt problem was a direct consequence of the 'oil shocks' of 1973 and 1979. The first 'oil shock' took the price of oil from $2.50 US a barrel in mid-1973 to $11.50 a year later ... Some simple arithmetic conveys a notion of the massive scale of the financial problem created by a $10-a-barrel jump in the price of oil. For a country like Saudi Arabia producing 10 million barrels of oil a day, an extra $10 a barrel meant increased revenues of $100 million a day which is $36.5 billion a year. Not all the Organization of Petroleum Exporting Countries (OPEC) were in the Middle East; the 'cartel' included countries like Nigeria and Venezuela, but the dominant country in the financial transformation was Saudi Arabia. The governments of these countries had no capacity to reinvest their windfall in global securities markets – nor any inclination to do so. They put most of their huge savings in short-term bank deposits in United States dollars. The world's commercial banking system suddenly had a huge inflow of savings to put to work. Instead of requiring OPEC depositors to put the money on deposit for extended terms, the world's banks fell over each other in a competitive rush to get thirty-day term deposits. This money was then recycled to the developing countries in Latin America, mostly on what was supposed to be a short-term basis" (p. 190).

lending jumped from $2 billion in 1972 to $90 billion in 1981 before falling to $50 billion in 1985" (pp. 111–12). The loans were based on the simple idea that "countries don't go bankrupt" (Kuczynski, 1988, p. 5). Porter (2005) recalls "stories told of young bankers flying around the world eagerly urging developing governments to borrow, on the assumption that governments could never go bankrupt" (p. 53). As MacIntosh (1991) notes, however, sovereign nations "cannot be forced to pay back money, especially in a foreign currency" (p. 190). Despite this, both Canadian and US governments lent official support to these loans. As Canada's minister of finance, John Turner, told the IMF in a speech one year after the first oil shock in 1973, "The mammoth scale of financing necessary to alleviate Third World payments imbalances implies that recycling of oil funds is crucial to the effective financing of the payments deficits" (as cited in MacIntosh, 1991, p. 192). After the second shock in 1979 brought the price of oil from roughly USD$13 a barrel to USD$35 in 1981, the numbers involved became ridiculous. As MacIntosh (1991) reports, "every single day another $500 million flowed into the OPEC coffers and was recycled into the world's money markets through the banks" (p. 191).

Supported by the finance ministers of these developing countries, the high rates of return on the debt disguised its true form: it was not the sort of long-term bonded debt underwritten by merchant banks that these countries were used to but rather short-term debt subject to volatile interest rates and economic performance. With countries such as Brazil, Argentina, and Mexico entering periods of strong growth, initially all seemed well: "Real growth exceeded 5 percent a year and exports were sufficient to pay the interest on the 'petro-dollar' loans" (MacIntosh, 1991, p. 191). But this was not to last, as large amounts of capital soon began to flow out of the debtor countries only to end up in the accounts of military and government elites in New York, London, and Zurich: "In effect the commercial banks of the world were lending the LDCs money through the front door, but most of it was going straight out the back door in the hands of a few citizens in the borrowing countries" (p. 191).[33] With creditors reluctant to provide new funds without substantial changes to limit capital flight, previously

---

33 As MacIntosh (1991) notes, "In the years 1975 to 1986, accumulated capital outflows from Argentina alone were estimated by Morgan Guaranty Trust Company economists to be $33 billion, compared to the country's gross external debts of $49 billion. In Mexico, capital outflows of $54 billion exceeded the country's gross debt of $38 billion" (p. 191).

supportive governments began to change their tune, as expressed by Pierre Trudeau in 1983:

> The massive lending by commercial banks to LDCs, viewed at the time as a surprisingly successful recycling of petro dollars ... has come back to haunt us as a formidable debt and liquidity problem ... which threatens the stability of the international system. (as cited in MacIntosh, 1991, p. 193)

When Mexico defaulted on its debt payment in 1982 (with Argentina following shortly after), the international credit system was thrown into crisis. The total external debt of the developing countries involved, which included Mexico, Argentina, Brazil, and Venezuela, totalled more than USD$500 billion: "Of this, about $285 billion was owed to commercial banks and of that about $24 billion was owed to the Canadian banks" (MacIntosh, 1991, p. 195).

While the Royal had been aware of the coming crisis since the late 1970s, by the 1980s it was already too late. The Bank of Montreal, the Royal, and the Canadian Imperial Bank of Commerce (CIBC) had already "loaned more funds to Latin American states than they had to their respective provincial governments" (Sweeny, 1997, p. 336). To take one example, in 1979, a group of international banks led by the Chase Merchant Banking Group, the Royal Bank of Canada, and the Banco de Reservas de la Republica Dominicana gave a loan of up to USD$185 million to the Dominican Republic ("Dominican Republic Is Lent", 1979, p. D18). In the aftermath of the debt crisis, international losses for the Royal totalled more than $318 million by 1983. With the subsequent devaluation of many Caribbean currencies, the Royal began "an almost total pull out" (P.J. Hudson, 2010, p. 44) from the region, prompting the *Financial Times* to remark in 1986 that "the Canadian banks' 'Caribbean holiday' was over" (as cited in McDowall, 1993, p. 406). Similar retail banking operations were closed in Germany, France, and Britain.

The Royal's official historian, Duncan McDowall (1993), interprets the LDC crisis as teaching the bank that this new world of global banking was complex, highly volatile, and full of competitors who were "keen and well honed" (p. 420). Seen from a critical vantage point, however, it also provided the legitimacy to further discipline developing countries by way of structural adjustment policies mediated through the remaining Bretton Woods institutions.[34] By the end of 1984, the Royal

---

34 Germain (2010) notes that "in the early 1980s, it was the US Treasury – ably assisted by an IMF that was casting about for a new role in a world of floating exchange rates – which took the lead in organizing debt negotiations" (p. 60).

was already preparing for loan losses of $2.7 billion; as such, the bank "refused to give ground on the issue of absolute forgiveness of the debt" (McDowall, 1993, p. 417). In the case of Brazil, for instance, the Royal's CEO, Allan Taylor, argued that Brazil was "the eighth biggest industrial economy in the world and to think in terms of forgiveness of the debt ... Where would you stop?" (as cited on p. 417). The world's largest banks argued that developing country governments had been irresponsible to borrow so much without making sure "that it was used to generate the revenue needed to pay back the loans" (Porter, 2005, p. 53). Later, the Royal would claim in its 1989 *Annual Report* that, due to "dealing aggressively" with its LDC loans, it had "cleared the way for strong earnings growth" (p. 5).[35] "Dealing aggressively" was not an individual task, however; all the world's largest banks, including the Royal, worked together to resolve the impacts of their self-made crisis through the IIF.

The IIF was created in 1983 after a meeting a year earlier between 38 senior bankers, public officials, and representatives of international institutions, who all agreed that having a transnational financial association "that could help banks by producing and sharing information about sovereign risk would be very useful. Within two years its membership had expanded to nearly 188 banks" (McKeen-Edwards & Porter, 2013, pp. 38–9).[36] Headquartered in Washington, DC, to be near the IMF and the WB, the IIF at first worked to assemble "information that would assist banks in managing their loans to developing country governments, such as statistics on government indebtedness" (Porter, 2005, p. 111). As the globalization of financial capital expanded over the 1980s, the IIF would take on a more prominent role as the largest

---

[35] It also helped that there continued to be a market for the loans: "In October 1989, for example, the resale value of loans to Brazil was around 28 percent of their face value; loans to Argentina fetched only about 18 percent, and loans to Mexico about 40 percent. In the case of Mexico, which is the largest LDC borrower from the Canadian banks, there was a special international debt restructuring scheme in July 1989. This also helped some of the Canadian banks to reduce their exposure to Mexico" (MacIntosh, 1991, p. 197).

[36] McKeen-Edwards & Porter (2013) explain further: "The senior public officials at that meeting included three from the IMF, and one from each of the World Bank, the US Comptroller of the Currency, the Bank of Japan, and the Bank of England. The Bank of England's representative was Peter Cooke, who had been the first chair of the Basel Committee on Banking Supervision. William Donough, who subsequently would also chair the BCBS and head the New York Federal Reserve, was also present as a representative of the First National Bank of Chicago" (p. 38).

financial sector lobby group, eventually becoming "the most important private sector interlocutor for public authorities, especially those in the Basel Committee and the IMF" (McKeen-Edwards & Porter, 2013, p. 39). As Blom (2019) notes, the IIF's lobbying is "organised in such a way as to mirror the structure of the global public policymaking forum, the Basel Committee on Banking Supervision" (p. 53). The IIF has since expanded to over 450 members in over 70 countries around the world, and describes itself as "the leading voice for the financial services industry on global regulatory issues" (IIF, n.d.).[37]

As stated on the BIS's website, "the Latin American debt crisis of 1982 highlighted the danger of undercapitalised banks being over-exposed to sovereign risk" (BIS, n.d.-b, para. 4). As such, the BCBS sought to revise their earlier Concordat in 1983 to provide "a fuller elaboration of principles for handling the problems posed by divergent supervisory standards and the complex structures of many international banking groups" (Rost, 2009, p. 320). Reissued as *Principles for the Supervision of Banks' Foreign Establishments* (BCBS, 1983), the revision was part of the ongoing quest "to clarify who was responsible for what in terms of international banking supervision" (Germain, 2010, p. 186, n. 1). Like the first Concordat, which was created in response to two failed banks, the 1983 revision was not only due to the consequences of the LDC crisis but also "the difficulties surrounding the failure of Banco Ambrosiano, when Italian authorities refused to honour the obligations of the failed bank's Luxembourg subsidiary" (p. 186, n. 1).[38] As such, the revised Concordat extended its calls for further collaboration and information sharing between regulators as banking became more globally integrated, and it recommended that a bank's home regulatory authority monitor the bank's "total risk exposure and capital adequacy ... by reviewing the bank's total transnational operations" (K. Alexander, 2003, p. 8) under the banner "that no foreign banking establishment should escape supervision" (BCBS, 1983, p. 2).

A major component of the supervisory and regulatory regime of our emerging global epoch is a division of labour between the IMF and the central banks of the most powerful capitalist countries, "whereby the IMF resolves financial crises in the periphery by imposing austerity, while the major central banks resolve financial crises in the centre by

---

37 For more on the IIF, see Blom (2019, 2021); Kalaitzake (2017); Mckeen-Edwards (2010); McKeen-Edwards & Porter (2013); Surrey & Nash (1984).
38 For a summary of this event, see Kapstein (1994).

easing credit" (Rude, 2005, p. 90). While the core powers were busy engaging in attempts to standardize authority over global banking activities, the world's largest banks, including the Royal, were attempting to get the IMF and the BIS to ensure that their LDC loans would be repaid via a series of short-term loans to debtor nations. The loans operated under the condition that debtor countries (1) increase labour flexibility via caps on minimum wages alongside other policies to weaken trade unions and workers' bargaining power; (2) increase taxes while cutting social spending; (3) privatize public sector enterprises; and (4) remove restrictions on the flow of capital in and out of the country as well as on what foreign corporations and banks could buy (Harvey, 2005). As William H. Rhodes, the Citibank official in charge of Latin American debt negotiations, put it in 1984, "the banks want to be assured that the [debtor] country is going to be pursuing the necessary adjustment program to take it out of its external debt situation to monitor what it is doing" (as cited in Wachtel, 1986/1990, p. 125). The banks claimed that institutions like the IMF and BIS were "better equipped" (p. 125) for such a role than they were individually.[39] In the case of Guyana, for instance, a group of globalizing banks headed by the Royal helped the country to defer and refinance some $28.5 million of its maturing Eurocurrency debt as long as it agreed to more loans from the IMF to start paying off its $400 million foreign debt.[40] Similarly, at the annual meeting of the IMF and WB, Canada's minister of finance, Michael Wilson, "expressed full confidence in the game plan devised by the US and gave lots of advice to developing countries to tighten their belts, privatize, and seek more foreign ownership" (Crane, 1986, p. B2).

The transformed role of these international institutions was thus a central way through which pre-existing protectionist measures and explicitly domestic markets were eliminated throughout the 1980s via the direct subordination of developing countries to the demands of globalizing capital.[41] It would only take a short time before the demands

---

39 For more on the LDC crisis and the changed role of the IMF and BIS, see Bederman (1988); Helleiner (1994, pp. 175–83).
40 The banks included in the group were the Bank of Nova Scotia, Barclays Bank International; Libra Bank; Orion Bank; RoyWest Banking Corp; and two other Royal Bank of Canada subsidiaries, Royal Bank of Canada (International) and RBC Finance BV. As part of the restructuring, Guyana also agreed to another $10-million, seven-year loan agreement with the Royal Bank "designated for general purposes and essential imports" ("Guyana to Restructure," 1980, p. 3).
41 It is important to note that this process continues today, albeit sometimes more directly. See, for instance, the article "She Is BlackRock's New Star" (Millan & de Rosario, 2020), which details the process by which BlackRock – one of the world's

of globalizing capital began to initiate significant changes to the most powerful capitalist countries as well. In 1987, for instance, under the Louvre Accord, all the G7 countries except Italy agreed to coordinate their economic policies, which meant that Canada was ultimately agreeing "to keep reducing its budget and balance of payments deficits" (Crane, 1989, p. D3). As part of the agreement, the IMF was tapped for a surveillance role to monitor the steps that countries were taking to achieve coordination, which "included the development of economic indicators as yardsticks that would signal when individual countries should alter their policies" (p. D3). It would only take until 1989 for both the OECD and the IMF to warn the federal government that "Canada was building up too much debt and leaving itself 'vulnerable' to problems in servicing its foreign debt in the future" (p. D3). These warnings would precipitate Canada's largest ever experiment with austerity politics after the election of the Chrétien Liberals in 1993.[42]

Big and Little Bangs

Money attaches itself to velocity.

– Lewis Lapham (1988/2018, p. 93)

Another shift in TAR that set the stage for our emerging global epoch was the granting of new rights to financial institutions in the 1980s and 1990s that dissolved the historical boundaries between banks, trust companies, insurance firms, and securities dealers. Commonly referred to simply as "deregulation," this process has not only enabled the creation of immense financial conglomerates, but has greatly contributed to the "onion-like layers of transnational ownership" (W.I. Robinson, 2014, p. 34) that continue to blur the lines and meaning of corporate nationality. For these reasons, deregulation has considerable overlap among the various literatures on financialization, globalization, and

---

largest investment management companies, responsible for more than $7 trillion in assets – restructured Argentina's loans after it defaulted on $65 billion held by a dozen investment firms, including BlackRock.

42 Finkel (2006) notes: "Reduction in government deficits and debt remained paramount in government policy, resulting in further tightening of UI payments; additional cuts to health care, post-secondary education, and social assistance payments; and an end to family allowances. Paul Martin's budget speech in 1995 slashed government spending by $25 billion in three years, including $7 billion in transfers to provinces. That amounted to a 40 per cent cut in federal transfers. A modest daycare program was announced but then withdrawn when the provinces, which would have to match federal funds, responded unfavourably" (p. 292).

imperialism (Bienefeld, 1992; Helleiner, 1994; Panitch & Gindin, 2012; Lapavitsas, 2013b; Sassen, 2014b; Strange, 1998/2015; Teeple, 2011; Varoufakis, 2011). Despite different definitions as to what exactly constitutes deregulation, there is a shared appreciation among scholars that whatever it is that we are referring to regarding globalization, it is surely wrapped up with this process.

In explaining his theory of global capitalism, for instance, William Robinson (2014) writes that with

> the deregulation and liberalization of financial markets worldwide in the 1980s and 1990s and the introduction of [computer information technologies], national financial systems have merged into an increasingly integrated global financial system – a monstrous global complex that allows for hitherto unknown concentrations of social power, including the ability to dictate to states and to other circuits of accumulation. (p. 135)

Similarly, in expressing his view that Canada is a secondary imperialist power, Klassen (2009) notes that "the circuits of money, productive and commodity capital, have been globalized as governments have deregulated currency markets and liberalized capital and current accounts" (p. 164). Vital to this discussion is the extent to which deregulation is responsible for allowing money to "move virtually frictionlessly and instantaneously around the world" (W.I. Robinson, 2014, p. 136) as it attempts to reach out to investments with the highest rate of return, engaging in increasingly speculative financial activities. Even the Royal's 1985 *Annual Report* notes that "the business environment continued to become more complex in 1985 as the flow of capital around the globe accelerated in its quest for markets offering the best rate of return" (p. 22). As such, in most accounts of globalization, there is an implicit recognition of the denationalization of money capital. In *The Oxford Handbook of the Sociology of Finance*, the reference is explicit, with G.F. Davis (2012) writing that over the 1980s and 1990s, finance "became increasingly unconstrained by state control as the effortless flow of funds through electronic means enabled a new placelessness" (p. 44).

While all these claims are no doubt due to the fact that "the fastest sector to 'globalize' was finance" (Streeck, 2016, p. 23), what is neglected when we use words like deregulation to suggest a novel placelessness of money is that both phenomena are the result of new rights for capital and, thus, the transformation of national systems of property relations. If we recall that policies that function to regulate (and thus deregulate) corporations fall under the ambit of property relations, since they are rules that regulate what can be done with what is owned (corporations), then deregulation is simply the removal of a prior restriction on how that particular property can be used – or, in the case of the corporation, how it is able to use itself as a rights-bearing, collective subject. Cleaver (2017) puts the matter simply:

> Financial deregulation amounted to capitalists freeing themselves from previous constraints by getting legislators to change the laws regulating what they could and could not do with their, and our, money. Those legal changes opened up previously barred channels of speculation, and they substantially increased the leverage of the wealthy in shaping politics and policies. (pp. 221–2)

As such, it is not so much that money has become placeless, but rather that it flows more easily around the world by virtue of the rights won by financial institutions to form together into huge, multi-service corporations able to operate across multiple territories. Here, Sassen (2012) explains the distinction in terms of TAR:

> Territory does not disappear from our global electronic financial system; rather it is repositioned as a network of a hundred plus global cities with major financial centres. And so are authority and rights: neoliberal policy transfers not only power, but also authority to global financial markets and away from national states, and it develops a range of new types of rights for global firms in foreign countries. (p. 16)

The point is that under globalization not everything changes. National territorial boundaries remain in existence, and nation states continue to protect and defend the property relations that sustain capitalist activity. But the ways in which financial firms can operate within this space has been radically transformed because of the new rights they gained in the 1980s. As Harvey (2005) puts it, "neoliberalization has meant, in short, the financialization of everything" (p. 33). Let us examine these rights.

What we refer to as deregulation can be traced back to what the business press refers to as the "Big Bang." The Big Bang was the eventual result of a 1983 agreement between the Thatcher government and the London Stock Exchange (LSE) to settle an earlier anti-trust lawsuit initiated against the LSE during the previous administration.[43] When the

---

43 The case was initiated by the Office of Fair Trading against the LSE under the Restrictive Trade Practices Act of 1956. These practices included the LSE's rules establishing fixed minimum commissions; the single capacity rule (which enforced

new rules came into effect on 27 October 1986, they effectively swept away the historical legislation barring banks from owning securities dealers; they also allowed for 100 per cent outside ownership of member firms within the City of London. As Tony Norfield (2016), a former London trader, points out, the Big Bang not only destroyed the "cosy cartel of British financial firms" but also significantly increased the volume of dealing as "international banks flocked to the City of London" (p. 13). The political economist Susan Strange (1998/2015) notes, for example, that by the late 1990s, almost nothing remained "of the old, informal, cosy system of self-regulation under the watchful eye of the Old Lady (of Threadneedle Street – i.e., the Bank of England)" (p. 153). In other words, those gentlemanly capitalists who figured prominently in Canada's early history "were either long gone or remained only as figureheads" (p. 154), replaced instead by "greedy young Turks with a command of financial technology beyond the comprehension of an older generation – and probably quite beyond the control of the regulators" (p. 154). As journalist Peter C. Newman (1999) outlines in *Titans: How the New Canadian Establishment Seized Power*, these interrelated transformations of class, technology, and corporate structure were taking place in Canada as well, reflecting the larger transformation of banking into finance.[44]

This so-called revolution in finance has since led to a number of digitally mediated financial innovations, such as derivatives (from swaps to futures markets), hedge funds, institutional investment funds, mortgage-backed securities, collateralized debt obligations, Ponzi

---

a separation between brokers acting as agents for their clients on commission and jobbers who made the market and would theoretically provide liquidity by holding lines of stocks and shares on their books); the requirement that both be independent and not part of any larger group; and, most importantly, the stock exchange's exclusion of all foreigners from stock exchange membership (Centre for Policy Studies, 2006).

44 Sassen (2017) notes: "Over the last 30 years, finance has inserted itself in more and more domains of traditional banking. It has taken over functions from traditional banking that should have stayed there. Beyond banking, it has gained control over the logics organising many large corporations via its critical role as an intermediary economic sector – for instance, facilitating the merger of two large corporations, providing financing and specialised advise to firms that want to expand their global network of affiliates. Increasingly, it is also one of the best sectors for negotiating on behalf of client firms for better conditions by a host government. In short, besides the core financial function, the leading financial firms in any country today have economic and political roles. Finance has become a critical vector especially in the economies of developed countries" (p. 4).

schemes, and more.[45] As writers in the political economy of finance literature note, these innovations have made possible a sort of global casino (Strange, 1997) in which "the circuits of financial accumulation steadily take over in the capitalist system, since money capital is universally convertible to any other commodity form of capital" (W.I. Robinson, 2014, p. 136). It is important to reiterate, however, that all this has become possible by virtue of the new rights granted to banks and other financial institutions over this period, enabling the transformation "of any current or *future* stream of earnings (dividends, interest, mortgages, credit card payments, state and private bond maturities, commodity deliveries, and so forth) into an easily tradable capital asset" (p. 136). This shift has enabled financial institutions to begin speculating through trades taking place at a second (or more) degree of separation from the original origin of the stream of earnings being traded. These new forms of intangible, but still exchangeable, private property have not only had the effect of speeding up the general pace of capital accumulation but also of enabling a massive concentration and centralization of capital, as evidenced by the immense growth of financial corporations over this period.

As Norfield (2012) points out, the decision by London to liberalize its financial market was the result of the United Kingdom "seeing the financial sector as a key area of the global economy in which they had a competitive advantage" (p. 14). This is backed up by Strange (1998/2015), who writes that the decision was,

> in a nutshell, because of competition, of two kinds: transnational competition between the City and Wall Street, and between American and Japanese and British banks; and domestic competition between the insiders who belonged to the cosy clubs and new interlopers who didn't, but were eager to share in the profits. (p. 154)

There is thus no need to see these developments as they are currently presented in the debate on globalization: as either the result of a transnational capitalist class that has taken over various economic and political institutions (W.I. Robinson, 2004, 2014), or because of the City of London's satellite status compared to Wall Street (Gowan, 1999; Panitch & Gindin, 2012). Norfield (2016) notes, for instance, that while major US banks do operate from London, "the UK enjoys significant economic

---

45 For a good overview of these so-called innovations, see "Glossary of Technical Terms" (2009).

gains from hosting the biggest international banking centre, and its own banks also take an important share of this business" (p. 18).[46] As such, it seems more accurate to view deregulation – like the reorientation of international institutions – as the result of the overall growth of national capitals to such a degree that their continued expansion ran up against the existing system of property relations. This is especially the case when considering the wider context of capitalist competition in which these changes emerged. The Royal's CEO confirms this view in the bank's 1985 *Annual Report*, writing that "in a turbulent world, profit is the ultimate source of financial soundness – the staying power which provides the foundation for consistently being capable of doing our job in society well" (p. 6). To better understand the extent to which the continued quest for profits led to new rights for globalizing capital, let us once again return to the case of the Royal Bank of Canada.

The Royal took advantage of the UK's Big Bang almost immediately, using Orion to acquire full ownership of Kitcat and Aitken, a London brokerage house. Having already gained access to Australian retail banking earlier that year through a joint venture with the National Mutual Life Assurance Association of Australasia, the Royal would take advantage of similar policies in Australia to form the National Mutual Royal Bank, giving it access to Australian investment banking. Back in Canada, a similar form of deregulation referred to as the "Little Bang" was stirring as a result of the long-term struggle between Toronto and Montreal to become capital of Canada's financial system. Having given way to Toronto's Bay Street in the 1970s, Montreal started to pressure Ottawa in the early 1980s to become "a mecca for offshore banking, a kind of 'New York North,' where international bankers could shelter from taxes" (McDowall, 1993, p. 428).[47] Despite the fact

---

46 It should be noted, however, that due to Brexit, there are concerns that London may soon lose its position as the world's financial capital (Belger, 2019). It is likely that London will offer further concessions to financial firms to stay, thus keeping the deregulatory race to the bottom going.

47 MacIntosh (1991) provides more details: "In 1981, the Montreal Chamber of Commerce and the Board of Trade commissioned a study by some tax lawyers and accountants which advocated the creation of an International Banking Centre (IBC) in Montreal. These tax experts had noted the creation of international banking facilities in New York City, which were designed to encourage the booking of non-resident international banking transactions in New York rather than abroad (that is, recording the loans and deposits of US banks within the US, even though the actual transactions were with non-residents at offshore locations). The legislation had succeeded in transferring hundreds of billions of dollars of offshore banking business to the books of the banks in New York City" (p. 264).

that "few had really thought out the actual economic benefit of such a centre" (p. 428), the federal government gave the scheme the go-ahead in February of 1986, adding Vancouver as another of these international banking centres.[48] In order to avoid losing tax revenue from the inevitable dislocation of the financial sector from Bay Street along with rumours of British deregulation, Ontario's minister of financial institutions, Monte Kwinter, announced in June of 1986 that the province was going to loosen its regulations to allow banks, trust companies, and offshore financial companies to acquire up to 30 per cent of any investment company that was domiciled in the province.[49] The chartered banks responded immediately by buying up regional securities firms in Ontario in an attempt to copy Germany's universal banks, with the end goal of competing with smaller American banks in the American market (Darroch, 1992, p. 167).[50]

With deregulation emerging through the provincial back door, the chartered banks set up a conference at Château Montebello in October of 1986 with Michael Wilson, Canada's minister of finance, and Stanley Hartt, the deputy minister of finance, to demand that the federal barrier

---

48 As MacIntosh (1991) notes, despite the fact that "Mulroney was given a standing ovation in Montreal," when the legislation passed, "there was no stampede to open an international banking centre. Most of the applicants were not commercial banks at all, but private Swiss investment banks and the like. In Vancouver, the Canadian Imperial Bank of Commerce, banker to the province for more than a century, was among the first to open an IBC. Late in 1988, the Royal Bank and the Bank of Montreal followed suit ... The significance of the international banking centre controversy was not the predictable failure of the legislation to achieve anything worthwhile for the Canadian financial system: the importance was the political fallout on securities legislation" (p. 268).
49 Martin and Srikantiah (2012) note: "The investment dealers' weakened position, the threat of international competition, and the mounting Quebec-Ontario feud, provided the combination of factors that Kwinter needed. In June 1986, Kwinter announced that Ontario would be the first province to allow banks, trust companies and foreign financial institutions to acquire up to 30 per cent ownership in a broker or investment dealer licensed in Ontario" (p. 9). MacIntosh (1991) adds: "Kwinter's announcement set in motion a train of events which would not stop until most of the big investment firms in Canada had been swallowed up by the major banks. This was certainly not what either Ontario or the other provinces or the federal government had intended" (p. 269).
50 Universal banking refers to "the ability of the bank to be involved not just in taking in deposits and lending for commercial activities but in other financial activities, including short-term money-market securities, derivatives, equities and equity-linked instruments like mutual funds, trusts and estate management, currency trading, insurance, and investment advising and portfolio management" (Coleman & Porter, 2003, p. 249).

between commercial banking and investment banking be taken down. As McDowall (1993) reports,

> One of the men waiting for Michael Wilson's helicopter at Montebello that fall weekend in 1986 was Allan Taylor, the Royal Bank's new CEO. Throughout the Montebello consultations, Taylor had spoken forcefully on the need for new "ground rules" in Canadian finance, rules that would preserve public confidence and, at the same time, make Canada's banks globally competitive. (p. 429)

This message was one that the chartered banks had been making for a few years by this point: that without access to the Canadian securities market, they would not be able to compete against banks in London and New York, which had already started to offer securitized loan products:

> In November 1984, for example, Rowland Frazee, the chairman of the Royal Bank, told the Canadian Tax Foundation that banks should be allowed to underwrite securities, and that the traditional separation of functions in the Canadian financial market was coming apart, with or without government policy changes. (MacIntosh, 1991, p. 272)

The Royal's 1985 *Annual Report* said something similar: "So-called securitization has spawned a host of new products. Interest rates and currency swaps are typical. These two capital-market products accounted for international financial transactions in excess of $100 billion over the past year" (p. 22). The report continues, noting that "the ability to trade and deal in negotiable securities – on an almost instantaneous basis worldwide – is now a dominant feature" (p. 22) of the global financial system, and that the blending of commercial and investment banking has become the "major force in the pressure for deregulation in a number of financial markets" (p. 22).[51]

---

51 Deputy Minister of Finance Stanley Hartt (2005) noted the following: "The bankers made a plea to be allowed to enter the securities business, which had been denied them for decades so as to minimize the risk to bank capital resulting from securities market volatility. Their thesis was that lending had become securitized: the banks' best customers could finance themselves directly in the London Interbank Market, in essence in competition with the banks themselves, by issuing Eurodollar securities, leaving to the banks the worst credits, on which spreads could be as little as 3/8 percent. Dick Thomson of the Toronto-Dominion Bank, speaking for the group, pointed out that while we were still dealing with the frightening implications of the

In conveying all this to the finance minister, the chartered banks got Wilson to agree "in principle that banks should be able to increase their access to securities either through acquisition of an investment bank, or by creating one, *de novo*" (Martin & Srikantiah, 2012, p. 10). This position was made official in December 1986, when *New Directions for the Financial Sector* (commonly referred to as the "Blue Paper") was released by Thomas Hockin, minister of state for finance, which advocated for a similar type of deregulation as in the United Kingdom:

> The government is proposing that, in principle and subject to the ownership policy described below, there be no restrictions on common ownership of regulated financial institutions. Such institutions will be allowed to hold financial subsidiaries in other pillars (including securities dealers) or to be affiliated with other financial institutions through a holding company structure. (Hockin, 1986, p. 6)

In 1987, the Mulroney government thus began a process that would eventually allow Canada's investment dealers to be wholly owned (up to 100 per cent) by Canadian banks, trust companies, and insurance companies; a year later, the 50 per cent ownership ceiling on foreign companies was lifted, allowing foreign firms to own up to 100 per cent of a Canadian investment bank (Martin & Srikantiah, 2012, p. 11). The move would predate the repeal of similar legislation in the United States (the Glass-Stegall Act) by 12 years.

As a country with one of the highest levels of concentration in the retail financial sector, foreign financial firms never had a chance; the one-year head start allowed the chartered banks to quickly swallow up small, regional securities dealers. The decision essentially gave "80 per cent of the Canadian financial sector to the five chartered banks" (Darroch & McMillan, 2007, p. 7). For its part, the Royal immediately

---

recent run on virtually all of the country's smaller banks, the government needed to consider the possibility of failures among the Big Six" (para. 9).

This interpretation is supported by MacIntosh (1991), who notes that prior to the Montebello meeting, a group of 25 bankers from Toronto and Montreal got together to discuss their priorities: "Dick Thompson of the Toronto-Dominion and Allan Taylor of the Royal Bank had made speeches in which they had urged Ottawa to reconsider its opposition to the banks being more fully involved in the investment business ... In 1986, about 85 percent of cross-border transactions in the global money markets were in the form of securities. This 'securitization' of world banking was likely to leave the big Canadian banks out in the cold, and the Canadian investment dealers were too small to compete with the major securities firms in New York and London" (p. 276).

acquired a 75 per cent interest stake in Dominion Securities (then Canada's largest securities dealer) to act as the Canadian base for Orion's investment activities.[52] The Royal Bank's 1987 *Annual Report* describes the merging of Canada's largest financial institution with its largest securities dealer as creating "a uniquely Canadian force in the market" (p. 6). While we might dispute the extent to which this force should be considered explicitly Canadian, there was no denying that the partnership made the Royal into a force to be reckoned with. By 1989, it was not only three times larger than its nearest non-bank financial rival, Trilon Financial, but also three times larger than the next largest non-financial corporation, Bell Canada (Van Houten, 1991, p. 95). By the mid-1990s, *The Banker* would accurately point out that deregulation had made it much "harder than it was in the past to define what exactly is meant by a 'bank' as the barriers between different types of financial institutions break down" ("25th Anniversary Listings," 1994, para. 3).

These transformations were also mirrored by domestic changes to the way in which banks and other financial firms were regulated. Having witnessed the failure of seven insurance company failures and 11 trust and mortgage loan company failures between 1981 and 1985, it was clear to the federal government that the existing regulatory framework, "which did not include on-site examinations and placed a great deal of reliance on self-regulation" (OSFI, n.d., para. 5), needed to change.[53] In response, Barbara McDougall, Prime Minister Mulroney's minister of state for finance, put together an independent industry working group in 1985 (the Wyman Committee) to study the Canadian Deposit Insurance Corporation (CDIC).[54] While waiting for the results of that report,

---

52 MacIntosh (1991) provides more details on the purchases of all the chartered banks: "The Bank of Montreal bought 75 percent of Nesbitt Thomson at 2.4 times the book value for a price of $291 million. Even the stock market crash of October 1987 did not discourage the bidding. The Bank of Nova Scotia paid $419 million for 100 percent of McLeod Young Weir in November 1987. In December, the Royal Bank bought 75 percent of Dominion Securities for $385 million, and in January 1988 the CIBC bought 65 percent of Wood Gundy for $190 million, after a deal with the First National Bank of Chicago aborted. The National Bank of Canada bought 73 percent of Levesque Beaubien for $100 million. Only the Toronto-Dominion stood aside from the rush to pay premium prices for discount merchandise. A few of the foreign banks joined the rush: the Security Pacific Bank of California bought 49 percent of Burns Fry, and later on some of the medium-size brokerage firms were bought by Deutsche Bank, Sanwa of Tokyo, and Citibank" (p. 278).
53 For more on trust company failures, see MacIntosh (1991, pp. 203–15).
54 A full list of CDIC member institution failures from 1970 onwards can be found at https://www.cdic.ca/about-us/our-history/history-of-failures.

McDougall and her staff also prepared a green paper, *The Regulation of Canadian Financial Institutions: Proposals for Discussion*. More reflective of the Mulroney government's focus on competition and expanding credit, the stated goal of the green paper was to develop "a regulatory approach that encourages, rather than inhibits, innovation and efficiency in our financial sector while at the same time protecting the public" (Department of Finance Canada, 1985, p. 1). Although the two reports came to different conclusions as to the role of CDIC, both recommended a more significant role for a stronger regulatory body.[55] As these discussions were playing out, however, two Western banks – the Canadian Commercial Bank (CCB) and the Northland Bank – would fail, marking the first bank failures in Canada since the failure of the Home Bank in 1923.

The two banks were the outcome of the Western Economic Opportunities Conference that took place in July 1973. At the conference, the governments of the four Western provinces made a joint submission in which they argued that the chartered banking system, "with branches coast to coast, and head offices in central Canada, [had] not been adequately responsive to Western needs" (as cited in Estey, 1986, p. 365). Their solution was to create several independent Western banks "in which there was a degree of public participation," enabling them to be "more sympathetic to the needs of the residents of the West" (p. 365). They claimed that these new banks would provide more "financial capital than in the past to rural and urban communities," thereby facilitating "an expansion in the productive capacities of the Western provinces' economies" (p. 365). Supported by Liberal Finance Minister John Turner, the CCB and the Northland Bank were granted charters by Parliament in 1975; two smaller banks would follow in 1983 and 1984.

By the summer of 1985, however, the failure of the CCB was imminent, as "falling oil prices and the resultant reduction in drilling meant that many of the bank's loans were in default" (Kyer, 2017, p. 129). To avoid overseeing the first bank failure in over 60 years, the Mulroney government approved a rescue package of $255 million.[56] While the

---

55 The Wyman Committee, for instance, saw new regulatory powers going to CDIC. The CBA would also play a significant role in these discussions. For more on this process, see Kyer (2017, pp. 111–26). For a comparison between reports, see Savage (2014).

56 Kyer (2017) provides details of the bailout: "It was tentatively agreed that the federal government, the government of Alberta and the syndicate would each put in $60 million for a total of $180 million. CDIC was called upon to contribute an additional $75 million, bringing the assistance being offered to $255 million. CDIC,

bailout would initiate "much self-congratulatory shaking of hands and slapping of backs" (Kyer, 2017, p. 132), it was not enough to save the CCB and in fact "created as many problems as it solved" (p. 132). This is because the similarly struggling Northland Bank was in the middle of a public offering, attempting to sell both preferred shares alongside a debenture issue to raise funds. With the bailout of the CCB derailing the confidence of investors in Western banks, the market for Northland's offerings dried up, forcing it "to draw on the Bank of Canada as a lender of last resort" (p. 132). The CCB was also relying on the Bank of Canada at this point to maintain liquidity as institutional investors lost confidence; as such, "the OIGB [Office of the Inspector General of Banks] concluded that both CCB and Northland were not viable. A curator was appointed for each and within ten days, steps were taken through CDIC to initiate the winding up of both" (p. 134).

As Kyer (2017) notes, "the public reaction was swift and negative" (p. 134), with significant criticism aimed the Mulroney government's handling of the collapse, which was now being referred to in the media as the CCB "debacle" (Drohan, 1985, p. D3). To save face, Justice Willard Estey (1986) of the Supreme Court of Canada was appointed on 29 September 1985 "to inquire into and report on the state of affairs surrounding the cessation of operations of the Canadian Commercial Bank and the Northland Bank, and to make any consequential recommendations for changes in the control of the banking industry in Canada" (p. iii). In October, Parliament also "introduced a bill to pay out the uninsured depositors in full. In effect, the government acknowledged that its assurances had misled large depositors" (MacIntosh, 1991, p. 25).

Despite the hopes of both the Western premiers and the federal government that the new Western banks would "lend money where the established banks refused to lend" (as cited in Estey, 1986, p. 71), the *Report of the Inquiry into the Collapse of the CCB and Northland Bank* (or, the Estey Report) stated the nature of the Canadian market plainly: "The evidence predominantly favours the conclusion that there was no market niche which had been overlooked by the existing banking

---

of course, had no such money. It was already more than a billion dollars in debt. Its contribution would come from the federal Consolidated Revenue Fund, as did the other government bailout money. But unlike that other money, CDIC's contribution could be recovered from Canada's financial institutions through premiums. It was effectively a levy on these institutions, a way to roughly balance the public sector and private sector contributions to the package. Because its share was intended to be recovered in this fashion, CDIC was not given a claim on the assets of CCB" (p. 131).

industry" (p. 71). With the chartered banks dominating almost the entire domestic market, "there were only two ways to grow: one was to assume unacceptable risks and the other was to drive profit margins down to the point at which the long-term viability of the institution was questionable" (MacIntosh, 1991, p. 224). Having used creative accounting techniques to enable the misrepresentation of assets, the Estey Report noted that "this oversight was perpetuated by the general 'wink and nod' practice employed by the Office of the Inspector General of Banks, which tended to rely on the external auditor's reports as the basis of its regulatory activities" (Puri, 2012, p. 169).[57] Like the April 1985 green paper, the Estey Report recommended consolidating the OIGB "with a strengthened CDIC to improve the banking supervision system" (Granger, 2013, para. 4).

When the new minister of state for finance, Thomas Hockin, released *New Directions for the Financial Sector* in December 1986, he followed course and recommended the merger of the OIGB and the Department of Insurance (DOI) on the basis "that the activities of the different types of regulated institutions were converging and that the supervisory system should be similarly integrated" (OSFI, n.d., para. 13). In 1987, the federal government followed these recommendations and introduced a bill to create the Office of the Superintendent of Financial Institutions (OSFI) by merging the OIGB and DOI into a single entity; it also "established the Financial Institutions Supervisory Committee (FISC), composed of the Superintendent of Financial Institutions (as chairperson), the Governor of the Bank of Canada, the Deputy Minister of Finance and the Chairman of the CDIC" (OSFI, n.d., para. 14), to allow for the confidential exchange of information relating to the supervision of financial institutions. Parliament also expanded the mandate of CDIC:

> From that of a simple paybox institution (confined to paying the claims of creditors after a member is closed) to one aimed at reducing or averting a threatened loss to CDIC. Accordingly, CDIC was given the power to act as an inspector, receiver, or liquidator of a member institution. (Engert, 2005, p. 68)

---

57 As MacIntosh (1991) notes, "by 1983, [Northland Bank's] internal inspector described the loan portfolio as a 'time bomb.' In order to avoid disclosing the true conditions of the bank to the public, the management developed original techniques of 'creative accounting.' As the later inquiry revealed, 'both banks dealt in the future tense in connections with loan valuations because the present tense, by 1983 at least, represented insolvency'" (pp. 221–2).

The end result of the CCB and Northland failures was thus not only "the virtual elimination of regional banks in Canada" (MacIntosh, 1991, p. 225) but also the strengthening of domestic regulation and the extension of that regulation across "all the federally regulated deposit-taking institutions and insurance companies" (p. 227) in Canada. These national regulations would quickly be strengthened by the adoption of the more globally oriented Basel Capital Accord of 1988.

Referred to today simply as "Basel I," the 1988 Basel Capital Accord was the result of the crumbling barriers between commercial banking and the securities business, which "forced the regulators to work out completely new arrangements to cover their responsibilities" (MacIntosh, 1991, p. 279) as well as the ongoing fallout from the LDC debt crisis, which made it crystal clear "that the capital ratios of the main international banks were deteriorating at a time of growing international risks" (BCBS, n.d., "Basel I," para. 1).[58] With G10 governors approving the BCBS's *International Convergence of Capital Measurement and Capital Standards*, it was released to banks in July 1988 as the Basel Capital Accord, calling "for a minimum ratio of capital to risk-weighted assets of 8% to be implemented by the end of 1992" (para. 3).[59] As pointed out by many commentators, the Accord was a means "to harmonize national standards ... aimed at facilitating the global banking system" (Teeple, 2000, p. 210, n. 15). In doing so, it not only represented "the most ambitious and successful example of international financial regulation" (Porter, 2005, p. 35), but it also furthered the transnationalization of political authority by strengthening "international cooperation and cohesion

---

58 As MacIntosh (1991) points out, the destruction of the barriers between commercial banking and the securities business led to several regulatory issues: "What would be the relationship between a bank and its controlled investment subsidiary if the bank had to supply capital to the underwriting part of the business, thereby possibly eroding the capital requirements of the bank under the Basle Concordat? (p. 279).

59 The 1988 Accord was revised over the 1990s to fill various regulatory gaps: "It was amended in November 1991 to more precisely define the general provisions or general loan loss reserves that could be included in the capital adequacy calculation. In April 1995, the Committee issued another amendment, to take effect at the end of that year, to recognise the effects of bilateral netting of banks' credit exposures in derivative products and to expand the matrix of add-on factors. In April 1996, another document was issued explaining how Committee members intended to recognise the effects of multilateral netting" (BCBS, n.d., "Basel I," para. 4). One of the more significant revisions was the Market Risk Amendment, which came into effect at the end of 1997. As the BCBS (n.d.) notes, "an important aspect of the Market Risk Amendment was that banks were, for the first time, allowed to use internal models (value-at-risk models) as a basis for measuring their market risk capital requirements" ("Basel I," para. 5).

between national monetary authorities" (Major, 2013, p. 42). This interpretation is shared by bankers such as MacIntosh (1991), who notes that "the final terms, accepted by all, became a form of international law" (p. 198). In this sense, "it is more than a symbol of the international global village – it is the reality of it" (p. 198). This is especially true given that the WB and IMF both incorporated the Basel Accord standards into their own assessments of the strength of potential borrowers' financial institutions (K. Alexander et al., 2006). By harmonizing national standards, the Accord helped to reorient nation states towards being capabilities for globalizing financial capitals through the design of "a global financial system that is, in principle, resilient enough to survive its own disorder" (Rude, 2005, p. 93).

This was particularly the case in Canada, which, having just dealt with the CCB and Northland failures, "did not permit banks to use a risk-adjusted measure of capital to discount the total assets on a bank's balance sheet" (Puri, 2012, p. 171). Having just witnessed a scenario in which "what were originally regarded as low risk mortgages and loans to the natural resource sector became extremely vulnerable by the recession in western Canada" (p. 171), Canadian regulators decided instead to "mandate that Tier 1 capital consist of 75 per cent common equity and retained earnings for the purposes of assessing capital adequacy requirements, and impose a simply, non-risk-adjusted, leverage ratio on Canadian banks" (p. 169). By not allowing the chartered banks to "remove certain assets from their balance sheets" (p. 171), the goal was to avoid a similar situation to the CCB and Northland failures, in which the removal of particular assets could "distort a bank's true liquidity and mislead consumers" (p. 171).

Despite these harsher restrictions on the chartered banks, the deregulation that accompanied Canada's Little Bang allowed them, as well as the Royal specifically, to make large leaps in size by increasing their hold on the domestic market.[60] In its 1992 *Annual Report*, for instance, the Royal notes that not only were domestic operations becoming more dominant in its overall business mix, "with domestic average assets representing 80% of total average assets in 1992, compared to 73% in 1988," but that residential mortgages also "accounted for almost half of

---

60 This process was aided by the collapse of Canadian real estate in the early 1990s, which "caused particular distress to the trust company sector, which had lent considerably to that industry. These financial troubles presented the opportunity for chartered banks to acquire almost all of Canada's troubled trust companies, to the extent that the trust company industry all but disappeared. This gave the chartered banks a tremendous growth spurt" (Bonham, 2024, "Deregulation," para. 5).

the increase in total assets since 1988" (p. 3). Most of this growth was, as the Royal reports, the result of its newfound ability to enter financial areas long off-limits to the chartered banks:

> The Bank's mutual fund assets have grown from $1.2 billion in 1988 to $4.8 billion in 1992, now ranking them fourth largest in Canada. In insurance, the Bank provides its clients with creditor life insurance and other related products, generating premiums of over $180 million annually. The acquisition of Voyageur Travel Insurance Limited, Canada's largest supplier of travel insurance to the retail travel insurance market, announced shortly after year-end 1992, will further enhance the Bank's insurance capabilities. These, and other new non-banking businesses, such as investment management, discount brokerage and retirement income services, are expected to be the high-growth areas of the Bank's operations over the next few years. (p. 4)

Reflecting on the overall impact of 1980s-era deregulation, development scholar Manfred Bienefeld (1992) predicted that insofar as large foreign banks were able to continue to enter the Canadian market, the chartered banks would be forced "to become fully internationalized in their activities and their orientation ... they must either perish or cease to be Canadian in any meaningful sense of the word, their Canadian origins soon being of interest only to historians" (p. 53). While the assets of foreign bank subsidiaries in Canada would only total $54 billion in 1990 (compared to the Royal's $116.9 billion in 1991), the second portion of Bienefeld's claim would hold true, as reflected in the Royal's own publications. Having referred to itself as simply "a bank" as late as 1988, by 1992 it was referring to itself a "financial services institution." It would only take until 1996 for the adjective "global" to be added, matching the bank's 1,600 branches scattered across 35 countries.

Constructing Bigger Markets

A further indicator of the centrifugal dynamic that characterizes our global epoch is the movement of the rights of capital and the authority over those rights to the transnational level: in other words, across the territory of multiple nation states. While many contemporary scholars of globalization argue that there is nothing new about globalization given the inherent expansionary tendencies of capital and, thus, the long-standing existence of a world market, such a view tends to downplay the stages of development of capitalism and the transformation of what constitutes that market over time.⁶¹ What is typically being referred to as a world market is a collection of national markets that are linked together. This is because markets are constituted by enforceable private property relations within a bounded space. The boundaries of this space are the limits beyond which the institutions of a particular authority are no longer able to enforce the private property relations necessary for the market to function (and thus, exist). If the reader recalls our discussion from chapter 2, the national epoch of capitalism was concerned with the making of a domestic market (i.e., the nation state) that involved the drawing in of TAR towards the national level. The world market of this period was thus one that was "still more or less international, a trading system by and large framed by international relations" (Teeple, 2000, p. 173).

In contrast, our global epoch has so far been characterized by the proliferation of trade and investment agreements that have established larger, regional markets across the territories of multiple nation states.⁶² Emerging in the 1980s, these agreements began giving foreign corporations new domestic rights – chief among them, the ability to sue national or subnational governments via private tribunals. As Unifor economist Jordan Brennan (2013) suggests, these tribunals are essentially exclusive courts for capitalists that enable global "investors and corporations to constrain government policy and regulation by submitting damage claims for alleged 'interference' with their 'rights'" (p. 24).⁶³ While the recent Canada–United States–Mexico Agreement

---

61 Teeple (2000) notes: "There is no such thing as an independent world market, except as an abstraction. Just as there is no society without its constituent members, so too there is no market without its member capitals, and no international market without nation-states. And just as the history of capital evolves through many qualitatively distinct stages, so too does the corresponding world market" (p. 173). If we want to make the case with Marx (1867/1991) in volume 1 of *Capital*, "It is otherwise on the world market, whose integral parts are the individual countries" (p. 702).

62 As Pistor (2019) notes, global capitalism is sustained by getting nation states to recognize and enforce the legal code of capital, which "is built around two domestic legal systems, the laws of England and those of New York State, complemented by a few international treaties and an extensive network of *bilateral* trade and investment regimes, which themselves are centred around a handful of advanced economies" (p. 132).

63 Pistor (2019) expands on this process: "Despite their resistance to divest control over property rights, states ended up giving away more than they may have intended. They have done so not through legal harmonization of substantive law or even of conflict-of-law rules, but by signing on to regional or bilateral investment treaties. These treaties rarely talk about property rights and instead focus on the investments made by foreign investors and their protection in the host state ... The Trojan horse

(CUSMA) has removed these controversial investor–state dispute settlement (ISDS) mechanisms between Canada and the United States, such mechanisms are still found in numerous multilateral and bilateral agreements, indicative of how global property regimes "only become operative, or performative, when they enter the national domain" (Sassen, 2006, p. 2). It is in this sense, as Pistor (2019) notes, that the holders of globalizing capital have been able to create "their own world of law, stitched together from different domestic legal systems with international or bilateral treaty law thrown into the mix" (p. 154).

The first of these new, larger markets was the Canada–United States Free Trade Agreement (CUSFTA) agreed to in 1987 and brought into force on 1 January 1989; it not only granted Canadian and American corporations new domestic rights in each other's home territory, but it also phased out several restrictions on trade over a 10-year period. The second was the incorporation of Mexico into the agreement in 1994 via the North American Free Trade Agreement (NAFTA), and its modification and renaming to CUSMA in 2018.[64] While CUSMA and the Canada–European Union Comprehensive Economic and Trade Agreement (CETA) have altered the way in which some of these dispute settlement mechanisms work – using a panel appointed by a joint committee selected by the countries involved, rather than independent arbitrators selected by the members of the dispute – the long-standing trend has been towards the use of national legal systems to remove barriers to trade in goods and services by creating new legal frameworks to manage the transnational flow of capital.[65] As historian Quinn Slobodian

---

in these treaties is a dispute settlement mechanism that goes by the initialism ISDS (investor–state dispute settlement). It allows a foreign investor to bring a case for damages against the host state in an arbitral tribunal outside its territory. The language of the treaties is sufficiently open-ended to give arbitrators the power to grant damages for 'unfair and inequitable treatment' that are on par with damages for expropriation. In doing so, they effectively confer property rights status on contractual commitments and curtail the powers of states to determine the claims they wish to recognize as property rights" (pp. 136–7).

64 A study by Mertins-Kirkwood (2022) notes that since the signing of NAFTA in 1994, "Canada has concluded 15 bilateral or regional free trade agreements as well as 38 foreign investment promotion and protection agreements. These 53 active agreements govern trade and investment relations with 75 countries that are together host to 89% of Canadian and direct investment abroad. Twelve countries, including Jordan, Peru, and Ukraine, are covered by both an active FTA and an active FIPA with Canada" (p. 7).

65 As reported in the *Globe and Mail*, the Liberal government wanted to keep ISDS mechanisms in CUSMA but make them more similar to those in CETA, using "set rosters of judges to hear these cases rather than ad hoc appointments of independent

(2018) notes in his book, *Globalists: The End of Empire and the Birth of Neoliberalism*, these sorts of agreements are central to the neo-liberal project, which seeks "to insulate market actors from democratic pressures" (p. 4).[66] And it is through this process, I argue, that the nation state has jumped the tracks and is becoming a capability for globalizing capitals.

As Mertins-Kirkwood (2014) suggests, for instance, both CUSFTA and NAFTA "represented an important shift from mere market access to an all-encompassing market presence for foreign capital" (p. 20). Against the international trading system initiated by the Bretton Woods system and the General Agreement on Tariffs and Trade (GATT) that involved the strengthening of the powers of the nation state to regulate capital, NAFTA and other similar agreements not only extend far beyond trade in goods, including investments, services, non-tariff barriers, and the protection of intellectual property rights, but also involve the de facto rewriting of national constitutions such that the capacity of the nation state to legislate against capital is reduced; as McBride (2005) notes, "simply put, they serve to protect almost all forms of economic activity and capital investments from 'excessive' state intervention"

---

arbitrators" (Fife & Chase, 2017, para. 2). With their removal by July 2023, dispute settlement will return to a system whereby each country selects a panel, rather than letting investors sue for monetary damages. Canadian investors are still able to sue Mexico under the ISDS mechanisms of the Comprehensive and Progressive Agreement for Trans-Pacific Partnership (CPTPP). For more on CUSMA, see Lai (2021); L. Macdonald (2020); Sinclair (2018).

66 As Slobodian (2018) points out, trade agreements are not the only way that this occurs: "The clearest-eyed academic observers of the neoliberal philosophy of global ordering have been not historians but social scientists. For the last twenty years, political scientists and sociologists have elaborated a sophisticated analysis of the neoliberal project. They have identified efforts to insulate market actors from democratic pressures in a series of institutions from the IMF and the World Bank to port authorities and central banks worldwide, including the European Central Bank, governance structures like the European Union, trade treaties like the North American Free Trade Agreement (NAFTA), and the WTO. They have also seen efforts to insulate in the expansion of international investment law designed to protect foreign investors from diverse forms of expropriation and to provide a parallel global legal system known as the transnational law merchant. They have traced the emergence of an 'offshore world' of tax havens and the proliferation of zones of many types, all designed to provide safe harbor for capital, free from fear of infringement by policies of progressive taxation or redistribution. 'Insulation of markets' is a useful metaphorical description of the aim of neoliberalism as a specific institution-building project rather than as a nebulous 'logic' or 'rationality'" (pp. 4–5).

(p. 88).[67] This not only means that private actors, such as TNCs, have acquired rights that have strengthened their hand against Canadian citizens, but also that "many capacities used in the national policies under which Canada developed are now beyond the reach of governments" (p. 186). As such, the meaning of national political rights is reduced as the nation state is forced to defend the rights of globalizing capital, reducing the potential for a diversity of policy options to be presented to the voting public.

While many scholars view these trade agreements as expressions of American domination (Hurtig, 2003; Ikeda, 2004; Jackson, 2007; McQuaig, 2007; Seccareccia, 2007), it is important to point out that, from the start, these agreements were promoted by globalizing Canadian firms who were not able to support the scale of their enterprises via the domestic market alone.[68] McBride (2005) notes, for example, that a delegation from the BCNI "broached the free-trade idea with American officials as early as 1982 and began to publicly promote the idea in Canada from 1983" (p. 58). During the Royal Commission on Economic Union and Development Prospects for Canada, both the BCNI and the Canadian Manufacturers Association (CMA) argued "that they could compete with the United States if given the chance" (McBride, 2005, p. 62). Despite referring to the proposed trade agreement as a "leap of faith," the head of the Commission, former Liberal MP Donald Macdonald, concluded that "if these people say they can compete in a free market, who am I to say they cannot?" (as cited on p. 62). In his history of corporate Canada, Van Houten (1991) agrees, noting that CUSFTA "was advanced as the solution to Canadian monopoly's predicament and hence it was prepared to make whatever compromises and

---

67 As Pistor (2019) notes, for instance, "NAFTA also created rights for private parties, specifically for foreign investors, and these rights are armed with a powerful enforcement mechanism. If a foreign investor believes that his 'investments' have been infringed by a host state, it can lodge a complaint with an arbitral tribunal and seek compensation for damages" (p. 139).

68 Sweeny (1997) explains: "Over the 1980s there was a very significant reduction in the relative importance of American direct investment. Nor was this simply a matter of fewer firms, the characteristic feature of a concentration in the middle ranks was eliminated. In part this was the result of continued corporate concentration, the scale of which was very impressive. The most important factor was, however, a complex and on-going process of democratisation of the capital markets in Canada. In short, this dramatic change was largely made in Canada and rather than representing a legacy of dependency the Canadian and Québécois bourgeoisies' enthusiastic endorsement of free trade was to a significant degree the result of this changed situation" (p. 334).

sacrifices necessary to protect its interest in the US" (p. 154). With the support of the Commission, CUSFTA was signed on 2 January 1988 and passed into law by the House of Commons later that year.

Despite meaning the removal of size restrictions on the subsidiaries of American banks,[69] the Royal's 1989 *Annual Report* commended the move, noting that "a strong North American base is fundamental to our vision of becoming a major North American 'corporate' bank and leading Canadian bank in the United States," and that "the prospects for developing new, quality business in the United States have been enhanced by the Canada–US Free Trade Agreement" (p. 5).[70] In attempting to capture part of the American middle market (smaller corporations with annual sales of $50–250 million), James Walker, the general manager of the Royal's New York branch, would issue a prescient warning: "It's a competitive field and it's very tempting to go for a little more risk for a better reward" (as cited in Burton, 1990, para. 11). It was, as Jonathan Burton (1990) put it in *The Banker*, "a world where barriers and borders are sand castles waiting to fall" (para. 31).

Shortly afterwards, in 1992, the *Bank Act* was again up for revision. Continuing the process of removing the legal barriers that divided Canadian finance, the 1992 revisions gave the chartered banks the "power to diversify into new lines of business through financial institution subsidiaries, as well as through increased in-house powers" (F. Daniel, 2002, p. 5). The revisions gave banks and insurance companies the right to own trust companies; bank, trust, and loan companies the right to own insurance companies; and widely held non-bank financial institutions the right to own Schedule II banks, or closely held banks. It also relaxed the conflict-of-interest provisions, enabling the chartered banks "to create investment bank subsidiaries, participate in the distribution and underwriting of securities, and offer investment

---

69 As Freedman (1998) notes, "the ceiling was originally 8 per cent of the total domestic assets of all banks in Canada but was raised to 16 per cent in 1985 when it appeared that the ceiling might become a binding constraint. When the US bank subsidiaries were exempted from the limitation in 1989, it was reduced to 12 per cent for the remaining foreign bank subsidiaries" (p. 9, n. 14).

70 As MacIntosh (1991) recalls, not all the chartered banks were supportive of CUSFTA: "Most of the banks took the view that the Free Trade Agreement should be supported. Allan Taylor of the Royal Bank was the most positive, while Cedric Ritchie of the Bank of Nova Scotia opposed it. Although most of the top bankers stayed out of the political debate, I felt there was enough agreement to make the following comment to the House Committee in November 1987: 'For the banking industry, what is good for Canada is good for the banks. The banking industry is supportive of the free trade deal'" (p. 283).

counselling services that were traditionally provided by investment houses, trust companies, and insurers" (Puri, 2012, p. 173).[71] As Seccareccia and Pringle (2020) conclude, "this resulted in the large chartered banks acquiring weaker trust companies, such as wealth management services" (p. 327). For the Royal, this meant buying up Royal Trustco – the parent company of the Royal Trust, one of Canada's oldest trust companies – for $1.6 billion dollars. At the time, Royal Trustco ranked among the 10th largest financial institutions in Canada and offered trust, financial, real estate, and deposit services spread across its 100 branches in Canada, the US, and abroad (Sawyer, 2014). Long associated with the Bank of Montreal, the acquisition of Royal Trustco not only provided the Royal Bank with a "huge block of assets" but also immediately transformed it into "the fourth-largest financial institution in North America" (McDowall, 1993, p. 431). More important, perhaps, is that the acquisition of Royal Trustco gave the Royal "access to wealth management, which is another way of saying getting your hands on all of a customer's assets, including RRSPs. This [was] hugely attractive to banks because profit margins are much higher than for traditional services" (Kingston, 1998, p. 14).

The 1992 *Bank Act* also abolished reserve requirements on the chartered banks. Although still required to "maintain non-negative settlement balances with the [Bank of Canada] on a daily basis" (Handa, 2002, p. 262), the chartered banks were no longer required to keep deposits with the Bank of Canada, with the BCBS instead setting capital requirements on global banks and financial institutions since 1988.[72] As such, the 1992 Act continued the process by which previously divided Canadian financial institutions – namely, the chartered banks, but also the large insurance companies – were transformed into huge, multi-service conglomerates.[73] The revision schedule was also shortened to five

---

71 Puri (2012) further discusses how the decision to offer these services through subsidiaries meant that the chartered banks had "direct ownership and responsibility for their investment portfolio's risk" (p. 173). They claim that this "promoted greater conservatism in Canadian lending behaviour and fund management, more diversity within a financial institutions portfolio, and reduced risk of collective action problems arising from a financial crisis in the securities market" (p. 173).

72 At the beginning of the 1980s, Duncan Cameron (1983) observed that "in the evolving global order, the importance of official reserves acquired in the market has declined, and the significance of international credit provided by transnational financial capital has increased" (p. 105).

73 The 1992 revisions were not entirely a win for the chartered banks: "Despite the broad liberalization of permitted banking activities, strong lobbying by

years to better match the quickening pace of change as well as to give both the government and interest groups time "to organize strategies to influence any amendments of the Act" (Seccareccia & Pringle, 2020, p. 327).

Having survived the bankruptcy of Canadian-based real estate firm Olympia & York in 1992, the Royal Bank was well positioned by the time NAFTA came into effect on 1 January 1994.[74] More forward looking than CUSFTA, NAFTA was crafted in such a way as to be extended to other countries over time; it has since provided the model for other multilateral trade agreements, such as CETA and the Comprehensive and Progressive Agreement for Trans-Pacific Partnership (CPTPP), among others. For its part, Canada was initially alarmed at the prospect of including Mexico, worried that this "would threaten Canada's privileged access to the US market" (L. Macdonald, 2020, p. 155). As White (1994) notes, however, the US government had different concerns. As the representative of the world's largest and most powerful financial firms, the US hoped that the provisions about the exchange of financial services "might establish a global model" (p. 12) that could be used in negotiations relating to the General Agreement on Trade in Services (GATS). Their goal was to use NAFTA and the GATS as a means of forcing other countries to open their financial sectors by giving foreign firms new domestic rights that would ensure equal access to markets subject to non-discriminatory regulation. As Gould (2010) notes, one aspect of the Doha Round of negotiations to expand the WTO is the attempt to get developing countries "to further liberalize their financial sectors" (p. 1) by giving foreign interests the right to acquire existing companies as well as establish new ones. National governments would then be responsible for guaranteeing those rights by making binding

---

industry-specific commercial financing companies such as the automotive financing sector prevented banks from being able to acquire downstream links to commercial companies" (Puri, 2012, p. 173).

74 Puri (2012) elaborates on the situation surrounding Olympia & York: "The 1992 bankruptcy of Canadian-based real-estate firm Olympia & York provided the first major test for Canada's Big-Five banks, and in particular the Royal Bank of Canada and Canadian Imperial Bank of Commerce, who were highly exposed as major creditors and investors to Olympia & York. Upon insolvency, Canada's Big-Five banks held over $2.3 billion of the nearly $17 billion outstanding liabilities declared by Olympia & York upon bankruptcy in 1992 ... The refusal of the government of Canada to intervene to assist the banks during the bankruptcy set a clear policy precedent that the government will not bail out large banks if their loans default" (p. 174).

commitments under the GATS, which would be "enforceable through the WTO dispute system" (p. 1).

It is important to recall that such agreements provide rights to foreign corporations *located* in member jurisdictions; as such, the firms involved may not even be "Canadian" or "American" by most measures of corporate nationality. As William Robinson (2012a) notes, the regional markets created by contemporary trade agreements do not "carve out separate regions" of capitalist activity; instead, they act as "regional transnational platforms for furthering capitalist globalization" (p. 411). One way this occurs is through the attached ISDS mechanisms, which compel countries who break the terms of the agreement to change their policies according to the ruling of a tribunal. Understood as such, trade agreements are less about trade and more about granting globalizing capital new rights that work to constrain the legislative options available to the host nation.

Under NAFTA's Chapter 14, for instance, the governments of Canada, the United States, and Mexico all agreed to refrain from discriminatory behaviour against financial institutions based in each other's countries, regardless of whether those companies "are investing in actual foreign premises or providing cross-border services from their home countries" (Clarkson, 2008, p. 315). NAFTA also required that member countries that run into macroeconomic trouble must "remedy the situation by seeking *and taking* the advice of the International Monetary Fund and such other relevant bodies as the World Bank" (p. 316). This ultimately means following the same sort of austerity policies previously pushed on developing nations along with the further privatization of public resources. Member countries are also restricted from excluding certain services from the market (such as education, health care, etc.) via the creation of new social rights; in other words, national governments only have two options: (1) status quo; or (2) more privatization. This is the reason why there is little chance of going back to any form of welfare state under the terms of these agreements; they ultimately restrict the range of policy options available to governments. Put another way, they restrict what national governments are entitled to govern.

This is not to suggest that there is not resistance, however, or that capital always gets its way. As Calvert et al. (2022) note, "governments have won more cases than they have lost. Of the 674 ISDS proceedings concluded by the end of 2019, 37 per cent were decided in favour of the state and 29 per cent in favour of the investor" (p. 789). The point, rather, is that these agreements serve as an indicator of the level and power of capital's expansionary thrust; in following their interests, the holders of globalizing capital are attempting to create a system of global rules for the accumulation of capital that puts their activities outside the realm of government intervention. As Stephen Clarkson (2008) remarks, by reducing "the authority of constitutionally established national authorities," NAFTA has increased the autonomy and capacity of TNCs by liberating them "from national control" (p. 470). Few Canadians know, for example, that Canada's federal government had already paid out NAFTA damages totalling over $172 million to a variety of TNCs by 2015 (Sinclair, 2015).[75] While the sum is relatively small, it is useful to remember that these payments were to compensate investors for decisions made by democratically elected governments at both the federal and provincial levels. The United Nations Conference on Trade and Development (UNCTAD, 2020) also notes that these settlements have risen significantly since the 1990s, with the total number of publicly known ISDS claims increasing to 1,023 as of 1 January 2020 (p. 110). They note, however, that "as some arbitrations can be kept confidential, the actual number of disputes filed in 2019 and previous years is likely to be higher" (p. 110).[76] What we are witnessing is thus a slow and complicated struggle to make the nation state into a capability

---

[75] One example is given by Pistor (2019), who highlights the case of Eli Lilly. After having patents revoked by Canadian courts as part of a legal dispute with another firm, "Eli Lilly did not seek dispute settlement under NAFTA right away. It first battled in the Canadian courts for recognition of its (second) patent ... After having lost its case, Eli Lilly now argued that the patent's revocation by the Canadian courts amounted to 'unfair and inequitable treatment' and 'indirect expropriation' under the NAFTA treaty. The reason given was that the Canadian court's interpretation of the *Canadian Patent Act* deviated from its earlier case law in a 'dramatic' fashion" (p. 140). Pistor goes on to show that the Eli Lilly case highlights "how traditional law enforcement agencies, such as courts and regulators, have been put in the service of capital. The holders of capital do not always win their first battle; rather, they chip away at existing legal barriers slowly but stubbornly until little stands in the way for principles that, not too long ago, appeared – to use Justice Cardozo's words – as 'unbending and inveterate,' to erode into sand" (p. 152).
[76] UNCTAD (2020) also notes that "about 70 per cent of investment arbitrations in 2019 were brought under BITs and TIPs [treaties with investment provisions] signed in the 1990s or earlier. The remaining cases were based on treaties signed between 2000 and 2011. The ECT [Energy Charter Treaty] (1994) was the IIA [International Investment Agreement] invoked most frequently in 2019, with seven cases, followed by the North American Free Trade Agreement (NAFTA [1992]) with three cases. Looking at the overall trend, about 20 per cent of the 1,023 known cases have invoked the ECT (128 cases) or NAFTA (67 cases)" (p. 111).

for globalizing capital via already existing national legal frameworks. Sassen (2006) explains:

> In this process, particular legal protections get detached from their national territorial jurisdictions and become incorporated into a variety of often highly specialized or partial global regimes and thereby often become transformed into far more specialized rights and obligations. I also see in this dynamic capabilities jumping tracks and becoming lodged into a novel organizing logic. One example is the bundle of rights granted by host states to foreign firms under the WTO which unsettles older national regimes. Many of these rights and guarantees derive from what were once national rights and guarantees used precisely to distinguish national firms from foreign firms; these rights and guarantees were also one critical component in the building up of the state's exclusive authority over its national territory. (p. 417)

In chapter 2, we explored the creation of the national market, which consisted of the construction of a national system of rights for the ownership of private property. Under this earlier system, foreign corporations were typically subject to the laws (and arbitrary decisions) of the host government under which business took place. Under investment and free trade agreements, however, the rights of capital are spread across multiple jurisdictions, forcing member nation states to increasingly protect the interests of all "local" corporations. The purpose of such agreements is thus to protect corporations (and, more importantly, their investors) from national legislation that could potentially impact their accumulation activities. As a result, these agreements ultimately reinforce the concentration and centralization of capital since corporations must grow larger and larger to survive against their globalizing rivals operating in new domains.

In the case of the Royal Bank, for instance, NAFTA not only gave it new rights in the American market, which had been a significant source of revenue for all the chartered banks over the 1990s, but also an immediate impetus to get much larger. The Royal's need to expand was the result of a worldwide mergers and acquisition (M&A) boom in the mid-1990s. As the Royal notes in its 1996 *Annual Report*, "consolidation is a worldwide industry trend. In Japan, the merger of the Bank of Tokyo and Mitsubishi Bank has created the world's largest bank with more than $700 billion US in assets" (p. 15). The report recommended that Canadian banks "consider the merits of mergers" (p. 15). With NAFTA putting pressure on the Canadian government to allow cross-border branching, the chartered banks were all too aware that they might soon have to compete at home with larger, more powerful American banks.

Up to this point, the Canadian government had been able to avoid the issue by stating that Canada would only allow cross-border branching "when the restrictions on nation-wide branching in the United States were lifted – in effect, refusing national treatment for US banks in Canada, but demanding reciprocity for Canadian banks in the United States" (Clarkson, 2008, p. 307). With the passing of the Riegle–Neal Act in 1994, which permitted nationwide branching in the United States, "Canada's position became much harder to defend" (p. 307), especially since Canada was now the only member of the OECD to not permit cross-border branching. The fears of the chartered banks were confirmed in late 1997 when the Canadian subsidiaries of both Citibank and American Express won large contracts with the Canadian government instead of the Bank of Montreal. With an amendment to the *Bank Act* in 1997 allowing foreign-owned banks to operate full-service branches, the late 1990s also saw ING, Maryland Bank of North America (MBNA), Fidelity Investment, Merrill Lynch, and Wells Fargo enter the Canadian market.[77] A report from Statistics Canada summarizes the period well: "Financial institutions are stretching over national boundaries. Canadian banks are investing abroad, while foreign banks are increasing their presence in Canada" (Hinchley, 2006, p. 3).

In response to the arrival of American banks in Canada, the chartered banks began quickly acquiring domestic subsidiaries. For their part, the Royal purchased Richardson Greenshields Limited (a Canadian investment dealer) for $480 million in 1997, as well as the remaining minority shares of the recently purchased RBC Dominion Securities Limited. The recently acquired Royal Trust also "purchased the institutional and pension custody business of Montreal Trust and the Bank of Nova Scotia, garnering $120 billion in client assets" (R.A. Williams, 2004, p. 165). And despite the fact that the earlier acquisition of Royal Trustco had made the Royal the fourth-largest financial institution in North America, the CEOs of both the Royal and the Bank of Montreal would announce their plans to merge into a single super bank on 23 January 1998.

---

[77] A report from Statistics Canada notes that "between 1997 and 2004, foreign bank operations slowly increased their market share in the Canadian deposit-taking industry. In 1997, foreign bank subsidiaries and full-service branches accounted for 5.7% of the value of services produced in this industry. By 2004, this proportion had edged up to 7.9%" (Hinchley, 2006, p. 3).

In a case study of the attempted merger, Russell Williams (2004) notes that the banks involved saw their actions as "the logical, or necessary, consequence of the government's previous decision to open the market up to competition, particularly competition from foreign and non-traditional financial services companies" (p. 156). For the federal government, though, the announcement came as a huge surprise. The CEOs of the two banks had called the finance minister, Paul Martin, at 8 a.m. to deliver the news, but were told to call back at 9 a.m. because Martin was in a meeting. Fifty minutes later, "an aide handed him a copy of a newswire story on the announcement" (Noble, 1998a, para. 20). Having decided to avoid giving earlier notification to Martin due to legal advice,[78] aides close to the finance minister described him as being "'steamed' by the way the banks handled the matter" (para. 21). Another official said that the merger announcement came "like a bolt from the clear blue sky" (Greenspon, 1998, para. 2).

Martin was particularly upset because he saw the two banks as having "jumped the queue on the orderly process of his task-force review" (Greenspon, 1998, para. 2). Two years earlier, in 1996, the government had appointed Saskatchewan lawyer and former director of the Bank of Canada Harold MacKay to head a task force investigating how technology and foreign competition would impact the Canadian financial sector moving forward. With the final report expected in the latter half of 1998, and with both the Senate and Commons standing committees still to respond to it, new legislation was unlikely to emerge for at least another year. By announcing their merger plans when they did, the banks "threatened to throw the entire policy process off the rails" (R.A. Williams, 2004, p. 157). In a press conference held the same afternoon as the merger proposals, Martin announced that any approval "would have to await a full investigation by the Competition Bureau and the OSFI as well as the final report of the MacKay Task Force" (p. 174). Tensions would only increase after rival banks TD and CIBC proposed a second merger a few weeks later.

"That other banks would feel pressure to follow suit 'was entirely predictable,'" claims Martin; "what proved harder to anticipate was the

---

[78] As Noble (1998a) explains, John Cleghorn, CEO of the Royal, and Matthew Barrett, CEO of the Bank of Montreal, had received legal advice warning them not to notify the finance minister until they went public with the news: "For their part, the bankers say they had no choice but to keep Martin in the dark until the last minute. Otherwise, Barrett said, they might have been accused of leaking insider information. 'We had legal advice – we had to go public before we told anybody'" (p. 45).

strength of the backlash" (Bradshaw, 2018, para. 14). With the unpopularity of the banks growing due to "rising service fees, complaints of meagre financing for small business, sweeping workforce reductions, billion-dollarplus [sic] profits, and the multimillion-dollar salaries and bonuses enjoyed by bank executives" (Noble, 1998a, p. 44), the proposed mergers brought forth a renewed chorus of alarm from citizen and consumer groups, unions, left-wing think tanks, small business groups, politicians, as well as some members of the financial industry, who all noted that, if approved, the two new banks would control over 70 per cent of Canada's banking assets.[79] Investors, however, were elated with the Bank of Montreal's stock shooting up "18% the day the deal was announced, while Royal Bank rallied by 5%. The love affair continued for three months, with the Bank of Montreal rising 50% on optimism over the merger and Royal climbing by 28%" (Willis, 2000, para. 6). To change their public image, the banks spent millions on legal fees, advertising, cross-country travel, as well as "retainers for lobbyists, pollsters, communications experts, consultants, and other assorted spin doctors, whose fees started at an estimated $15,000 a month even before the operating expenses were added on" (Whittington, 1999, p. 198).[80]

---

79 If the Royal Bank and the Bank of Montreal merger had gone through, the new bank would have had $497 billion in total assets. The merger between TD and CIBC "would have resulted in total assets of $463 billion" (Bradshaw, 2018, para. 19). This potential concentration of corporate power brought criticism from both the left and the small business community. The Council of Canadians, for example, waged a successful anti-merger campaign in 1998 called Stop the Mergers (B. Patterson, 2013), and several polls found that "most Canadians thought that bank executives, not customers, stood to gain the most from such deals" (Crary, 1998, para. 12). The president of the Canadian Federation of Independent Business, Catherine Swift, would also come out against the mergers, stating, "We want a better banking system ... But better banks does not have to mean bigger banks and fewer competitive choices" (as cited in Crary, 1998, para. 15). Paul Martin himself stated that "the business community was not in favour [of the mergers], by and large" (as cited in Bradshaw, 2018, para. 14).

80 In his book about the mergers, Whittington (1999) provides more detail as to the cast of characters involved: "As might be expected for the biggest corporate gamble ever undertaken in Canada, the supporting cast was a kind of influence-peddling all-star team. It included some of the most experienced, well-known practitioners of the art: Bill Neville, the grainy Tory operative, one-time aide to former prime minister Joe Clark, and ultimate Ottawa insider, was brought in by TD; Rick Anderson, a former Liberal and public-relations powerhouse, who went over to Reform as a key adviser ... assisted the Royal-BMO group; David MacNaughton, the erstwhile organizer for Paul Martin and a former Hill & Knowlton PR executive, was also in the Royal-BMO line-up; and Bank of Montreal chairman Matthew Barrett relied on Patrick Gossage, the ebullient former press secretary to Pierre Trudeau. The

The unpopularity of the chartered banks at the time of the merger announcement was compounded by the changing nature of global finance. Having already embraced neo-liberalism in the sector in the 1980s through the belief that "more competition and more market participants would enhance the efficiency and competitiveness of the sector" (R.A. Williams, 2004, p. 159), the government's decision to deregulate the sector in 1987 produced opposite results, with the big banks instead using "their superior resources to squeeze out smaller competitors and [behave] in a monopolistic fashion" (p. 159). This basic tension between the policy goals of the federal government and the major players in the financial sector was further challenged by Canada's ongoing participation in several trade agreements. Through CUSFTA, NAFTA, as well as the GATS Accord on Financial Services, "Canadian trade officials gradually committed the Canadian government to remove barriers to foreign banks and non-traditional financial services companies seeking to do business in Canada" (p. 158). As such, the Senate Standing Committee on Banking, Trade and Commerce was focused on "bringing Canada into compliance with the financial institutions' provisions of [the various trade agreements] and on enhancing the ability of foreign banks to fully participate in Canadian markets" (Puri, 2012, p. 175). The chartered banks would use these changes as ammunition in their public quest to get bigger, with the Royal's CEO, John Cleghorn, telling more than one reporter, "'We've got to get them in the water before they land on our beach' ... referring to the threat posed by any incoming US banks" (as cited in Kingston, 1998, p. 14). As noted in many publications, these claims were also used as threats, with the chartered banks arguing that if they were disallowed to merge, they might lose their Canadian identity – or even worse, gain an American one:

> Says Cleghorn: "We had to do it this way, or we will sit here and sometime in the next century we will lose our own identity, we will not be Canadian-based. To be able to compete, we will have to join forces – maybe with a big American institution." (Noble, 1998a, p. 45)[81]

---

on-the-ground work in Ottawa was carried out by the likes of Herb Metcalfe, whose well-connected Capital Hill Group lobbying firm assisted CIBC, and by Larry Mohr, another CIBC operative. The stylish James Lorimer, of Humphreys Public Affairs Group, toiled for the Royal-BMO contingent, as did Rick Kuwayti, Steven Bright, and former MP David Walker" (p. 198).

81 CEO of TD, Charles Baillie, made roughly the same argument about the mergers to Prime Minister Jean Chrétien, claiming that if the mergers were refused it would lessen Canada's standing in international circles, and that Canada might no longer

While the MacKay Task Force continued its investigation, Scotiabank CEO Peter Godsoe dismissed the other banks' arguments as fearmongering: "I do not believe Canadian banks face a crisis or that foreign competition is about to overrun us" (as cited in Whittington, 1999, p. 24). Godsoe was, in fact, correct; by 1998, foreign banks made up only 10 per cent of the total assets of Canada's banking sector. Of this 10 per cent, 7.3 per cent was business credit and 2.8 per cent was credit to small and medium-sized business (Whittington, 1999, pp. 96–7). As Clarkson (2008) notes, foreign financial subsidiaries had actually been losing market share in Canada for some time (p. 307). The president and CEO of Manulife Financial, Dominic D'Alessandro, also publicly questioned the claims of the merger partners, noting that there is no evidence "that in the financial services sector we're falling behind anybody. On the contrary. The opposite is true" (as cited in Newman, 1998, p. 46).[82] D'Alessandro was pointing to the obvious reality: not only had the overseas holdings of the chartered banks been growing year after year, but "the number of players in the domestic financial services industry [had] rapidly declined" as well (R.A. Williams, 2004, p. 165).

The chartered banks did have an argument when considering the size of American financial firms, however. Mergers in 1997 and 1998 had led to the creation of a small group of American super banks:

> Five giant financial-services merger proposals in the early months of 1998 doubled the value of all 1997 transactions. These were deals to join NationsBank and Bank America ($60 billion U.S.), Banc One and First Chicago ($30 billion US), Norwest and Wells Fargo ($34 billion US), Sun Trust Banks and Crestar ($10 billion US), and Citicorp and Travelers Group ($70 billion US). (Whittington, 1999, p. 69)

As noted in *The Banker*, however, this trend was "by no means confined to the US" (Blanden, 1999, para. 5). Similar to the wave of mergers that characterized the age of imperialism at the turn of the twentieth

---

be a G7 country. Chrétien replied that "Canada didn't deserve to be in the G-7 anyway ... Canada was brought in only because the US wanted an ally at the table to even the score with France, which had insisted on including Italy to offset the influence of Britain" (as cited in Whittington, 1999, p. 197).

82 A few sentences earlier, D'Alessandro questions whether Canadian financial institutions truly need to get larger: "To say that Canada, with 30 million people, should have financial institutions the same size as countries 10 times our size is crazy. What are the bank mergers really about? Are we getting value? Are these guys creating jobs? Are they competitive? Is our society all that we want it to be?" (as cited in Newman, 1998, p. 46).

century, this new wave "defied all expectations and catapulted ahead with a fury that left investors, analysts, and average citizens in awe, and sometimes in fear" (Whittington, 1999, p. 70). While worldwide M&A totalled only USD$1.6 trillion by 1997, by mid-1998 merger values had already reached USD$1.3 trillion, "double the total for the same period of 1997 and almost equal to the value of all deals recorded in 1997" (p. 71). As Whittington (1999) notes, this merger activity was so intense that on 18 May 1998, 11 mergers worth roughly USD$17 billion took place. While the chartered banks had grown dramatically over the 1990s when measured by their capital, they were starting to lose ground internationally.[83] In this context, Matthew Barrett, the CEO of the Bank of Montreal, took to the press to argue that "Canadian banks risked ending up like 'the corner hardware store waiting for Home Depot to arrive to put it out of business'" (as cited in Bradshaw, 2018, para. 7).

There were several factors behind the 1990s M&A wave. The most significant was the belief that "bigger is better in the global marketplace" (Whittington, 1999, p. 70). As national markets were increasingly opened to global competition, capitalist logic dictates that only the largest firms should survive. As Strange (1998/2015) notes, "it is the larger enterprises that are less at risk from their competitors" (p. 182). As such, globalization substantially accelerated the pace of economic concentration, a process that has had the subsequent effect of diluting "the national identity of business enterprise" (p. 182). Even the chartered banks admitted that they wanted to merge so that they could "cut expenses, share the high costs of future capital investment and boost their capital for expansion outside the Canadian market" (Bowley, 1999, p. 16).[84] The reality of these global pressures were reflected in the Royal's acquisition of Credit Suisse's Private Banking North America in

---

83 As noted in *Policy Options*, "[Canada] had three banks among the global top 50 banks in 1990, none in 2003. Whereas Royal Bank of Canada was number 38 in 1990, with CIBC number 40 and TD Bank number 49, by 2003 Royal had dropped to 51st, and Scotiabank was in 54th place, with BMO at 62nd. CIBC had become 65th in the global bank size sweepstakes, and TD was 70th. By contrast, foreign competitors, including Citibank, JPMorgan Chase, Bank of America, HSBC and Mizuho have grown exponentially through consolidation" ("Good Policy," 2004, para. 7).

84 This was further described in an article in *Report on Business Magazine*: "On the cost side, takeovers mean big-ticket expenses such as technology get spread over a larger number of clients; Royal Bank spent $376 million on computers last year. And, of course, coming together allows for the ruthless elimination of duplication in areas such as back offices and branch networks. Again, looking back two years, Royal Bank and Bank of Montreal predicted that a merger would shave 10% off their combined annual costs, as they slashed at least 9,200 jobs" (Willis, 2000, para. 9).

1998, just prior to the federal government's decision on domestic mergers. The move was part of a larger strategy by the bank to strengthen its "US wealth management capabilities" (Morrison, 1998a, p. 16) in the context of the merger decision. The Royal also formed a strategic alliance with the now infamous Koch Industries, the second-largest privately held company in the US and leading commodities derivatives trader, "to market their energy-related trading and derivatives products" (Morrison, 1998b, p. 40).

At the same time that the merger wave was happening, the 1997–8 Asian financial crisis was unfolding. As geographer Jim Glassman (2003) argues, the crisis was not really "Asian" in the sense that (1) it was influenced by forces outside the region, mainly "those generating large flows of capital from places such as Japan, Europe, and North America into (especially) Southeast Asia" (p. 31); and (2) because "the crisis was not an Asia-wide phenomenon, striking far more severely in Southeast than Northeast Asia, and having far worse effects in certain Southeast Asian countries than others" (p. 31). Set off by the devaluation of the Thai baht in July 1997, by the summer of 1998 the crisis had gone global, sweeping through Southeast Asia, Russia, and Brazil, among other so-called emerging market economies. Initially joining in with other G7 countries in offering financial relief to impacted countries if IMF funds were insufficient,[85] Canada's Chrétien government would play a significant role in pushing for a reduction to the pace of privatization, capital account liberalization, and greater fiscal flexibility in the IMF adjustment program so that impacted countries could increase spending on "targeted social programmes, development programmes, and public infrastructure" (Kirton, 1999, p. 613). Having developed a "strong scepticism toward unrestricted capital flows" (p. 608) after the 1994 Mexican financial crisis, Martin and Chrétien would also push for stronger supervision of national financial sectors through a new

---

85 "When a support package for a beleaguered Indonesia was assembled, the United States joined Japan as a contributor to a 'second line of defence' of national funds if those of the IMF and other international financial institutions (IFIs) proved insufficient. In November, Canada and its G-7 colleagues formalized the second line of defence and moved to ensure that they all had the legislative authority to contribute to it. In early December, they agreed to a support package for South Korea of USD$35 billion from the IFIs, to be reinforced, if necessary, by a second line of defence, to which Japan committed USD$10 billion, the United States USD$5 billion, each of the European G-7 members USD$1.25 billion, and Canada USD$1 billion" (Kirton, 1999, p. 609).

international supervisory authority, as well as private-sector burden sharing.[86]

At the Cologne G7/G8 Summit of 1999, many of the Canadian government's suggestions were adopted in some form, including the removal of rapid capital account liberalization.[87] The move reflected a growing shift against free capital mobility spurred on by the globalized nature of the crisis. As Soederberg (2002) notes, this emerging countermovement included several "high-profile US policymakers and economic pundits, such as the former Federal Reserve Chairman, Paul Volcker, and the former Chief Economist of the World Bank, Joseph Stiglitz," who began to "question not only the wealth-creating power of free capital mobility but also whether the structure of the global financial system is sufficiently coherent for continued capital accumulation" (p. 177).[88] As such, the G7/G8 now invited these so-called emerging economies "to carry out a 'careful and well sequenced approach to capital account liberalization' and to do so only after they had stronger, better regulated national financial systems in place" (Kirton, 1999, p. 622). To aid in the latter, the G8 would also create new organizations, such as the G20 and the Financial Stability

---

86 The former governor of the Bank of Canada, Gordon Thiessen (1999), would also remark that "the main, and somewhat contentious, issue here is to ensure that private lenders have the incentive to participate in crisis prevention and that they bear their fair share of the financial burden of dealing with crisis" (p. 5).

87 The following was reported in the *Toronto Star* in October of that year: "Canada appears to have headed off a move by the International Monetary Fund that could have given it broad powers on foreign direct investment rules – in effect, a Multilateral Agreement on Investment by the back door. For several years now, IMF managing director Michel Camdessus has been campaigning to broaden the powers of the IMF through an amendment to its Articles of Agreement to promote liberalization of capital flows. Initially, this would have included foreign direct investment. Under the original proposal, the IMF could have forced complete capital account liberalization as a condition of membership, with a phase-in for developing countries. But Finance Minister Paul Martin objected to the inclusion of foreign direct investment. Canada's executive director at the IMF, Tom Bernes, has led the fight within the IMF on this issue, along with the French. Canadian and some IMF officials say Canada won the debate" (Crane, 1999, p. 1). For more on Canada's role, see Baker (2006); Kirton (1999); Rowlands (1999).

88 This list also included Alexandre Lamfalussy, the former general manager of the BIS, who noted that "the exuberant behaviour of lenders and investors from the industrialized world played a major role in spurring on the past several crises in the emerging markets" (as cited in Soederberg, 2002, p. 177). Similarly, by this point the economist, Paul Krugman, had been arguing for several years that "most economists today believe foreign exchange markets behave more like the unstable and irrational asset markets described by Keynes than the efficient markets described by modern finance theory" (as cited on p. 177).

Forum (FSF), to further the incorporation of "systematically important" emerging market countries into the global financial system by means of increased surveillance of their national financial systems and adherence to core country standards and practices.[89]

The G20 includes the G7, EU representatives, the WB and their Development Committee, as well as several "systematically important" emerging economies: Argentina, Australia, Brazil, China, India, Indonesia, Mexico, Saudi Arabia, South Africa, South Korea, and Turkey. While the official goal of the G20 was to help integrate these countries into the global economy by increasing the transparency and surveillance of their financial systems, Soederberg (2002) notes that it also represented a new attempt at core-periphery coercion by coopting an increasing number of countries "into the rules and standards of the core alliance by involving them in official, and thus more tightly integrated relations with the IMF and World Bank" (p. 183). Similarly, Soederberg (2002) sees organizations like the FSF as a new attempt at core-alliance coercion. Made up of G7 members and with a secretariat based at the BIS in Basel, Switzerland, the FSF was meant to bring together "national authorities responsible for financial stability ... sector-specific inter-national groupings of regulators and supervisors ... and committees of central bank experts" (FSB, 2023, para. 4) in order to "strengthen financial systems and increase the stability of international financial markets" (FSB, 2020, para. 2). These organizations were also aided by the Financial Stability Institute (FSI), which was created by the BIS and the BCBS in July 1998 "to provide practical training to financial sector supervisors worldwide" (Borio et al., 2020, p. 218). As a means of reproducing globalizing capital, it is more accurate to state that these

---

89 Historian Adam Tooze (2018) notes the following: "The G20 owed its existence to an initiative launched in December 1999 by then US Treasury secretary Larry Summers and Canadian prime minister Paul Martin. Their vision was to create a forum for global governance that was more representative than the Bretton Woods institutions, such as the IMF and the World Bank, but not so unmanageable as the United Nations. Twenty members seemed like a round number. As the story is told, the list was drawn up by Summers's assistant, Timothy Geithner (then in charge of international affairs at the Treasury), and Caio Koch-Weser, former managing director at the World Bank and then at the German finance ministry. With data for GDP, population and world trade to hand, they went down the list 'ticking some countries and crossing others: Canada in, Spain out, South Africa in, Nigeria and Egypt out, Argentina in, Colombia out, and so on.' Once the list had been approved by the G8, the invitations were then dispatched to the relevant finance ministries and central banks. There was no prior discussion or consultation. The rich countries decided to form a bigger club and asked twelve new members to join. It was global governance made simple." (pp. 161–2).

new organizations helped preserve existing power relations in the global political economy by linking developing economies more closely with the IMF and WB through increased financial surveillance and control. A few months prior to the 1999 Cologne G7/G8 Summit, the former governor of the Bank of Canada, Gordon Thiessen (1999), would make a speech summing up the general position of the state managers in the capitalist core tasked with the ongoing reproduction of globalizing capital:

> It would be all too easy to blame globalization and unhindered, large, cross-border capital flows for the recent financial problems, and to suggest that we retreat behind national borders and place restrictions on the flow of capital. But it would be unwise ... What we must do is find ways to minimize the risks, without surrendering the benefits. (p. 3)

It was in this conjuncture that Martin was making his decision about the mergers. Despite their pre-merger announcement acquisitions, the Royal, along with the other chartered banks, continued to argue that the US's largest banks had a cost advantage that would allow them to deliver financial services more efficiently through new technology.[90] The major problem, however, was that the public's hostility towards the banks was mirrored by the ruling Liberal government. In the years leading up to the merger proposals, for example, former Trade Minister Roy MacLaren told the *Toronto Star*,

> There's nothing that brings the caucus on its feet cheering like a good attack on the banks ... Who are those sons of bitches to be telling us how to run the country when they're hauling in so much money?" (as cited in Ferguson, 1995a, p. D1)

---

90 The chartered banks were, of course, lying. As pointed out in a study by Ernst & Young, cited in the Competition Bureau's findings, Canada's banks were in actual fact well ahead of other countries – especially the United States – when it came to using new information and computer technologies: "A study by the consulting firm Ernst & Young found that the Canadian financial sector, far from being a vulnerable laggard, is out in front when it comes to exploiting new ways to reach customers, including use of the Internet. One finding: 78 per cent of those Canadian financial firms responding to the survey planned to offer services through electronic channels, compared with only 30 per cent of US financial companies. The report, released last week, surveyed more than 100 banks, mutual funds, insurance companies and other financial institutions in 26 countries. In Canada, 15 companies participated. They were found to be spending nine per cent of their total information technology budgets on developing electronic commerce compared with just three per cent overall for their foreign rivals" (Geddes, 1998a, p. 55).

Martin himself shared the sentiment, having already ripped into the chartered banks at a previous meeting about their lack of lending to small businesses, referring to them as 'fuckers'" (as cited in Ferguson, 1995b, p. A1).[91] He also cut them off from the research tax incentive and brought in an additional capital tax that cost the banks (and other large, deposit-taking institutions) a "mostly symbolic" $60 million in 1995, and $40 million in 1996 (Ferguson, 1995a, p. D1). Helen Sinclair, president of the Canadian Bankers Association, argued these were political moves "designed to kick us in the shins and say to the public that we're hitting the big and famous as hard as we're hitting you" (as cited on p. D1). She claimed that the real reason for the tax was because "Martin and others in the cabinet are worried about the impact that their fiscal restraint measures are having on the economy," suggesting instead that more bank credit could offset "the impact of the downsizing of government programs ... Some of the pain of what Martin had to do would be blunted nicely" (p. D1). In other words, flooding the national market with more credit would help offset the pain of neo-liberal austerity measures.

Almost a year later, on 14 September 1998, the MacKay Task Force released its report. As Russell Williams (2004) notes in his case study, the report "made a host of complex recommendations regarding the future of the industry in Canada," its most significant being the "endorsement of the CBA's recommendation that the 'big should not buy big' rule should be abandoned – that, in theory, the big banks should be allowed to merge" (p. 179). The report also suggested further deregulating the financial sector, embracing the idea long promoted by the CBA that the chartered banks be allowed to provide a full range of services, including "automobile leasing, one lucrative sector from which the banks were still excluded" (p. 179). Despite telling *Maclean's* magazine that he "could not afford to be distracted by the particular needs of the banks" and that the report was meant to uncover "what will benefit Canadian consumers" (as cited in Geddes, 1998b, p. 44), MacKay's report was

---

91 This specific dispute would erupt again at a Liberal fundraising dinner at the Westin Hotel in Toronto, with Royal CEO Jim Cleghorn launching "into a public tirade against Industry Minister John Manley, whom he had just met. Cleghorn was furious about the politician's critical remarks about the banks' inadequate lending practices to small businesses" (Kingston, 1998, p. 14). According to Stephen LeDrew, "president of the Liberal Party of Canada in Ontario, who witnessed the scene, 'It wasn't very politic. What no one reported was that Manley gave back as good, if not better, than he got.' After the exchange, they shook hands" (as cited on p. 14). For a comprehensive overview of the merger saga, see Whittington (1999).

nothing other than "a major victory for the banks" (R.A. Williams, 2004, p. 179). Responding to the potential approval of the mergers in a speech to the C.D. Howe Institute in early October, TD CEO Charles A. Baillie made sure to point out that "Canadian ownership of global concerns means, ultimately, keeping more jobs in Canada" (as cited in R.A. Williams, 2004, p. 181).

In early October 1998, the mergers would receive another endorsement from the Senate Standing Committee on Banking, Trade and Commerce (1998), which released its report, *Comparative Study of Financial Regulatory Regimes*. While the report disagreed with the claim that bigger is better in the global marketplace, it did note that in certain countries (the United States, the Netherlands, Switzerland), having a "domestic bank that is a 'world-class player'" (part 2, para. 13) was an important contributor to the success of the transnational firms operating there. The report thus suggested that "having a domestic bank that is a global player may ensure a reliable source of capital on a large scale for multinational companies based in Canada" (part 2, para. 13). Although the two reports did little to sway public opinion about the mergers, they certainly made the merger partners optimistic about their chances.

As one of Martin's advisors shared with *Maclean's* magazine, "MacKay's recommendations are on the technical level ... Now, we need political scrutiny" (as cited in Geddes, 1998b, p. 45). This type of scrutiny would not be as kind to the banks. Despite the favourable ruling on mergers, the MacKay Report also recommended that "merger participants undergo a detailed Public Interest Review Process, which would examine the implications for employment, costs, and benefits to consumers, and other factors" (Whittington, 1999, p. 203). Martin deemed this part of the process mandatory, responding in a public statement "that no major bank merger would be allowed to proceed without public hearings on that specific merger proposal" (as cited in Whittington, 1999, p. 203).

The first of such hearings took the form of the Ianno Report, an investigation into the mergers created by a committee of Liberal backbenchers, chaired by Liberal MP Tony Ianno.[92] Released on 4 November 1998 and signed by 50 Liberal MPs and four senators, the report "bluntly

---

[92] Ianno would step into the spotlight again in 2011 for engaging in trades to inflate the share price of medical device company Covalon Technologies Inc. He was forced to pay $100,000 to the Ontario Securities Commission, banned from trading for five years, and prohibited from serving as a director, officer, or promoter of a publicly traded company for five years (Trichur, 2011).

recommended that the finance minister reject the mergers" (R.A. Williams, 2004, p. 182). The report cited the usual concerns: that the mergers would lead to large-scale job loss, reduced consumer choice, limited small business loans, and, most importantly, the concentration of "too much political and economic power in the hands of the two post-merger conglomerates" (Whittington, 1999, p. 207). Unsurprisingly, the banks did not react favourably to the report. The Royal's vice-president, David Moorecraft, for instance, responded by trotting out the usual claim that rejecting the mergers was a sure-fire road to American domination, stating,

> I would imagine today in Boston and Delaware and San Francisco there are smiling faces and parties being held. Because they will be able to expand and grow in our country. We're not being given the same right to grow and expand and take them on as competitors. (as cited in R.A. Williams, 2004, pp. 182–3)[93]

Similarly, at a speech at the Empire Club in late November entitled, "The Business of Bank Mergers," TD CEO Charles A. Baillie argued that Ianno's oft-repeated claim that "banking is not a right, it's a privilege" (Tedesco, 1998, p. A1) was a belief only held in totalitarian states.[94]

---

93 Such comments were typical of bankers during the merger debate. Noble (1998b) notes: "One banker likened the process of seeing the competition rulings made public to having 'open-heart surgery on The Learning Channel so everybody can watch and say, "Ooh, look at all the blood here."' Another warns that while Canadians might think they hate bankers now, they have not seen anything yet. 'They're going to like it even less when they're stuck dealing with American institutions,' he grumbled, arguing that Martin's decision to postpone merger talks until after the federal government completes its lengthy review of the financial services sector means there will be no Canadian banks left by the time the Liberals get around to letting them join forces. Some are even more apocalyptic. 'So, how do you think you'll like living in Indonesia?' asked one senior banker, suggesting that any country that rejects banks mergers is somehow headed for dictatorship and financial chaos" (pp. 71–2).

94 Baillie's (1998) full response is as follows: "That statement is profoundly revealing – and profoundly wrong ... Laws and regulations exist to set the rules according to which that right can be exercised. Although the unique nature of financial institutions brings unique regulations, this does not detract from the fact that as with any other business, we should be able to conduct our affairs freely – within the law and without interference. This is not a narrow and invalid point. It goes to the very heart of how we conceive ourselves as a democratic, free-market society. Indeed, I believe it is telling to note that the only countries in which operating a business is considered to be a privilege – and not a right – are, in fact, totalitarian" (paras. 55–7).

Other players, such as insurance brokers and automobile dealers, welcomed the report's findings, with the president of the Canadian Automobile Dealers Association, Richard Gauthier, calling it "a victory for Main Street over Bay Street" (as cited in R.A. Williams, 2004, p. 183). Following on the heels of several research surveys indicating the unpopularity of the mergers,[95] the Ianno Report made clear the major political difficulty: "Regardless of what happened in either parliamentary committee or at the OSFI and Competition Bureau, one-third of the government's sitting members had signed this report calling for a rejection of the mergers" (p. 183). Martin responded coyly, telling reporters that it was "an important report; it's good work," and that it was only one of many reports that the "government is going to take into consideration when we make a final decision" (as cited in Whittington, 1999, p. 207). Seeing the writing on the wall, NDP finance critic Lorne Nystrom told the press "the mergers are dead" (p. 207).

Despite a multi-million public media blitz to improve their image,[96] the mergers ultimately "landed like a lead balloon in the court of public opinion" according to Konrad von Finckenstein, commissioner of the Competition Bureau (as cited in Bradshaw, 2018, para. 12). While rejecting the mergers "might seem at odds with the broader neoliberal policy legacy of the Chrétien years, with its support of the North American Free Trade Agreement in 1993 and fiscal retrenchment beginning with the sharp budget cuts of 1995," economists Mario Seccareccia and David Pringle (2020) point out that the ruling Liberals feared significant

---

[95] Whittington (1999) highlights that there were a number of polls suggesting that the mergers were generally unpopular with the Canadian public: "Around the time of the Ianno Report, various interest groups released polls indicating that national opinion for the Insurance Brokers Association of Canada found that 59 percent of respondents opposed or strongly opposed mergers. The Canadian Federation of Independent Business said its small business members opposed the banks deals by a similar majority. And the Council of Canadians reports that two-thirds of Canadians surveyed in a BBM/Comquest poll said bank consolidations would be bad for them personally" (p. 209).

[96] Whittington (1999) here outlines the details of the media campaign: "The new Royal–BMO information blitz, rumoured to cost millions of dollars, included national newspaper ads headlined 'Two Banks. One Pledge.' If allowed to join forces, the two banks promised, they would reduce service charges, hire more customer-service staff, keep rural branches open, set up a new small business bank to make $40 billion available in loans, and increase staffed bank outlets. The two banks' chequing-account customers were sent a six-page blurb amplifying these promises in their bank statements. And a twenty-four-page booklet covering the same information was made available in Royal and Bank of Montreal branches" (p. 210).

"voter backlash at the next election if financial services declined as a result of the mergers" (p. 328). As such, Martin invited Royal CEO John Cleghorn to his Montreal home on 29 November 1998 to inform him that while he had yet to make up his mind (reports from OSFI and the Competition Bureau were still to be released), they should prepare for bad news. When asked directly whether the mergers were going to be allowed to proceed, Martin simply said, "No." When pushed by Cleghorn to clarify, "Martin repeated his first answer. 'No'" (Noble, 1998b, p. 70). According to government officials, Cleghorn lost it: "His face grew red and he pounded the table, while giving the minister an earful" (p. 71).

The finance minister's private decision was solidified by the results of the reports by OSFI and the Competition Bureau, which were both released in early December. The OSFI report combined an analysis of the involved bank's current financial situation, risk profile, and the likely effects of the mergers. Much like the MacKay Report, the OSFI investigation found no "prudential reasons why the finance minister should not consider the mergers" (R.A. Williams, 2004, p. 187). It did note, however, that if one of the newly created super banks ran into trouble, it would likely have to involve a buyout from a large, non-Canadian bank, an issue that might cause political problems. The Competition Bureau, in contrast, had more stringent requirements; rather than looking at risk profiles or impacts, it had attempted to determine whether the mergers would reduce competition for consumers:

> If either of the two merged banks would command more than 35 per cent of a certain local market for a financial service, such as credit cards in one city or home mortgages in another, the bureau's guidelines assume that competition might be seriously threatened. It would also consider a situation in which any four banks have more than 65 per cent of a particular market to be too much concentration. (Geddes, 1998a, p. 55)

The Bureau's findings were unsurprising to many, noting that, if allowed to merge, there would be a "substantial" reduction of competition, which would lead to "higher prices and lower levels of service and choice for several key banking services in Canada" (von Finckenstein, 1998, para. 2). It also noted that smaller banks and credit unions in Canada would likely be unable to compete with the two new super banks without merging with other banks. The Bureau thus confirmed the major fear of the critics: that "rather than ending up with two superbanks and a host of smaller traditional and new competitors, Canada might end up with only two big banks" (R.A. Williams, 2004, p. 189).

On 14 December 1998, at a press conference in Ottawa, Martin finally delivered the news that the chartered banks had been dreading: "I am announcing today that the bank mergers will not be allowed to proceed because they are not in the best interests of Canadians" (as cited in Whittington, 1999, p. 228). Martin was particularly concerned with the chartered banks' rationale for the mergers. He pointed out that the global competitors that the chartered banks kept warning everyone about were not actually banks at all but "the big investment operations such as Goldman Sachs and Merrill Lynch, and 'these [mergers] weren't going to make them a Goldman Sachs or a Merrill Lynch'" (as cited in Whittington, 1999, p. 237). With a personal net worth of roughly $225 million (Radia, 2013), Martin was no stranger to this world, remarking, "I've spent twenty-five years in business, and I've dealt with all of these firms all around the world, and I know damn well what the hell a global financial institution does and [it's not what the Canadian banks were talking about]" (as cited in Whittington, 1999, p. 237).

Celebrated by critics and panned by bankers,[97] Martin's decision was not so much a firm "no," however, but rather, as the Canadian Centre for Policy Alternatives (CCPA) pointed out, an invitation to "regroup, re-grease their public relations machinery and then make him an offer he can't refuse" (as cited in R.A. Williams, 2004, p. 192). Despite rejecting these specific mergers, Martin was still seen as being relatively "merger friendly" (Sinclair, 2003, p. B3), and within two years, the Liberals "not only passed new legislation that created a specific process for banks when pursuing mergers, but also approved the largest financial services merger in Canada to date – the Toronto Dominion/Canada

---

[97] The Council of Canadians, for example, called the rejection "welcome – if overdue – news to the vast majority of Canadians" (as cited in Whittington, 1999, p. 235). Similarly, Catherine Swift, the president of the Canadian Federation of Independent Business, called the rejection "a defeat for the banks but a victory for small business" (as cited in R.A. Williams, 2004, p. 191). The banks, meanwhile, were more sober with their response, for fear of alienating Martin further. In a joint statement, the CEOs of the Royal and the Bank of Montreal held that "history will judge if Mr. Martin has made the right decision for Canada" (as cited in Whittington, 1999, p. 231). A leaked memo by Brian Steck, CEO of Nesbitt Burns and vice-chairman of BMO, was not so kind, however: "You will excuse me for offering the views of my friends on Wall Street. They wish to applaud our government for its 'internationally surprising stand' and giving them a delightful Christmas present. To Tony Ianno, they wish to collectively thank him for his naiveté and complete lack of comprehension" (as cited in Whittington, 1999, p. 234).

Trust merger" (R.A. Williams, 2004, p. 156).[98] Put into place in 2001 via Bill C-8 (*An Act to Establish the Financial Consumer Agency of Canada, and to Amend Certain Acts in Relation to Financial Institutions*), the merger process recognized the legal right of the chartered banks to merge, but required that any merger proposal "be evaluated by the OSFI, the Competition [Bureau], *and by Parliament*" (Williams, 2004, p. 200).[99] Bill C-8 also created the Financial Consumer Agency of Canada (FCAC), which "effectively removed from OSFI's mandate the responsibility for overseeing consumer protection" (OSFI, n.d., para. 29).[100] Despite these new hurdles, some banking analysts still argued that "mergers are going to happen. The only question is when" (Warn, 2000, p. 33). Others were more nuanced in their forecasts. In an interview, Dominic D'Allesandro, president of Manulife Financial, predicted that "the thrust of the banking system into related activities such as insurance is going to be more pronounced as a result of their frustration at not being allowed to merge" (as cited in Whittington, 1999, pp. 246–7). From the Royal's point of view, incoming CEO Gordon Nixon announced that

---

98 Despite the passing of the TD/Canada Trust merger, Liberal Finance Minister John Manley – Martin's replacement – rejected two other proposals, including Manulife Financial's attempt to take over CIBC, and Scotiabank's attempt to take over BMO. See R.A. Williams (2004, pp. 200–4) for more details.

99 Under the terms of Bill C-8, "the three criteria on which the government based its rejection of the 1998 bank merger proposals would continue to apply: merger proposals would have to demonstrate that they would not unduly concentrate economic power, significantly reduce competition, or restrict flexibility to reduce prudential concerns. The Minister could allow the proposed merger to proceed subject to certain conditions. Should the Minister find the concerns too great to be remedied, the proposal would be rejected. The Competition Bureau and OSFI would negotiate competition and prudential remedies with the parties. These two agencies would work with the Department of Finance to co-ordinate an overall set of prudential, competition and other public-interest remedies. It would then be left to the merging parties to decide whether they wished to proceed in light of the conditions imposed upon the transaction. If they decided to proceed, final approval of the merger would be sought from the Minister" (Haggart et al., 2001, pp. 28–9).

100 In taking over the consumer-protection related aspects of banking, FCAC was meant to serve "as a consumer advocate and public interest watchdog by directly negotiating with banks to ensure the interests of consumers are considered in any strategic changes or branch closures, and requires banks with equity over $1 billion to publish annual statements describing their contribution to the Canadian economy and society" (Puri, 2012, p. 177). With the addition of FCAC, the regulatory responsibilities of each institution are as follows: "prudential supervision (OSFI), lender of last resort (Bank of Canada), deposit insurance (CDIC), and consumer protection (FCAC)" (Seccareccia & Pringle, 2020, p. 326, n. 3).

the bank was "preparing for all eventualities" (as cited in R.A. Williams, 2004, p. 201).

Although they lost the merger battle, this period was not entirely absent of legislative gains for the chartered banks. Despite the new rules about mergers and the creation of a new consumer protection agency (FCAC), Bill C-8 massively liberalized the Canadian banking industry by moving the widely held ownership cap from 10 to 20 per cent for voting shares and to 30 per cent for non-voting shares of domestic banks and foreign bank subsidiaries. While the move was welcomed by foreign governments and investors frustrated by the federal government's long-standing rule that the chartered banks be widely held,[101] "the impetus behind it lay in the Canadian banking industry's desire to raise more capital to boost their international competitiveness" (Clarkson, 2008, p. 308). In 1999, the federal government had allowed foreign-owned banks to establish full-service branches, rather than forcing them to create subsidiaries. As a result, "between 1997 and 2004, foreign bank operations slowly increased their market share in the Canadian deposit-taking industry" (Hinchley, 2006, para. 4), with the value of services produced by foreign banking subsidiaries operating in Canada rising from 5.7 per cent in 1997 to 7.9 per cent in 2004. Where previously foreign investors were barred from holding more than 25 per cent of the share issue of federally regulated financial institutions, "successive international trade agreements have led to the elimination of this restriction" (Haggart et al., 2001, p. 3).

As the legislative summary of Bill C-8 makes clear, the legislation was meant to enable "domestically based financial institutions to become large enough to compete internationally" (Haggart et al., 2001, p. 26). In other words, despite the rejection of the mergers, the government recognized that the chartered banks would have to get much larger if they wanted to compete with the new era of global super banks. An article in the *Globe and Mail* put the matter bluntly:

> As the [merger] deal died, so did Royal's chances of becoming a global financial institution ... Not so many years ago, Royal was one of the world's biggest banks; so big, in fact, that it could have bought any of

---

101 Canada is currently the only country in the OECD that does not allow cross-border branching. So far, Canada has been able to hold on to the widely held rule by virtue of its non-discriminatory wording in respect to nationality, as no one person (Canadian or foreign) may own more than 20 per cent. It is unclear how long this rule will last given the extent to which other countries have criticized it as an indirect form of protectionism.

the top names in American banking, including Citibank. Now, in relative terms, it is a bit player, a global non-entity. Today, Royal barely makes the list of the top 50 banks. According to a *Financial Times of London* survey of the biggest companies by market value, it ranked 251st last year. (Reguly, 2001, para. 5)

With trade agreements creating larger domestic markets, the chartered banks were increasingly unable to hide behind the series of protective walls built up during the national epoch. With the merger deal dead, the Royal's only choice was to try and draw in foreign capital and to continue expanding abroad – and expand it did. As a report from Statistics Canada records, "between 1997 and 2004, the total real value of services produced by the domestic banks rose at an annual average rate of 1.8% in Canada. Worldwide, however, the gain was more than double that pace, 4.8%" (Hinchley, 2006, para. 8). With large Canadian-based firms increasingly choosing to list on the New York Stock Exchange instead of the Canadian exchanges, the federal government also decided to reorganize Canada's financial markets in 1999, making the Toronto Stock Exchange for senior securities, the Montreal Exchange for exchange-traded derivative products, and the merged Alberta and Vancouver Stock Exchange taking responsibility for all junior securities (Coleman & Porter, 2003, p. 252).

As Stephen Clarkson (2008) points out, the concessions included in Bill C-8 were the result of lobbying from the CBA, whose membership includes banks from all over the world, with lobbying efforts "based on individual issues, not on the geographical position of their headquarters" (p. 320).[102] With the CBA responsible for dealing with national issues relating to banking (regardless of the origin of the banks involved), influence over global issues has shifted in recent years to the IIF, of which the Royal is a member along with the other chartered banks. As Heather McKeen-Edwards and Tony Porter (2013) note, for instance, "the IIF submitted the largest number of pages, three reports totalling 169 pages" (p. 175, n. 2), to the BCBS as part of the second consultative process of the new Basel Capital Accord (Basel II) in 2001.[103] From its founding in 1983, the IIF has since "become the most important private-sector interlocutor for public authorities, especially those

---

102 As Clarkson (2008) further remarks, "foreign banks from a wide variety of countries constitute the Foreign Bank Executive Committee, in which British HSBC, Canada's largest foreign bank subsidiary, is the most influential member" (p. 321).
103 On the making of Basel II, see Claessens et al. (2008); King & Sinclair (2003); Tsingou (2007); Underhill et al. (2010).

in the Basel Committee and the IMF" (p. 39). In fact, the BCBS directly asked the IIF to organize private-sector input "due to its specific expertise as a representative of the most 'sophisticated' internationally active banks" (Blom, 2019, p. 50). The IIF helped the BCBS, for example, to create "quantitative studies that were used as prototypes of the final accord and it facilitated the sharing of information about internal bank risk models by acting as a trusted guardian of the proprietary information that they involved" (p. 39).

All this does not necessarily mean that the BCBS was captured by the IIF.[104] A study by Young (2012), for instance, demonstrates that Basel II was much stricter than if it had simply reflected the preferences of the banking industry. Rather, as McKeen-Edwards and Porter (2013) point out, the outcome of Basel II was the result of "a flow of intense interactions between regulators, competing models, and empirical data produced by the actual ongoing experiences of banks with defaults and losses" (p. 39). In any case, the existing regulations in Canada and the standard practices of the chartered banks were already similar to the requirements of Basel II, which was, as Puri (2012) points out, "primarily a shift in the way banks reported their assets and a formalization of their internal risk management protocols" (p. 178).[105] The point remains, however, that as capital continues to globalize, the character of these associations has shifted, with the CBA now lobbying on behalf of globalizing banks operating in Canada (a category that includes the chartered banks), and the IIF lobbying for globalizing banks dealing with global regulatory regimes. As Blom (2019) suggests, this role "was as much a consequence of demand from the Basel Committee for a counterpart with a compatible outlook on global financial regulation as of the preferences of its membership" (p. 50).

Despite the influence of such associations on banking in Canada, the requirement that any merger proposal be evaluated by Parliament has since "braked any rekindled movement towards disrupting the

---

104 For studies reflecting this view, see Baker (2006); Blom (2019); Claessens et al. (2008); Lall (2012); Underhill et al. (2010).

105 As Puri (2012) further notes, Canada's regulations and standard banking practices were already similar to Basel II because "Canadian banks have been required, since the 1980s, to meet individually established leverage ratios based on their total, non-risk weighted assets to Tier I and Tier II capital reserves. The continued use of a simple leverage ratio combined with OSFI's requirement that Tier I capital be composed of 75 per cent common equity and retained earnings ensures that the capital reserves of Canadian banks are able to serve their intended purpose of providing liquid, loss bearing capital, which can effectively absorb financial shocks" (p. 179).

structure of the banking industry" (Seccareccia & Pringle, 2020, p. 328), with the chartered banks instead attempting "to reduce 'political interference' in the sector" (R.A. Williams, 2006, p. 37). As noted in the *Globe and Mail*, "today, there is broad agreement that a merger between any of Canada's largest banks is still verboten, no matter the government of the day, except in a crisis in which a major Canadian bank would need rescuing" (Bradshaw, 2018, para. 31).[106] Stephen Harris (2004) points out the following, however:

> Historically, policy change in finance, globally and in Canada, is such that finance will get what it wants ... This occurs only after finance takes steps to work around the obstacles established by the state when it responds to the struggle of interests. (p. 180)

To put this a different way, when economic actors come up against property relations that thwart their activities, they attempt to overturn or sidestep them – typically both simultaneously. This is compounded by the reality of ongoing financial globalization; even the Competition Policy Review Panel (2008) notes that due to the merger rejection, "reaching the scale of the world's largest institutions will depend on how well Canadian banks fare in the contest to acquire foreign banks" (p. 51). It is thus not surprising to find that after being denied the right to merge, the chartered banks began to pursue strategies of exit "in reaction to the internationalization of finance and the domestic obstacles to pursuing global forms of financial organization" (S.L. Harris, 2004, p. 180). For its part, the Royal immediately cut "6,000 full-time jobs, or more than 10 per cent of the workforce" (Bowley, 1999, p. 16) and began looking outside Canada for acquisition targets.

This meant moving deeper into the United States, the Royal's largest domestic market due to NAFTA. As Clarkson (2008) notes, the American market was especially attractive due to its own version of deregulation, which enabled the chartered banks to acquire several "niche service providers and large subregional banks" (p. 308). Beginning in 1998, the Royal purchased the Atlanta-based Internet-only bank, Security First Network Bank, and the New York discount brokerage firm Bull & Bear Group Inc. to compete with TD subsidiaries "Green Line

---

[106] The work of business scholars Meredith and Darroch (2017) reflects the changing discourse used to support mergers today: "not because bigger is better but ... because allowing the weakest to play on carries the risk of hobbling the entire system" (p. 178).

and Waterhouse Investor Services, as well as giant Charles Schwab & Co Inc. of San Francisco" (Noble, 1998b, p. 72). These initial acquisitions were followed by a phased strategy that mirrored the Royal's early growth in Canada: get an initial foothold through the acquisition of smaller firms and then, in the Royal's own words, "build scale and achieve cost synergies" (Royal Bank of Canada, 2001a, p. 9). To this effect, between 2000 and 2001, the Royal purchased the Chicago-based mortgage originator, Prism Financial Corporation, for USD$115 million; South Carolina-based Liberty Life Insurance Company and Liberty Insurance Services Corporation for USD$650 million; North Carolina-based Centura Bank for USD$2.2 billion; the Minneapolis-based investment bank, Dain Rauscher Corporation, for USD$1.4 billion; and Boston-based retail brokerage firm Tucker Anthony Sutro Corporation for USD$625 million. The merging of the latter two made the Royal the ninth-largest US retail brokerage firm, and overall, these acquisitions gave the Royal 2 million additional clients (compared to a client base of 10 million in Canada), highlighting "the substantial size and potential of the US market" (p. 9). Reflecting the larger transformation of banking into finance, the Royal's 2001 *Annual Report* also made clear that the bank now positioned itself as "a diversified financial services company" that saw "value in remaining diversified as we grow beyond our borders" (p. 9). By focusing "on building an integrated, broad-based financial services company in the US, expanding via acquisitions, alliances and organic growth" (Royal Bank of Canada, 2000, p. 6), the Royal's international revenues and earnings continued to grow, with "16 per cent of revenues and 30 per cent of net income originated outside Canada" (p. 6) by the year 2000.

To reflect these changing territorial circumstances, the Royal finally decided to remove all vestiges of its colonial heritage, changing the bank's name to a tech-suited initialism, RBC, and removing the crown on top of the globe – a long-standing nod to the British Empire – from its logo.[107] As the bank noted in its own press release, the move symbolized "the evolution that the organization has undergone in recent years, expanding beyond its Canadian base into the United States and other international markets" (Royal Bank of Canada, 2001b, para. 1). The bank certainly wasn't lying. By the early 2000s, RBC was "the largest global private banking business among the Canadian banks" (Royal Bank of Canada, 2000, p. 15), with a global network that included "724

---

107 The change can be seen on RBC's website: https://www.rbc.com/en/about-us/history/celebrating-our-history.

offices in more than 30 countries" (Royal Bank of Canada, 2001a, p. i). That said, RBC was also slipping relative to other globalizing firms, sitting at only 303 on the *Fortune* Global 500 index (McKenna, 2004). China had also recently "nudged out Canada for sixth spot among countries with the largest number of Global 500 companies" (para. 15).

The growing globalization of RBC's operations was the result of the competitive realities of financial globalization: "with global players operating in Canada and the financial borders fading" (Royal Bank of Canada, 2001a, p. 8), the bank was forced to attempt to become, in its own words, "a leading North American financial services organization, pre-eminent in Canada, with global niche businesses in those areas where we have a competitive advantage" (p. 4). To this end, RBC acquired the Ernst & Young Trust Company (Jersey) Limited in the Channel Islands in 2000,[108] integrating it into its Global Private Banking business, and Perpetual Fund Services (the custody, investment administration, and unit registry business of Perpetual Trustees Australia Limited) in 2001, allowing RBC to expand its securities offerings in Australia and the Asia–Pacific region. RBC also continued to expand its Global Equity Derivatives business in London, "delivering to the world a growing array of structured equity products" (Royal Bank of Canada, 2001a, p. 10), as well as create RBC Dexia Investor Services with Banque Interantionale Luxembourg S.A., holding "$1.9 trillion in client assets under administration" (Royal Bank of Canada, 2006, p. 11).[109] The bank's most notable purchase over this period, however, was the acquisition of Royal Bank of Trinidad and Tobago Financial Group (RBTT). Started in 1902 by the Union Bank of Halifax and acquired by the Royal in 1910, by 1987, the Royal had divested itself from its remaining shares in RBTT as part of its earlier pullout from the Caribbean. The reacquisition of RBTT not only marked the return of RBC to Trinidad and Tobago after 20 years, but, more importantly, created "one of the most expansive banking networks in the Caribbean with a presence in 18 countries and territories across the region" (Royal Bank of Canada, 2007, p. 13). RBC was clear to note that the acquisition of RBTT "significantly advances us towards our objective to grow outside Canada" (p. 13).

Alongside RBC's global excursions, growth and expansion also continued in the continental market. In 2007, for instance, RBC purchased

---

108 Jersey, the largest of the Channel Islands, is considered a tax haven since it has no inheritance, wealth, corporate, or capital gains taxes (States of Jersey, n.d.). Financial services companies, however, pay a 10 per cent tax rate.
109 RBC would later buy the other 50 per cent stake of RBC Dexia for CAD$1.1 billion (Royal Bank of Canada, 2012).

J.B. Hanauer, a privately held financial services firm specializing in "retail fixed income and wealth management services" (IE Staff, 2007, para. 3). Holding USD$10 billion in assets, the purchase helped RBC expand its presence in New Jersey, Pennsylvania, and Florida. RBC also acquired the Alabama National BanCorporation (ANB) in 2008 for USD$1.6 billion, further expanding its retail operations in the Southern US by giving it "45 locations in Alabama, 45 locations in Florida, and 13 locations in Georgia" (Jarvis, 2008, para. 5). As RBC put it in its 2007 *Annual Report*, "the competition for capital is global and [our customers'] investment decisions reflect whether they have confidence in our ability to deliver returns that are superior to others" (Royal Bank of Canada, 2007, p. 4). With its earlier domestic merger hopes dashed, and the pressure to globalize continuing apace, it is not a surprise to find the bank referring to itself in the period leading up to the 2008 financial crisis "as a complex, global financial services company" (p. 5) rather than just a bank.

The 2008 Financial Crisis

RBC's obsession with becoming globally competitive did not come from simple geographic pressures alone, but also from sectoral pressures relating to the new rights gained by financial institutions in the 1980s. While these new rights enabled the chartered banks to transform into huge financial service conglomerates, they fundamentally "changed the structure of the financial sector and greatly extended the range of its products" (Dow & Dow, 2014, p. 115). As Lapavitsas (2013a) notes, what we commonly refer to as financialization more accurately refers to the way in which these new rights shifted the entire corporate sector towards open profit-making activities on financial markets.[110] With the growth of electronic markets in the 1980s, large non-financial corporations began to retain their own funds to engage in financial trading, thereby reducing their dependency on banks for loans, a process referred to as disintermediation.[111] In Canada, for instance, between

---

110 For an in-depth look at the qualitative nature of this shift, see Coleman and Porter (2003); Henwood (1998); Marazzi (2010); Porter (2005); Strange (1998/2015).
111 In a research paper written by the Task Force on the Future of Canadian Financial Services Sector (1998), this shift is highlighted: "Global forces are changing the traditional relationship banks have had with their customers. With new competitors constantly striving to deliver higher value products in new and different ways, customers have an increasing number of options for where and how to invest their money. More and more often, banks are being left out of the loop" (p. 30).

1988 and 1998, the level of corporate debt held as a proportion of the chartered banks' loans went from 44 per cent to 34 per cent (Kalman-Lamb, 2017, p. 303). Having lost their primary source of revenue, all of the world's largest banks pivoted from traditional borrowing and lending to "transacting in open financial markets with the aim of making profits through financial trading" (Lapavitsas, 2013a, p. 794). By 1999, *The Banker* would remark that the

> trend has now reached epidemic proportions. Commercial banks have moved into the securities business and capital markets. They have forayed – with more or less success, usually the latter – into investment banking. And in a number of countries ... the barriers between banking and the insurance business have been extensively broken down. (Blanden, 1999, para. 17)

The result was an immense rise in financial speculation. In 2000, for instance, worldwide trade in goods and services was less than USD$10 trillion for the entire year, whereas "*daily* movements in currency speculation stood at $3.5 trillion, so that in just a few days more currency circulated as speculation than the international circulation of goods and services in an entire year" (W.I. Robinson, 2014, p. 145). As William Robinson (2014) notes, this transformation has blurred the "boundaries between industrial, commercial, and money capital" (p. 22) by drawing non-financial corporations into the financial sector. In Canada, these changes are reflected in the shift towards corporate financing by pension funds belonging to groups such as the Ontario Municipal Workers and the Ontario Teachers' Federation (OTF), as well as the decision by retailers such as Loblaws, Walmart, and Canadian Tire to offer their own financial services (Darroch & McMillan, 2007). Becoming globally competitive for RBC in this context was thus no mere matter of being able to compete against rival banks, but to do so in an environment in which the dominant form of wealth was made by trading on electronic markets by any entity who had the financial means to do so.

Like many firms, RBCs efforts at growth were momentarily stalled in 2007 with the beginnings of what would later become known as the 2008 financial crisis. The crisis was, without question, the result of the new rights granted to banks and other financial institutions in the 1980s, and, as economists Dow and Dow (2014) note, it was "the power exercised by the banks over governments" (p. 115) that eventually forced the transformation of these rights through deregulation, enabling the creation of huge financial services conglomerates that continue to dominate the global economy.[112] In the 20 years leading up to the crisis, the financial sector had become the world's largest industry: "bigger than oil, autos, and consumer electronics combined. The largest financial institutions had a market capitalization well in excess of $200 billion, more than 25 per cent of Canada's annual GNP" (Darroch & McMillan, 2007, p. 5). As part of the same process, the long-standing relationship between borrowers and lenders had become inverted. Seccareccia and Pringle (2020) note: "Traditionally, Canadian households had been net savers in the aggregate, thereby building up financial assets within the bank-dominated financial system, while Canadian businesses generally were net borrowers whose debt normally went towards financing their capital expenditures" (pp. 320–1). From the 1990s onwards, however, this relationship had reversed, "with households becoming net borrowers and firms becoming net lenders" (p. 321). The new rights gained by the banks, as well as the increasing use of information technology, enabled them to engage in a particular type of commoditization unique to finance, in which loans were immediately treated as assets to be sold on global financial markets "with no intention of establishing a relationship with the borrower" (S.L. Harris, 2010, p. 70).[113]

This shift from relationship banking to transactional banking gave rise to further innovations that facilitated the transformation of high-yielding, highly risky assets like mortgage loans and credit card receivables into complex, above-average yielding financial products.[114] As Kalman-Lamb (2017) notes, from 2001 to 2010, a number of different programs established by the Canada Mortgage and Housing Corporation

---

112 Through an analysis of transnational ownership networks, a group of computer scientists have discovered that "nearly 4/10 of the control over the economic value of TNCs in the world is held, via a complicated web of ownership relations, by a group of 147 TNCs in the core, which has almost full control over itself. The top holders within this core can thus be thought of as an economic 'super-entity' in the global network of corporations. A relevant additional fact at this point is that 3/4 of the core are financial intermediaries" (Vitali et al., 2011, p. 4).

113 It is important to note the distinction between commodification and commoditization. *Commodification* is a Marxist term that ultimately refers to the process whereby things become commodities. *Commoditization*, on the other hand, refers more specifically to the process whereby goods that may have previously been distinguishable in terms of their attributes (or, in the case of banking, relationships) are transformed into mere commodities, with the only distinguishable feature being their price. For more on this recent shift in financial terminology, see Rushkoff (2005).

114 See Tooze (2018) and Fligstein (2021) for more details on the rise of asset-backed securities.

(CMHC)[115] created an extremely profitable revenue stream for financial institutions by enabling the creation of government-insured mortgage-backed securities,

> which increased from just $35 billion in 2002 during the first year of the [Canada Mortgage Bonds] programme to an average of $178 billion from 2008 to 2010. By the end of 2010, Canadian chartered banks held $506 billion in residential mortgages, almost doubling their $281 billion in commercial debt. (p. 306)

Sold mainly to institutional investors like pension funds, these products were generally hard to decipher, leaving regulators, risk committees, rating agencies, and more importantly, the investors themselves, scratching their heads as to how they worked. Furthermore, global banks increasingly made their loans based on "credit-scoring rather than the exercise of judgement and used quantitative models to represent their risk profile (as required by the Basel capital adequacy rules)" (Dow & Dow, 2014, pp. 115–16). In the end, it became apparent that the world's banks had essentially created much of the value of these assets themselves. In Canada, for instance, the total size of the market for these products "was about $116 billion before the global financial collapse and the chartered banks had originated some 75 percent of the total" (S.L. Harris, 2010, p. 71). Put simply, Canada's chartered banks, like the rest of the world's financial institutions, had figured out how to make money from nothing.

The crisis as it occurred in Canada, however, was slightly different than how things unfolded in the United States, despite being linked. Whereas the American crisis was more about disintermediated financing in subprime markets, Canada's crisis specifically had to do with asset-backed commercial paper (ABCP).[116] As Mary Brown (2022)

---

115 As Kalman-Lamb (2017) notes, these are the "Canada Mortgage Bonds program in 2001, and the Insured Mortgage Purchase Program (IMPP) in 2008, which massively expanded the 1987 National Housing Act-Mortgage Backed Securities (NHA-MBS) programme" (p. 303). For more on the securitization of the Canadian housing market, see Walks (2014, 2016); Walks & Clifford (2015).

116 For an overview of the Canadian ABCP crisis, see Halpern et al. (2016). It is also important to point out that prior to the 2008 financial crisis, Canada was moving in a similar direction to the United States in respect to subprime mortgages. Meredith and Darroch (2017) note the following: "Going back to 2003, CMHC agreed to allow home buyers to borrow their minimum 5 per cent down payment and 1.5 per cent closing costs. This concession meant that, in practice, buyers needed no down-payment at all, and that the government would insure 95 per cent of any new

explains, ABCP "is like traditional commercial paper, in that it is issued with maturities of one year or less (typically less than 270 days) and is highly rated" (para. 4). Whereas commercial paper is typically "used as short-term vehicles for investing cash" (para. 4), ABCP differs in that "instead of being an unsecured promissory note representing an obligation of the issuing company, ABCP is backed by securities. Therefore, the perceived quality of the ABCP depends on the underlying securities" (para. 5).

The first ABCP was issued in 1997 by CIBC through the RAC Trust, "a conduit created by the bank to securitize receivables (i.e., loan payments) on behalf of different companies" (Halpern et al., 2016, p. 7). When RAC Trust was established in 1997, "the total amount of ABCP issued in Canada stood at $10 billion" (p. 7). By August 2007, when the market for ABCP collapsed after investors discovered that the "alleged safe product was, in fact, quite risky since some of the paper was tied to US mortgage-backed securities" (Roberge, 2013, p. 143), the total value of Canadian-issued ABCP "had grown to $115 billion" (Halpern et al., 2016, p. 7). As the market ground to a halt, many of Canada's largest financial institutions were left holding billions in ABCP.[117] As Puri (2012) notes, the ABCP crisis "revealed that Canada's financial markets are not immune from the risk of catastrophic failure" (p. 156). More important, perhaps, is that it made clear that the state would use public funds to support banks and other financial institutions when the house of cards finally came crashing down. Despite the common refrain from the former minister of finance, Jim Flaherty, that Canada has one of "the most sound banking systems in the world" (as cited in D. Macdonald,

---

mortgage. The agency's next move, in 2006, was to allow a zero down payment and to extend amortization periods from a maximum of twenty-five years to as much as forty years. The result of these changes was that more than a third of mortgages issued in 2006 and 2007 had amortization periods longer than twenty-five years and high loan-to-value ratios. By 2008, these riskier mortgages made up 9 per cent of the total mortgage market" (p. 62). As a result of the financial crisis, "Canada's mortgage insurance rules looked pretty much the same by 2012 as they had before 2004. The maximum amortization had reverted to twenty-five years, and the government had withdrawn insurance backing on lines of credit secured by homes and had raised the maximum refinancing to 80 per cent of the value of the home. The authorities also capped the CMHCs outstanding insurance commitments at $600 billion, restricted banks' ability to buy bulk insurance to reduce capital requirements, and curtailed the use of government-backed insurance for securities sold to the private sector" (p. 63).

117 When the ABCP market froze, the Caisse de dépôt et placement du Québec, for instance, held almost $13 billion worth of ABCP notes (Roberge, 2013).

2012, p. 5), or that the Canadian government "has not had to put any taxpayers' money into our financial system" (p. 8), in actual fact, the federal government started making provisions to buy insured mortgage pools from the chartered banks as early as 2008.[118] Referred to as a liquidity support instead of a bailout,[119] the financing extended to the banks was immense, with both the chartered banks as well as a couple non-Canadian banks taking advantage.[120] Political economist Heather Whiteside (2012) noted the following:

> In Canada, Budget 2009 outlined the decision to spend up to $125 billion CAD to buy up shaky mortgages from the country's largest banks (via the Canada Mortgage and Housing Corporation [CMHC]), and to establish a $200 CAD billion fund, called the Emergency Financing Framework, to support these banks should they need to borrow money. (p. 59)

---

118 One can find numerous accolades for Canada's handling of the financial crisis, whether from the IMF, the World Economic Forum (WEF), President Obama, or newspapers with headlines reading, "What Toronto can teach New York and London" (Freeland, 2010). Stephanie Flanders, the BBC's economics editor, similarly gave Canada the award for "Best Prepared Country Going into the Crisis" (see Gunter, 2009, p. A14). See T. Porter (2010) for more examples. Walks (2014) provides a more accurate analysis: "While Canada's mortgage markets might appear robust in comparison with international peers, their true character is disguised by particular institutional features of the Canadian system, which has merely been more successful than others in encouraging releveraging, in socializing private debt, and attracting new flows of investment into the housing market. Indeed Canada's experience is illuminating, and buttresses the case for both a systemic interpretation of the global credit crisis and a nuanced understanding of its uneven articulation across national contexts. The primary driver is the unprecedented availability of credit, generated and channeled by financial 'innovations,' and like other de-industrializing nations in the developed world, it has been expressed through the inflation of residential housing assets, rapidly growing household indebtedness, and the vulnerability of its financial institutions (pp. 277–8).
119 Interpretations of this spending seem to hinge on what word is used. The federal government and CBA argue against the CCPA's interpretation of the spending as a bailout, which they claim is about saving failing banks, rather than simply extending financing: "Funding measures were put in place to ensure credit was available to lend to business and consumers to help the economy through the recession, not because the banks were in financial difficulty" (Canadian Press, 2012, para. 7).
120 As D. Macdonald (2012) notes, "Despite having access to the Canadian programs and being heavy users of the US Fed programs, most of the Canadian subsidiaries of [foreign] banks ... did not access the Bank of Canada support programs. In almost all cases, the Canadian dollar repurchase agreements liability line on the balance sheet was zero, the telltale sign of accessing the Bank of Canada programs. The only two banks that had non-zero values for their Canadian repurchase agreements and saw spikes during the Bank of Canada loan program were ING and HSBC" (p. 15).

Regardless of whether we call it liquidity support or a bailout, the chartered banks received funds from the federal government that went up to $114 billion in March 2009 during the peak support period: "to put that into perspective, that would have made up 7% of the Canadian economy in 2009 and was worth $3,400 for every man, woman and child in Canada" (D. Macdonald, 2012, p. 6).

With three of the country's biggest banks – CIBC, Bank of Montreal, and Scotiabank – receiving support equal to or more than the value of their shares, CCPA Senior Economist David Macdonald remarked in the *Financial Post* that the government "could have just purchased every single share in those banks instead of providing support ... [but] that's not the story Canadians were told. There was a massive failure in the private-sector market" (as cited in Postmedia News, 2012, paras. 16–17). The claim put forward by both the CBA and the federal government that this was not a bailout has similarly been challenged by journalists (Livesey, 2012), as well as mortgage analysts (Rabidoux, 2012), who argue that the ability to offload mortgages to the CMHC "looks very much like a simple ploy to strengthen Canadian banks' balance sheets by offloading risk to the Canadian taxpayers. *This* is the real Canadian bank bailout" (paras. 6–9).[121] In the years since the crisis, the ability to argue that there was no bailout has been legitimized by the fact that the government made a slight amount of money: "By the time the program ended, the IMPP [Insured Mortgage Purchase Program] generated an estimated C[AD]$2.5 billion in net revenues for the government" (Van Hasselt, 2012, para. 7). In any case, the real reason for the bailout was simple, and expressed by Flaherty himself: "This is

---

121 Livesey (2012) asks: "But was this reputation for fiscal prudence really warranted? First, it's not true that Canada's big banks hadn't been bailed out during the credit crisis. In the fall of 2008, through the Canada Mortgage and Housing Corporation (CMHC), the federal government created a unique program that allowed the banks to move tens of billions of dollars of mortgage assets off of their balance sheets – anywhere from $69 billion to $125 billion, depending on whose estimates you believe. (Originally, the amount was supposed to be just $20 billion, a figure that had to be ratcheted upwards – and substantially so – once it was clear this was not going to be enough to help the banks.) The plan was designed to ensure the banks had enough liquidity to keep lending – although it's unclear if they actually loaned out any of that money. Banks were also called upon to honour their financial commitments to all of the subprime mortgage debt they had insured through credit default swaps (CDSs – insurance contracts that promise to pay for the credit losses on subprime mortgage and other 'toxic' debts). These 'margin calls' happened just as the banks were facing write downs on other risky forays into the US subprime mortgage market, bringing their losses from the credit crisis to roughly $17 billion" (p. 114).

a time to protect Canadian investors and protect our system" (as cited in CBC News, 2008, para. 13).

For RBC specifically, which "received the third highest level of support for Canadian banks after TD Bank and Scotiabank" (D. Macdonald, 2012, p. 22), the bank hit its first peak borrowing in March 2009 at approximately $25 billion; a second peak appeared in July of 2009, hitting just under $23 billion. Having accessed liquidity support programs from the US Federal Reserve, the CMHC, and the Bank of Canada, it is somewhat shocking that RBC was able to receive "63% of its market cap in February 2009" (p. 22), considering that the official view at the time was that Canada's banks did not receive, nor require, a bailout. It is similarly difficult to take seriously the suggestion from corporate lawyers and management scholars that "Canada's ABCP crisis – unlike the crisis in other countries – was not about institutions holding too many toxic subprime assets. Rather, it was about a crisis of confidence in the market and liquidity problems" (Halpern et al., 2016, p. 201). If one simply asks where the crisis of confidence and liquidity problems come from, we end up back at square one: that globalizing financial institutions created and were holding toxic assets that needed to be removed from their balance sheets – and that they eventually required the assistance of nation-state institutions (both their own and others) to help them do this. That this help was eventually required by the state was due to the failure of financial institutions to offload their toxic assets onto other entities.

In just one example of many from Bruce Livesey's *The Thieves of Bay Street*, RBC was sued in 2008 by five Wisconsin school boards for deliberately moving toxic mortgage assets off their own books and transferring that risk onto the school boards. As Livesey (2012) explains, the school boards

> were convinced by RBC and the St. Louis-based brokerage firm Stifel, Nicolaus & Co. to borrow USD$163 million from a European bank with the idea of investing it in a synthetic CDO [collateralized debt obligation] constructed by RBC. The CDO was a witch's brew of complexity, containing portfolios of credit default swaps pegged to corporate bonds. The school boards said the bankers led them to believe this was a safe and secure investment when, in fact, it was quite risky. Indeed, the corporate bonds were linked to subprime mortgage debt. Sure enough, after the credit crisis struck, the investments tanked and the foreign bank seized the school board's collateral underlying the investments. (pp. 115–16)

Despite its efforts to get the lawsuit thrown out of the Milwaukee courts, RBC was eventually forced to pay "more than USD$30 million to the SEC [Securities and Exchange Commission] after the commission charged the bank with failing to explain the risks of the CDOs to the boards" (p. 116). Similarly, after the City of Detroit went bankrupt in 2008 due to the purchase of questionable financial products (Gaist, 2014; Hanover, 2013), the creditors, which included RBC, JPMorgan Chase & Co., and the Bank of America, among others, unsuccessfully attempted to get the Detroit Institute of Art to sell off its entire collection (which includes paintings by Van Gogh, Matisse, and Picasso, alongside Rodin's *Thinker*) to pay them back (Fisher, 2014). Given this sort of behaviour, it seems clear that Canada's crisis was at least in part about holding too many toxic assets, regardless of their specific makeup.[122]

That bailouts happened at all reflects the growing power and size of financial capital within the contemporary global economy. As political sociologist Bob Jessop (2015) has pointed out, "If financial capital is well-entrenched in the state apparatus, then the capacity to rescue 'too big to fail' financial institutions also exists when states can create fiat money and engage in other credit manoeuvres to socialize toxic assets and losses" (p. 35).[123] Where previously "too big to fail" meant that an institution was so large that it would not fail, "now it meant that the institution was too large for a government to permit it to fail in the usual way" (Kyer, 2017, p. 231). With one of the world's most concentrated banking sectors, the obvious reality in the Canadian case is the one suggested by David Macdonald (2012): that "Canada's big banks are too big to fail. The Government of Canada, the Bank of Canada, and the big banks themselves understand that Canada's banks will be bailed out irrespective of the cost" (p. 30). This was made explicitly clear after the crisis when Flaherty argued against an international campaign to impose taxes and levies on banks to create a fund in the case of future bailouts, claiming that "such taxes create an incentive for banks to behave recklessly, since they know they'll be bailed out if worst comes to worst" (S. Kilpatrick, 2010, p. A14).

---

122 For an overview of the range of questionable financial practices characteristic of our present epoch, see Teeple (2011).

123 Christophers (2022) suggests that "financial institutions enjoy power vis-à-vis the state because it is increasingly through financial markets themselves that the state pursues certain important policy objectives. If markets constitute an infrastructure of governance, safeguarding markets in times of economic crisis takes on a significance that the state diminishes at no small risk, not least to itself; and to one degree or another, safeguarding markets always entails backstopping those institutions holding the systemically important assets and liabilities circulating in those markets" (p. 148).

Another important aspect of the bailouts that has been neglected is that these were not simply bailouts of Canada's chartered banks but rather *any bank* that has the *right* to access the Canadian market. Despite Flaherty's (2008) remark that the reason for the bailout was "to ensure the Canadian banks – which have weathered the global credit crunch better than their competitors – are not put at a competitive disadvantage because other countries have provided borrowing guarantees to restore or protect the stability of their own financial systems" (para. 26), the bailout was offered to, and taken by, both domestic and foreign banks, even though the number of foreign banks and the amount taken by them was relatively small. Similarly, Canada's chartered banks participated in bailout programs provided by the US government (Kuntz & Ivry, 2011). Such practices indicate that today's nation-state institutions are less a capability for explicitly national capitals, as they were historically, and increasingly a capability for globalizing capitals, wherever they might reside. In referring to the American response, Simon Johnson and James Kwak (2011) remark that "never before has so much taxpayer money been dedicated to saving an industry from the consequences of its own mistakes" (p. 164).

The crisis predictably set off another round of regulatory tweaks at both the global and national levels. New macroprudential regulations for the so-called too big to fail banks, for instance, were unveiled by the G20-created Financial Stability Board (FSB), which is managed by a small administrative office at the BIS in Switzerland ("Too Big to Fail," 2014). Formed in 2009 as a successor to the FSF, the FSB immediately set out new too-big-to-fail (TBTF) reforms for what they referred to as "systemically important firms" (FSB, 2020, para. 3). Endorsed by the leaders of the G20 and eventually put into place as part of the recent Basel III Accord, the most significant of these reforms has been the new capital adequacy rules, which require global systemically important banks (G-SIBs) to hold additional capital as a shock absorber in the event of another global financial crisis. Since the November 2012 update, the FSB has sorted G-SIBs into five risk buckets that correspond to the "level of additional common equity loss absorbency as a percentage of risk-weighted assets" (FSB, 2014, p. 2, n. 7) for each listed bank. In a recent report from the FSB (2022), G-SIBs in the lowest bucket are supposed to maintain a capital/asset ratio 1 per cent higher than that required by their national authorities. This ratio is raised by 0.5 per cent from buckets two to four. An additional 1 per cent is required for any bank put into the top risk tier (although this bucket has been intentionally left empty to allow for the tightening of capital requirements in the case that a bank's riskiness pushes it past the fourth bucket). None of

Canada's chartered banks were placed on the list at the time of its creation, but they were still subject to new capital adequacy requirements as domestic systemically important banks (D-SIBs) ("Canadian Banks Don't," 2012).[124] Since then, however, both RBC and TD have moved into the first bucket as G-SIBs (FSB, 2022).[125] The FSB has also required "each country to establish a resolution authority with appropriate powers to 'resolve' large, complex bank failures" (Kyer, 2017, p. 227), a role taken on by CDIC, alongside other new powers.[126] If one wants to know how banks responded to these changes, one need only look at the response of Jamie Dimon, CEO of JPMorgan Chase: "He condemned the new capital rules and challenged Mark Carney, the chairman of the Bank of Canada and head of the FSB, so violently that Lloyd Blankfein of Goldman Sachs felt it necessary to personally intercede" (Tooze, 2018, p. 402).

The response of commentators to the macroprudential regulations coming out of the financial crisis is varied. While some authors take a positive view – highlighted by the existence of titles such as *The System Worked* (Drezner, 2014) – the general consensus is that there are still significant gaps in the global regulatory system, especially as it pertains to the identification and containment of risk (Barth et al., 2012; Halpern et al., 2016; O'Halloran & Groll, 2019). As Puri (2012) notes, this is particularly the case in Canada since the Supreme Court ruled

---

124 Anand and Peihani (2019) note: "In the banking sector, Canadian policy makers have implemented the Basel III capital and liquidity reforms that represent a central part of the G20 post-crisis agenda. Under the new regulations issued by OSFI, banks are required to hold common equity tier one (CET1) of at least seven percent and a total capital buffer of at least 10.5 percent against risk-weighted assets. Canadian banks are also expected to meet a leverage ratio of at least three percent ... The six largest Canadian banks have also been named by OSFI as D-SIBs. This designation means that these institutions are subject to enhanced disclosure requirements and intense supervision and must hold an additional one percent of CET1 capital" (p. 18).

125 The most recent FSB list is as follows: (1) Agricultural Bank of China, Bank of New York Mellon, China Construction Bank, Credit Suisse, Groupe BPCE, Groupe Crédit Agricole, ING, Mizuho FG, Morgan Stanley, Royal Bank of Canada, Santander, Société Générale, Standard Chartered, State Street, Sumitomo Mitsui FG, Toronto Dominion, Union Bank of Switzerland (UBS), UniCredit, Wells Fargo; (2) Bank of China, Barclays, BNP Paribas, Deutsche Bank, Goldman Sachs, Industrial and Commercial Bank of China, Mitsubishi UFJ FG; (3) Bank of America, Citigroup, HSBC; (4) JPMorgan Chase; (5) empty (see FSB, 2022, p. 3).

126 As Kyer (2017) notes, CDIC is also working to "develop legislation increasing its toolkit, including the concept of the bridge bank; work with the Department of Finance on 'bail-in' legislation; and adopt a data requirements bylaw" (p. 8).

in 2011 that the federal government does not have the jurisdiction to create a new national securities regulator. Going against the recommendations of the IMF (2019), this means that Canada remains "vulnerable to regulatory gaps between banking and securities regulators – similar to what occurred in the ABCP crisis" (Puri, 2012, p. 182).[127] While some writers in the United States have suggested entirely new regulatory institutions, such as "The Sentinel," which is supposed to "provide an informed, expert, and independent assessment of financial regulation that will both assist financial regulators and enhance the ability of the public and its representatives to govern financial regulators" (Barth et al., 2012, p. 216), most scholars point to the impact of industry lobbying, the toothless nature of the new reforms, and why institutions like The Sentinel are thus unlikely to be created in the first place (Chon & Fleming, 2014; Courville, 2012; Helleiner, 2013, 2014; M. Wolf, 2010). It is in this sense that we can return to Schenk's (2020) comments quoted in the introduction: that these new reforms are simply "another turn of the wheel" (p. 8) in the long history of the regulation of banking and finance – "from regulation to deregulation and then to reregulation" (p. 12).

Given this reality, it seems more accurate to suggest, as Rogers (2018) does, that these new rules do nothing more than reproduce capitalist social relations by disciplining banks and other financial institutions into being more careful in their accumulation activities; these rules certainly do not alter the fundamental growth of such institutions, nor the global sweep of their interests. As a group of scholars in the UK demonstrate, most of the TBTF banks, including RBC, are now much larger than they were at the start of the crisis, calling into question

> why this global megabanking sector –a sector comprised of institutions whose very scale, complexity, and interconnectedness, and risk-tolerance have already proven to be a toxic mix – is still so large and powerful ten years after the global financial crisis. (Ioannou et al., 2019, p. 376)

Far from the system of nation-state authority over financial actors that characterized the Bretton Woods system, the FSB is simply the newest organization to join the patchwork system of national and international institutions that work to prop up global capitalism. There is thus

---

127 As the IMF (2019) suggests, "modernization of the financial stability architecture would help enhance systemic risk oversight and crisis preparedness. A single body in charge of systemic risk oversight would be the first-best solution" (p. 8).

good reason to question claims that because of the crisis, "the historical sweep of financial governance is about to experience a renewed assertion of the nation-state as the central locus of regulatory authority" (Germain, 2010, p. 12). As we have already seen, the networks through which financial regulation and governance flow encompass both transnational organizations such as the BCBS, FSB, IMF, and so on, as well as national regulatory agencies such as OSFI that put them into practice. While national governments no doubt have to deal with the outcomes of future financial crises, much of the work of financial regulation in the post-crisis period has been under the direction of transnational organizations, signalling a continuation of the centrifugal organizing dynamic that defines our age. As Porter (2014a) observes, "the experience of transnational regulatory reform after the crisis indicates that the trends of the past three decades, which have involved a growth in transnational interdependence in financial transactions and governance, is continuing rather than reversing" (p. 5).

This is further compounded by the relationship between increasingly complex transnational regulations and big data. As the former chief economist of the Bank of England, Andy Haldane (2012), notes, keeping compliant with Basel III reforms "has meant a rise in the number of calculations required from single figures a generation ago to several million today" (p. 7). Campbell-Verduyn et al. (2017) point out that this change has driven tech firms to offer automated monitoring systems, furthering a global dynamic of accumulation within the regulatory system itself. And this is in addition to the point that Basel III does not go nearly far enough in preventing another global financial crisis, subject as it was to pushback from the world's largest banks (Chon & Fleming, 2014; M. Wolf, 2010).

Conclusion

This chapter set out to explore how our present conjuncture differs in its constitution of TAR in respect to financial capital as compared to the earlier national epoch of capitalism analyzed in chapters 2 and 3. I argued that our current period can be distinguished by the emergence of a centrifugal organizing dynamic of TAR. My main claim is that the ongoing shift of the rights of capital and the authority over those rights to the transnational level represents the making of global capital – that is, the making of a legal infrastructure for a global system of private property relations. This infrastructure is still in the making, but it rests on the wide variety of rights granted to capital over this period that not only push the legal institutions of member nation states to enforce the rights of foreign firms but also increasingly restrict the ability of governments everywhere to legislate against corporate interests. The role of the nation state over this period has thus been one of transformation, changing from a capability geared towards the growth of national capitals to a capability geared towards globalizing capitals, since its work is increasingly oriented towards the protection of the rights of global corporate private property over and against the rights of national citizens. As Teeple (2007) notes, this is evident in the anti-democratic makeup of the transnational institutions that regulate globalizing capitals:

> They are staffed by bureaucrats and appointed officials, and decisions about policies and practice are often determined by the relative weight of national economic power. There is no meaningful access to the decision-making process other than by career bureaucrats and representatives of governments and TNCs. Most of their business, moreover, is conducted in camera, out of view of the world's public. The working classes and other subordinate groups and peoples have little or no recourse to decisions and policies at the global level other than extra-parliamentary or extra-legal action. (p. 143)

That any of this occurs at all is the result of the continuous expansion of capital and the consequent process of its concentration and centralization in a small number of interlocked, globalizing firms that must constantly grow to survive – "the ideology of the cancer cell" (p. 98), as environmental activist Edward Abbey (1991) once put it.

To demonstrate the empirical reality of the change, I provided an analysis of the transformation of Canadian banking via the history of RBC from 1975 to 2008. I identified three shifts in TAR – the movement of authority over banking to transnational institutions, financial deregulation, and free trade agreements – to represent this emerging centrifugal dynamic of TAR as it relates to the chartered banks. Through these three shifts, Canada's chartered banks gained new rights that enabled them to become huge, global financial institutions, a process which has subsequently led to numerous financial crises requiring new forms of transnational coordination and macroprudential regulation to keep the whole system afloat (i.e., keep the global credit taps open). While transnational civil society groups may have influenced the agenda, Kastner (2014) notes that the implementation phase of post-crisis reform has "turned out to be largely dominated by industry lobbying" (p. 1316). Indeed, as Teeple (2007) points out, these regulations "are not political, but rather are the formalization of the rules of global competition between capitals" (p. 129).

As such, I suggest that we interpret all this as the transformation of the nation state into a capability for globalizing capitals through the movement of the rights of capital and the authority over those rights to the transnational level – a level in which there are no mechanisms for democratic intervention, and, thus, "the accumulation of capitalist private property can be pursued without political interference" (Teeple, 2007, p. 129). This is not to suggest that this process is complete at the global level, or without resistance; rather, it is to suggest, as Christophers (2022) does, that "states' freedom of action with regards to finance today is clearly constrained by the extent to which the state and state-policymaking has itself become operationally entangled with market mechanisms" (p. 148). As this dynamic continues to transform the property relations of national capitalisms, it will also chip away at the remaining privileges held by the chartered banks in Canada. In the next and final chapter, I look at some emergent trends in relation to banking and finance and explore some of their political, economic, and social implications.

Chapter Five

Emerging Tendencies and Trajectories: 2009–2022

All we can do is study the present epoch in an attempt to discern within it those tendencies leading into the next epoch.
– C. Wright Mills (1962, p. 38)

Introduction

The previous chapters in this book have been concerned with asking where we have been so as to understand where we are now. In contrast, this chapter is an attempt to understand where we are going. In the last chapter, I demonstrated that our present epoch is characterized by an emerging centrifugal logic that is drawing elements of territory, authority, and rights (TAR) away from the nation state, despite still being coded as national or operating through national domains. If, as political scientist Randall Germain (2010) notes, "financial governance is most effective when it is organized predominantly at the national level" (p. 1), then these dynamics are representative of a worrisome trend in respect to capital's ability to escape national regulation and oversight. In this chapter, I focus on a number of recent developments in banking and finance that are not only representative of this centrifugal dynamic but also of where capitalist societies are heading more generally. In particular, I focus on new forms of escape from the nation state, such as dark pools and temporary foreign worker programs; new free trade agreements, such as the Canada–European Union Comprehensive Economic and Trade Agreement (CETA), and the Comprehensive and Progressive Agreement for Trans-Pacific Partnership (CPTPP); and new, so-called institutional technologies, such as blockchain.

What I want to stress, here, is that while all these trends move elements of TAR away from the national level, this does not mean that they do not involve nation states; in many cases, these globalizing processes were the result of national regulations or policies. The question is therefore not whether these emergent trends reduce the importance of the nation state within the global political economy – clearly, they do not. Rather, we should ask whether they are contributing to a global property regime that works to cement the power of globalizing capital by restricting the extent to which nation states can oppose corporate interests. This global property regime is undoubtedly still in the making; as such, the best we can do is attempt "to detect shapes and construct objects of study around what is ultimately a roving animal moving with increasing vigour and velocity" (Sassen, 2007, p. 213). The need to detect and examine these shapes and trends is extremely important, however, given their potential implications. If all human societies are defined by their respective property relations, and those relations are the result of social and political struggles, then it is the job of the critical social scientist to determine in which direction these struggles are heading in order to have a better understanding of their likely outcomes. The goal of this chapter is therefore to try to see the future in the present; to identify those tendencies of the new order that are not yet prevalent but that have the potential to induce systemic change.

The chapter proceeds as follows. First, I explore two contemporary means of escaping national restrictions: dark pools and temporary foreign worker programs. Next, I explore two of the new free trade agreements: CETA and the CPTPP. I then explore the emergence of blockchain technology, a digital public ledger that eliminates the need for trusted third parties (like banks) to verify transactions. In each instance, I explore how RBC is wrapped up in these various shifts of TAR, and I conclude by reflecting on the COVID-19 pandemic and what all this means for the future.

Making Global Space in National Domains

Of the robber barons of the late nineteenth century, Thorstein Veblen observed, "It is not easy in any given case – indeed it is at times impossible until the courts have spoken – to say whether it is an instance of praiseworthy salesmanship or a penitentiary offense."

– Lewis Lapham (1988/2018, p. 114)

In the 1936 volume of *Canadian Banker*, J.V. Walters, an employee in the securities department of the Bank of Montreal (BMO) summed up the entire practice of banking when he wrote, "it goes without saying … the ultimate aim of the banker is to make a profit" (p. 51). Since the 1980s, however, profit-making in banking has increasingly involved a variety of different means to escape national-level regulations, such as tax havens and shadow banking (Ban et al., 2016; Bryan et al., 2016; Fichtner, 2016; Kalman-Lamb, 2017; Lysandrou & Nesvetailova, 2014; Plender, 2021; Streeck, 2016; Woyames Dreher, 2019). The historian Nils Gilman (2014) refers to this trend as a novel form of plutocratic insurgency. Unlike the insurgents of the twentieth century (whether rich or poor) who sought to take over the state apparatus in order to implement social reforms, the plutocratic insurgents of today

> do not seek to take over the state. Nor do they wish to destroy the state, since they rely parasitically on it to provide the legacy goods of social welfare: health, education, infrastructure, and so on. Rather, their aim is simpler: to carve out *de facto* zones of autonomy for themselves by crippling the state's ability to constrain their freedom of (economic) action. (p. 3)

In their quest to escape national constraints on the accumulation of capital, today's super-rich seek out or create "virtual zones of legal exception in the form of offshore tax havens and special economic zones allowing them to avoid tariffs as well as laws designed to protect labour or the environment" (p. 10). While tax havens have long been part of capital's global circuitry, they now exist all over the world, including within small jurisdictional zones subsumed within advanced capitalist countries, including Austria, Belgium, Canada, Ireland, the Netherlands, and the United States.

As Deneault (2018) explains, these "mixed" tax havens were created to avoid "the 'blacklists' of the OECD, the Financial Stability Forum (FSF) associated with the International Monetary Fund (IMF), and the Financial Action Task Force (FATF), which were officially intended to stigmatize the jurisdictions least likely to 'cooperate' with foreign authorities" (p. 59). By appearing as otherwise responsible states, governments of an increasing number of capitalist countries can "base entire sections of their jurisdictions on the offshore model" (p. 59) in an explicit example of nation states being transformed into a capability for global capital accumulation. RBC, for instance, has many of its principal subsidiaries incorporated in known tax havens, such as Delaware, Luxembourg, the Channel Islands (medieval territories turned into global financial centres), and the Caribbean, a region that the chartered banks helped transform into a series of tax havens in the late nineteenth century. And while there are many excellent studies of the offshore system (Deneault, 2011, 2015, 2018; Norfield, 2016), there has been less discussion of some of the more obtuse means by which capital escapes national constraints on accumulation by creating private zones of autonomy. Let us begin with one of the digital ones: dark pools.

In a discussion of the nature of global cities, Sassen (2006) argues that despite the fact that financial centres such as Wall Street and the City of London are located within national territories, they should not "be seen as simply national in the historical sense, nor can they be reduced to the administrative unit encompassing the actual terrain, one that is part of a nation-state" (p. 386). This is because, in their aggregate, "they house components of the global, partly electronic markets for capital," and are thus "denationalized in specific and partial ways" (p. 386). One of those ways is through the so-called shadow banking system, which sits just below the surface. The basic definition of shadow banking is lending, or other financial activities, that are conducted by unregulated institutions or under unregulated conditions. Despite the name, the system is not "informal, illegal, or clandestine. It is in the open, but it thrives on the opaqueness of investments," allowing for practices and activities that might be, "after the fact, viewed as bordering on the illegal" (Sassen, 2014a, pp. 142–3). A perfect example is the dark pool, a "key component of the shadow banking system" (p. 143).

A dark pool is simply a private exchange not accessible to the investing public. In the late 1990s and into the mid-2000s, a number of rules were changed by the American Securities and Exchange Commission (SEC) in order to help out ordinary investors. These rules essentially forced the various stock exchanges to compete against one another for orders. As Jacob Goldstein (2013) explains in the *New York Times*, the new rules meant that "exchanges could no longer hoard orders; if a better offer existed on another trading platform, they'd have to send it there" (p. SM15). In 2005, this change was accompanied by a transformation in the classification of American stock exchanges, which "went from being utilities owned by their members to public corporations run for profit" (Lewis, 2014, p. 35). The combination of these two changes led to the creation, and subsequent proliferation, of an alternative trading system (ATS) – more commonly known as dark pools.

First offered by financial giants such as Goldman Sachs and Credit Suisse, dark pools are especially notable because they all share one key component: "they do not display order size or price until after a trade has been completed" (Sassen, 2014a, p. 143). Michael Lewis (2014) explains the concept in *Flash Boys*:

> The amazing idea the big Wall Street banks had sold to big investors was that transparency was their enemy. If, say, Fidelity wanted to sell a million shares of Microsoft Corp. – so the argument ran – they were better off putting them into a dark pool run by, say, Credit Suisse than going directly to the public exchanges. On the public exchanges, everyone would notice a big seller had entered the market, and the market price of Microsoft would plunge. Inside a dark pool, no one but the broker who ran it had any idea what was happening. (p. 43)[1]

As sociologist Donald MacKenzie (2019) notes, the first generation of dark pools, which worked to break larger orders into smaller portions (or "child orders") before sending them out to the exchanges, meant that investment banks "would incur fees that would cut into the revenue earned by executing fund managers' orders"; they thus preferred "to 'internalise' those orders, for example buying shares from one fund manager and then selling them to another, without the use of external markets" (p. 10). After the SEC passed the Regulation National Market System (typically referred to as Reg NMS) in 2005, however, internalization became more difficult as trades could only be "conducted at a price no worse than the constantly fluctuating best prices on the registered exchanges" (p. 10). A second generation of dark pools thus emerged that automated the process, turning "the internal, manual matching of orders into automated dark pools" (p. 10). As one of MacKenzie's interview subjects put it, "everything was the same except we had a machine do it instead of having people do it," meaning that "existing social relations and practices were ... therefore preserved in a new technological form" (p. 10).

---

1 Sassen (2014a) provides another description: "In a public exchange with an open order book, the presence of a larger order can immediately move the price of a stock (for example, if ABC Co. has an average trading volume of 1 million shares a day, and there is an entry placed in the order book to buy 500,000 shares, it's an easy bet that ABC stock is going to go up, and the price that the purchaser will have to pay likely to be higher by the time the transaction is completed). To combat this, large investors had brokers 'work' trades, breaking large blocks of stock into smaller transactions carried out over an extended period of time. This solution was never entirely effective: it increased price volatility and transaction time, and market participants could still detect a general upsurge of demand. The introduction of computerized high-frequency trading (HFT) made the situation worse for institutional investors; algorithmic trading models could reliably detect even the most patiently distributed orders" (pp. 143–4).

The opacity of these digital territories represents a huge potential for abuse. Big banks have not only been caught giving unequal access to their own traders but also selling access to high-frequency trading (HFT) firms, which use algorithmic trading to buy and sell securities in the nanoseconds between trades, making money off the slight differences in price. As the rooms full of shouting traders were steadily replaced by stacks of computer servers with matching engines connecting buyers and sellers,

> it was only a matter of time before the stock exchanges figured out that, if people were willing to spend hundreds of thousands of dollars to move their machines around inside some remote data center just so they might be a tiny bit closer to the stock exchange, they'd pay millions to be inside the stock exchange itself. (Lewis, 2014, p. 63)

The sale of these highly valued locations inside the exchange is referred to as "co-location," and it provides a good example of the extent to which private property, and thus capital, is constitutive of different forms of space across multiple national domains.[2]

Dark pools are now a ubiquitous feature of the global financial system used as a means of escaping transparency: "Today it's not just the familiar New York Stock Exchange and Nasdaq, but also lesser-known ones with names like BATS and Direct Edge" (Goldstein, 2013,

---

2 As Lewis (2014) explains, this "Americanization" of stock exchanges was going on across the world, following a relatively similar pattern: "A country in which the stock market had always traded on a single exchange – Canada, Australia, the UK – would, in the name of free-market competition, permit the creation of a new exchange. The new exchange was always located at some surprising distance from the original exchange. In Toronto it was inside an old department store building across the city from the Toronto Stock Exchange. In Australia it was mysteriously located not in the Sydney financial district but across Sydney Harbor, in the middle of a residential district. The old London Stock Exchange was in central London. BATS created a British rival in the Docklands, NYSE created another, outside of London, in Basildon, and Chi-X created a third in Slough. Each new exchange gave rise to the need for high-speed routes between the exchanges." (Lewis, 2014, pp. 66–7). One interlocutor in Lewis's book observed that "it was almost like they picked places to set up exchanges so that the market would fragment" (as cited in Lewis, 2014, p. 38).

As the former chief economist of the Bank of England, Andy Haldane (2011), points out, these trends will continue until zero latency between trades is reached: "It is clear from these trends that trading technologists are involved in an arms race. And it is far from over. The new trading frontier is nano-seconds – billionths of a second. And the twinkle in technologists' (unblinking) eye is pico-seconds – trillionths of a second. HFT firms talk of a 'race to zero.' This is the promised land of zero 'latency' where trading converges on its natural (Planck's) limit, the speed of light" (p. 3).

p. SM15). Despite the basis of their initial rationale – to allow institutional investors to place large orders anonymously without displaying them to the public to minimize their market impact – a 2010 position paper from the Joint Canadian Securities Administrators/Investment Industry Regulatory Organization of Canada (CAS/IIRCA) claims that dark pools are now being used for "orders of all sizes, small or large" (p. 5). Dark pools thus represent a private space in which the information about what is going on in the global financial system is hidden from the gaze of the nation state, even as it provides the very regulations and rules that allow them to function.

HFT firms are, like dark pools, the curious result of the way in which regulations meant to deal with some of the contradictions of capitalism often provide new, contingent avenues for accumulation. As mentioned above, in 2005, the SEC passed Reg NMS, which required brokers to find the best market prices for the investors they represented: "the regulation had been inspired by charges of front-running made in 2004 against two dozen specialists on the floor of the old New York Stock Exchange – a charge the specialists settled by paying a $241 million fine" (Lewis, 2014, p. 96). Reg NMS massively increased the significance of HFT since it forced brokers to find the best price for their investors – prices always offered by HFT firms. The combination of HFT firms and dark pools has thus played a massive role in distorting financial markets, something that is no small matter given that "by the middle of 2011, roughly 30 percent of all stock market trades occurred off the public exchanges, most of them in dark pools" (p. 60). A recent article in *The Economist* notes, for instance, that "America now has 13 equity exchanges and 44 off-exchange centres such as dark pools" ("Crashing the Party," 2019, para. 3). Accordingly, the New York Stock Exchange's (NYSE) "share of equity trading has shrunk from 72% to 24% in a decade; off-exchange venues account for 36%" (para. 3). Furthermore, as Sassen (2014a) notes, the opacity of dark pools has made possible new forms of financial abuse: big banks that run their own dark pools do not just give their own traders unequal access, but many have also been caught "running the same HFT strategies within their exchanges and sharing confidential trade information with investors" (p. 145).

As Canada's largest bank, RBC decided to plug itself into the world of dark pools and HFT to compete against other expanding firms. As discussed in chapter 4, the bank's failed merger bid with the Bank of Montreal in 1998 caused RBC to reorient its business strategy around the North American market, and as part of that process, it was able to acquire Carlin Financial, a small American electronic trading firm, in 2006 for $100 million. As narrated by Lewis (2014) in *Flash Boys*, one of

RBC's traders, Brad Katsuyama, discovered that when he used Carlin's software, his trading screens did not match the market price:

> Before RBC acquired this supposedly state-of-the-art electronic trading firm, his computers worked. Now, suddenly, they didn't. Until he was forced to use some of Carlin's technology, he trusted his trading screens. When his trading screens showed 10,000 shares of Intel offered at $22 a share, it meant that he could buy 10,000 shares of Intel for $22 a share. He had only to push a button. By the spring of 2007, when his screens showed 10,000 shares of Intel offered at $22 and he pushed the button, the offers vanished. In his seven years as a trader he had always been able to look at the screens on his desk and see the stock market. Now the market as it appeared on his screens was an illusion. (pp. 30–1)

Through trial and error, Katsuyama figured out that in the time it took for him to execute a trade, someone else was already front running the stock: "It was as if someone knew what he was trying to do and was reacting to his desire to sell before he had fully expressed it" (p. 21). Over time, Kastuyama would discover the cause: HFT.

HFT was introduced to the Canadian market in 2009, after CIBC sublet its license on the Toronto Stock Exchange (TSX) to several HFT firms (Shecter, 2012b). Within months, the bank was seeing "its historically stable 6–7 percent share of Canadian stock market trading triple" (Lewis, 2014, p. 54). As a result, American HFT firms began to fly to "Toronto with offers to pay Canadian banks to expose their customers to high-frequency traders" (p. 31). Not wanting to be outdone, senior managers at RBC argued that they should create their own dark pool, "route their Canadian stock market orders into it, and then sell to high-frequency traders the right to operate inside the dark pool" (p. 31). In doing so, they would have been following a path laid out for them by other big banks; as MacKenzie's (2019) interview subjects reported, "a bank's systems' first choice would often be its own dark pool. Only if a child order could not be executed there would it then be sent on to other banks' dark pools and perhaps eventually to public 'lit' markets" (p. 11). The idea was ultimately killed by Katsuyama, who argued that it made more sense to "expose the new game for what it was" (Lewis, 2014, p. 54). He subsequently created a new software program for RBC called THOR that foiled high-frequency traders by creating a delay on stock market orders.[3] The software was so

---

3 Katsuyama has since left RBC to start his own dark pool, IEX, based on similar delay tactics as THOR (Erman, 2013). IEX now trades more in value daily than the London

successful in thwarting HFT firms that it moved RBC from number 19 in 2009 to number one in 2011 on Greenwich Associates' stock market rankings (Lam & Alexander, 2014). The move was so significant that Greenwich phoned RBC to ask what was going on: "In the history of their rankings, they said, they had never seen a firm jump more than three spots" (Lewis, 2014, p. 87).

Lest the reader think this is a tale of "RBC Nice" – the culture of the bank as described by Lewis (2014) in *Flash Boys* – saving Wall Street, the creation of THOR more practically demonstrates how corporations are forced to respond to the expansion of capital as it takes on more obscure routes towards the production of profit. As Lewis (2014) points out, the question of how to respond to HFT for RBC could have gone either way, since "the RBC executives who wanted to join forces with high-frequency traders knew as little about high-frequency trading as [Katsuyama] did" (p. 55). While HFT algorithms are "the perfect match for the streams of electronic 'child' orders flowing from an investment bank's fund-manager clients into the bank's dark pool" (MacKenzie, 2019, p. 12), it also means that those banks must "contend with a pervasive fear among fund managers: that HFT firms' algorithms are profiting at the expense of their orders to buy or sell shares" (p. 12). Excluding HFT is not an attractive option, however, "because of the vital role those algorithms play in increasing the chance that a fund manager's order will be executed in the bank's own dark pool" (p. 12). As a result, many investment bank dark pools have chosen to instead "monitor and categorise the behaviour of the HFT and other algorithms trading in the pool" (p. 12).

The normalization of some of these trends can be witnessed through the transformation of Canada's own exchanges. On 9 February 2011, the London Stock Exchange (LSE) announced that it was merging with TMX Group, the parent company that operates the TSX, Toronto

---

Stock Exchange, according to Katsuyama, but it only has 3 per cent market share in the United States ("Crashing the Party," 2019, para. 9). As MacKenzie (2018) makes clear, however, IEX is not necessarily anti-HFT: "HFT market makers are welcome and active on IEX. The chief point of the coil is to make it impossible to profit from the sixth class of signal listed in table 1, in which orders are being matched at the midpoint of the highest bid and lowest offer, but the prices being used to calculate that midpoint are stale (much trading on IEX takes the form of midpoint matching). The data feeds from the other exchanges that IEX uses to calculate the midpoint of the national best bid and offer do not go through the coil (and thus are not delayed), but orders to IEX are delayed. By the time an order attempting to exploit a stale midpoint would arrive at IEX, the prices used to calculate the midpoint would thus already have been updated" (p. 1679).

Venture Exchange (TSXV), and the Montreal Exchange (MX), among others.[4] The LSE side of the deal was being advised by RBC's investment banking arm (with BMO advising TMX) and, if it had gone through, would have made the new exchange the second largest exchange in the world, with a market cap 47 per cent greater than Nasdaq. The deal was ultimately rejected by shareholders, however, due to a rival bid from Maple Group Acquisition Corp., a takeover vehicle consisting of the Alberta Investment Management Corp., Caisse de dépôt et placement du Québec, the Canada Pension Plan Investment Board, CIBC World Markets Inc., Desjardins Financial Group, Dundee Capital Markets Inc., Fonds de solidarité FTQ, National Bank Financial & Co. Inc., Ontario Teachers' Pension Plan, Scotia Capital Inc., TD Securities Inc., and Manulife Financial. By the summer of 2012, the Maple Group's deal was approved by all federal and provincial regulatory authorities, with a "mandate to act in Canadian interests" (Freeman, 2012, para. 12). As pointed out in the *Financial Post*, "one of the things that apparently gave comfort to regulators to allow the deal to go ahead is that two of Canada's big banks [RBC and BMO] were not part of the Maple consortium" (Shecter, 2013, para. 35). In a letter to the Ontario Securities Commission (OSC), Greg Mills, head of global equities for RBC Capital Markets, argued that there would have to be "a significantly different approach to the regulation of fees and fee models in Canada in order to compensate for the removal of effective competition for trading venues" (as cited in Shecter, 2012a, para. 2).

Further consolidation occurred after the TMX Group merged with "the alternative Alpha Trading System, and clearing and depository firm CDS Inc., which are owned by the major players in the Canadian securities industry, several of which are part of the consortium" (Shecter, 2012a, para. 18). With control of "some 90 per cent of trading in Canada" (para. 5), the deal has since enabled the TMX Group to introduce new exchanges, such as TSX Alpha Exchange, which "has a built in 'speed bump' to slow the execution of orders" (Flanagan, 2015, para. 2), as well as TSX DRK, an alternative dark pool that offers a wide range of "dark strategies" in order "to help prevent information leakage" (TSX Inc., 2022, p. 5). While the failed merger between the TMX Group and the LSE exemplifies the rifts between different segments

---

4 TMX Group also operates TSX Trust, TSX Alpha Exchange, Shorcan, Canadian Derivatives Clearing Company (CDCC), Canadian Depository for Securities (CDS), TMX Datalinx, TMX Insights, and Trayport. See https://www.tmx.com for more details.

of Canada's financial sector policy network (Roberge et al., 2015), it is also important to highlight the ways in which these new means of extracting capital involve new sets of rights (e.g., the privatization of exchanges) that obscure what is taking place. As RBC's Greg Mills makes clear in respect to the government's understanding of dark pools and HFT technology, "regulators don't have the in-house expertise that they require" (as cited in Shecter, 2012b, para. 24). Similarly, Stephen Piron, a director of Brightsun Group in the UK, notes that "the technology that regulators have to monitor market abuse is far, far behind the technology used by traders" (as cited in Shecter, 2012b, para. 25).

While the world's big banks have been quiet about the amounts of money they make off dark pools, Katsuyama claims that their use is "industry wide. It's systemic" (as cited in Lewis, 2014, p. 84). Lewis (2014) shows, for instance, that from 2006 to 2008, HFTs "share of total US market trading doubled, from 26 percent to 52 percent – and it has never fallen below 50 percent since then" (p. 108). The total amount of trades per day has also grown from 10 million in 2006 to just over 20 million in 2009. Jacob Goldstein (2013) of the *New York Times* similarly notes that "by 2009, high-frequency traders were making billions of dollars a year, and their transactions accounted for about 60 percent of US stock trades" (p. SM14). These figures are confirmed by Sassen (2014a), who points out that dark pool trading represents close to 13 per cent of *all* stock market action around the world and that "their numbers are increasing" (p. 144).

In Canada, it is estimated that only 10 per cent of trading activity occurs in dark pools as compared with over 50 per cent in the United States (Corcoran, 2015; J. Foster, 2019). This low number is the result of rules introduced by the federal government through the Investment Industry Regulatory Organization of Canada (IIROC), which regulates investment dealers and trading activity in the debt and equity markets across Canada. In 2012, the IIROC introduced new rules for dark trading in shares of inter-listed stocks (i.e., the 330 stocks listed on both the US and Canadian stock exchanges, representing at least 50 per cent of the Canadian market). The rules were designed to discourage Canadian investment dealers from funnelling all their transactions through dark pools by giving visible (or "lit") orders priority. While smaller retail orders can still be routed through dark pools, they need to show an improvement in the quoted price of at least half a cent per share.

To make sure that Canadian orders are not routed to US dark pools, the IIROC also proposed a Dark Rules Anti-Avoidance Provision, which would limit dealers' ability to do so. As might be expected, the chartered banks were against the proposed set of rules, which would put them at a serious disadvantage as compared to their rivals in the US, where dark pools provide an important source of liquidity. Scotiabank called the proposed rules an attempt "to prop up marketplaces with protectionist regulations" (Corcoran, 2015, para. 16). CIBC World Markets claimed that they are "akin to the creation of a non-tariff barrier to trade" (para. 18). In typically RBC Nice form, RBC Capital said that "while well-intentioned ... the proposed rule changes constitute a blunt tool" (para. 17). The IIROC (2017) has since withdrawn the proposed amendment. In any case, the development of these sorts of new financialized means of extracting profit forces banks to either adapt or die, as evidenced by the recent release of Aiden, a new AI trading platform created by RBC Capital Markets (n.d.) that adapts to market conditions on the fly through deep learning techniques. RBC has also acquired WayPay, a cloud-based payments fintech; Dr. Bill, a mobile billing platform for physicians; as well as Ownr, a platform enabling businesses to automate legal tasks (Royal Bank of Canada, 2019, 2020a, 2020b). We should expect the digitalization of finance to continue.

While we will return to the realm of technology shortly, there are also other, more explicit means of escape that RBC participates in, along with other sectors of globalizing capital. As political scientist David McNally (1999) notes, "interest-bearing money capital cannot escape its ties to the mundane world of labor and production" (para. 14). A good example is Canada's Temporary Foreign Worker Program (TFWP). First created in 1973 to bring high-skilled workers to Canada, the program was expanded in 2002 to include a low-skilled worker category. The total number of temporary foreign workers (TFW) in Canada doubled between 1993 and 2013 to 338,189 workers (Pfeffer, 2013), and from 2006 to 2014 more than 500,000 TFWs have been brought into Canada under the program (Wingrove, 2014). Despite having the same employment rights as Canadian citizens, TFWs are often treated far worse than their Canadian counterparts since their residency is tied to their employer. It is also against federal rules to bring in TFWs if Canadian workers are available for the same job. Even with these limits, RBC, along with 33,000 other companies and agencies from across all sectors of the Canadian economy, have applied to bring in TFWs as part of the program (Robertson et al., 2013).

In the case of RBC, the bank contracted iGate Corp. to handle the outsourcing of specific technology jobs. To rub salt in the wound, RBC expected their Canadian workers to train the very staff who were going to replace them (Tomlinson, 2013). RBC initially denied the charges, but it was eventually forced to issue a public apology (see Royal Bank of Canada, 2013). In standard corporate form, RBC's president and CEO,

Gord Nixon (2013), said that although the bank was technically "compliant with regulations," the outcry was clearly about something else: "The question for many people is not about doing only what the rules require – it's about what employees, clients, shareholders, and Canadians expect of RBC" (para. 5). The significant backlash that accompanied the discovery of RBC's activities led the federal government to amend its TFWP in 2014 and 2016, including new rules restricting access to the program, tougher penalties on employers that break the rules, and greater transparency on labour assessments (Employment and Social Development Canada, 2014; Menon, 2014). The amendments also removed the "four-in, four-out' rule that limited foreign workers to four years in Canada, and low-wage employers are now required to advertise positions first "to under-represented groups in the workforce: youth, persons with disabilities, Indigenous people, and newcomers" (Ly, 2017, para. 8).

The response from Canada's business community was overwhelmingly negative, with pro-business groups claiming that the amendments were "purely political and completely impractical" (Cohen, 2013, para. 1). For example, Dan Kelly, president of the Canadian Federation of Independent Business, argued that the reforms

> were little more than a knee-jerk reaction to intense pressure over recent revelations that a BC mining company hired 201 Chinese workers after an ad seeking Mandarin-speaking miners failed to turn up Canadian candidates, and a group of Royal Bank of Canada employees found themselves training foreigners to replace them after their jobs were outsourced by a contractor. (Cohen, 2013, para. 4)

As many scholars point out, it is unsurprising that these reforms are seen as political and impractical from the perspective of capital because they essentially allow capital to escape the rules of the national labour market, which involve significant regulations on labour gained after more than a century of struggle (Binford, 2013; Lenard & Straehle, 2012; Quintana, 2011). Furthermore, TFW programs provide a convenient solution to some of the problems faced by contemporary national governments: not only do they provide a means of dealing with an aging and declining domestic population by enabling the import of low-wage workers, but the requirement that jobs first be advertised to under-represented groups also represents a means of dealing with Canada's relative surplus population through low-wage employment rather than more significant social welfare reforms or higher paid work.

The response from Canada's corporate sector is thus demonstrative of the extent to which the expansion of capital today is constrained by the continued existence of national labour markets and their associated rights. And despite the response of the federal government to public outcry, the new reforms do nothing to deal with the fundamental reasons why programs like this exist in the first place: to allow capital relatively quick and easy access to flexible, cheap labour for the purposes of extracting greater surplus than is currently possible within the confines of the national labour market. This is exemplified by the federal government's commitment to expand the TFWP in the context of COVID-19 instead of focusing on raising wages. As the executive director of Migrant Workers Alliance for Change, Syed Hussan, points out, "there is no shortage of workers. There's a shortage of more exploitable workers" (as cited in CBC Radio, 2022, para. 3). As Sassen (2006) notes, this is one way in which new forms of territory are constituted "through the development of new jurisdictional geographies" that rely on the earlier framework for rights and guarantees that was "developed in the context of the formation of national states" (p. 388). Rather than working to strengthen the national political economy, however, in our present epoch these instruments work to strengthen a global organizing dynamic of accumulation that not only alters the valence of older nation-state capabilities but also pushes "national states to go against the interests of national capital" (p. 388). This can happen, for instance, when the largest firms are allowed to purchase cheap labour from abroad while smaller businesses operating at the local scale are forced to rely on higher-paid domestic labour, thereby reducing one aspect of their competitiveness. While small tweaks have been made to reduce the harshness of the TFWP, that it exists at all is emblematic of the ways in which capital must now escape the property relations of the national epoch to expand. A recent example can be seen with the Canadian-based fast-food company Freshii, which now uses iPads to outsource cashier jobs to workers in Nicaragua who are paid only USD$3.75 an hour (Lorinc, 2022a).

Attempts to escape national regulations can also be seen in the increasingly illicit activities that have become a part of the normal workings of the global financial system, as evidenced by the numerous examples provided by RBC. In 2009, for instance, the minister of national revenue, Jean-Pierre Blackburn, revealed that

> 106 wealthy people had used RBC Dominion Securities Inc., the brokerage house of the Royal Bank of Canada, to set up offshore accounts in the European principality of Liechtenstein. As much as $100 million in total

was sitting in these accounts. One account alone held $12 million. (Livesey, 2012, p. 151)

As a result of an investigation by the Canada Revenue Agency (CRA), the federal government was eventually able to recover "$6 million in taxes from these accounts, but nobody was charged or fined" (p. 151). In a similar vein, RBC was accused by US regulators in 2012 of orchestrating a complex wash and trade scheme through its various subsidiaries from 2007 to 2010, allowing the bank to earn lucrative tax credits by purchasing dividend-paying stock in the US and Canada. According to the Commodity Futures Trading Commission (CFTC), the scheme was the largest "ever brought forward based on the value of the securities traded, which it said were in the 'hundreds of millions of dollars'" (Robertson & Kiladze, 2012, para. 3). RBC eventually ended up paying USD$35 million to settle the lawsuit (Reuters, 2014).

The same year, RBC was also suspected of manipulating interest rates as part of the London Interbank Offered Rate (LIBOR) scandal (Nelson, 2012). While RBC managed to avoid the criminal charges and fines levied on its competitors by US, UK, and European regulators,[5] the manipulation enabled several global banks, including Deutsche Bank, Barclays, Citigroup, JPMorgan Chase, Union Bank of Switzerland (UBS), and the Royal Bank of Scotland, to make millions from financial derivatives in what has been described as "big banking's 'tobacco moment' – when informed commentators could no longer ignore or explain away the depredations of an industry" (Pasquale, 2015, p. 122).[6] As a complex form of debt that derives its value from another source, derivatives can range "from other types of debt to material goods such as buildings and crops" (Sassen, 2014a, p. 117). Since the value of a derivative depends on the prevailing rate of interest, which is commonly calculated based on the LIBOR (Lapavitsas, 2013b, p. 9), the

---

[5] Almost two dozen people were charged, and fines totalled near $9 billion (CBC News, 2016a; Fernando, 2021; Freifeld, 2015).

[6] Interestingly, Tom Hayes, a trader working for UBS who was sent to prison as part of the scandal, had previously worked at RBC, where he "had taken ambitious trading positions using dubious models that exaggerated his success" (Bradshaw, 2017, para. 4). A spokesperson for RBC claimed that the bank "made the appropriate disclosure to the regulator regarding the termination of Mr. Hayes' employment at RBC, and then to UBS as a professional courtesy" (para. 18). A UBS employee, however, wrote a file note, stating that RBC "was, if not backtracking, at least playing down the severity of the seriousness of the issues … One surmises that if UBS were to take significant action this may place RBC … in an uncomfortable position" (as cited in Bradshaw, 2017, paras. 19–20).

conflict of interest should be clear. Having previously kept its distance from the process of setting Canada's version of LIBOR, the Canadian Dealer Offered Rate (CDOR), the Office of the Superintendent of Financial Institutions (OSFI) announced in 2014 that it "would take more of an active role in oversight and would examine the 'governance and risk controls' of the banks involved" (McLannahan, 2018, para. 8).

More recently, the Fire and Police Pension Association of Colorado has accused nine large banks, including RBC, of manipulating CDOR over a period of seven years to boost their profits from derivatives trading.[7] Like the LIBOR scandal, the suit claimed that

> the banks conspired to "suppress" CDOR by making artificially low submissions that did not reflect the actual rates at which they were lending ... By lowballing submissions, the banks stood to make more money from their derivatives business, from which they "aggressively" marketed and sold interest-rate swaps, forward-rate agreements and other CDOR-based products to pension funds, hedge funds and companies in North America. (McLannahan, 2018, paras. 4–5)

Alleging violations of "the Sherman Act, a landmark antitrust statute; the Commodity Exchange Act, which governs futures trading; and the Racketeer Influenced Corrupt Organization Act" (para. 12), the case was eventually thrown out, since "the wrongful conduct occurred in Canada, which is not covered by the US anti-racketeering law known as RICO, and the plaintiff failed to show that any rigging left it worse off" (Stempel, 2019, para. 7).

Similarly, in 2019, both RBC and TD were forced to pay the OSC a combined USD$18.4 million in fines as part of the foreign exchange market (FX) rigging scandal that emerged in 2013, in which global banks colluded over a decade to manipulate foreign exchange rates to their benefit (Abdel-Qader, 2019).[8] While RBC has so far managed to avoid any damage to its reputation as a result of these scandals, the

---

7 The other banks involved are BMO, Bank of America, Merrill Lynch, Deutsche Bank, Scotiabank, CIBC, HSBC, National Bank of Canada, and TD (McLannahan, 2018).
8 Although a less significant sum, RBC was also fined by the Financial Consumer Agency of Canada (FCAC) for $350,000 for a failure to obtain consent from customers to increase their credit limits. The judgement was reached in 2019, and RBC "asked for the penalty to be halved and that it not be named" (Consumers Council of Canada, 2021, para. 5). The agency has also released a report, *Mystery Shopping at Domestic Retail Banks* (FCAC, 2022), suggesting that the chartered banks offer inappropriate financial products to racialized customers.

website Violation Tracker (n.d.) notes that the bank and its subsidiaries have been forced to pay up to $981,987,409 in penalties in the United States alone since 2000.[9] As sociologist Alain Deneault (2018) points out, "economic globalization means that businesses delocalize and register their operations in a fragmented manner, so that they can bypass the social and taxation laws of the countries where their head offices and the markets for their products are located" (p. 51). At almost every turn, the tendency today is towards escaping national restrictions on accumulation activities; that is, of course, unless firms can restrict the nation state from even possessing the legal right to do so. Enter the new free trade agreements.

The New Free Trade Agreements

The astute reader will note that I have been somewhat reticent to talk specifically about the ways in which Canada fits into or is affected by this emerging centrifugal dynamic. While I have pointed out that this movement increasingly reduces the meaning and efficacy of Canadian liberal democracy, I have said less about where Canada is going and what we might expect of the country's economy in the years to come. To explore those questions, let us begin by reflecting on some of the larger shifts from the political economy of Canada's past. This will help make clearer some of the epoch-level changes that are occurring today by way of globalization.

While foreign direct investment (FDI) and Canadian direct investment abroad (CDIA) have long been a barometer of Canada's location in the global political economy, they operate in qualitatively different ways than in the past. Not only have FDI *and* CDIA tripled since 1996, but the main sectors for investment both abroad *and* in Canada are in finance, insurance, and management, not branch-plant manufacturing, as was the case historically. In 2012, for instance, 52.9 per cent of total

---

9 For instance, Deneault (2018) notes that "in 2014, the Royal Bank of Canada (RBC) was accused of illegal transactions in its Cayman Islands and Bahamas subsidiaries. The bank had breached the law by failing to produce, in a timely manner, all of the documents requested by the Commodity Futures Trading Commission (CFTC), the independent federal agency that regulates commodity exchanges in the United States" (p. 53). A year later, RBC was forced to pay the same agency "USD$35 million for having pretended to sell derivatives to its offshore subsidiaries in the Bahamas, the Cayman Islands, and Luxembourg, in order to reduce taxes owed in Canada" (p. 53). For examples of other illegal activities conducted by the chartered banks, see IE Staff (2021); Livesey (2012); Marchese (2021); Nikolova (2021); SEC (2021).

CDIA was in the finance, insurance, and management industries, followed by the mining, oil, and gas extraction sector at 18.8 per cent:

> Meanwhile, the share of investment in manufacturing fell below 10% for the first time, continuing a decline which has seen that sector's share of Canadian investment abroad decline from a peak of 31.9% in 2000. The finance, insurance and management industries also accounted for a significant share of foreign direct investment in Canada with 32.6% of total investment in 2012. The manufacturing sector remained a significant destination of foreign direct investment in 2012 with a 28.7% share, while the mining and oil and gas extraction industry accounted for a further 19%. (Statistics Canada, 2013)

Although direct investment, both in and outside of Canada, remains tied to the US, the UK, and Europe, it is important to note that the next highest amount of outgoing FDI is invested in known tax havens. As Klassen (2009) accurately points out, the circuits of capital in Canada mirror the wider globalization and financialization of the circuitry of capital at the world scale; foreign ownership of Canadian assets and revenues also remains low by historical and comparative standards: in 2009, foreign ownership of Canadian assets and revenues was 19.7 per cent and 28.9 per cent, respectively (Statistics Canada, 2011). While transnational enterprises represent less than 1 per cent of enterprises in Canada, they own 67 per cent of total assets in both the financial and non-financial sectors (Schaffter & Fortier-Labonte, 2019). To better account for these changes, let us once again reflect on what RBC has been up to since 2008 and how its activities reflect the larger transformation of global capitalism.

In the last decade, RBC has shifted its focus towards "high net worth and ultra-high net worth clients in key areas of expansion, including Canada, the US, the British Isles and Asia" (Canadian Press, 2014, para. 6). The move reflects larger global shifts in class composition, as evidenced by a now infamous 2005 memo from Citibank. In the memo, Citibank argued that the world was being divided into two blocs: "the plutonomies, where economic growth is powered by and largely consumed by the wealthy few, and the rest" (Kapur et al., 2005, p. 1). The memo projected that the key plutonomies – the US, the UK, and Canada – would likely see "even more income inequality, disproportionately feeding off a further rise in the profit share of their economies, capitalist-friendly governments, more technology-driven productivity, and globalization" (p. 2). No longer made up of national consumers, plutonomies are divided between the rich, "few in number but disproportionate in the gigantic slice of income and consumption they take," and "the rest, the 'non-rich,' the multitudinous many" that account for "surprisingly small bites of the national pie" (p. 2). Citibank's advice for their wealthy clients was not to worry, since "the plutonomy is here [and] is going to get stronger, its membership swelling from globalized enclaves in the emerging world" (p. 2). Their concluding recommendation was that "a 'plutonomy basket' of stocks should continue to do well. These toys for the wealthy have pricing power and staying power" (p. 2). A more recent analysis by UBS and PricewaterhouseCoopers (PwC) demonstrates that in response to these economic forces, billionaires were also increasing their investments in art and sport franchises prior to the COVID-19 pandemic (see Stadler et al., 2017).

RBC's post-2008 strategy confirms the unfortunate reality of Citibank's memo. Unwilling to spend the necessary funds to compete with larger regional players, RBC abandoned its US retail strategy with the sale of Centura Bank to PNC Financial in 2011,[10] deciding instead to focus on its two remaining US divisions, RBC Wealth Management and RBC Capital Markets. As the tenth largest global investment bank, RBC Capital Markets has since "expanded its sales and research coverage from nine to thirteen industry sectors and has added more than 270 new borrowing clients, bringing its US loan portfolio to USD$65 billion" (Meredith & Darroch, 2017, p. 159). RBC Wealth Management also received a boost with the purchase of City National, Hollywood's banker to the stars. Purchased for USD$5.4 billion after RBC's official year-end on 21 October 2015 – a year in which the bank earned record profits of $10 billion – the acquisition was seen by commentators as a hedge against slumping oil prices "in the face of withering growth prospects at home" (Trichur & Steinberg, 2015, para. 1).

As much has been admitted by RBC's president and CEO, Dave McKay, who has repeatedly complained about the state of Canada's economy in a series of speeches across the country. At the Canadian Club of Montreal, for instance, McKay (2018a) pointed to the increasing flow of capital leaving the country, arguing that "we need to take stock of our competitive conditions" (p. 4). In a speech to the Calgary Chamber of Commerce, he linked these concerns to the development

---

10 As Meredith and Darroch (2017) note, RBC Centura's 439 branches and USD$27 billion in assets "was no match for SunTrust, a strong regional player with 1,685 branches and USD$130 billion in assets" (p. 158). Centura was sold by RBC to PNC Financial in 2011 for USD$3.6 billion, "less than Centura's book value" (p. 158).

of Canada's oil sector, noting that the rise of America's oil industry has transformed the main buyer of our country's oil and gas products into "our major competitor, not only because of what they are producing, but also how cheaply they are producing it" (McKay, 2018b, p. 7). In response to those who might claim that we should restrict, rather than enhance, our production of such products, he apathetically concludes that "as we approach 2030, oil and gas consumption will be 10 percent higher than today. This remains true no matter what Canada does as a country" (McKay, 2018b, p. 7). In an address to shareholders at the 150th Annual Meeting of the Royal Bank in Halifax, McKay (2019) similarly starts off by claiming – after first highlighting a record $12.4 billion in earnings – that he often hears "concerns from investors about Canada's falling position in the world" (p. 6). Arguing that "we need to be honest with ourselves – about our economic growth and our ability to compete globally in an era of disruption" (p. 5) – he concludes a section entitled "Build New Foundations for a Global Canada" with the following statement: "Canada's lost $100 billion in energy projects in the last two years alone. We simply can't afford to lose any more" (p. 6).

As the co-directors of the Corporate Mapping Project point out, it is not particularly surprising that RBC is "anxious for a return to a booming Canadian oil and gas sector" (Daub & Carroll, 2016, para. 6). Despite the CEO's constant refrain that the bank is "active in supporting clients in renewable energy, clean transportation, and other low carbon sectors" (McKay, 2019, p. 3) – a process the Care Collective (2020) refers to as "care-washing" (p. 11), where corporations pretend to act like they care about relevant social issues – RBC is also "the world's largest financier of the oil sands, the second-largest investor in 'extreme' fossil fuels (over USD$26 billion since 2015) and the second-largest direct owner of the fossil fuel industry in Canada" (Yunker, 2021, para. 1).[11] With the exception of the three major private oil companies – Nexen, Talisman Energy/Repsol, and Shell Canada – RBC has an ownership stake over 5 per cent in every single one of the other 12 publicly traded companies operating in Alberta's oil sands, all of which are predominantly foreign owned (Carroll & Huijzer, 2018; Daub & Carroll, 2016; Laxer, 2021).

Political economist Gordon Laxer (2021) points out that these fully or majority foreign-owned corporations (that typically get loans from the chartered banks) maintain and assert "their power through control

---

11 For more details on how RBC funds the fossil fuel sector, see its profile on BankTrack (https://www.banktrack.org/bank/rbc) and the Corporate Mapping Project (https://www.corporatemapping.ca/profiles/royal-bank-of-canada).

over the apex oil and gas lobby group, the Canadian Association of Petroleum Producers (CAPP)" (p. 4). By wrapping themselves in the Canadian flag and promoting a discourse of supporting the national interest, an agglomeration of foreign and domestic corporations has not only been able to influence provincial governments of all stripes in Alberta but also gaslight the Canadian population into believing that foreign funds have been flowing to Indigenous communities, environmentalists, and other groups opposing the continued development of the Canadian oil industry (p. 4). In the context of the current climate crisis, the protestors that showed up to RBC's Bay Street headquarters on 29 October 2021, promoting the hashtag #RBCIsKillingMe and spray-painting an image of a bear devouring the RBC lion next to a world on fire, were simply telling it like it is (Sharp & Winter, 2021).[12] Despite beginning its annual shareholders meeting with land acknowledgements, and having an entire page on its website devoted to its relationships with Indigenous communities,[13] RBC funds the Coastal GasLink pipeline against the wishes of Wet'suwet'en hereditary chiefs. Described as a "carbon bomb" by Marc Lee, a senior economist with the Canadian Centre for Policy Alternatives (Britten, 2018), the project is meant to transport natural gas to a plant in Kitimat, where it will be processed and exported to global markets.

As McKay (2019) puts it himself, RBC is a bank, and banks move to where the money is: "That's why we've gone where our clients have gone – expanding across Canada, the United States, and to select global markets" (p. 2). It is also why RBC recently decided to sell its Eastern Caribbean banking operations. Despite having been in the region for over 100 years, an outlook of only moderate growth meant that the sale was necessary for the bank as means of de-risking its holdings (Canadian Press, 2019). While RBC may be able to move where the money is, its current strategy suggests a more dire future for working-class Canadians. In referring to the bank's renewed focus on what it refers to as "high ultra net worth individuals" (Fukakusa, 2013, p. 2) via its purchase of City National, McKay pointed out that "the combined high-net population of these three markets [New York, Los Angeles,

---

12 More recently, celebrities have begun boycotting City National due to its support for the Coastal GasLink project (Judd, 2022). In Montreal, a group of eco-anarchists torched cars belonging to Michael Fortier, a former Harper cabinet minister and current vice chairman of RBC Capital Markets (Goldenberg, 2022). The bank is also being investigated by the Competition Bureau over its deceptive marketing strategies regarding climate change (Lagerquist, 2022).
13 See https://www.rbc.com/indigenous.

San Francisco] is over 4½ times the entire high-net-worth population of Canada (as cited in Pittis, 2015, para. 16). As such, RBC is also looking to move into "other places with a lot of rich people such as Houston and London" (para. 17), a reality borne out by the bank's recent purchase of Brewin Dolphin, one of the largest British wealth management firms (Royal Bank of Canada, 2022), and its $13.5-billion purchase of HSBC Canada. McKay hopes that the move will make RBC "the bank of choice for commercial clients with international needs ... affluent clients who need global banking and wealth management capabilities" (as cited in P. Evans, 2022, para. 3). While the press repeatedly suggests that "Canadians of all walks of life will benefit if McKay's strategy turns out to be profitable" (Pittis, 2015, para. 17), since RBC is the largest asset in most Canadian stock portfolios, including the Canada Pension Plan Investment Fund and the Quebec Pension Plan, this position neglects how the ongoing financialization of capitalism has impacted the balance sheets of working-class Canadians.

As Seccareccia and Pringle (2020) point out, the continued expansion of household credit "has partly compensated for the slowdown in private business investment that has been associated with Canada's relatively anemic overall real GDP growth since the 1980s" (p. 333). The problem with this strategy, of course, is that – as Margaret Thatcher once said about socialism – you eventually "run out of other people's money" ("Margaret Thatcher," 2016). Business scholars Meredith and Darroch (2017) note that "with many of their customers now maxed out on mortgages, credit card debt, and auto and student loans, the banks have limited scope to boost revenues through new lending products and services" (p. 66). With most Canadians caught in an unsustainable debt trap – even middle-income groups were unable to reduce their debt after the 2008 financial crisis (Seccareccia & Pringle, 2020, p. 340) – it is no surprise that the banks are looking upwards and abroad for new profit opportunities.

McKay has attempted to downplay concerns about rising debt levels, arguing that a housing crisis in Canada is unlikely since "higher interest rates are only likely if the overall economy is doing well" (as cited in Shecter, 2017, para. 4). Besides, added BMO CEO Bill Downe, people only walked away from their mortgages during the 2008 financial crisis "when they lost their jobs, got a divorce, or if the value of their home fell to 60 per cent or less than the mortgage" (para. 6). Comforting words. Over the last few years, the BIS, IMF, Moody's, and the S&P Global Ratings have all warned that Canada's record-high levels of consumer debt have the potential to collapse Canada's biggest banks in the event of another financial crisis (Onoszko, 2018), and there is nothing to suggest that this overall trend will reverse anytime soon. As Kalman-Lamb (2017) points out, since the chartered banks are still committed to "mortgage securitization as a key profit source" (p. 308), there is a clear incentive not only to increase national home prices but also "to pursue profits by further bundling mortgages with [Mortgage Investment Corporations] or even experimenting with new forms of riskier securitization" (p. 313).[14] Over the course of the COVID-19 pandemic, Canadians took on an additional $193 billion in new mortgage debt, bringing total household debt to a record $2.5 trillion (Hussain, 2021). Although the Bank of Canada has slowly begun creeping up interest rates to tame inflation, and various foreign homebuyer bans are being explored (Ferreira, 2023), the damage has already been done; mortgage debt in Canada is currently growing at double the rate of the economy and currently sits at over 100 per cent of the country's GDP (P. Evans, 2023).

As RBC and the other chartered banks attempt to hedge their bets against an anemic Canadian economy, we should do well to take note of the institutional framework that allows them to do so. As pointed out by a wide variety of scholars, investment and free trade agreements represent a significant means by which the nation states' ability to constrain globalizing capital is restricted (Cutler, 2011; Gill, 1992; Harmes, 2006; McBride, 2011; Slobodian, 2018; Streeck, 2014). Take, for example, the Comprehensive Economic Trade Agreement (CETA) agreed by the Harper government and the European Union in 2013 and signed by the Trudeau administration in 2016 – a process ironically negotiated by then Liberal Minister of Trade Chrystia Freeland (2012), author of *Plutocrats: The Rise of the New Global Super-Rich and the Fall of Everyone Else*. Supported by the Canadian Bankers Association, and thus, all of Canada's major banks, CETA is like NAFTA in that it utilizes existing national legal systems to protect and enforce global corporate private property. It does this by giving European firms operating in Canada (and vice versa) new rights to launch legal challenges against the government over policy or regulatory changes that inhibit their ability to accumulate capital.

---

14 As Kalman-Lamb (2017) further notes, the chartered banks issue their own mortgage-backed Canadian covered bonds (CCBs), and "from 2010 to 2014, the volume of CCBs issued more than tripled from a small volume of $22 billion to $75 billion, with almost 90 percent going to US and Eurozone capital markets (p. 308). The National Bank of Canada and RBC have also explored "the bundling of uninsured subprime 'alt-A' mortgages originated within the shadow banking sector by Equitable Group and Home Capital, the same alternative lender found to have originated almost $2 billion in fraudulent mortgages in 2014" (p. 313).

Since Canada has already been subject to 35 of these challenges under NAFTA (Sinclair, 2015), it is likely that this number could rise substantially over the coming decades. We might expect this because CETA goes much further than NAFTA as an instrument of corporate power. Covering a significantly broader range of investor protections, the agreement gives European banks the right to sue the Canadian government if they believe that they are being discriminated against relative to other Canadian or foreign investors. They can also sue on the broader basis of not being offered fair and equitable treatment. With the potential to win millions, or even billions, if they succeed, there is little chance that Canada's state managers fail to take account of this when drafting financial policy. As international investment law professor Gus Van Harten remarks, "with billions of dollars at stake, you're going to think very carefully about what an unknown trio of arbitrators is going to do with the fair and equitable treatment clause as applied to the financial sector" (as cited in Whittington, 2014, para. 15). While the federal government has so far been able to negotiate a carve out that allows them to preserve the widely held ownership rule – thus barring any direct foreign takeover of Canada's banks – as well as their ability to regulate the financial sector, this provision only goes so far as is necessary to stabilize the Canadian financial system. To regulate the financial sector, the government must first demonstrate "before a 'financial services committee' that its actions were indeed to reduce risks and contagion, rather than a back-door to restriction competition" (Beltrame & Blanchfield, 2013, para. 18). Unless that committee comes to a consensus that "the government's use of prudent measures was legitimate and therefore not a breach of the foreign investors' rights" (Whittington, 2014, para. 19), the case moves forward to a tribunal consisting of "a panel of fifteen members who will be appointed for a renewable 5-year term by a joint committee of the two parties to the treaty (i.e., the EU and Canada) rather than selected members of the dispute" (Pistor, 2019, p. 157). While this is certainly an upgrade over the existing process, it remains to be seen whether this change will have any effect on the overall outcome.

As instruments of corporate power, so-called free trade agreements like CETA are used to restrict the ability of nation states to regulate the activities of TNCs, no matter where they are based. Although these agreements have so far been limited to regional blocs, larger, more wide-ranging agreements, such as the CPTPP, seek to continue the trend of creating economic megaregions.[15] As the constitutional basis for

---

15 The countries involved with the CPTPP are Australia, Brunei, Canada, Chile, Japan, Malaysia, Mexico, New Zealand, Peru, Singapore, and Vietnam. China, Taiwan,

"quasi-states for capital, detached from any formal or legitimate means of countervailing political leverage" (Teeple, 2007, p. 136), these agreements are ultimately the institutional and political mechanisms used to consolidate a system of global corporate private property. They essentially function as supra-constitutions that work to defend the economic freedom of corporate actors against democratic attempts to challenge their right to devastate the environment and privatize government services. Why else would investors need agreements that supersede the democratic decisions of the citizens of particular countries?

Given what we've already covered, it should be little surprise that Canada's chartered banks support such agreements. An early report from BMO, for instance, notes that if the original Trans-Pacific Partnership (TPP) had gone forward, it would have not only improved the bank's access to high-growth markets in Asia, such as Malaysia, Vietnam, and Singapore, but also "temper[ed] the dominance of state-owned enterprises in banking and insurance" (Chen et al., 2015, p. 9). With Canada officially joining the CPTPP in October 2018, Canadian corporations now enjoy preferential access to almost 90 per cent of its export markets, and Canada is the only G7 country to have free trade access to the United States, Europe, and the Asia–Pacific region, all at the same time.[16] This is no small matter given that the export of Canadian financial services has more than doubled over the past decade (Sutherland, 2014). It is thus no surprise that in the middle of NAFTA renegotiations, RBC CEO Dave McKay (2018a) made sure to comment that "with the world at risk of turning inward, taking advantage of our trade agreements is something we need to execute" (p. 8). Continuing, he added: "We're at risk of losing our competitive edge. Canada remains a great place to do business, but it's not the only great place in the world" (p. 9).

While it is certainly up for debate as to whether this overall trend will continue, I am sceptical that events like Brexit, or Donald Trump pulling out of the first iteration of the CPTPP, are relevant indicators of a return to a more nation-centred politics. As popular responses to

---

and the UK have also applied to join. Canada is also in talks with Taiwan to sign a foreign investment agreement (Reuters, 2022).

16 Mertins-Kirkwood (2022) also notes that "Canada has started but not yet concluded negotiations toward 11 new free trade agreements (covering 40 countries) and 15 new bilateral investment treaties ... If all these agreements were to come into force, they would provide coverage for an additional 3% of Canadian foreign investment, as well as creating overlapping coverage for several countries, such as Argentina, Barbados, and the Philippines" (pp. 7–8).

global capitalism, they do not appear to fundamentally challenge the trajectory identified here. For instance, despite pulling out from the CPTPP, the Biden administration unveiled in May 2022 the Indo-Pacific Economic Framework (IPEF), a new agreement involving 13 countries in the Indo-Pacific region ("America's New," 2022; "US Will Not Join CPTPP," 2021). Similarly, while many financial institutions were happy to see Trump's rejection of the Basel III regulations, even financial consultants in Washington know that such accords "are there to prevent global financial catastrophes, not boost short-term growth" (as cited in "Basel Is on Life Support," 2016, para. 11); as such, they tend not to be ignored for long, as demonstrated by the Biden administration's renewed focus on implementing them.

Brexit is similar in that analysts worry that the United Kingdom will react to a loss of investment in the City of London by reducing financial, tax, and labour regulations, leading to a race to the bottom with other jurisdictions that could ultimately lead to more crises in the future (Barber, 2017; D. Thomas & Stafford, 2021). Far from signalling the demise of globalization, Brexit has merely enabled new bilateral trade agreements, containing many of the same corporate rights, to take the place of larger, multilateral agreements, as evidenced by the one made between Canada and the UK in 2021. As Prime Minister Justin Trudeau pointed out, now the two countries can "work on a bespoke agreement, a comprehensive agreement, over the coming years that will really maximize our trade opportunities" (as cited in McGregor & Patel, 2020, para. 2). With the rights of financial institutions in the balance, it should be no surprise that a 2017 analysis by the CBC found that since Trudeau's election, there have been 410 communication reports filed with the Office of the Commissioner of Lobbying of Canada by the six largest banks and the CBA (Thompson, 2017).

As should be clear, trade and investment agreements do nothing more than move the rights of capital upwards, far away from any countervailing policy mechanisms. In doing so, they reduce the ways in which the citizens of nation states can legitimately challenge capital's inherent drive to turn the entire world into a single, unified market. All of this does not mean that nation states no longer protect their own firms,[17] or that existing

---

17 This is made clear by Canada's rejection of the Aecon takeover by state-owned China Communications Co. Ltd. (Fife & Chase, 2018), its banning of Huawei from Canada's 5G network (Hertzberg & Platt, 2022), and its moves to tighten foreign investment rules for state-owned entities, or firms investing in companies related to public health or critical goods and services in the wake of COVID-19 (Walsh et al., 2020).

imperialist relations are disrupted.[18] As Jessop (2018) notes, "while the world market is the ultimate horizon of capital accumulation, integration proceeds in an uneven, combined manner that, using a contemporary scientific term, can be described as fractal" (p. 210). Though much has been made of the effort to leave China out of the first iteration of the CPTPP (of which they applied to join in 2021),[19] far less has been made of the numerous bilateral trade deals pursued by China, as well as its membership in the Regional Comprehensive Economic Partnership (RCEP).[20] Despite disagreements leading to the removal of investor–state dispute settlement (ISDS) mechanisms in the initial version, member states have since agreed to restart ISDS negotiations in 2024 (Ranald, 2019).

Rather than asking the old question of whether Canadian or foreign capitalists dominate the domestic market, as is common in recent debates (see, for example, T. Gordon & Webber, 2018), it seems to me that we should instead be asking questions that help us better understand this ongoing transformation. How are the property relations that sustain capital changing? How do they alter the role and nature of the nation state? How do they alter the relationships between states, or between the core and periphery, or between ever-growing globalizing capitals and nationally delimited citizens? By granting globalizing capitals rights that protect their economic freedoms across multiple nation states, trade and investment agreements fundamentally rearrange the property relations of the national epoch of capitalism. In doing so, many of the capabilities used to develop Canada's economy in earlier historical periods are now restricted under the terms of these agreements, with others under threat as they reach even further "into the realm of domestic policy" (McBride, 2005, p. 186). This phenomenon is thus not simply something that is enacted on peripheral countries by

---

18 Mertins-Kirkwood (2022) notes the following in his study of how Canadian firms use trade and investment agreements: "Whatever the legal arrangement, there is a clear trend toward the ISDS system being used by wealthy corporations to punish poor governments for taking action to control their own resources, protect the environment or otherwise act in the public interest" (p. 21).

19 As Tooze (2018) notes, the goal of leaving China out of the first iteration of the CPTPP "was not to face China down, let alone to stop its economic growth. Everyone had too much to gain. The aim was to establish a bloc strong enough to offer a counterweight to China's rising strength. It was, as one of Hillary Clinton's indiscreet correspondents dubbed it, a 'de facto China containment alliance'" (p. 486).

20 The RCEP includes Australia, Brunei, Cambodia, China, Indonesia, Japan, South Korea, Laos, Malaysia, Myanmar, New Zealand, the Philippines, Singapore, Thailand, and Vietnam.

core ones, because the restriction of nation-state capabilities similarly impacts the governments of core countries as well.

Our emerging global epoch can thus be characterized as one in which, in continuing to grow, capital is attempting to craft a global system of rights that limits the ability of nation states to restrict its movement or legislate against corporate activity. Political economist Shawn Nichols (2018) notes:

> In adopting ISDS, states advance a legal narrative that directs and sanctions a particular set of production relations and exploitation, ultimately reproducing the power of transnational actors and entities seeking the most beneficial conditions for capital wherever it might flow or operate. (p. 264)

If we recall that capital is not a thing but "a definite social relation of production pertaining to a particular historical social formation" (Marx, 1894/1993b, p. 953), and that property relations are "a legal expression" (Marx, 1859/1978b, p. 4) of the relations of production, we should therefore understand this overall process as the much larger making of global capital(ism) – one that necessarily includes a fundamental reorganization of the assemblage of territory, authority, and rights that characterized the previous national epoch of capitalism that ended in the 1970s. As mentioned above, this is no doubt an uneven development, and there is significant resistance from certain quarters, including some national political parties. But critical scholars and activists should beware of the various ways in which the emerging property relations of global capitalism transform the role of the nation state, the meaning of liberal democracy, and the potential for anticapitalist struggle.

Blockchain: Making Global Property

> We're experimenting with taking an asset and breaking it into smaller pieces and registering that in a decentralized register called blockchain. You can take an asset or even a company and create a unit on a decentralized blockchain and then sell that into the marketplace.
> – Dave McKay, president and CEO of RBC (as cited in Schwartz, 2019, para. 15)

Another example of the centrifugal dynamic of our epoch can be seen in some of the new technologies being utilized by the financial sector, in particular, blockchain technology, which, according to some, has the potential to transform not only the financial system but the entire global political economy. On 21 October 2008, six weeks after the collapse of Lehman Brothers (the event typically associated with the start of the 2008 financial crisis), a mysterious figure known only by the pseudonym Satoshi Nakamoto released a white paper entitled, "Bitcoin: A Peer-to-Peer Electronic Cash System." The paper set out to solve a long-standing problem in the creation of digital money: the double spender problem. If digital money is simply a token, how does one ensure that it is only spent once? The solution was blockchain: a digital public ledger that is distributed and verified across an entire network. The significant change was the demise of an institution of trust (a financial institution) to verify the transaction, and the fact that "neither the purchaser nor supplier has control over the ledger. Rather, information about exchanges is distributed and available to all, rather than being centralized and often proprietary" (Klaus, 2017, p. 2). In this sense, all transactions have the potential to be transparent and traceable.

The innovation was heralded by many as groundbreaking. *The Economist*, for example, claimed that the blockchain was "on par with the introduction of limited liability for corporations, or private property rights, or the internet itself" ("Next Big Thing," 2015, para. 3). The world's techno-libertarians were especially convinced, claiming that the power of nation states and TNCs would dissolve due to the rise of non-state cryptocurrencies (Frank, 2015; Henwood, 2017; Karlstrøm, 2014). It is still not uncommon, for instance, to see headlines claiming to explain "how blockchain will eliminate banks and democratize money" (Roos, 2017). As smart contracts were added to blockchain (digital contracts enforced automatically by a set of computer protocols) via the Ethereum platform, these types of claims got much wider, with many supporters seeing decentralized autonomous organizations (DAOs) as the means to recreate global society itself (Garrod, 2016). Vitalik Buterin (2014), one of the co-founders of Ethereum, describes DAOs as "long-term smart contracts that contain the assets and encode the bylaws of an entire organization" (p. 1). As such, they are similar to corporations, except that the management function is automated, allowing them to manage themselves.

In a presentation at the Swiss Institute of New York, Buterin explains how all this might work through a description of a typical day in which your rent is automatically deducted from your wallet (and if you are unable to pay, your door no longer recognizes the validity of your smartphone's private keys); the government is a large decentralized organization, allowing you to track your automatic tax payments to their final destination; your transportation to work is in a self-driving car that owns itself (meaning it purchases its own insurance and repairs); and your work is at a hybrid living and working space where people labour as independent contractors for various DAOs (Buterin & Frank 2014). The idea behind DAOs, according to Buterin, is that "real reform isn't just about swapping out bad players for good players. It's really more about the structural ... [DAOs are] about figuring out how we can deinstitutionalize power; how we can ensure that, while power structures do need to exist, that these power structures are modular and they disappear as soon as they're not wanted anymore" (as cited in Frank, 2015, para. 71). As Sam Frank (2015) put it in an article in *Harper's Magazine*, it is a world in which "politics is an engineering problem and every person is a master of atoms and bits" (para. 4).

Supporters' excitement over the possibility of a rational, apolitical, technologically mediated society was dampened almost as soon as these ideas were put into practice. On 30 April 2016, Christoph and Simon Jentzsch, the co-founders of slock.it, a company aiming to connect material items to blockchain via smart locks, released the world's first public, stateless, crowd-sourced, venture capital fund called The DAO (Waters, 2016). The idea was that anyone could join by transferring Ethereum's cryptocurrency, ether, to The DAO, which was itself a smart contract that would give joiners the right to vote on investment proposals for projects to further develop blockchain technology. The DAO quickly became one of the largest crowdfunding successes of all time, raising more than USD$150 million before an oversight in the code allowed one user to siphon out USD$50 million worth of ether to their private account. Eventually, the Ethereum community agreed to a rollback of the software, allowing the original owners to withdraw their funds.

As economic sociologist Vili Lehdonvirta (2016) pointed out on Oxford's *Policy and Internet Blog*, the decision to initiate a rollback of The DAO not only highlighted the reality common to all blockchain systems – that "humans are still very much in charge of setting the rules that the network enforces" (para. 12) – but that the decision goes against the whole reason for having immutable smart contracts in the first place. An article for *The Economist* similarly pointed out that "if code is law, so are bugs in the code – and correcting them may itself mean a breach of contract" ("Not-So-Clever Contracts," 2016, para. 7). While the Jentzsch brothers may have been correct to view the corporation in legal terms as a bundle of contracts, it was clear that they failed to consider that although technology can be used to "enhance the processes of governance (e.g. transparency, online deliberation, e-voting) ... you can't engineer away governance as such" (Lehdonvirta, 2016, para. 16). This issue has similarly been highlighted by sociologist Karen Levy (2017), who notes that by focusing so intently on the technical aspects of contracts, blockchain developers continue to fail to grasp the "social contexts within which contracts operate, and the complex ways in which people use them" (p. 4).

Despite these failures, there remains a persistent discourse among the business press that suggests that while the blockchain may not be as revolutionary as once thought, it still possesses the capability to solve a number of problems associated with global capitalism: online advertising, financial exclusion, fake news, and the existence of huge, monopolistic middle-men tech corporations, like Airbnb and Uber (Casey & Vigna, 2018; Tapscott & Tapscott, 2016). An article in the *New York Times*, for example, argued that "in its potential to break up large concentrations of power and explore less-proprietary models of ownership," blockchain still has the potential to "distribute wealth more equitably" and "break up the cartels of the digital age" (S. Johnson, 2018, para. 65). In other words, blockchain might still produce "an alternative to the winner-take-all model of capitalism than [sic] has driven wealth inequality to heights not seen since the age of the robber barons" (para. 16). In an article in *Forbes*, Joe Lubin, the co-founder of Ethereum and Consensys, makes a similar claim, arguing that blockchain technology will cause the world to shift "'from a scarcity to an abundance mindset' … by 'enable[ing] a self-determined, sovereign identity'" (as cited in Bambrough, 2018, paras. 1–3).

While these sorts of claims may be expected of a business press hoping to sell magazine subscriptions by creating buzz about The Next Big Thing, they can also be witnessed in a growing academic literature on blockchain technology produced by economists, computer scientists, and business and legal scholars (Allen et al., 2018; Bell, 2017; Catalini & Gans, 2019; Fairfield, 2015, 2017; Ishmaev, 2017; Jun, 2018; Nair & Sutter, 2018; Swan, 2015; Tasca & Ulieru, 2016). The basic idea is that because a blockchain is able to enforce property rights "independently of any legal institutions" (Ishmaev, 2017, p. 681), it functions as a sort of "social operating infrastructure" (Jun, 2018, p. 10) that can produce new types of peer-to-peer (p2p) organizations.[21] By

---

21 As management scholars Christian Catalini and Joshua Gans (2019) note, "the ability to track transaction attributes, settle trades and enforce contracts across a wide variety of digital assets is what makes blockchain technology a general purpose technology. Entries on a distributed ledger can represent ownership in currency, intellectual property, equity, information, contracts, financial and physical assets" (p. 3). Similarly, law professor Joshua Fairfield (2017) writes that "using the blockchain, we can recreate the power of everyday property in the online context.

blending "features of competitive markets with the more nuanced forms of governance used within vertically integrated firms and online platforms" (Catalini & Gans, 2019, p. 22), these scholars claim that these new p2p organizations will "open possibilities of 'prosperity for the many' through distribution of value creation (entrepreneurship) and value participation (through distributed ownership of the firm) solving the 'wealth for the few' prosperity paradox plaguing our lives today" (Tasca & Ulieru, 2016, p. 8). In more simple terms, by using a blockchain to "trade, track, and transfer" (Fairfield, 2017, p. 167) money, goods, and services without intermediaries (including our own data), we will finally gain the freedom that was supposed to be part of capitalism all along. These views are shared by blockchain developers, as well. In a review of Eric Posner and E. Glen Weyl's book *Radical Markets* (2018), Ethereum co-founder Vitalik Buterin (2018) writes: "Blockchains may well be used as a technical backbone for some of the solutions described in the book, and Ethereum-style smart contracts are ideal for the kinds of complex systems of property rights that the book explores" (para. 3).

While these lofty claims of an emerging sharing economy may be attractive to some, actual practice shows that the technology is primarily being taken up to enhance business as usual. For instance, at the same time that economist Paolo Tasca and computer scientist Mihaela Ulieru were busy proclaiming in an interview on Nasdaq's website that blockchain will let us "organize our economic life around p2p decentralized sharing economy platforms, with the potential to dramatically narrow the income divide, democratize the global economy and create a more ecologically sustainable society" (as cited in Prisco, 2016, para. 12), Nasdaq was creating a venture capital firm to discover "investment opportunities and partnerships across fintech, including blockchain, machine intelligence, data analytics and cloud" (Cummings, 2017, para. 1). Part of that work has already resulted in a partnership with cryptocurrency exchange Gemini, founded by the Winklevoss twins (of Facebook fame). An article on CNBC notes that "the deal gives Gemini access to Nasdaq's surveillance technology to help make sure the platform provides a fair and 'rules-based marketplace'" (Rooney, 2018, para. 6).

Remember, property interests are simply information: who owns what. We can record those property interests in a public, decentralized blockchain. Transferring MP3s, games, smartphones, even cars and land, can become as simple and low-cost as the transfer of slots on a blockchain" (p. 180).

All across the blockchain universe, examples abound of powerful economic actors investing in, and ultimately co-opting, the technology to speed up and secure the exchange of assets and data and lower labour and overhead costs through automation – a far cry from blockchain's initial purpose to radically dismantle state and corporate power. One need only look at some of the names that were first involved in the R3 consortium, a global payments system: Bank of America, Bank of New York Mellon, Citibank, Deutsche Bank, HSBC, RBC, Société Générale, TD Bank, Barclays, Banco Bilbao Vizcaya Argentaria (BBVA), JPMorgan Chase, and Goldman Sachs (Perez, 2015). While some of these firms have since left R3 to create their own payment systems – such as JPMorgan Chase's Quorum, which involves over 200 of the world's largest financial institutions – R3 still includes companies such as Accenture, Amazon, Intel, Microsoft, Oracle, and KPMG, among others (Andreasyan, 2016; Ho, 2017; Noto, 2017). Other consortiums include Ripple, a global payments network that includes large financial institutions such as RBC, American Express, UBS, BMO, CIBC, BBVA, and Santander, as well as Microsoft's Confidential Consortium Framework (now CCF, but previously referred to affectionately as Coco), which aims to link up public and private blockchains while also enabling individual firms to control what can be seen on their networks; adopters include R3, Intel, JPMorgan Chase, and their respective blockchains (Dollentas, 2017). Amazon has also started offering blockchain templates, allowing their customers to create blockchain-based decentralized applications (dApps); Oracle, IBM, and Huawei offer similar services, as well (Shu, 2018). Ant Financial, affiliate of Chinese e-commerce conglomerate Alibaba and operator of the digital payment service Alipay, has also developed its own blockchain platform to underpin a number of new exchange-related and tracking products (Orcutt, 2019). More recently, JPMorgan Chase has been using Onyx Digital Assets, its private blockchain platform, to allow "banks to lend out US government bonds for a few hours as collateral, without the bonds leaving their balance sheets" (Szalay, 2022, para. 6).[22] Since December 2020, more than USD$300 billion worth of short-term loans have been exchanged via the platform, which uses smart contracts to ensure "that the cash is in the borrower's

---

22 This move solves an interesting problem for large banks. As the article explains, "post-crisis regulatory requirements demand that banks hold large amounts of liquid assets – which can be bought and sold easily even during times of market stress – such as Treasuries as a safety buffer. By tokenising these assets banks can temporarily turn them into collateral for a few hours, but without lowering their safety buffers, which are calculated at the end of each day" (Szalay, 2022, para. 7).

account and that collateral locked up against loans is released at the end of the deal" (para. 9).

Though blockchain was created to reduce the power of financial institutions, it is clear that such institutions are its earliest and most empowered corporate actors, a reality that contradicts claims of an emerging sharing economy. For instance, despite claims of creating a fair and transparent trading ecosystem, scholars demonstrate that many blockchain-based decentralized exchanges are also subject to HFT strategies (Daian et al., 2020; Zhou et al., 2021). Furthermore, as historian Quinn Slobodian (2021b) notes, "the future for crypto now looks less like a techno-utopian dream or libertarian fantasy, and more like subordination to the very thing it was designed to overthrow: the nation state's monopoly over the money supply" (para. 10). This is perhaps best exemplified by El Salvador's adoption of bitcoin as legal tender, a trend that is being followed by some other governments (Renteria & Esposito, 2021).[23] As a recent report from Fidelity Digital Assets notes, "even if other countries do not believe in the investment thesis or adoption of bitcoin, they will be forced to acquire some as a form of insurance" (Kuiper & Neureuter, 2022, para. 9). The authors of the report also make a poignant observation about the history of capital: "History has shown that capital flows to where it is treated best" (para. 9).

RBC, for its part, has been experimenting with the technology since 2017 to move payments between its banks in Canada and the US, and to verify client identities (D. Alexander, 2019a; Scuffham, 2017). As indicated by the opening quote for this section, CEO Dave McKay has

---

23 There are numerous examples of blockchain adoption by various levels of government. Some US states, for instance, recognize smart contracts as legal contracts (Bronsdon, 2019; De, 2018; Neuburger, 2017). Estonia now offers most of its government services online via digital ID cards secured by blockchain technology, allowing identifying information to move effortlessly between different government organizations (Kaljulaid, 2019). One Russian oblast wants to start using blockchains to allow its citizens to distribute their own taxes ("Russia to Implement," 2019). Dubai is planning to use them to create smart courts and, eventually, a blockchain-based judicial system (Debusmann, 2018). The Bank of Canada and the Monetary Authority of Singapore have recently sent each other digital currencies using blockchain technology, marking the first successful trial between two central banks (D. Alexander, 2019b). The mayor of Rio de Janeiro plans to allocate 1 per cent of the city's treasury to bitcoin (Dzhondzhorov, 2022). The mayor of Miami received one of their paychecks in bitcoin and wants to enable citizens to pay taxes and other fees in cryptocurrency (Bostick et al., 2021). Similarly, the mayor of New York will take their first three paychecks in bitcoin (Brooks, 2021). There are also examples of resistance, however, such as the IMF suggesting Argentina discourage the use of cryptocurrencies as part of a $45 billion bailout (W. Daniel, 2022).

also expressed that RBC is looking at using blockchains to tokenize a wide variety of assets. With 27 patents filed relating to blockchain-based means of providing "credit scores, vehicle records, digital rewards, smart contracts, loan offerings and a variety of investment vehicles" (Schwartz, 2019, para. 14), blockchain does not seem to be disrupting finance so much as it is aiding in the overall process of financialization. As McKay accurately points out, the adoption of the technology is "going to explode the number of transactions [and] the complexity of those transactions" (as cited in Orland, 2021b, para. 5). There are currently 64 crypto-related funds on the TSX,[24] and Fidelity has been approved by the IIROC to become Canada's first bitcoin custodian, paving the way for more institutional investors, such as pension funds, portfolio mangers, mutual funds, and exchange-traded funds (ETFs) to get involved with bitcoin (O'Hara, 2021). The approval signifies "that IIROC is prepared to regulate cryptoasset dealers, and that it is permissible for one IIROC member to operate both a traditional securities business and a crypto trading business" (Akhtar, 2021, para. 10).

Far from signifying the demise of traditional financial institutions or overcoming the power of the state, then, the regulation of blockchain-based financial services appears to instead prove correct a point made years earlier in a report made by the Chartered Professional Accountants of Canada (2016):

> To the extent blockchain technology becomes established, government and regulatory bodies, financial institutions, law enforcement agencies, businesses, CPAs, lawyers, technology experts and others will need to be involved. If the momentum of blockchain development continues at the rate indicated by the preceding discussion, new rules, controls, best-practice models and business skills will be needed to make a smooth transition to a blockchain-enabled future. (p. 20)

In the years since the report was released, the Canadian Securities Administrators (CSA) – the umbrella organization for the various provincial and territorial securities regulators – has created a registration regime for crypto asset trading platforms,[25] which includes

---

24 For the full list, see https://money.tmx.com/en/stock-list/CRYPTO_FUNDS_LIST.
25 As of 1 December 2021, there were five Canadian crypto asset trading platforms registered as restricted dealers under securities laws: Wealthsimple Crypto, Coinberry, Netcoins, CoinSmart, and Bitbuy (Akhtar, 2021).

the requirement of holding at least 80 per cent of client crypto assets in cold storage with a "qualified custodian," such as Gemini Trust Company, based in New York and owned by the Winklevoss twins, or Bitgo Trust Company, based out of California (Akhtar, 2021).[26] Similar to the safe-harbour rules proposed by SEC Commissioner Hester M. Peirce (2020) that would allow crypto asset trading platforms in the United States exemption from federal securities laws for three years, restricted dealer crypto asset trading platforms in Canada "are expected to transition to investment dealer registration and obtain membership with the IIROC within two years" (para. 8). As of 2021, the OSC reports that they have had 70 different platforms initiate compliance discussions with securities regulators, and that almost a quarter of them "are based outside of Canada" (OSC, 2021, para. 4). Since then, Coinsquare, Canada's longest-operating crypto asset trading platform, has received dealer registration from the IIROC, enabling the protection of investors' assets through use of "the Canadian Investment Protection Fund in the event of insolvency" (Atlee, 2022, para. 1). The IIROC also gave the firm approval to "operate as a regulated alternative trading system (ATS) in the future" (Ligon, 2022, para. 2) – in other words, a dark pool. In this way, an ostensibly global form of private property (a crypto asset) becomes protected and regulated by nation-state institutions.

Given the massive divide between supporters' claims of an emerging sharing economy and the evolving reality of the blockchain universe (that is, ever-increasing financialization), it is not surprising to see an attendant critical literature suggesting that what is being created is not so much the escape from tyranny, but rather, the techno-institutional framework for a crisis-ridden, hyper-capitalist society that is, as Nancy Fraser (2014) puts it, "commodities all the way down" (p. 545). Legal scholars, for instance, have questioned how blockchains should be regulated by governments, whether it will lead to the codification of law, and how that development might favour already powerful corporations and states (De Filippi & Hassan, 2016; De Filippi & Wright, 2018; Herian, 2018, 2019). This last point has been made forcefully by the urbanist Adam Greenfield (2017), who focuses on the difficulties of regulating dApps due to their non-placeness, the strict character

---

26 Montreal-based cryptocurrency exchange, Shakepay, for instance, uses a third-party custodian based in the US for its cold-storage needs, and it has also secured insurance through the British-American TNC Aon, underwritten by Lloyd's of London (De, 2020).

of smart contracts, their ability to enforce material property rights via smart locks, and the dystopian character of what appears is being created: a global, atomized, entrepreneurial labour force that will live in a world of automated locks. His conclusion, like others, is that blockchain will merely enhance capitalism, and that if "smart contracts work not to protect but to undermine working people, we must conclude that on some level this is what they are for" (p. 155).

While I agree that blockchain will enhance capitalism rather than disrupt it, the critics tend to treat their hypotheses (that blockchains are inherently a dystopian technology) as conclusions instead of initiating a more thorough analysis of the specific ways in which blockchains might work to transform the global political economy and, thus, lead to the hyper-capitalist dystopia that they believe is emerging. For instance, while the power of the platform model, like the blockchain, finds its source "in the way the platform's data and algorithms 'structure the rules and parameters' that are available to participants on the platform" (Rahman & Thelen, 2019, p. 3), platforms must first alter existing national and subnational rules and regulations surrounding their conduct as corporate entities, that is, as "creatures of property relations endowed with the rights of capital" (Clement, 1979, p. 232). Platforms like Uber and Airbnb provide good examples of this phenomenon, operating illegally in many jurisdictions until their widespread adoption forced legislators to change the rules around what could be done with one's private property (CBC News, 2016b; Fedio, 2016; Israel, 2017).

There is ample evidence that this is true in the blockchain universe as well. For instance, Bloomberg's Matt Levine (2022) notes that

> Tether is a hugely popular stablecoin that obeys no capital regulation, lied about its backing for a long time, did shady related-party transactions, got in trouble with regulators and kept on being a hugely popular stablecoin. Meanwhile, Libra/Diem [the stablecoin created by Facebook] asked for approval first, did everything right, and seems to have died a regulatory death. (para. 21)

Levine's point is that "if you just issue a stablecoin without asking the Fed, it probably won't stop you" (para. 22). The question, then, is not merely one of regulating blockchain, or whether the inflexible nature of code might end up frustrating "the legal provisions it purports to implement" (De Filippi & Hassan, 2016, para. 33), but rather the much more specific process whereby national and subnational laws and regulations get transformed into capabilities for transnational accumulation activities.[27] As Lawrence and Mudge (2019) point out, for example, it was only after the Internal Revenue Service (IRS) redefined bitcoin as property, rather than currency, that it became understood as a legitimate investment. As Levine (2022) highlights, however, there is nothing particularly new about this process:

> These are big important companies that try to comply with the law, and the SEC calls them and says "under our interpretation of our precedents you are not complying with the law," and so they change their behavior to comply with the law while also, of course, lobbying the SEC to change the rules to allow the things they want to do. All normal stuff, though normal stuff at the cutting edge of legal and financial developments, so nobody is quite sure what the right answers are. (paras. 4–5)

Before reaching conclusions as to the overall impact of blockchain technology, then, we should instead investigate the critics' hypotheses more closely by researching the ways in which blockchains are becoming embedded in national legal, political, and monetary systems, and how that process alters the configuration and meaning of national territory in a world of increasingly transnational flows of capital.

As Prudham and Coleman (2011) remind us, territory is always "the spatial expression of power relations in general and the more specific expression of property rights and their administration in the delineation of particular spaces" (p. 13). Given blockchain's technological potential to enforce property rights at the global level, we might then

---

27 This is clearest in respect to the attempt to use blockchains to mediate the transfer of material goods. Mattereum, for instance, is a company that aims to use the Ethereum blockchain to control the legal aspect of the exchange of material goods. In an interview, the CEO, Vinay Gupta, notes that for this to occur, there must be a melding of national legal systems and the (supposedly global) world of smart contracts: "Here are all the actors in the system that you actually wind up working with if you want to do this work – it's a big cast of characters. You have the blockchain, you have private courts or arbitrators, you have the national courts … The national courts are in this scheme, because the national court is what rules over the property in the system … We're no longer in a situation where we've just got crypto assets; what we have is crypto assets on one hand and fiat assets on the other, and our job is to join that stuff together seamlessly" (as cited in Shelupanov, 2019, para. 12). Americana Technologies is another company attempting to use microchips to turn material objects into non-fungible tokens (NFTs), not only enabling authentication but also the transfer of ownership and royalties without an intermediary (Lin, 2022). Similarly, while a project in Switzerland has seen 37 households use a blockchain to exchange surplus solar energy, further regulations are needed before the project can expand to the entire country (Chang, 2019).

ask: What new forms of territory do blockchains open up, and which actors are able to use them? How do the property rights that constitute the boundaries of these new territories complicate, frustrate, or contradict existing forms of national territory? How will the proliferation of placeless territories in the form of DAOs be absorbed, restricted, or dominated by nation states? And how might this process contribute to new forms of global integration, disintegration, or hegemony?

China's current development strategy, the Belt and Road Initiative, for instance, includes the creation of a global infrastructure network of blockchains, providing "software developers a cheaper alternative to current server storage space offerings" (Hillman & Sacks, 2021, p. 25). With major blockchain partners including Ethereum, Consensys, and Hyperledger involved, as well as cloud service providers such as Amazon Web Services and Google Cloud, a report from the Council on Foreign Relations notes that the integration of several different blockchains within this network will enable "Beijing to bring this 'international plumbing,' including the network infrastructure in Australia, Brazil, France, Japan, South Africa, and the United States, under its influence" (p. 25). Such concerns should be expected from the Council, of course, given its long-standing connections to big American capital and empire-building. But we should be wary of putting too much emphasis on these traditional geographic markers considering the changing nature of the property relations that sustain them. While we are no doubt a bit early to the party here, we should keep our eye on the ways in which blockchain's initial purpose – avoiding state constraints on economic freedom – transforms as it develops, contributing to new territories of accumulation, as well as resistance, and the ways in which this process both involves and reorients existing national institutions, complicating our understanding of the analytical categories we use to describe them. We might recall that many absolutist kings supported the activities of merchants thinking that it was contributing to their royal power, and not, as history would have it, providing the basis for an entirely different mode of production that would significantly reduce that power and reorient its dynamics. Perhaps this is more of the same?

COVID-19 and the New Normal

We live in a country where if you want to go bomb somebody, there's remarkably little discussion about how much it might cost. But when you have a discussion about whether or not we can assist people who are suffering, then suddenly we become very cost conscious.

– Andrew Bacevich (as cited in Boston University, 2014, para. 5)

If the COVID-19 pandemic is a rehearsal for climate change, as sociologist Bruno Latour (2020) suggests, we must ask: What does this dress rehearsal tell us about the possibilities or pitfalls of our current age? While Bacevich's quote above refers to the United States, it might as well be about Canada. Despite the strangely persistent image of Canada as a caring society, the COVID-19 pandemic has brought to light many of the country's long-standing inequalities, not least of which was the support offered to many Canadians during a global pandemic of unprecedented scale. One could point to the Canada Emergency Response Benefit (CERB) as evidence that the state is not in support of capital, but in many ways it makes the point. Following the path of the Canadian welfare state in offering few concessions to working classes,[28] CERB is more of the same, offering a minimum level of protection to avoid systemic collapse – as scholars point out, the amount offered to impacted workers was significantly more than the provincial disability benefits that people are expected to live on all the time.[29] At the same time that the corporate sector was telling workers that "We're all in this together!" and offering meagre "hero's pay" to poorly compensated front-line staff without benefits or sick pay, the same companies were racking up record profits; in 2022, for instance, Loblaws recorded first-quarter profits 40 per cent higher than in 2021, upping their quarterly dividend (Bundale, 2022). With concerns about inflation once again hitting the headlines, the forces of globalization and financialization (which are themselves the forces of concentration and centralization of capital at a more abstract level) are strangely absent from many commentators' analyses.[30] To understand what is before us, let us quickly review the political and economic conjuncture in which we find ourselves.

---

28 Despite having the image of being a social democratic country, most political economists label Canada as having a liberal welfare state along the lines of the US and the UK (Esping-Andersen, 1990/2013; O'Connor et al., 1999; Olsen, 2002).

29 As Ferdosi and Graefe (2021) note, "under the Ontario Disability Support Program, people continued to receive only $1,169 per month (with one-time pandemic top-ups of $100 per month until the end of July 2020). This is just two-thirds of the CERB level, but still above the $733 per month provided to Ontario social assistance recipients who did not qualify for CERB" (para. 3). Disabled individuals have also been using Canada's new medical assistance in dying (MAiD) legislation to end their lives after being unable to find housing that can accommodate their disabilities (Canadian Human Rights Commission, 2022).

30 For a good overview of the inflation debate in the US, see Vernengo (2022). Studies in Canada reflect the substance of Vernengo's analysis: that a substantial portion of inflation today is simply due to corporate price hikes (Lorinc, 2022b).

As we have already seen, over the past 40 years there has been an ongoing trend of reducing the taxes paid by corporations and wealthy individuals. Deneault (2018) provides a convenient list of the Canadian version:

1. Federal corporate tax rate slashed from 37.8 per cent in 1981 to 15 per cent in 2012.
2. Federal capital tax eliminated in 2006.
3. Federal capital gains inclusion rate lowered from 75 per cent in 1998 to 50 per cent in 2000.
4. Some exporters exempted from sales tax and customs duty (Canada's Strategic Gateways and Trade Corridors program).
5. Indefinite tax deferrals for some companies: "Between 1992 and 2005 the 20 largest income tax deferrals in Canada increased by $29.4 billion or 199 per cent, from $14.8 billion in 1992 to $44.2 billion in 2005."
6. Flow-through shares program enhanced for some mining, oil, and gas companies.
7. Possibility for some mining, oil, and gas companies to set themselves up as tax-free income trusts.
8. Tax rate on taxable Canadian property held by non-residents lowered. (p. 37)[31]

As we already know, the cumulative effect of these practices is a reduction of state revenue, meaning that governments must now borrow the money they no longer collect from financial institutions at higher interest rates. As state debt grows, funding is cut for services, user fees are added, and privatization once again becomes a possible "solution." This, of course, occurs within a context in which Canada's corporations are swimming in cash and the country's highest officials are using tax avoidance schemes themselves.[32]

---

31 In response to external pressure, the Nova Scotia government recently scrapped a plan that would have increased taxes on non-resident property owners by $2 per $100 of assessed value (Willick, 2022).

32 Deneault (2018) notes: "Even the Bank of Canada was moved to complain when it discovered in 2014 that Canadian companies were holding over $600 billion in their various bank accounts" (p. 49). The premier of Nova Scotia, Tim Houston, as well as former Prime Ministers Brian Mulroney, Jean Chrétien, Paul Martin, and Liberal Party fundraiser Stephen Bronfman, were all named in the Paradise Papers, a leak of documents related to offshore investment (CTVNews.ca, 2017; International Consortium of Investigative Journalists, 2017). They were among a

It is into this world that the COVID-19 pandemic emerged, and whose impacts it laid bare. In Ontario, for instance, Martine August (2021) has examined how welfare state retrenchment and deregulation in the 1980s and 1990s produced opportunities for finance capital to fill in the gaps in social provision by "consolidating ownership of low-cost housing and providing private-pay options for frail seniors in need of care" (p. 291). As her research demonstrates, this has led to the threat of eviction for low-income populations, as well as the loss of life, with COVID-19 death rates the "worst in corporate-owned chained and financialized properties, when compared to other forprofits [sic], non-profits, and public homes" (p. 298). Despite August's research being specific to Ontario, the same overall process can be witnessed across Canada (e.g., Annable et al., 2021), the result of neo-liberal reforms that have allowed "homes and care to be treated as financial investment products" (August, 2021, p. 300).[33] With significant state debts racked up to deal with the pandemic, Canadians should expect more waves of austerity that reduce the efficacy of existing state services and thus create the conditions to legitimize further privatization, as is already occurring with health care in Alberta and Ontario (C. Gilbert & Guénin, 2022; Herring, 2022; McQuaig, 2022).[34] And all this while household indebtedness in Canada continues to rise (IMF, 2019).[35]

---

group of transnational actors that included Queen Elizabeth II, Jeffrey Epstein, and corporations such as Apple and Nike.

33 August (2021) provides more background on the financialization of seniors' housing and multifamily rental units: "In Canada, the financialization of multifamily and seniors' housing began in the late 1990s and is rapidly transforming ownership in both sectors. In Canada, REITs [real estate investment trusts] went from owning zero to more than 194,000 multifamily suites between 1996 and 2020. Looking beyond just REITs, at least 330,000 apartments – about 20 percent of the country's stock – are owned by the country's top 25 largest financial firms. The financialization of seniors' housing is more profound. About 42 percent of all retirement homes are owned by financial firms, as are 22 percent of LTCs and 33 percent of seniors' housing overall. These trends raise important questions about the impacts of this new style of ownership in which housing is being managed by large, capital-rich entities to maximize returns for investors" (p. 291).

34 As C. Gilbert and Guénin (2022) remind us, "massive public debts are, in fact, central and vital to neoliberalism and the state interventions (and central bank use of quantitative easing) that we have witnessed recently are in accordance with usual neoliberal practices" (p. 1).

35 A report from RBC Economics notes that "the rate of consumers 90 or more days late on their instalment loans is rising" (Zadikian, 2023, para. 2), and they project a 30 per cent increase in consumer insolvencies in the next five years. The MNP Consumer Debt Index, which measures Canadians' attitudes about their debt, has also hit record lows (see MNP Ltd., 2022).

In such a context, we might ask: Well, how are the banks doing? Surely, they must be struggling too? Not quite. In 2021, the banks recorded record-breaking profits of $57.4 billion and paid out $18.8 billion in bonuses, making it their most profitable year yet (Darrah, 2021; P. Evans, 2021).[36] In fact, having stockpiled cash to deal with a potential financial crisis, the banks now have an excess of $70.4 billion that analysts expect will be used to purchase smaller American banks (Orland, 2021a), or reward their shareholders by increasing dividends or buying back shares (Darrah, 2021). For their part specifically, RBC netted $16.1 billion in profits at the end of 2021, having previously reported a record profit in 2019 of $12.9 billion, which was "the largest amount earned by any Canadian company in a single year to date" ("Breakdown of RBC's Record," 2019). While the banks did use some of their profits to offer credit card and mortgage payment deferrals to working Canadians, as well as loan payment deferrals for small businesses (FCAC, 2020), these supports were temporary and, as NDP finance critic Peter Julian (2020) pointed out, did not extend to credit card interest, or "interest, penalties and fees on loan deferrals" (p. 1). Instead, the banks decided for a more personal approach; as RBC President and CEO Dave McKay (2020a) noted in an address to shareholders, an account manager purchased 50 flower arrangements from a client with excess inventory due to cancellations and distributed them to local branches: "It was a small gesture. But it went a long way in saying 'we are in this together'" (p. 9). Of course, the bank also announced plans to repurchase up to 45 million of its common shares (Royal Bank of Canada, 2021).

Paltry gestures aside, the banks' dominant position is a result of the favourable business climate they've enjoyed now for over 70 years, with 1952 being the last year that corporations paid the same income tax as individuals (Oved et al., 2017). Not only do the chartered banks pay the lowest tax rate (16 per cent) of all G7 countries, but they also pay less than other businesses in Canada; a study by the *Toronto Star*, for instance, points out that the chartered banks paid three times less than other businesses in the rest of the economy, "including the banks' credit union cousins" (Oved et al., 2017, para. 30). While the CBA has argued that, in addition to paying taxes, the banks are among the country's top

---

36 Darrah (2021) notes: "In 2020, TD Bank CEO Bharat Masrani earned $8.9 million – consisting of a cash bonus, stock options, and deferred 'performance share units' – in addition to his $1.45-million salary. Dave McKay, President and CEO of RBC, earned $10.8 million on top of his $1.5-million salary. BMO CEO Darryl White topped his $1-million salary with $8.2 million in bonuses, including a $2.3 million cash bonus" (para. 31).

corporate donors, the study shows that from 2011 to 2016 their donations "amounted to less than one-tenth of what they avoided in tax" (para. 70). Lest we think that this is a case of the banks pulling one over on the government, the reality is, as tax expert Peter van Dijk notes, that their ability to dodge taxes is a "conscious policy decision to preserve the ability of Canadian companies to compete internationally" (as cited in Oved et al., 2017, para. 52). Canadian tax law currently allows a significant amount of the banks' foreign investments to go untaxed, and this is doubly so if that income is recorded in one of the banks' many subsidiaries located in offshore tax havens. As the study notes, from 2011 to 2017, "over and above their tax savings from 'international operations,' the Big Five saved an additional $8.6 billion in taxes from 'tax-exempt income'" (para. 48).[37]

In this globalizing age, contradictions abound. The governments of nation states claim to be doing something to deal with tax avoidance while being the same entities that create the legal means through which such avoidance is achieved. In such a context, Deneault (2018) asks a pertinent question:

> How can we escape the conclusion that governments are serving the interests of big capital? They are creating loopholes that enable large corporations and financial institutions to move hundreds of billions of dollars offshore and not pay tax on that money. Taking their cue from tax havens, they are lowering tax rates on the capital that corporations and wealthy individuals keep here. (p. 45)

These dual-sided practices are exactly what I am referring to when I suggest that the nation state is becoming a capability for globalizing capitals. On the one hand, nation states continue to remake their laws and regulations to attract foreign investment, while on the other they simultaneously work to create beneficial conditions for the TNCs headquartered here to compete abroad.[38] As part of both processes, the rights of globalizing capital are increasingly secured across multiple national jurisdictions, a process that increasingly straightjackets

---

[37] Similarly, a recent report by Canadians for Tax Fairness (Cochrane, 2022) pointed out that Canada's largest corporations avoided $30 billion in taxes in 2021.

[38] This even occurs at the subnational level as well. For example, Nova Scotia agreed to pay RBC $22 million in payroll rebates to open a financial services centre in Halifax (Tutton, 2015). Three years later, RBC would sign an agreement with Nova Scotia Business Inc. to expand its operations in the province (Communications Nova Scotia, 2018).

national governments regardless of party affiliation – the election of Syriza in Greece being a recent example. While one could point to the bank tax recently introduced by the Liberals as evidence against this interpretation (Aiello, 2022), one would have to neglect the fact that this idea has been floating around since 1997, when it was introduced in the *Report of the Technical Committee on Business Taxation* commissioned by former Finance Minister Paul Martin. The report suggested that a temporary surtax be put on financial institutions until taxes for that sector were made comparable to "those imposed on other large corporations in other industries" (p. 5.37). Having escaped the tax for over 20 years, the new version comes in the form of a 3 per cent surtax on banks and insurers who earn over $1 billion per year.

The banks hate it, of course,[39] but this highlights the fact that the globalization of capitalism is a process that inevitably involves conflict, struggle, and contradiction; as Demirović (2011) notes, "the state is not a subject with agency, nor is it an instrument. It is the terrain and the strategic field where conflicts occur" (p. 43). In the resolution of these conflicts, concessions are made, but the overall thrust is still towards reproducing capitalism; since it is an increasingly global form of capitalism, the nation state takes on a new role as a capability for globalizing capitals, increasingly enforcing their rights and mediating the crises and conflicts thrown off by their accumulation activities. In this sense, the new bank tax is more than it appears, as it is a preliminary domestic

---

39 In their ideological assault on such a tax, the banks and their supporters consistently refer to the fact that taxing the banks would send the wrong message to the "global investment community" (read: transnational capitalist class) and be bad for Canadians, since the banks are typically a large component of pension plans and mutual funds. Scotiabank CEO Brian Porter, for instance, called the bank tax a "knee-jerk reaction that sends the wrong message to the global investment community ... it is ultimately a tax on you, our shareholders – approximately 70 per cent of whom are Canadian. It's a tax on those who directly own our shares or participate through pension plans or mutual funds, index funds, or ETFs [exchange-traded funds]" (as cited in Aiello, 2022, para. 21).

Business professor Ian Lee makes similar statements: "Your instinctive reaction may be sock it to the banks ... sit back and go look at your company pension plan – if you have a private company pension plan – and ask them if they have investments in the banks" (as cited in Alini, 2021, para. 10). Outside of the fact that one might feel they get more back from having a well-supported society rather than a few extra dollars in the bank, Lee's comments highlight some important realities: not everyone has a pension, and the share of who owns stocks in Canada is not equally distributed. As the study by the *Toronto Star* notes, 46.5 per cent of Canadian stocks are owned by foreigners, with 36.5 per cent owned by the wealthiest 20 per cent of Canadians. Only 16.9 per cent are owned by the bottom 80 per cent of Canadians (Oved et al., 2017).

version of a much larger initiative through the OECD to establish a global minimum tax rate of 15 per cent for TNCs with more than $1 billion in revenue (Alini, 2021). While this may again appear as if the nation state is no close friend to globalizing capital, the reality is that it is merely a political attempt to slow down the devastation caused by over 40 years of neo-liberalism. Under this new initiative, for instance, the corporate tax rate in the United States would rise from 21 per cent to 28 per cent. Seems like a fair increase, right? Well, not really, if we consider that the Trump administration cut the corporate tax rate down to 21 per cent from 35 per cent, meaning that the corporate tax rate has actually fallen 7 per cent over that time (Curry, 2021).

We can see similar processes at work with the Liberal Party's adoption of modern supply-side economics. While an article from the CBC portrays the shift as an "attempt – by a Liberal government that has never gotten along particularly well with Bay Street – to expand the conversation about what counts as a focus on economic growth" (Wherry, 2022, para. 19), it is really just more of the same backsliding of social spending consistent with neo-liberalism and the global extension of capitalism. After suggesting that the move will reverse a two-decade trend of declining federal revenues and spending,[40] the article also points out that the rate of revenue will be lower than it was in 2004–5 (16 per cent), the last year of the Martin government, and spending lower than it was in 1994–5 (15.6 per cent), the year preceding significant cuts initiated by the Chrétien government.

Is this truly a reversal then? It seems more like the long-standing swing of neo-liberal politics within liberal welfare states; from the harshness of neo-conservatism (Thatcher, Reagan, Mulroney, Harper) back to the version of neo-liberalism with a happy face (Blair, Clinton, Chrétien, Martin, Trudeau) that includes slight spending increases, but no fundamental differences in terms of economic reform that would restrict the overall trajectory of the globalization and financialization of capital and its effects.[41] As Christophers (2022) notes, this is partly due to the infrastructural power of financial capital today:

> Financial institutions enjoy power vis-à-vis the state because it is increasingly through financial markets themselves that the state pursues certain

---

40 From 14 per cent of GDP to 15.7 per cent in terms of revenue. From 12.5 per cent of GDP to a projected 14.7 per cent increase in spending in 2026–7 (Wherry, 2022).
41 As Harvey (2005) highlights, the fundamental difference between these groups is mainly in how they understand questions of order and morality: "Neoconservatives favour corporate power, private enterprise, and the restoration of class power.

important policy objectives. If markets constitute an infrastructure of governance, safeguarding markets in times of economic crisis takes on a significance that the state diminishes at no small risk not least to itself; and to one degree or another, safeguarding markets always entails backstopping those institutions holding the systematically important assets and liabilities circulating in those markets. (p. 148)

In such a context, nation states are ultimately limited in their actions. But this is also about corporate power in general. As Hathaway (2020) points out, regardless of the specific institutional construction of the various neo-liberalisms around the world, national governments have time and time again "favoured increasing the size of corporations, increasing the scope of their activity, granting them new rights, allowing new forms of corporate organization and diminishing their responsibilities, all the while talking of freedom, consumer choice and a cosmopolitan global system" (p. 332). While right-wing political parties have found success by railing against the cosmopolitanism of the happy face version of neo-liberalism through a renewed nationalist discourse, the reality is that, in political and economic terms, the basic trajectories remain, as well as their consequences.[42]

We can see some of these contradictions at work in Canada. While RBC is providing $1.5 million to organizations that support Black communities, they are also donating money to police foundations across Canada.[43] At the same time that RBC's CEO Dave McKay (2020b) is telling investors that "climate change is one of the most pressing issues of our age," and that "the financial system needs to be leading efforts to support clean economic growth and the transition to the low-carbon economy" (p. 1), RBC is one of the world's largest lenders to oil and

---

Neoconservatism is therefore entirely consistent with the neoliberal agenda of elite governance, mistrust of democracy, and the maintenance of market freedoms. But it veers away from the principles of pure neoliberalism and has reshaped neoliberal politics in two fundamental respects: first, in its concern for order as an answer to the chaos of individual interests, and second, in its concern for an overweening morality as the necessary social glue to keep the body politic secure in the face of external and internal dangers" (p. 82).

42 See, for instance, Streeck (2017). Wendy Brown (2018) also provides a useful analysis of the "authoritarian freedom" that has resulted from the development arc of neo-liberalism.

43 According to a report by *The Tyee*, for instance, RBC, along with LNG Canada and several real estate companies, donated $3 million over five years to the Vancouver Police Foundation (Lukacs & Groves, 2020).

gas companies (Greenpeace, 2020).[44] In fact, the Big Five banks actually increased their fossil fuel financing by 70 per cent, or around $61 billion, in 2021, according to the annual *Banking on Climate Chaos* report put together by several prominent environmental organizations (Rainforest Action Network et al., 2022). As such, it is no surprise to find that there are currently many different groups committed to action against the banks, whether that be through divestment campaigns or alternative forms of banking, such as postal banking.[45]

But the question remains whether these proposals go far enough. While the regulation of the Canadian financial system is no doubt a question of sovereignty,[46] it is just one part of a larger capitalist mode of production, whose historical development has been accompanied by the extension of corporate rights across multiple jurisdictions, the making of autonomous spaces for capital deep within national domains, and a deepening financialization of new areas of social life. In this book, I have attempted to provide an alternative account of the historical development of Canadian capitalism to make clearer some of the qualitative changes that make our current global age fundamentally different than the national one that came before it; put simply, there are far

---

44 Barnea (2020) notes that at the UN Climate Action Summit in 2019, banks representing a third of the global banking sector signed the *Principles for Responsible Banking* "to align their business with the goals of both the Paris Agreement on Climate Change and the UN's Sustainable Development Goals" (para. 6). While the CEOs of the Desjardins Group and the National Bank signed the document, the Big Five were notably absent.

45 There are numerous divestment campaigns against the banks (e.g., https://www.stand.earth/climate-finance/rbc-and-fossil-fuels; https://bankingonabetterfuture.org; https://quit-rbc.ca/en/index.html; http://bctfdivestnow.com). There are also campaigns to bring back postal banking (e.g., https://www.postalbanking.ca/en/campaign/postal-banking).

46 Bienefeld (1992) notes: "The inescapable need to regulate financial systems at some level, raises the issue of sovereignty, partly because regulation is more likely to be feasible within a relatively coherent national society and partly because regulatory systems embody social and political choices which must be legitimated through a meaningful and effective political process. Financial regulation is an inherently political task because it determines: how effectively a society can mobilize resources to serve its collective concern with the welfare of future generations and that of its more disadvantaged members; where a society will maintain the delicate balance between the need to encourage entrepreneurial risk taking, the need to protect society from speculation and the need to encourage a concern with long-term outcomes; how easy it is to sustain a viable domestic compromise with respect to the sharing rewards between labour and capital; and to what extent a society can really choose between efficiency and leisure, or between growth and stability, social harmony or environmental protection" (pp. 50–1).

fewer mechanisms today by which non-corporate interests can express their rights to mitigate the economic, social, and ecological crises generated by the pre-eminence of corporate rights at the transnational level. These changes are so significant that some authors speculate that we may be exiting capitalism and entering something far worse (Dean, 2020; Wark, 2019).

In highlighting certain elements of this overall shift, my goal has been to redirect the question of struggle back to the more basic issue of property. As Canadian political economist C.B. Macpherson (1978) notes, it is difficult to speak about property in capitalist societies because it is typically talked about as a thing rather than as a right, entitlement, or obligation. In conflating the wider concept of property with private property (an exclusive right), it thus becomes difficult to even think about all the different ways in which property relationships have been or could be configured.[47] The significance of doing so is at once historical and practical. It is historical because changes to property are always reflected in different sorts of institutional configurations, as in the national and global epochs of capitalism, in which territory, authority, and rights are configured in different ways and with different dynamics, despite the continued existence of the nation state in both periods. Focusing on property can thus provide us with a more nuanced view of social change that enables us to see how even small changes to property can have a knock-on effect on territorial organization, political authority, class structure, and more.

The significance of identifying different configurations of property relations is also practical, however. If different configurations of property relations have different results – that is, if they have different outcomes for the ways in which real people live their lives and reproduce themselves socially – then it follows that we can use this understanding to change and shape our contemporary circumstances. We can use property as a lens to evaluate whether our current social order is just, and, if it isn't, to explore how different configurations of property might make it more equitable. We can use property to determine whether some people have too much power at the expense of others and evaluate whether they should. Assessing the outcome of any property regime is thus to make a judgement call on one of the most fundamental aspects of living

---

47 For instance, Greer (2018) highlights the immense variety of historical Indigenous property relations on Turtle Island. Today, there are many scholars envisioning new arrangements of property relations. See, for example, Gibson-Graham et al. (2013); Gindin (2018); Hardt & Negri (2017). It is also usefully explored in science fiction (see, for example, O'Brien & Abdelhadi, 2022; K.S. Robinson, 2020).

together as social creatures. Being able to see how property is changing means having the ability to see where we are going – and whether that is a direction we want to go.

Early in the twentieth century, the president of the Canadian Bank of Commerce, Sir Edmund Walker, stated that "as democracy does not love banks, progress is very limited" (as cited in MacIntosh, 1991, p. 1). But we might also ask why democracy doesn't love the banks, and why, as liberal democracy becomes less democratic, the power of the chartered banks keeps growing? These are not one-to-one causal mechanisms, but to suggest that they are unrelated would be similarly foolish considering the evidence. As pointed out by several scholars (W. Brown, 2018, 2019; Patnaik, 2021; Slobodian, 2021a; Streeck, 2017), the ascendance of right-wing illiberal democracy across the world is closely linked with the ongoing impacts and reproduction of globalization and financialization.[48] While the nation state was able to provide a reasonably high standard of living in many countries, including Canada, its ability to do so rested on several historical preconditions that are no longer with us.[49] To put it simply, we can no longer vote our way back to the days of the welfare state, and we're certainly not going to vote our way out of climate change and the end of human civilization. As the philosopher Slavoj Žižek (2012) suggests, this is why Marx never located the question of freedom in the political sphere:

> The key to actual freedom rather resides in the "apolitical" network of social relations, from the market to the family, where the change needed if we want an actual improvement is not a political reform, but a change in the "apolitical" social relations of production. We do not vote about who owns what, about relations in a factory, etc. – all this is left to processes outside the sphere of the political. It is illusory to expect that one can effectively change things by "extending" democracy into this sphere, say, by organizing "democratic" banks under people's control. In such

---

[48] Stewart (2020), for instance, argues that "the hegemonic project of FRC [far-right civilizationism] is one of renewal; it is a strategy to *prevent* contemporary crisis from inducing a systemic transformation away from neoliberal globalization and the capitalist mode of production" (p. 1217).

[49] As outlined in chapter 3, these preconditions are an expanding national economy supported by a limited labour market and relatively immobile capital. In countries where these conditions prevailed, parties of all stripes found the basis for social reform, albeit to different degrees depending on "the strength and impact of working-class mobilization" (McEwen, 2006, p. 59). For a good overview of why social democratic reform is an impossibility today, see Hardt & Negri (2017, pp. 251–67).

"democratic" procedures (which, of course, can have a positive role to play), no matter how radical our anti-capitalism is, the solution is sought in applying the democratic mechanisms – which, one should never forget, are part of the state apparatuses of the "bourgeois" state that guarantees undisturbed functioning of the capitalist reproduction. (para. 15)

Consequently, for us, the "multitudinous many" of the 2005 Citibank memo, it means that the struggle against capital must go beyond the nation state and focus more clearly on the widespread protection of global common properties relevant to our shared needs. A good start would be guaranteeing common rights to things like clean drinking water, food, housing, electricity, health care, clothing, Internet, public transportation, and education, among other basic needs. Doing so would not only reduce the precarity of our lives in a world in which one's employment status continues to be the bearer of whether we are able to live a full and joyous life, but it would also lead to the creation of "new democratic social relations based on freedom and equality" (Hardt & Negri, 2017, p. 279). Furthermore, as Andreas Malm (2021) notes, it is the right of private property that secures the infrastructure, land, and resources held by corporations in polluting sectors. Extending common property to these areas would thus mean taking democratic control over the earth as a common space all entities share and rely on to survive.

The major problem is how. While good points have been made about why entirely local solutions are inadequate,[50] they all tend to end up back at the same place: "there is no way that an anti-capitalist social order can be constructed without seizing state power, radically transforming it and reworking the constitutional and institutional framework that currently supports private property, the market system and endless capital accumulation" (Harvey, 2011, p. 256). Given the current state of left-wing politics in the capitalist core today, it is difficult to imagine a national working class movement able to do this, let alone one across national borders. In the face of an increasingly dire future, however, it is necessary to acknowledge that our shared crisis knows

---

50 The sociologist Ruth Levitas (2017) notes, for instance, that "moves to more localized production, such as farming on the roofs of buildings and in small urban spaces, will not remove the need for global and national coordination, and thus for global supranational and national institutions, and forms of public accountability. The state remains necessary, though not as the debt-collector for global capitalism that it has become. Basic income requires an enabling state, while a regulatory state is needed to curtail wasteful production and consumption or polluting practices" (p. 11).

no boundaries – as such, neither should our struggles. Despite sharing Sam Gindin's (2022) pessimism over the possibilities of a successful global movement for the creation of common property,[51] in my view we are far past the point of Marx and Engels's (1848/1978b) suggestion that the working class "first of all settle matters with its own bourgeoisie" (p. 482). Doing so today means coming into confrontation with a capitalist class that not only views the entire world as a site of accumulation but is also actively attempting to transform it into one, making urgently necessary more extensive forms of transnational anticapitalist coordination. *This* is the challenge for present and future generations, no matter where they reside. My hope is that this book has been able to provide us with a better knowledge of what is happening, so that we might be able to change it.

---

51 In a piece entitled, "Morbid Symptoms, Premature Obituaries: The American Empire," Gindin (2022) writes: "It is tempting to battle capitalist internationalization by countering it with a working-class internationalism. Specific acts of international solidarity are, of course, possible and an internationalist sensibility is paramount. But we cannot act substantively on the international stage without being strong at home. If we cannot build genuine solidarity across the class at home, it is an illusion to think we can skip this step and build it across borders" ("Confronting Capital and Capitalism," paras. 12–13).

References

Royal Bank of Canada Documents, Reports, and Websites

McKay, D. (2018a, May 7). *Our new competitiveness: Thriving in the age of disruption* [Speech transcript]. Canadian Club of Montreal. https://www.rbc.com/newsroom/_assets-custom/pdf/20180507-canadian-club-mtl.pdf.

– (2018b, October 26). *A new Silicon Valley* [Speech transcript]. Calgary Chamber of Commerce. https://www.rbc.com/newsroom/_assets-custom/pdf/20181026-calgary-chamber-commerce.pdf.

– (2019, April 4). *Address to shareholders* [Speech transcript]. 150th Annual Meeting of the Royal Bank of Canada, Halifax. https://www.rbc.com/newsroom/_assets-custom/pdf/20190404-shareholders-address.pdf.

– (2020a, April 8). *Creating value with a purpose* [Speech transcript]. 150th Annual Meeting of the Royal Bank of Canada, Toronto. https://www.rbc.com/newsroom/_assets-custom/pdf/20200408-shareholders-address.pdf.

– (2020b). *Royal Bank of Canada: Climate blueprint*. https://web.archive.org/web/20220303173148/https://www.rbc.com/community-sustainability/_assets-custom/pdf/RBC-Environmental-Blueprint.pdf.

Nixon, G. (2013, April 11). *RBC issues open letter to Canadians* [Press release]. Royal Bank of Canada. https://www.rbc.com/newsroom/news/2013/20130411-rbc-statement.html.

RBC Capital Markets. (n.d.). *Aiden: From artificial intelligence to trading intelligence*. Retrieved 31 July 2024, from https://www.rbccm.com/en/expertise/electronic-trading.page.

Royal Bank of Canada. (1920). *The Royal Bank of Canada: Fiftieth anniversary, 1869–1919*. Ronalds Press and Advertising Agency. https://archive.org/details/fiftiethanniversO0royauoft/page/n15/mode/2up.

– (1948). Canada's natural resources. *Royal Bank of Canada Monthly Letter*, 29(7), 1–4. https://www.rbc.com/en/wp-content/uploads/sites/4/1948/06/june1948.pdf.

– (1949). Canada is a world customer. *Royal Bank of Canada Monthly Letter*, *30*(6), 1–4. https://www.rbc.com/en/wp-content/uploads/sites/4/1949/06/june1949.pdf.
– (1953). Our banking system. *Royal Bank of Canada Monthly Letter*, *34*(11), 1–4. https://www.rbc.com/en/wp-content/uploads/sites/4/2022/07/november1953.pdf.
– (1966). *Annual report*. Royal Bank of Canada.
– (1976a). *Newsletter and interim report: First quarter*. Royal Bank of Canada.
– (1976b). *Newsletter and interim report: Second quarter*. Royal Bank of Canada.
– (1976c). *Newsletter and interim report: Third quarter*. Royal Bank of Canada.
– (1985). *Annual report*. Royal Bank of Canada.
– (1987). *Annual report*. Royal Bank of Canada.
– (1989). *Annual report*. Royal Bank of Canada.
– (1992). *Annual report*. Royal Bank of Canada.
– (1996). *Annual report*. Royal Bank of Canada.
– (2000). *Annual report*. Royal Bank of Canada. https://www.rbc.com/investor-relations/_assets-custom/pdf/ar_2000_e.pdf.
– (2001a). *Annual report*. Royal Bank of Canada. https://www.rbc.com/investor-relations/_assets-custom/pdf/ar_2001_e.pdf.
– (2001b, August 20). *Royal Bank of Canada updates brand name and logo* [Press release]. https://web.archive.org/web/20220208083038/http:/www.rbc.com/newsroom/brand.html.
– (2006). *Annual report*. Royal Bank of Canada. https://www.rbc.com/investor-relations/_assets-custom/pdf/ar_2006_e.pdf.
– (2007). *Annual report*. Royal Bank of Canada. https://www.rbc.com/investor-relations/_assets-custom/pdf/ar_2007_e.pdf.
– (2012, April 3). *Royal Bank of Canada to acquire full ownership of RBC Dexia Investor Services* [Press release]. http://www.rbc.com/newsroom/news/2012/20120403-dexia.html
– (2013, April 7). *RBC clarifies recent media reports* [Press release]. https://www.rbc.com/newsroom/news/2013/20130407-rbc-statement.html.
– (2019, July 9). *RBC acquires fintech startup WayPay* [Press release]. https://www.rbc.com/newsroom/news/article.html?article=125603.
– (2020a, February 24). *RBC Ventures eases the pain for physicians with acquisition of Dr. Bill* [Press release]. https://www.rbc.com/newsroom/news/article.html?article=125241.
– (2020b, September 30). *Ownr by RBC Ventures acquires leading legal tech platform Founded* [Press release]. https://www.rbc.com/newsroom/news/article.html?article=125343.
– (2021a). *Annual report*. Royal Bank of Canada. https://www.rbc.com/investor-relations/_assets-custom/pdf/ar_2021_e.pdf.

- (2021b, December 6). *Royal Bank of Canada to repurchase up to 45 million of its common shares* [Press release]. https://www.rbc.com/newsroom/news/article.html?article=125535.
- (2022, March 31). *Royal Bank of Canada announces proposed acquisition of Brewin Dolphin* [Press release]. https://www.rbc.com/newsroom/news/article.html?article=125671.

Government Documents and Reports

Competition Policy Review Panel. (2008). *Compete to win: Final report – June 2008*. Government of Canada. https://publications.gc.ca/collections/collection_2008/ic/Iu173-1-2008E.pdf.

Department of Finance Canada. (1985). *The regulation of Canadian financial institutions: Proposals for discussion*. https://publications.gc.ca/site/eng/9.830886/publication.html.

Dominion Bureau of Statistics. (1927). *Canada year book, 1927–28*. F.A. Acland, Printer to the King. https://publications.gc.ca/collections/collection_2017/statcan/11-202/CS11-202-1928-eng.pdf.

Employment and Social Development Canada. (2014). *Overhauling the Temporary Foreign Worker Program: Putting Canadians first*. https://publications.gc.ca/site/eng/469576/publication.html.

Estey, W.Z. (1986). *Report of the inquiry into the collapse of the CCB and Northland Bank*. Privy Council Office. https://publications.gc.ca/site/eng/471442/publication.html.

Financial Consumer Agency of Canada (FCAC). (2022). *Mystery shopping at domestic retail banks*. https://www.canada.ca/en/financial-consumer-agency/programs/research/mystery-shopping-domestic-retail-banks.html.

Haggart, B., Laurin, A., Kieley, G., Smith, M., & Wrobel, M.G. (2001). *Legislative summary: Bill C-8: An act to establish the financial consumer agency of Canada and to amend certain acts in relation to financial institutions*. Parliamentary Research Branch. https://lop.parl.ca/sites/PublicWebsite/default/en_CA/ResearchPublications/LegislativeSummaries/371LS387E.

Hinchley, C. (2006, May 3). *Foreign banks in the Canadian market*. Statistics Canada. https://www150.statcan.gc.ca/n1/pub/11-621-m/11-621-m2006041-eng.htm.

Hockin, T. (1986). *New directions for the financial sector*. Department of Finance. https://publications.gc.ca/site/eng/9.829803/publication.html.

McKeown, H.A. (1924). *Interim report: Royal Commission re home bank*. F.A. Acland, Printer to the King. https://epe.lac-bac.gc.ca/100/200/301/pco-bcp/commissions-ef/mckeown1924-eng/mckeown1924-eng.htm.

Mimoto, H., & Cross, P. (1991). The growth of the federal debt, 1975–1990. In P. Cross (Ed.), *Canadian economic observer* (pp. 3.1–3.17). Statistics Canada.

Royal Commission on Banking and Currency in Canada. (1933). *Report of the Royal Commission on banking and currency in Canada*. J.O. Patenaude, Printer to the King. https://epe.lac-bac.gc.ca/100/200/301/pco-bcp/commissions-ef/macmillan1933-eng/macmillan1933-eng.htm.

Royal Commission on Banking and Finance. (1964). *Report of the Royal Commission on Banking and Finance*. R. Duhamel, Queen's Printer. https://epe.lac-bac.gc.ca/100/200/301/pco-bcp/commissions-ef/porter1964-eng/porter1964-eng.htm.

Royal Commission on Canada's Economic Prospects. (1957). *Final report*. Privy Council Office. https://epe.lac-bac.gc.ca/100/200/301/pco-bcp/commissions-ef/gordon1957-eng/gordon1957-eng.htm.

Royal Commission on Corporate Concentration. (1978). *Report of the Royal Commission on Corporate Concentration*. Minister of Supply and Services Canada. https://publications.gc.ca/site/eng/472239/publication.html.

Schaffter, C., & Fortier-Labonte, A. (2019). *Multinational enterprises in Canada*. Statistics Canada. https://www150.statcan.gc.ca/n1/pub/11-621-m/11-621-m2019001-eng.htm#a2.

Standing Senate Committee on Banking, Trade and Commerce. (1998). *Comparative study of financial regulatory regimes*. Senate of Canada. https://sencanada.ca/content/sen/committee/361/bank/rep/report15-cov-e.htm.

Statistics Canada. (2009, August 28). *Federal government debt, for fiscal year ending March 31*. https://www150.statcan.gc.ca/t1/tbl1/en/tv.action?pid=1010004801.

– (2011, October 13). *Foreign control in the Canadian economy*. https://www150.statcan.gc.ca/n1/daily-quotidien/111013/dq111013b-eng.htm.

– (2013, May 9). *Foreign direct investment, 2012*. https://www150.statcan.gc.ca/n1/daily-quotidien/130509/dq130509a-eng.pdf.

– (2017, March 29). *Federal net debt per capita since 1867*. https://www150.statcan.gc.ca/n1/daily-quotidien/170329/dq170329h-eng.htm.

– (2021, April 27). Foreign direct investment, 2020. *The Daily*. https://www150.statcan.gc.ca/n1/daily-quotidien/210427/dq210427a-eng.htm.

– (2024, April 29). *International investment position, Canadian direct investment abroad and foreign direct investment in Canada, by country, annual*. https://doi.org/10.25318/3610000801-eng.

Task Force on the Future of the Canadian Financial Services Sector. (1998). *The changing landscape for Canadian financial services: New forces, new competitors, new choices*. Department of Finance Canada. https://publications.gc.ca/site/eng/408879/publication.html.

Technical Committee on Business Taxation. (1997). *Report of the technical committee on business taxation*. Department of Finance. https://publications.gc.ca/collections/Collection/F32-5-1998E.pdf.

References

Abbey, E. (1991). *A voice crying in the wilderness (vox clamantis in deserto): Notes from a secret journal*. St. Martin's Press.

Abdel-Qader, A. (2019, August 30). *Canada regulator fines RBC and TD Bank in FX Rig cases*. Finance Magnates. https://www.financemagnates.com/institutional-forex/regulation/canada-regulator-fines-rbc-and-td-bank-24m-in-fx-rig-cases.

Abrams, P. (1982). *Historical sociology*. Cornell University Press.

– (1988). Notes on the difficulty of studying the state (1977). *Journal of Historical Sociology*, 1(1), 58–89. https://doi.org/10.1111/j.1467-6443.1988.tb00004.x.

Acheson, T.W. (1972). The national policy and the industrialization of the Maritimes, 1880–1910. *Acadiensis*, 1(2), 3–28. https://id.erudit.org/iderudit/acad1_2art01.

Ackerman, S. (2012, December 20). The red and the black. *Jacobin*. https://www.jacobinmag.com/2012/12/the-red-and-the-black.

Adkins, L., Cooper, M., & Konings, M. (2020). *The asset economy*. John Wiley & Sons.

Aiello, R. (2022, April 5). *Federal budget 2022: Ottawa to make big banks to pay more*. CTV News. https://www.ctvnews.ca/politics/federal-budget-set-to-include-surtax-on-big-banks-pandemic-profits-1.5850053.

Akhtar, A. (2021, December 13). *Decoding crypto: Providing regulatory clarity to cryptoasset businesses*. Osler. https://legalyearinreview.ca/decoding-crypto-providing-regulatory-clarity-to-cryptoasset-businesses.

Albo, G., & Klassen, J. (Eds.). (2013). *Empire's ally: Canada and the war in Afghanistan*. University of Toronto Press.

Alexander, D. (2019a, May 1). *Blockchain adopted by Canadian banks to verify client identities*. Bloomberg. https://www.bloomberg.com/news/articles/2019-05-01/blockchain-adopted-by-canadian-banks-to-verify-client-identities.

– (2019b, May 1). *Central banks use blockchain for first time to swap currency*. Bloomberg. https://www.bloomberg.com/news/articles/2019-05-02/central-banks-use-blockchain-for-first-time-to-swap-currency.

Alexander, K. (2003, April 11). *The Basel Committee and global governance* [Paper presentation]. International Monetary Fund: Meeting of the G24, Washington, DC, United States. https://www.g24.org/wp-content/uploads/2016/01/THE-BASEL-COMMITTEE-AND-GLOBAL-GOVERNANCE.pdf.

– (2009). Bank for international settlements. In C. Tietje & A. Brouder (Eds.), *Handbook of transnational economic governance regimes* (pp. 305–18). Martinus Nijhoff Publishers.

Alexander, K., Dhumale, R., & Eatwell, J. (2006). *Global governance of financial systems: The international regulation of systemic risk*. Oxford University Press.

Alini, E. (2021, August 26). *"Nothing good to say about the policy": Experts slam Trudeau's bank tax promise*. Global News. https://globalnews.ca/news/8142492/trudeau-election-bank-tax-reaction.

Allen, D.W.E., Berg, C., & Novak, M. (2018). Blockchain: An entangled political economy approach. *Journal of Public Finance and Public Choice, 33*(2), 105–25. https://doi.org/10.1332/251569118X15282111163993.

Altman, R.C. (2009). Globalization in retreat: Further geopolitical consequences of the financial crisis. *Foreign Affairs, 88*(4), 2–7. https://www.jstor.org/stable/20699617.

America's new Asian economic pact: Just don't call it a trade deal. (2022, May 24). *The Economist*. https://www.economist.com/finance-and-economics/2022/05/24/americas-new-asian-economic-pact-just-dont-call-it-a-trade-deal.

Anand, A., & Peihani, M. (2019). Regulating systemic risk in Canada. In D.W. Arner, E. Avgouleas, D. Busch, & S.L. Schwarcz (Eds.), *Systemic risk in the financial sector: Ten years after the great crash* (pp. 11–30). McGill-Queen's University Press.

Andreasyan, T. (2016, November 25). *More banks to opt out of R3 blockchain consortium*. FinTech Futures. https://www.bankingtech.com/2016/11/more-banks-to-opt-out-of-r3-blockchain-consortium.

Anievas, A. (2008). Theories of a global state: A critique. *Historical Materialism, 16*(2), 190–206. https://doi.org/10.1163/156920608X296123.

Annable, K., Kubinec, V.-L., Barghout, C., & Levasseur, J. (2021, March 17). *For-profit care homes have higher COVID-19 death rates among Winnipeg nursing homes*. CBC News. https://www.cbc.ca/news/canada/manitoba/for-profit-care-homes-coronavirus-deaths-wfpcbc-cbc-1.5952171.

Armstrong, C., & Nelles, H.V. (1988). *Southern exposure: Canadian promoters in Latin America and the Caribbean, 1896–1930*. University of Toronto Press.

Armstrong, F.H. (1967). Approaches to business history in Canada: The historian's approach. *Proceedings of the Annual Meeting of the Business History Conference, 14*, 16–33. https://www.jstor.org/stable/43916904.

Arrighi, G. (2001). Global capitalism and the persistence of the north-south divide. *Science & Society, 65*(4), 469–76. https://www.jstor.org/stable/40403915.

– (2010). *The long twentieth century: Money, power, and the origins of our times*. Verso. (Original work published 1994)

Associated British Foods. (2021). *Annual report*. https://www.abf.co.uk/content/dam/abf/corporate/Documents/investors/annual-and-interim-reports/ar2021.pdf.downloadasset.pdf.

Atlee, D. (2022, November 26). *Canada crypto regulation: Bitcoin ETFs, strict licensing and a digital dollar*. Cointelegraph. https://cointelegraph.com/news/canada-crypto-regulation-bitcoin-etfs-strict-licensing-and-a-digital-dollar.

August, M. (2021). Financialization of housing from cradle to grave: COVID-19, seniors' housing, and multifamily rental housing in Canada. *Studies in Political Economy, 102*(3), 289–308. https://doi.org/10.1080/07078552.2021.2000207.

Baillie, A.C. (1998, November 20). *The business of bank mergers: A sound strategy for Canada* [Speech transcript]. Empire Club of Canada, Toronto. https://speeches.empireclub.org/61909/data.

Baker, A. (2006). *The Group of Seven: Finance ministries, central banks and global financial governance.* Routledge. https://doi.org/10.4324/9780203001493.

Bal, S.S. (2017). Banking on identity: Constructing a Canadian banking identity one branch at a time. *Journal of Historical Sociology, 31*(2), 196–212. https://doi.org/10.1111/johs.12169.

Balakrishnan, G. (2015). The abolitionist – II. *New Left Review, 91,* 69–100. https://newleftreview.org/issues/ii91/articles/gopal-balakrishnan-the-abolitionist-ii.

Bambrough, B. (2018, November 12). Ethereum co-founder predicts a radical overhaul of society. *Forbes.* https://www.forbes.com/sites/billybambrough/2018/11/12/ethereum-co-founder-predicts-a-radical-overhaul-of-society/#4e71be8ef60c.

Ban, C., Seabrooke, L., & Freitas, S. (2016). Grey matter in shadow banking: International organisations and expert strategies in global financial governance. *Review of International Political Economy, 23*(6), 1001–33. https://doi.org/10.1080/09692290.2016.1235599.

Banaji, J. (2007). Islam, the Mediterranean and the rise of capitalism. *Historical Materialism, 15*(1), 47–74. https://doi.org/10.1163/156920607X171591.

– (2020). State and capital in the era of primitive accumulation. *Historical Materialism.* https://www.historicalmaterialism.org/book-review/state-and-capital-era-primitive-accumulation.

Bank for International Settlements (BIS). (n.d.-a). *History: The BIS during the Second World War (1939–48).* Retrieved 31 July 2024, from https://www.bis.org/about/history_2ww2.htm.

– (n.d.-b). *History: The BIS going global (1961–).* Retrieved 31 July 2024, from https://www.bis.org/about/history_4global.htm.

– (n.d.-c). *History: Foundation and crisis (1930–39).* Retrieved 31 July 2024, from https://www.bis.org/about/history_1foundation.htm.

Baragar, F., & Seccareccia, M. (2008). Financial restructuring: Implications of recent Canadian macroeconomic developments. *Studies in Political Economy, 82*(1), 61–83. https://doi.org/10.1080/19187033.2008.11675064.

Barber, T. (2017, March 23). Brexit and the city. *Financial Times.* https://www.ft.com/content/be6dbd66-0fc6-11e7-b030-768954394623.

Barnea, A. (2020, January 28). How Canada's banks can help reduce the "collateral damage" of capitalism. *Toronto Star.* https://www.thestar.com

/business/opinion/2020/01/28/canadas-big-5-banks-need-to-move-from-climate-change-statements-to-real-action.html.

Barrow, C.W. (1993). *Critical theories of the state: Marxist, neo-Marxist, post-Marxist*. University of Wisconsin Press.

– (2005). The return of the state: Globalization, state theory, and the new imperialism. *New Political Science, 27*(2), 123–45. http://dx.doi.org/10.1080/07393140500098235.

Barth, J.R., Caprio, G., & Levine, R. (2012). *Guardians of finance: Making regulators work for us*. MIT Press.

Basel Committee on Banking Supervision (BCBS). (1975, September 28). *Report to the governors on the supervision of banks' foreign establishments*. Bank for International Settlements. https://www.bis.org/publ/bcbs00a.pdf.

– (1983, May 28). *Principles for the supervision of banks' foreign establishments*. Bank for International Settlements. https://www.bis.org/publ/bcbsc312.pdf.

– (1988, July 15). *International convergence of capital measurement and capital standards*. Bank for International Settlements. https://www.bis.org/publ/bcbs04a.pdf.

– (n.d.). *History of the Basel Committee*. Bank for International Settlements. https://www.bis.org/bcbs/history.htm.

"Basel is on life support" in Trump era. (2016, November 28). *American Banker*. https://www.americanbanker.com/news/basel-is-on-life-support-in-trump-era.

Baum, D.J. (1974). *The banks of Canada in the Commonwealth Caribbean: Economic nationalism and multinational enterprises of a medium power*. Praeger.

Beaulieu, E., & Cherniwchan, J. (2014). Tariff structure, trade expansion, and Canadian protectionism, 1870–1910. *Canadian Journal of Economics/Revue Canadienne d'économique, 47*(1), 144–72. https://doi.org/10.1111/caje.12065.

Bederman, D.J. (1988). Bank for International Settlements and the debt crisis: A new role for the central bankers' bank. *Berkeley Journal of International Law, 6*(1), 92–121. https://doi.org/10.15779/Z38XM05.

Belger, T. (2019, May 28). *Global financial capital: Why New York is "replacing London."* Yahoo Finance. https://finance.yahoo.com/news/new-york-is-replacing-london-as-the-worlds-financial-capital-105526842.html.

Bell, T.W. (2017). *Your next government? From the nation state to stateless nations*. Cambridge University Press. https://doi.org/10.1017/9781316676387.

Beltrame, J., & Blanchfield, M. (2013, November 1). *EU boasts of huge gains in Canadian trade deal*. CBC News. https://www.cbc.ca/news/business/eu-boasts-of-huge-gains-in-canadian-trade-deal-1.2325983.

Bennett, R.A. (1979, September 12). Canadian bank's US role grows. *New York Times*, D1. https://www.nytimes.com/1979/09/12/archives/canadian-banks-us-role-grows-canadian-bank-increases-its-role-in-us.html.

Berle, A.A., & Means, G.C. (1968). *The modern corporation and private property* (Rev. ed.). Harcourt, Brace & World. (Original work published 1932)

Best, J. (2018). Technocratic exceptionalism: Monetary policy and the fear of democracy. *International Political Sociology, 12*(4), 328–45. https://doi.org/10.1093/ips/oly017.

Better late. (1964, June 12). *Globe and Mail*, 6.

Beynon, T.G. (1959). Canada as a welfare state. *Canadian Banker, 66*(3), 44–52.

Bieler, A., & Morton, A.D. (2014). The will-o'-the-wisp of the transnational state. *Journal of Australian Political Economy, 72*, 23–51. https://www.ppesydney.net/content/uploads/2020/05/The-will-o-the-wisp-of-the-transnational-state.pdf.

Bienefeld, M. (1992). Financial deregulation: Disarming the nation state. *Studies in Political Economy, 37*(1), 31–58. https://doi.org/10.1080/19187033.1992.11675433.

Binford, L. (2013). *Tomorrow we're all going to the harvest: Temporary foreign worker programs and neoliberal political economy*. University of Texas Press.

Binhammer, H.H. (1988). *Money, banking and the Canadian financial system*. Nelson Canada. (Original work published 1968)

Birch, K., & Springer, S. (2019). Peak neoliberalism? Revisiting and rethinking the concept of neoliberalism. *Ephemera, 19*(3), 467–85. https://ephemerajournal.org/sites/default/files/pdfs/contribution/19-3editorial_0.pdf.

The birth of a new mining town. (1909, February 15). *Globe and Mail*, 5.

Blackstone, W. (1893). *Commentaries on the laws of England in four books* (Vol. 1). J.B. Lippincott Company. (Original work published 1753)

Blanden, M. (1999, July 1). 30th anniversary listing: Reversal of fortune. *The Banker, 149*(881).

Bliss, M. (2006). Has Canada failed? *Literary Review of Canada, 14*(2), 3–5. https://reviewcanada.ca/magazine/2006/03/has-canada-failed.

– (2018). *Northern enterprise: Five centuries of Canadian business* (Rev. ed.). Rock's Mills Press. (Originally published 1987)

Block, F. (2001). Using social theory to leap over historical contingencies: A comment on Robinson. *Theory and Society, 30*(2), 215–21. https://doi.org/10.1023/A:1011050008960.

Block, F., & Somers, M.R. (2014). *The power of market fundamentalism*. Harvard University Press.

Blom, J. (2019). Banking on public power: Lessons of the Institute of International Finance. In N. Buxton & D. Eade (Eds.), *State of power 2019: Finance* (pp. 38–57). Transnational Institute.

– (2021). The Institute of International Finance: From poacher to gamekeeper? *Business and Politics, 23*(1), 153–78. https://doi.org/10.1017/bap.2020.6.

Blomley, N. (2011). Cuts, flows, and the geographies of property. *Law, Culture and the Humanities, 7*(2), 203–16. https://doi.org/10.1177/1743872109355583.

Boffey, D. (2013, February 9). British sugar giant caught in global tax scandal. *The Guardian.* https://www.theguardian.com/business/2013/feb/09/british-sugar-giant-tax-scandal.

Bonham, M.S. (2024, April 24). Chartered banks in Canada. In *The Canadian encyclopedia.* Retrieved 31 July 2024, from https://www.thecanadianencyclopedia.ca/en/article/chartered-bank.

Borch, C., & Wosnitzer, R. (Eds.) (2020). *The Routledge handbook of critical finance studies.* Routledge. https://doi.org/10.4324/9781315114255.

Boreham, G.F. (1989). The changing landscape of the financial services industry in Canada: Some implications for managers. *Service Industries Journal, 9*(2), 191–204. https://doi.org/10.1080/02642068900000024.

Borio, C., Claessens, S., Clement, P., McCauley, R.N., & Shin, H.S. (Eds.). (2020). *Promoting global monetary and financial stability: The Bank for International Settlements after Bretton Woods, 1973–2020.* Cambridge University Press. https://doi.org/10.1017/9781108856522.

Bostick, R., Riggs, T., & Hyde, C. (2021, December 3). *Miami mayor seeks wider crypto use after taking pay in Bitcoin.* BNN Bloomberg. https://www.bnnbloomberg.ca/miami-mayor-seeks-wider-crypto-use-after-taking-pay-in-bitcoin-1.1691005.

Boston University. (2014, June 2014). *Prof. Bacevich on Iraq, Isis, and more* [Press release]. https://www.bu.edu/pardeeschool/2014/06/28/bacevich-on-iraq-isis-and-more.

Bowley, G. (1999, November 22). Canadian banks reveal strong profits. *Financial Times,* 16.

Boyer, R., & Drache, D. (1996). *States against markets: The limits of globalization.* Routledge.

Bradshaw, J. (2017, March 22). Face of Libor rate manipulation scandal cost RBC millions. *Globe and Mail.* https://www.theglobeandmail.com/report-on-business/streetwise/face-of-libor-rate-manipulation-scandal-cost-rbc-millions/article34390842.

– (2018, December 27). How blocked mergers foiled banks' ambitions – and forced the Big Six to innovate. *Globe and Mail.* https://www.theglobeandmail.com/business/article-20th-anniversary-of-the-failed-royal-bank-of-canada-and-bank-of.

A breakdown of RBC's record $12.9B profit this year, down to the second. (2019, December 4). BNN Bloomberg. https://www.bnnbloomberg.ca/a-breakdown-of-rbc-s-record-12-9b-profit-this-year-down-to-the-second-1.1357588.

Breckenridge, R.M. (1894). *The Canadian banking system, 1817–1890.* American Economic Association.

Brennan, J. (2013). The power underpinnings, and some distributional consequences, of trade and investment liberalisation in Canada. *New Political Economy, 18*(5), 715–47. https://doi.org/10.1080/13563467.2013.736955.

Brenner, N., Peck, J., & Theodore, N. (2010). Variegated neoliberalization: Geographies, modalities, pathways. *Global Networks, 10*(2), 182–222. https://doi.org/10.1111/j.1471-0374.2009.00277.x.

Brenner, R. (2003). *Merchants and revolution: Commercial change, political conflict, and London's overseas traders, 1550–1653*. Verso.

Brewer, T. (2002). *Marxist theories of imperialism: A critical survey*. Routledge. (Original work published 1980)

Bridges, M. (2021). Branching out: Banking, credit, and the globalizing US economy, 1900s–1930s. *Enterprise & Society, 22*(4), 930–8. https://doi.org/10.1017/eso.2021.51.

Britten, L. (2018, October 3). *LNG Canada could be "carbon bomb" that blows up BC's climate goals, critic warns.* CBC News. https://www.cbc.ca/news/canada/british-columbia/lng-canada-carbon-greenhouse-environment-climate-1.4848237.

Bromley, S. (2003). Reflections on empire, imperialism and United States hegemony. *Historical Materialism, 11*(3), 17–68. https://doi.org/10.1163/156920603770678300.

Bronsdon, C. (2019, April 30). *Washington State's "blockchain bill" signed into law.* Coinlaw. https://coinlaw.io/washington-states-blockchain-bill-signed-into-law.

Brooks, K. (2021, November 22). *NYC mayor-elect Eric Adams says he'll "take" his first three paychecks in crypto.* CBS News. https://www.cbsnews.com/news/eric-adams-mayor-paycheck-bitcoin-cryptocurrency.

Brown, M. (2022, June 30). *Asset-backed commercial paper carries high risk.* Investopedia. https://www.investopedia.com/articles/bonds/08/commercial-paper.asp.

Brown, W. (1992). Finding the man in the state. *Feminist Studies, 18*(1), 7–34. https://doi.org/10.2307/3178212.

– (2018). Neoliberalism's Frankenstein: Authoritarian freedom in twenty-first century "democracies." *Critical Times, 1*(1), 60–79. https://doi.org/10.1215/26410478-1.1.60.

– (2019). *In the ruins of neoliberalism: The rise of antidemocratic politics in the West*. Columbia University Press.

Brummer, C. (2014). *Minilateralism: How trade alliances, soft law and financial engineering are redefining economic statecraft*. Cambridge University Press.

Bryan, D., Harvie, D., Rafferty, M., & Tinel, B. (2020). The financialized state. In C. Borch & R. Wosnitzer (Eds.), *The Routledge handbook of critical finance studies* (pp. 261–77). Routledge. https://doi.org/10.4324/9781315114255.

Bryan, D., Rafferty, M., & Wigan, D. (2016). Politics, time and space in the era of shadow banking. *Review of International Political Economy, 23*(6), 941–66. https://doi.org/10.1080/09692290.2016.1139618.

Buckley, K. (1974). *Capital formation in Canada, 1896–1930*. McGill-Queen's University Press.

Bundale, B. (2022, January 7). *Grocers pressured to bring back "hero pay" amid Omicron surge.* CBC News. https://www.cbc.ca/news/business/grocers-hero-pay-unifor-1.6307698.

Burbach, R., & Robinson, W.I. (1999). The fin de siecle debate: Globalization as epochal shift. *Science & Society, 63*(1), 10–39.

Burgess, B. (2000). Foreign direct investment: Facts and perceptions about Canada. *Canadian Geographer, 44*(2), 98–113. https://doi.org/10.1111/j.1541-0064.2000.tb00696.x.

– (2002). *Canada's location in the world system: Reworking the debate in Canadian political economy* [Doctoral dissertation, University of British Columbia]. UBC Theses and Dissertations. https://doi.org/10.14288/1.0090586.

Burton, J. (1990, March 1). North America (US): Melding into the landscape? Foreign banks in the US are going native, moving away from their natural habitat and winning acceptance alongside local competitors. *The Banker, 140*(769).

Buterin, V. (2014). *Ethereum white paper: A next generation smart contract and decentralized application platform.* https://www.weusecoins.com/assets/pdf/library/Ethereum_white_paper-a_next_generation_smart_contract_and_decentralized_application_platform-vitalik-buterin.pdf.

– (2018, April 20). *On* Radical Markets. Vitalik Buterin's Website. https://vitalik.eth.limo/general/2018/04/20/radical_markets.html.

Buterin, V., and Frank, S. (2014, December 16). *Decentralized autonomous society* [Speech transcript]. Triple Canopy. https://www.canopycanopycanopy.com/contents/decentralized-autonomous-society?sub=decentralized-autonomous-society-transcript.

Cain, P.J., & Hopkins, A.G. (1986). Gentlemanly capitalism and British expansion overseas: The old colonial system, 1688–1850. *Economic History Review, 39*(4), 501–25. https://doi.org/10.1111/j.1468-0289.1986.tb01254.x.

– (1993). *British imperialism: Innovation and expansion, 1688–1914.* Longman.

Calhoun, C. (2002). Imagining solidarity: Cosmopolitanism, constitutional patriotism, and the public sphere. *Public Culture, 14*(1), 147–71. https://doi.org/10.1215/08992363-14-1-147.

Callinicos, A. (2009). *Imperialism and global political economy.* Polity Press.

Calvert, J., Rommerskirchen, C., & van der Heide, A. (2022). Does ownership matter? Claimant characteristics and case outcomes in investor-state arbitration. *New Political Economy, 27*(5), 788–805. https://doi.org/10.1080/13563467.2021.2013792.

Cameron, D. (1983). Order and disorder in the world economy: International finance in evolution. *Studies in Political Economy, 11*(1), 105–26. https://doi.org/10.1080/19187033.1983.11675664.

Cameron, R.E., Bovykin, V.I., & Anan'ich, B.V. (Eds.). (1991). *International banking, 1870–1914*. Oxford University Press.

Cammack, P. (2009). Forget the transnational state. *Geopolitics, History, and International Relations*, 1(2), 79–97. https://www.jstor.org/stable/26803994.

Campbell-Verduyn, M., Goguen, M., & Porter, T. (2017). Big data and algorithmic governance: The case of financial practices. *New Political Economy*, 22(2), 219–36. https://doi.org/10.1080/13563467.2016.1216533.

Canada picks head for central bank. (1934, September 6). *New York Times*, 37. https://www.nytimes.com/1934/09/07/archives/canada-picks-head-for-central-bank-gf-towers-of-royal-bank-of.html.

Canadian bank buys 15-story home here. (1919, February 1). *New York Times*, 6. https://www.nytimes.com/1919/02/01/archives/canadian-bank-buys-15story-home-here-the-royal-pays-more-than.html.

Canadian Bankers Association. (1960). The chartered banks and inflation: A submission to the Senate Finance Committee from the Canadian Bankers' Association. *Canadian Banker*, 67(1), 20–8.

– (1975). *Bank Act 77: The industry's brief*. Canadian Bankers Association.

Canadian banks don't need too-big-to-fail reserves. (2012, August 28). *Globe and Mail*. https://www.theglobeandmail.com/globe-debate/editorials/canadian-banks-dont-need-too-big-to-fail-reserves/article4507085.

Canadian banks hold two spots among top 20. (1966, July 26). *Globe and Mail*, B1.

Canadian banks to merge: Stockholders asked to ratify union of the Royal and Union institutions. (1910, July 18). *New York Times*, 8. https://www.nytimes.com/1910/07/18/archives/canadian-banks-to-merge-stockholders-asked-to-ratify-union-of-the.html.

Canadian explains bank credit curb. (1959, August 18). *New York Times*, 45. https://www.nytimes.com/1959/08/18/archives/canadian-explains-bank-credit-curb.html.

Canadian Human Rights Commission. (2022, May 10). *MAiD cannot be an answer to systemic inequality*. https://www.chrc-ccdp.gc.ca/en/resources/maid-cannot-be-answer-systemic-inequality.

Canadian law limits foreign bank growth. (1980, December 2). *New York Times*, B1. https://www.nytimes.com/1980/12/02/archives/canadian-law-limits-foreign-bank-growth-cumbersome-system-canada.html.

Canadian Press. (2012, April 30). Canadian banks got billions in support, report says. *Globe and Mail*. https://www.theglobeandmail.com/globe-investor/canadian-banks-got-billions-in-support-report-says/article4103645.

– (2014, November 21). Royal Bank exits Caribbean wealth management business. *CBC News*. https://www.cbc.ca/1.2844864.

– (2018, December 13). Moody's downgrades Ontario's credit rating. *Toronto Star*. https://www.thestar.com/politics/provincial/2018/12/13/moodys-downgrades-ontarios-credit-rating.html.
– (2019, December 12). *RBC selling Eastern Caribbean banking operations to consortium*. BNN Bloomberg. https://www.bnnbloomberg.ca/rbc-selling-eastern-caribbean-banking-operations-to-consortium-1.1361705.
Canova, T.A. (2000). Financial liberalization, international monetary dis/order, and the neoliberal state. *American University International Law Review*, 15(6), 1279–319.
The Care Collective. (2020). *Care manifesto: The politics of interdependence*. Verso.
Carr, J., Mathewson, F., & Quigley, N. (1995). Stability in the absence of deposit insurance: The Canadian banking system, 1890–1966. *Journal of Money, Credit and Banking*, 27(4), 1137–58. https://doi.org/10.2307/2077794.
Carroll, W.K. (1982). The Canadian corporate elite: Financiers or finance capitalists. *Studies in Political Economy*, 8(1), 89–114. https://doi.org/10.1080/19187033.1982.11675689.
– (1985). Dependency, imperialism and the capitalist class in Canada. In R.J. Brym (Ed.), *The structure of the Canadian capitalist class* (pp. 21–52). Garamond Press.
– (1986). *Corporate power and Canadian capitalism*. University of British Columbia Press.
– (1989). Neoliberalism and the recomposition of Finance Capital in Canada. *Capital & Class*, 13(2), 81–112. https://doi.org/10.1177/030981688903800106.
– (2002). Does disorganized capitalism disorganize corporate networks? *Canadian Journal of Sociology/Cahiers Canadiens de Sociologie*, 27(3), 339–71. https://doi.org/10.2307/3341548.
– (2012). Global, transnational, regional, national: The need for nuance in theorizing global capitalism. *Critical Sociology*, 38(3), 365–71. https://doi.org/10.1177/0896920511434265.
– (2013). Global capitalism, American empire, collective imperialism? *Studies in Political Economy*, 92(1), 93–100. https://doi.org/10.1080/19187033.2013.11674977.
– (2017). Canada's carbon-capital elite: A tangled web of corporate power. *Canadian Journal of Sociology/Cahiers Canadiens de Sociologie*, 42(3), 225–60. https://doi.org/10.29173/cjs28258.
Carroll, W.K., & Daub, S. (2018). Corporate power, fossil capital, climate crisis: Introducing the Corporate Mapping Project. *Studies in Political Economy*, 99(2), 111–13. https://doi.org/10.1080/07078552.2018.1492074.
Carroll, W.K., & Huijzer, M.J. (2018). *Who owns Canada's fossil-fuel sector? Mapping the network of ownership*. Canadian Centre for Policy Alternatives.

https://canadacommons.ca/artifacts/1197603/who-owns-canadas-fossil-fuel-sector/1750727.

Carroll, W.K., & Klassen, J. (2010). Hollowing out corporate Canada? Changes in the corporate network since the 1990s. *Canadian Journal of Sociology/Cahiers Canadiens de Sociologie, 35*(1), 1–30. https://doi.org/10.29173/cjs6184.

Carroll, W.K., & Sapinski, J.P. (2016). Neoliberalism and the transnational capitalist class. In K. Birch, J. MacLeavy, & S. Springer (Eds.), *The handbook of neoliberalism* (pp. 39–49). Routledge.

Carruthers, B.G. (1996). *City of capital: Politics and markets in the English financial revolution*. Princeton University Press.

Carruthers, B.G., & Ariovich, L. (2004). The sociology of property rights. *Annual Review of Sociology, 30*(1), 23–46. https://doi.org/10.1146/annurev.soc.30.012703.110538.

Carruthers, B.G., & Kim, J.-C. (2011). The sociology of finance. *Annual Review of Sociology, 37*(1), 239–59. https://doi.org/10.1146/annurev-soc-081309-150129.

Casey, M.J., & Vigna, P. (2018). *The truth machine: The blockchain and the future of everything*. St. Martin's Press.

Catalini, C., & Gans, J.S. (2019, June). *Some simple economics of the blockchain* (National Bureau of Economic Research Working Paper No. 22952). https://doi.org/10.3386/w22952.

CBC News. (2008, October 9). *Canada positioned to weather global crisis: Flaherty*. CBC. https://www.cbc.ca/news/canada/canada-positioned-to-weather-global-crisis-flaherty-1.704481.

– (2016a, May 24). *Lawsuits revived against Royal Bank of Canada and 15 other banks in LIBOR-rigging case*. CBC. https://www.cbc.ca/news/business/libor-rigging-banks-1.3597254.

– (2016b, September 30). *Uber's bumpy ride to regulation in Ottawa*. CBC. https://www.cbc.ca/news/canada/ottawa/uber-regulated-ottawa-1.3784570.

CBC Radio. (2022, April 6). *Expanding temporary foreign worker program just means "more exploitable workers": Advocate*. CBC. https://www.cbc.ca/radio/thecurrent/the-current-for-april-6-2022-1.6410000/expanding-temporary-foreign-worker-program-just-means-more-exploitable-workers-advocate-1.6410422.

Centre for Policy Studies. (2006). *Big Bang 20 years on: New challenges facing the financial services sector*. Centre for Policy Studies. https://cps.org.uk/research/big-bang-20-years-on-new-challenges-facing-the-financial-services-sector.

Cerri, L. (2018). Birth of the modern corporation: From servant of the state to semi-sovereign power. *American Journal of Economics and Sociology, 77*(2), 239–77. https://doi.org/10.1111/ajes.12212.

Chandler, A.D. (1977). *Visible hand: The managerial revolution in American business*. Harvard University Press.

Chang, O. (2019, April 18). *Meet the Swiss town using blockchain to trade solar energy*. CNN Money. https://www.cnnmoney.ch/shows/blockchain/videos/meet-swiss-town-using-blockchain-trade-solar-energy.

Chant, J. (1979). The banks and the concentration of corporate power. In P.K. Gorecki & W.T. Stanbury (Eds.), *Perspectives on the Royal Commission on Corporate Concentration* (pp. 191–200). Institute for Research on Public Policy.

Chartered Professional Accountants of Canada. (2016). *Technological disruption of capital markets and reporting? An introduction to blockchain*. https://www.cpacanada.ca/-/media/site/business-and-accounting-resources/docs/g10157-rg-technological-disruption-of-capital-markets-reporting-introduction-to-blockchain-october-2016.pdf.

Chen, C., Koustas, A., & Goertzen, A. (2015). *The Trans-Pacific Partnership: A landmark trade deal for Canada*. Bank of Montreal.

Chodos, R. (1977). *The Caribbean connection*. James Lorimer & Company.

Chon, G., & Fleming, S. (2014, January 13). Banks win Basel concessions on debt rules. *Financial Times*. https://www.ft.com/content/d920db5e-7bb6-11e3-84af-00144feabdc0.

Christophers, B. (2013). *Banking across boundaries: Placing finance in capitalism*. John Wiley & Sons.

– (2022). The role of the state in the transfer of value from Main Street to Wall Street: US single-family housing after the financial crisis. *Antipode, 54*(1), 130–52. https://doi.org/10.1111/anti.12760.

Claessens, S., Underhill, G.R.D., & Zhang, X. (2008). The political economy of Basle II: The costs for poor countries. *World Economy, 31*(3), 313–44. https://doi.org/10.1111/j.1467-9701.2007.01090.x.

Clarkson, S. (2001). The multi-level state: Canada in the semi-periphery of both continentalism and globalization. *Review of International Political Economy, 8*(3), 501–27. https://doi.org/10.1080/09692290110055858.

– (2008). *Does North America exist? Governing the continent after NAFTA and 9/11*. University of Toronto Press.

Clarkson, S., & Wood, S. (2010). *A perilous imbalance: The globalization of Canadian law and governance*. UBC Press.

Cleaver, H. (2017). *Rupturing the dialectic*. AK Press.

Clement, W. (1975). *The Canadian corporate elite: An analysis of economic power*. McClelland & Stewart.

– (1977a). *Continental corporate power: Economic elite linkages between Canada and the United States*. McClelland & Stewart.

– (1977b). The corporate elite, the capitalist class, and the Canadian state. In L. Panitch (Ed.), *The Canadian state: Political economy and political power* (pp. 225–48). University of Toronto Press.

– (1979). An exercise in legitimation: Ownership and control in the report of the Royal Commission on Corporate Concentration. In P.K. Gorecki

& W.T. Stanbury (Eds.), *Perspectives on the Royal Commission on Corporate Concentration* (pp. 215–36). Institute for Research on Public Policy.

Clune, M.W. (2013, February 26). What was neoliberalism? *Los Angeles Review of Books.* https://lareviewofbooks.org/article/what-was-neoliberalism.

Cochrane, D.T. (2022, October 4). *Unaccountable: How did Canada lose $30 billion to corporations?* Canadians for Tax Fairness. https://www.taxfairness.ca/en/resources/reports/unaccountable-how-did-canada-lose-30-billion-corporations.

Cohen, T. (2013, April 30). *Temporary foreign worker reforms a political solution that will hurt the economy, business community says.* Postmedia News.

Coleman, W., & Porter, T. (2003). "Playin' along": Canada and global finance. In W. Clement & L.F. Vosko (Eds.), *Changing Canada: Political economy as transformation* (pp. 241–64). McGill-Queen's University Press.

Communications Nova Scotia. (2018, May 11). *Financial services sector expands with RBC* [Press release]. https://novascotia.ca/news/release/?id=20150311001.

Consumers Council of Canada. (2021, February 6). *RBC fined $350,000 for failing to get clear consent for credit limit hikes.* https://www.consumerscouncil.com/rbc-fined-350000-for-failing-to-get-clear-consent-for-credit-limit-hikes.

Corbett, P.E. (1938). The British North America Act and our crippled constitution. *Canadian Banker, 45*(2), 155–64.

Corcoran, T. (2015, June 22). Dark pools vs protectionism. *Financial Post.* http://business.financialpost.com/fp-comment/terence-corcoran-dark-pools-vs-protectionism.

Courchene, T.J. (1976). *Monetarism and controls: The inflation fighters.* C.D. Howe Research Institute.

Courville, L. (2012, May 8). *Financial crisis: A perfect storm or regulatory failure.* https://www.hec.ca/iea/seminaires/120508_leon_courville.pdf.

Cox, R. (1981). Social forces, states and world orders: Beyond international relations theory. *Millennium: Journal of International Studies, 10*(2), 126–55. https://doi.org/10.1177/03058298810100020501.

Crane, D. (1986, October 4). Canada has abandoned its role as a friend of the Third World. *Toronto Star,* B2.

– (1989, March 8). IMF not the only group warning Canada to cut deficit. *Toronto Star,* D3.

– (1999, October 1). Plan to open capital flows suffers blow: Canada credited with heading off IMF power move. *Toronto Star.*

Crary, D. (1998, December 15). Banks cancel mergers after opposition forms. *Pittsburgh Post-Gazette,* B2.

Crashing the party: Wall Street firms take aim at America's stock-exchange oligopoly. (2019, January 12). *The Economist.* https://www.economist.com/finance-and-economics/2019/01/12/wall-street-firms-take-aim-at-americas-stock-exchange-oligopoly.

Creighton, J.H. (1933). *Central banking in Canada*. Clarke & Stewart.
Crouch, C. (2009). Privatised Keynesianism: An unacknowledged policy regime. *British Journal of Politics and International Relations*, 11(3), 382–99. https://doi.org/10.1111/j.1467-856X.2009.00377.x.
Crow, J.W., & Fischer, S. (2002). *Making money: An insider's perspective on finance, politics, and Canada's central bank*. Wiley.
CTV News.ca. (2017, November 5). *Top Liberal Party fundraiser, 3 former PMs named in Paradise Papers*. CTV News. https://www.ctvnews.ca/politics/top-liberal-party-fundraiser-3-former-pms-named-in-paradise-papers-1.3664328.
Cummings, D. (2017, April 19). *Nasdaq to invest in blockchain technology*. ETH News. https://www.ethnews.com/nasdaq-to-invest-in-blockchain-technology.
Curry, B. (2021, April 6). Trudeau open to discussions after Yellen calls for global minimum corporate tax rate. *Globe and Mail*. https://www.theglobeandmail.com/politics/article-trudeau-open-to-discussions-after-yellen-calls-for-global-minimum.
Curtiss, C.A. (1948). Banking. In W.S. Wallace (Ed.), *The encyclopedia of Canada* (Vol. 1, pp. 151–64). University Associates of Canada. http://faculty.marianopolis.edu/c.belanger/quebechistory/encyclopedia/BankinginCanada-CanadianBanks-CanadianHistory.htm.
Cutler, A.C. (2011). The privatization of authority in the global political economy. In S. McBride & G. Teeple (Eds.), *Relations of global power: Neoliberal order and disorder* (pp. 41–59). University of Toronto Press.
Daian, P., Goldfeder, S., Kell, T., Li, Y., Zhao, X., Bentov, I., Breidenbach, L., & Juels, A. (2020). Flash Boys 2.0: Frontrunning in decentralized exchanges, miner extractable value, and consensus instability. In *2020 IEEE Symposium on Security and Privacy (SP)* (pp. 910–27). IEEE. https://doi.org/10.1109/SP40000.2020.00040.
Daniel, F. (2002). Recent changes to Canada's financial Sector legislation. *Bank of Canada Review*, 3–16. https://www.bankofcanada.ca/wp-content/uploads/2010/06/daniele.pdf.
Daniel, W. (2022, March 18). *Argentina's IMF bailout deal includes a wild clause that rips cryptocurrencies*. Yahoo Finance. https://finance.yahoo.com/news/argentina-imf-bailout-deal-includes-190748787.html.
Darrah, D. (2021, December 3). *Canada's big banks pay out $19 billion in record bonuses*. The Breach. https://breachmedia.ca/canadas-big-banks-pay-out-19-billion-in-record-bonuses.
Darroch, J.L. (1992). Global competitiveness and public policy: The case of Canadian multinational banks. *Business History*, 34(3), 153–75. https://doi.org/10.1080/00076799200000086.

– (1994). *Canadian banks and global competitiveness.* McGill-Queen's University Press.

Darroch, J.L., & McMillan, C. (2007). Globalization restricted: The Canadian financial system and public policy. *Ivey Business Journal, 71*(3), 1–9. https://doi.org/10.1108/sd.2007.05623gad.010.

Daub, S., & Carroll, W.K. (2016, October 6). *Why is the CEO of a big Canadian bank giving speeches about climate change and pipelines?* Corporate Mapping Project. https://www.corporatemapping.ca/rbc-ceo-speech-climate-pipelines.

Davis, G.F. (2012). Politics and financial markets. In K.K. Cetina & A. Preda (Eds.), *The Oxford handbook of the sociology of finance* (pp. 33–51). Oxford University Press.

Davis, G.F., & Kim, S. (2015). Financialization of the economy. *Annual Review of Sociology, 41*(1), 203–21. https://doi.org/10.1146/annurev-soc-073014-112402.

Davis, L.E., & Gallman, R.E. (2001). *Evolving financial markets and international capital flows: Britain, the Americas, and Australia, 1865–1914.* Cambridge University Press.

De, N. (2018, March 23). *Smart contracts now recognized under Tennessee law.* CoinDesk. https://www.coindesk.com/blockchain-bill-becomes-law-tennessee.

– (2020, August 26). *Canadian exchange Shakepay gets cold wallet insurance to protect customer funds.* CoinDesk. https://www.coindesk.com/markets/2020/08/26/canadian-exchange-shakepay-gets-cold-wallet-insurance-to-protect-customer-funds.

De Filippi, P., & Hassan, S. (2016). Blockchain technology as a regulatory technology: From code is law to law is code. *First Monday, 21*(12). https://doi.org/10.5210/fm.v21i12.7113.

De Filippi, P., & Wright, A. (2018). *Blockchain and the law: The rule of code.* Harvard University Press.

Dean, J. (2020). Communism or neo-feudalism? *New Political Science, 42*(1), 1–17. https://doi.org/10.1080/07393148.2020.1718974.

Debusmann, B., Jr. (2018, July 30). *Smart Dubai, DIFC Courts to launch world's first Court of the Blockchain.* Arabian Business. https://www.arabianbusiness.com/technology/401774-smart-dubai-difc-courts-to-launch-worlds-first-court-of-the-blockchain.

Demirović, A. (2011). Materialist state theory and the transnationalization of the capitalist state. *Antipode, 43*(1), 38–59. https://doi.org/10.1111/j.1467-8330.2010.00810.x.

Deneault, A. (2011). *Offshore: Tax havens and the rule of global crime* (G. Holoch, Trans.). New Press. (Original work published 2010)

– (2015). *Canada, a new tax haven: How the country that shaped Caribbean offshore jurisdictions is becoming one itself*. Talonbooks.

– (2018). *Legalizing theft: A short guide to tax havens*. Fernwood Publishing.

Deneault, A., & Sacher, W. (2012). *Imperial Canada Inc.: Legal haven of choice for the world's mining industries* (R. Philpot & F.A. Reed, Trans.). Talonbooks.

Denison, M. (1967). *Canada's first bank: A history of the Bank of Montreal* (Vols. 1–2). McClelland & Stewart.

Desai, R. (2013). *Geopolitical economy: After US hegemony, globalization and empire*. Pluto Press.

Dilley, A. (2012). *Finance, politics, and imperialism: Australia, Canada, and the City of London, c. 1896–1914*. Palgrave Macmillan.

Dodd, N. (2014). *The social life of money*. Princeton University Press.

Dollentas, N. (2017, August 12). *Microsoft's Coco to speed up blockchains for enterprise*. crypto.news. https://crypto.news/microsofts-coco-to-speed-up-blockchains-for-enterprise.

Dominican Republic is lent $185 million. (1979, March 20). *New York Times*, D18. https://www.nytimes.com/1979/03/21/archives/dominican-republic-is-lent-185-million.html.

Dow, A., & Dow, S. (2014). The staples approach and the financial crisis. In J. Stanford (Ed.), *The staple theory @ 50: Reflections on the lasting significance of Mel Watkins' "A staples theory of economic growth"* (pp. 114–17). Canadian Centre for Policy Alternatives.

Drache, D. (1977). Staple-ization: A theory of Canadian capitalist development. In C. Heron (Ed.), *Imperialism, nationalism, and Canada: Essays from the Marxist Institute of Toronto* (pp. 15–33). New Hogtown Press.

Drainville, A.C. (1991). *Monetarism in Canada and the world economy* [Unpublished doctoral dissertation]. York University.

– (1995). Monetarism in Canada and the world economy. *Studies in Political Economy*, 46(1), 7–42. https://doi.org/10.1080/19187033.1995.11675365.

Draper, H. (1977). *Karl Marx's theory of revolution: Vol. 1. State and bureaucracy*. Monthly Review Press.

Drezner, D.W. (2014). *The system worked: How the world stopped another Great Depression*. Oxford University Press.

Drohan, M. (1985, December 28). The Canadian Commercial Bank debacle: Worthless but costly bailout strained relations between banks and government. *The Gazette*, D3.

Dubinsky, Z. (2016, June 18). *How Canada got into bed with tax havens*. CBC News. https://www.cbc.ca/news/business/canada-offshore-treaties-barbados-tax-avoidance-1.3641278.

Dzhondzhorov, D. (2022, January 14). *Rio de Janeiro's mayor to invest 1% of The City's treasury in Bitcoin*. CryptoPotato. https://cryptopotato.com/rio-de-janeiros-mayor-to-invest-1-of-the-citys-treasury-in-bitcoin.

Eayrs, J. (1975, May 6). Royal commission: Psychoanalyst to Canada. *The Gazette*, 9.

Eckardt, H.M.P. (2016). *Manual of Canadian banking*. Leopold Classic Library. (Original work published 1914)

Eichengreen, B.J. (2008). *Globalizing capital: A history of the international monetary system* (2nd ed.). Princeton University Press. (Original work published 1996)

Elias, N. (2000). *The civilizing process* (2nd ed.). Wiley-Blackwell. (Original work published 1939)

Engert, W. (2005). On the evolution of the financial safety net. *Financial System Review*, 67–73.

Erman, B. (2013, June 25). New exchange to take on TSX. *Globe and Mail*. https://www.theglobeandmail.com/report-on-business/new-exchange-to-take-on-tsx/article12790216.

Esping-Andersen, G. (2013). *The three worlds of welfare capitalism*. John Wiley & Sons. (Original work published 1990)

Evans, J. (2019). Colonialism, racism, and the transition to capitalism in Canada. In X. Lafrance & C. Post (Eds.), *Case studies in the origins of capitalism* (pp. 191–214). Palgrave Macmillan. https://doi.org/10.1007/978-3-319-95657-2.

Evans, P. (2021, May 27). *Earnings bonanza continues at big banks as RBC, TD and CIBC profits up by more than 100%*. CBC News. https://www.cbc.ca/news/business/bank-earnings-thursday-1.6042217.

– (2022, November 29). *RBC to take over HSBC Canada in biggest ever deal for a domestic banks*. CBC News. https://www.cbc.ca/news/business/rbc-buying-hsbc-canada-1.6667564.

– (2023, May 23). *Households now owe more than Canada's entire GDP, housing agency warns*. CBC News. https://www.cbc.ca/news/business/household-debt-gdp-1.6852027.

Fairfield, J.A.T. (2015). Bitproperty. *Southern California Law Review*, 88(4), 805–74. https://scholarlycommons.law.wlu.edu/wlufac/492.

– (2017). *Owned: Property, privacy, and the new digital serfdom*. Cambridge University Press. https://doi.org/10.1017/9781316671467.

Fedio, C. (2016, April 13). *Uber barges in: Company gets green light to operate legally in Ottawa*. CBC News. https://www.cbc.ca/news/canada/ottawa/uber-legalization-city-council-vote-passes-1.3533537.

Ferdosi, M., & Graefe, P. (2021, May 2). *CERB was luxurious compared to provincial social assistance*. The Conversation. http://theconversation.com/cerb-was-luxurious-compared-to-provincial-social-assistance-158501.

Ferguson, J. (1995a, June 25). How the banks blew it. *Toronto Star*, D1.

– (1995b, June 25). Why Martin used f-word at banks. *Toronto Star*, A1.

Ferland, J. (1989). Business history and the buried treasures of the theory of value. *Labour/Le Travail*, 23, 235–45. https://doi.org/10.2307/25143144.

Fernando, J. (2021, February 24). *The LIBOR scandal*. Investopedia. https://www.investopedia.com/terms/l/libor-scandal.asp.

Ferreira, J. (2023, March 29). *Canada makes amendments to foreign homebuyers ban – here's what they look like*. CTV News. https://www.ctvnews.ca/business/canada-makes-amendments-to-foreign-homebuyers-ban-here-s-what-they-look-like-1.6334287.

Fichtner, J. (2016). The anatomy of the Cayman Islands offshore financial center: Anglo-America, Japan, and the role of hedge funds. *Review of International Political Economy, 23*(6), 1034–63. https://doi.org/10.1080/09692290.2016.1243143.

Fife, R., & Chase, S. (2017, September 13). Canada pushing to revamp NAFTA lawsuit provision. *Globe and Mail*. https://www.theglobeandmail.com/news/politics/canada-pushing-to-revamp-nafta-chapter-11-lawsuit-provision/article36255908.

– (2018, May 23). Trudeau cabinet blocks Chinese takeover of Aecon over national security concerns. *Globe and Mail*. https://www.theglobeandmail.com/politics/article-ottawa-blocks-chinese-takeover-of-aecon-over-national-security.

Financial Stability Board (FSB). (2014, November 6). *2014 update of list of global systemically important banks (G-SIBs)*. https://www.fsb.org/2014/11/2014-update-of-list-of-global-systemically-important-banks.

– (2020, November 16). *About the FSB*. https://www.fsb.org/about.

– (2022, November 21). *2022 list of global systemically important banks (G-SIBs)*. https://www.fsb.org/2022/11/2022-list-of-global-systemically-important-banks-g-sibs.

– (2023). *History of the FSB*. https://www.fsb.org/about/history-of-the-fsb.

Finkel, A. (2006). *Social policy and practice in Canada: A history*. Wilfrid Laurier University Press.

Fisher, D. (2014, November 7). How Detroit saved its art collection from the bill collectors. *Forbes*. https://www.forbes.com/sites/danielfisher/2014/11/07/how-detroit-saved-its-art-collection-from-the-bill-collectors.

Flaherty, J. (2008, October 29). *Speech by the Honourable Jim Flaherty, Minister of Finance, to a joint meeting of the Empire Club of Canada and the Canadian Club of Toronto* [Speech transcript]. Empire Club of Canada, Toronto. https://www.canada.ca/en/news/archive/2008/10/speech-honourable-jim-flaherty-minister-finance-joint-meeting-empire-club-canada-canadian-club-toronto.html.

Flanagan, T. (2015, November 4). *Canadian traders adjust to TSX Alpha*. Markets Media. https://www.marketsmedia.com/canadian-traders-adjust-to-tsx-alpha.

Fligstein, N. (2002). *The architecture of markets: An economic sociology of twenty-first-century capitalist societies*. Princeton University Press.

– (2021). *The banks did it: An anatomy of the financial crisis*. Harvard University Press.

Foster, J. (2019, August 19). *TMX POV: It's time to rethink Canadian dark pools*. TMX Inc. https://www.tmx.com/pov?id=25&lang=en.

Foster, J.B. (2003). *Imperialism now*. Monthly Review Press.

Frank, S. (2015, January). Come with us if you want to live. *Harper's Magazine*. http://harpers.org/archive/2015/01/come-with-us-if-you-want-to-live.

Fraser, N. (2014). Can society be commodities all the way down? Post-Polanyian reflections on capitalist crisis. *Economy and Society, 43*(4), 541–58. https://doi.org/10.1080/03085147.2014.898822.

Freedman, C. (1998). *The Canadian banking system* (Technical Report No. 81). Bank of Canada. https://doi.org/10.34989/tr-81.

Freeland, C. (2010, January 29). What Toronto can teach New York and London. *Financial Times*. http://www.ft.com/content/db2b340a-0a1b-11df-8b23-00144feabdc0.

– *Plutocrats: The rise of the new global super-rich and the fall of everyone else*. Doubleday Canada.

Freeman, S. (2012, July 31). Maple Group wins control of TMX, with 91 per cent of shares tendered. *Globe and Mail*. https://www.theglobeandmail.com/report-on-business/maple-group-wins-control-of-tmx-with-91-per-cent-of-shares-tendered/article4453456.

Freifeld, K. (2015, May 20). *Five global banks to pay $5.7 billion in fines over rate rigging*. Reuters. https://www.reuters.com/article/us-banks-forex-settlementa-usa-idUSKBN0O51PY20150520.

Fuchs, C. (2010). Critical globalization studies: An empirical and theoretical analysis of the new imperialism. *Science & Society, 74*(2), 215–47. https://doi.org/10.1521/siso.2010.74.2.215.

Fukakusa, J. (2013, September 10). *Royal Bank of Canada Barclays Global Financial Services conference speech* [Speech transcript]. Barclays Global Financial Services Conference. https://web.archive.org/web/20210228135602/https://www.rbc.com/investorrelations/pdf/barclays2013notes.pdf.

Fullerton, D.H. (1986). *Graham Towers and his times: A biography*. McClelland & Stewart.

Gaist, T. (2014, January 8). *Wall Street swindles, not pensions, behind financial crisis in Detroit and other US cities*. World Socialist Web Site. https://www.wsws.org/en/articles/2014/01/08/swap-j08.html.

Galbraith, J.A. (1970). *Canadian banking*. Ryerson Press.

Gamble, A. (2019). Why is neo-liberalism so resilient? *Critical Sociology, 45*(7–8), 983–94. https://doi.org/10.1177/0896920519832648.

Gardner, B.C. (1938). Some aspects of banking. *Canadian Banker, 45*(2), 187–95.

Garrod, J.Z. (2016). The real world of the decentralized autonomous society. *TripleC: Communication, Capitalism & Critique, 14*(1), 62–77. https://doi.org/10.31269/triplec.v14i1.692.

- (2018). Imperialism or global capitalism? Some reflections from Canada. *Studies in Political Economy, 99*(3), 268–84. https://doi.org/10.1080/07078552.2018.1536359.
Garrod, J.Z., & Macdonald, L. (2016). Rethinking "Canadian mining imperialism" in Latin America. In D. Kalowatie & M.L. Dougherty (Eds.), *Mining in Latin America: Critical approaches to the "new extraction"* (pp. 100–15). Routledge.
Geddes, J. (1998a, September 21). The battle begins. *Maclean's*. https://archive.macleans.ca/article/1998/9/21/the-battle-beings.
- (1998b, September 28). Rules of the game. *Maclean's*. https://archive.macleans.ca/article/1998/09/28/rules-of-the-game.
George Weston Limited. (2020). *Annual report*. https://www.annualreports.com/HostedData/AnnualReportArchive/g/TSX_WN_2020.pdf.
Germain, R. (2010). *Global politics and financial governance*. Palgrave Macmillan.
Gibson, J.D. (1938). The changing character of bank assets. *Canadian Banker, 45*(2), 145–54.
Gibson-Graham, J.K., Cameron, J., & Healy, S. (2013). *Take back the economy: An ethical guide for transforming our communities*. University of Minnesota Press.
Gilbert, C., & Guénin, H. (2022). The COVID-19 crisis and massive public debts: What should we expect? *Critical Perspectives on Accounting, 98*, Article 102417. https://doi.org/10.1016/j.cpa.2022.102417.
Gilbert, E. (2002). Forging a national currency: Money, state-making and nation-building in Canada. In E. Gilbert & E. Helleiner (Eds.), *Nation-states and money: The past, present and future of national currencies* (pp. 25–46). Routledge.
Gill, S. (1992). Economic globalization and the internationalization of authority: Limits and contradictions. *Geoforum, 23*(3), 269–83. https://doi.org/10.1016/0016-7185(92)90042-3.
Gill, S., & Law, D. (1989). Global hegemony and the structural power of capital. *International Studies Quarterly, 33*(4), 475–99. https://doi.org/10.2307/2600523.
Gill, S., & Cutler, A.C. (Eds.). (2014). *New constitutionalism and world order*. Cambridge University Press.
Gilman, N. (2014). The twin insurgency. *American Interest, 9*(6), 3–11. https://www.the-american-interest.com/2014/06/15/the-twin-insurgency.
Gindin, S. (2018). Socialism for realists. *Catalyst, 2*(3). https://catalyst-journal.com/2018/12/socialism-for-realists.
- (2022, November 22). Morbid symptoms, premature obituaries: The American empire. *The Bullet*. https://socialistproject.ca/morbid-symptoms-premature-obituaries.

Glassman, J. (2003). The spaces of economic crisis: Asia and the reconfiguration of neo-Marxist crisis theory. *Studies in Comparative International Development*, 37(4), 31–63. https://doi.org/10.1007/BF02686271.

Glossary of technical terms. (2009). *Historical Materialism*, 17(2), 109–13. https://doi.org/10.1163/156920609X443407.

Goldenberg, J. (2022, May 7). Eco-anarchists torch former minister's cars in TMR. *The Suburban*. https://www.thesuburban.com/news/city_news/eco-anarchists-torch-former-ministers-cars-in-tmr/article_d4647f48-0a0a-5059-b93f-d19ff1ba28af.html.

Goldstein, J. (2013, October 8). Putting a speed limit on the stock market. *New York Times*, SM14–15. https://www.nytimes.com/2013/10/13/magazine/high-frequency-traders.html.

Good policy is good politics: Why Canada needs bank mergers now. (2004, May 1). *Policy Options*. https://policyoptions.irpp.org/magazines/governance-and-scandal/good-policy-is-good-politics-why-canada-needs-bank-mergers-now.

Goodhart, C.A.E. (2011). *The Basel Committee on Banking Supervision: A history of the early years, 1974–1997*. Cambridge University Press.

Gorecki, P.K., & Stanbury, W.T. (Eds.). (1979). *Perspectives on the Royal Commission on Corporate Concentration*. Institute for Research on Public Policy.

Gordon, D. (1988). The global economy: New edifice or crumbling foundations? *New Left Review*, 168, 24–64. https://newleftreview.org/issues/i168/articles/david-gordon-the-global-economy-new-edifice-or-crumbling-foundations.pdf.

Gordon, T. (2010). *Imperialist Canada*. Arbeiter Ring Publishing.

Gordon, T., & Webber, J.R. (2008). Imperialism and resistance: Canadian mining companies in Latin America. *Third World Quarterly*, 29(1), 63–87. https://doi.org/10.1080/01436590701726509.

– (2011). Canada and the Honduran coup. *Bulletin of Latin American Research*, 30(3), 328–43. https://doi.org/10.1111/j.1470-9856.2010.00499.x.

– (2013). Post-coup Honduras: Latin America's corridor of reaction. *Historical Materialism*, 21(3), 16–56. https://doi.org/10.1163/1569206X-12341316.

– (2014). Canadian geopolitics in post-coup Honduras. *Critical Sociology*, 40(4), 601–20. https://doi.org/10.1177/0896920513482149.

– (2016). *Blood of extraction: Canadian imperialism in Latin America*. Fernwood Publishing.

– (2018). Canadian capital and secondary imperialism in Latin America. *Canadian Foreign Policy Journal*, 25(1), 72–89. https://doi.org/10.1080/11926422.2018.1457966.

Gould, E. (2010). *Nobody's poster child: Why the "Canadian model" cannot be used to promote financial liberalization at the World Trade Organization*. Canadian Centre for Policy Alternatives. https://www.policyalternatives.ca/sites/default/files/uploads/publications/reports/docs/Nobodys_Poster_Child.pdf.

Gowan, P. (1999). *The global gamble: Washington's Faustian bid for world dominance*. Verso.

Graeber, D. (2011). *Debt: The first 5000 years*. Melville House Publishing.

Granger, A. (2013, December 15). Estey Commission. *The Canadian encyclopedia*. Retrieved 31 July 2024, from https://www.thecanadianencyclopedia.ca/en/article/estey-commission.

Gray, J.N. (1977). On the contestability of social and political concepts. *Political Theory*, 5(3), 331–48. https://doi.org/10.1177/009059177700500304.

Greater money market: President Royal Bank says time is now ripe for forward move. (1954, January 15). *Globe and Mail*, 22.

Greenfield, A. (2017). *Radical technologies*. Verso.

Green Party of Canada. (2019). *Platform 2019: Costing*. https://www.poltext.org/sites/poltext.org/files/plateformesV2/Canada/CAN_PL_2019_GREEN_EN_COSTING.pdf.

Greenpeace. (2020). *It's the finance sector, stupid*. https://media.greenpeace.org/archive/Report--It-s-the-Finance-Sector--Stupid-27MZIFJ8ZCWOC.html.

Greenspon, E. (1998, March). St Paul among the philistines: When you're Paul Martin and planning quietly to undergo a political facelift, a gigantic bank merger is extremely inconvenient. *Report on Business Magazine*, 14(9), 25–8.

Greer, A. (2018). *Property and dispossession: Natives, empires and land in early modern North America*. Cambridge University Press.

Grossman, R.S. (2010). *Unsettled account: The evolution of banking in the industrialized world since 1800*. Princeton University Press.

Gunter, L. (2009, April 5). "Boringly consistent" wins in banking; IMF, others note that Canada's cautious approach has proven its value. *Edmonton Journal*, A14.

Guyana to restructure its Eurocurrency debt. (1980, February 6). *American Banker*, 3.

Hager, S.B. (2015). Corporate ownership of the public debt: Mapping the new aristocracy of finance. *Socio-Economic Review*, 13(3), 505–23. https://doi.org/10.1093/ser/mwv013.

Haldane, A. (2011, July 8). *The race to zero* [Speech transcript]. International Economic Association Sixteenth World Congress, Beijing. https://www.bis.org/review/r110720a.pdf.

– (2012, August 31). *The dog and the frisbee* [Speech transcript]. Federal Reserve Bank of Kansas City's 366th Economic Policy Symposium, Jackson Hole, Wyoming. https://www.bis.org/review/r120905a.pdf.

Hall, C. (2015, September 12). "Liberals in a hurry"? That's Trudeau, not Mulcair's NDP. *CBC News*. https://www.cbc.ca/news/politics/canada-election-2015-chris-hall-liberals-ndp-1.3225365.

Hall, W. (1982, February 9). Orion's bid for stardom. *Financial Times*, 18.
Halpern, P., Cakebread, C., Nicholls, C.C., & Puri, P. (2016). *Back from the brink: Lessons from the Canadian asset-backed commercial paper crisis*. University of Toronto Press. https://www.jstor.org/stable/10.3138/j.ctvg253b2.
Handa, J. (2002). *Monetary economics*. Routledge.
Hann, C.M. (1998). Introduction: The embededness of property. In C.M. Hann (Ed.), *Property relations: Renewing the anthropological tradition* (pp. 1–47). Cambridge University Press.
Hanover, N. (2013). Who are Detroit's creditors? World Socialist Web Site. https://www.wsws.org/en/articles/2013/06/14/cred-j14.html.
Hanson, E.J., Boothe, P.M., & Edwards, H. (2003). *Eric J. Hanson's financial history of Alberta, 1905–1950*. University of Calgary Press.
Hardt, M., & Negri, A. (2000). *Empire*. Harvard University Press.
– (2017). *Assembly*. Oxford University Press.
Harmes, A. (2006). Neoliberalism and multilevel governance. *Review of International Political Economy*, 13(5), 725–49. https://doi.org/10.1080/09692290600950621.
Harris, J. (2005). To be or not to be: The nation-centric world under globalization. *Science & Society*, 69(3), 329–40. https://doi.org/10.1521/siso.69.3.329.66517.
Harris, S.L. (2004). Financial sector reform in Canada: Interests and the policy process. *Canadian Journal of Political Science*, 37(1), 161–84. https://doi.org/10.1017/S0008423904040053.
– (2010). The global financial meltdown and financial regulation: Shirking and learning – Canada in an International Context. In G.B. Doern & C. Stoney (Eds.), *How Ottawa spends, 2010–2011: Recession, realignment, and the new deficit era* (pp. 68–86). McGill-Queen's University Press.
Hart, K., & Ortiz, H. (2014). The anthropology of money and finance: Between ethnography and world history. *Annual Review of Anthropology*, 43(1), 465–82. https://doi.org/10.1146/annurev-anthro-102313-025814.
Hart, N.G. (1951). A Canadian banker abroad – France. *Canadian Banker*, 58(2), 100–14.
Hartt, S.H. (2005, September 1). From a bang to a whimper: Twenty years of lost momentum in financial institutions. *Policy Options*. https://policyoptions.irpp.org/magazines/the-un-at-60/from-a-bang-to-a-whimper-twenty-years-of-lost-momentum-in-financial-institutions.
Harvey, D. (2000). *Spaces of hope*. University of California Press.
– (2003). *The new imperialism*. Oxford University Press.
– (2005). *A brief history of neoliberalism*. Oxford University Press.
– (2007). In what ways is "the new imperialism" really new? *Historical Materialism*, 15(3), 57–70. https://doi.org/10.1163/156920607X225870.

- (2009). The art of rent: Globalisation, monopoly and the commodification of culture. *Socialist Register, 38*, 93–110. https://socialistregister.com/index.php/srv/article/view/5778/2674.
- (2011). *The enigma of capital: And the crises of capitalism*. Oxford University Press.

Hathaway, T. (2020). Neoliberalism as corporate power. *Competition & Change, 24*(3–4), 315–37. https://doi.org/10.1177/1024529420910382.

Havana bank is bombed. (1931, September 2). *New York Times*, 8. https://www.nytimes.com/1931/09/02/archives/havana-bank-is-bombed-branch-of-the-royal-bank-of-canada-is-badly.html.

Hayes, S.L., & Hubbard, P.M. (1990). *Investment banking: A tale of three cities*. Harvard Business School Press.

Hazlitt, T. (1967, January 12). First step by Ottawa to protect depositors. *Toronto Star*, 11.

Helleiner, E. (1994). *States and the reemergence of global finance: From Bretton Woods to the 1990s*. Cornell University Press.
- (1995). Explaining the globalization of financial markets: Bringing states back in. *Review of International Political Economy, 2*(2), 315–41. https://doi.org/10.1080/09692299508434322.
- (1997). Braudelian reflections on economic globalisation: The historian as pioneer. In S. Gill & J.H. Mittelman (Eds.), *Innovation and transformation in international relations theory* (pp. 90–104). Cambridge University Press.
- (1999). Sovereignty, territoriality, and the globalization of finance. In D.A. Smith, D.J. Solinger, & S.C. Topik (Eds.), *States and sovereignty in the global economy* (pp. 138–57). Routledge.
- (2003). *The making of national money: Territorial currencies in historical perspective*. Cornell University Press.
- (2013). Did the financial crisis generate a fourth pillar of global economic architecture? *Swiss Political Science Review, 19*(4), 558–63. https://doi.org/10.1111/spsr.12060.
- (2014). *The status quo crisis: Global financial governance after the 2008 financial meltdown*. Oxford University Press.

Helleiner, E., Pagliari, S., & Zimmermann, H. (2010). *Global finance in crisis: The politics of international regulatory change*. Routledge.

Heller, H. (2012). Imperialist Canada, Todd Gordon, Winnipeg: Arbeiter Ring Publishing, 2011. *Historical Materialism, 20*(2), 222–31. https://doi.org/10.1163/1569206X-12341239.

Henwood, D. (1998). *Wall Street: How it works and for whom*. Verso.
- (2017, December 26). What's behind Bitcoin mania? *Jacobin*. http://jacobinmag.com/2017/12/bitcoin-price-crypto-currency-explainer.

Herian, R. (2018). Taking blockchain seriously. *Law and Critique, 29*(2), 163–71. https://doi.org/10.1007/s10978-018-9226-y.

– (2019). *Regulating blockchain: Critical perspectives in law and technology*. Routledge.

Heron, C., & Storey, R.H. (1986). *On the job: Confronting the labour process in Canada*. McGill-Queen's University Press.

Heron, J. (1969). *The first hundred years: The Royal Bank of Canada, 1869–1969*. Royal Bank of Canada.

Herring, J. (2022, February 22). Health-care advocates worry wave of privatization incoming in Budget 2022. *Calgary Herald*. https://calgaryherald.com/news/politics/public-health-advocates-worry-wave-of-privatization-incoming-in-budget-2022.

Hertzberg, E., & Platt, B. (2022, May 19). *Canada bans China's Huawei, ZTE from 5G wireless networks*. Bloomberg. https://www.bloomberg.com/news/articles/2022-05-19/trudeau-government-said-to-ban-huawei-from-5g-in-canada.

Hillman, J., & Sacks, D. (2021). *China's Belt and Road: Implications for the United States* (Independent Task Force Report No. 79). Council on Foreign Relations. https://www.cfr.org/task-force-report/chinas-belt-and-road-implications-for-the-united-states.

Hirst, P., & Thompson, G. (2015). *Globalization in question*. John Wiley & Sons. (Original work published 1996)

Ho, S. (2017, May 31). *Canadian trial finds blockchain not ready for bank settlements*. Reuters. https://www.reuters.com/article/business/canadian-trial-finds-blockchain-not-ready-for-bank-settlements-idUSKBN18L26L.

Hoang, K.K. (2022). *Spiderweb capitalism: How global elites exploit frontier markets*. Princeton University Press.

Hobsbawm, E. (1987). *The age of empire: 1875–1914*. Pantheon Books.

Hudson, G. (1959, June 25). Bank chief says time is nearing to loosen tight money situation. *Globe and Mail*, 3.

Hudson, P.J. (2010). Imperial designs: The Royal Bank of Canada in the Caribbean. *Race & Class*, 52(1), 33–48. https://doi.org/10.1177/0306396810371762.

Hurtig, M. (2003). *The vanishing country: Is it too late to save Canada?* McClelland & Stewart.

Hussain, Y. (2021, December 7). Posthaste: Canadians embarked on a $193B mortgage binge during the pandemic. Now comes the reckoning. *Financial Post*. https://financialpost.com/executive/posthaste-canadians-embarked-on-a-193b-mortgage-binge-during-the-pandemic-now-comes-the-reckoning.

Hymer, S. (1979). *The multinational corporation: A radical approach*. Cambridge University Press.

Iacobucci, E., Trebilcock, M.J., & Winter, R.A. (2006). The Canadian experience with deregulation. *University of Toronto Law Journal*, 56(1), 1–74. https://doi.org/10.1353/tlj.2006.0001.

IE Staff. (2007, March 13). *RBC Dain Rauscher to acquire J.B. Hanauer & Co.* Investment Executive. https://www.investmentexecutive.com/news/industry-news/rbc-dain-rauscher-to-acquire-j-b-hanauer-co.

– (2021, July 27). *RBC Dominion Securities fined $350K for supervisory failings.* Investment Executive. https://www.investmentexecutive.com/news/industry-news/rbc-dominion-securities-fined-350k-for-supervisory-failings.

Investment Industry Regulatory Organization of Canada (IIROC). (2017, July 13). *Withdrawal of proposed Dark Rules Anti-Avoidance Provision.* https://www.ciro.ca/news-room/publications/withdrawal-proposed-dark-rules-anti-avoidance-provision.

Ikeda, S. (2004). Zonal structure and the trajectories of Canada, Mexico, Australia, and Norway under neo-liberal globalization. In S. Clarkson & M.G. Cohen (Eds.), *Governing under stress: Middle powers and the challenge of globalization* (pp. 263–90). Zed Books.

Ince, C.H. (1970). *The Royal Bank of Canada: A chronology 1864–1969.* Royal Bank of Canada.

Ingham, G. (1999). Capitalism, money and banking: A critique of recent historical sociology. *British Journal of Sociology, 50*(1), 76–96. https://doi.org/10.1111/j.1468-4446.1999.00076.x.

Institute of International Finance (IIF). (n.d.). *About us.* Retrieved 31 July 2024, from https://www.iif.com/about-us.

International Consortium of Investigative Journalists. (2017, November 5). *Paradise Papers: Secrets of the global elite.* https://www.icij.org/investigations/paradise-papers.

International Monetary Fund (IMF). (2019, June 24). *Canada: Financial system stability assessment* (Country Report No. 2019/177). IMF. https://www.imf.org/en/Publications/CR/Issues/2019/06/24/Canada-Financial-System-Stability-Assessment-47024.

Ioannou, S., Wójcik, D., & Dymski, G. (2019). Too-big-to-fail: Why megabanks have not become smaller since the global financial crisis? *Review of Political Economy, 31*(3), 356–81. https://doi.org/10.1080/09538259.2019.1674001.

Ishmaev, G. (2017). Blockchain technology as an institution of property. *Metaphilosophy, 48*(5), 666–86. https://doi.org/10.1111/meta.12277.

Israel, S. (2017, June 17). *Toronto and Vancouver move to regulate Airbnb, but compliance hard to enforce.* CBC News. https://www.cbc.ca/news/business/airbnb-municipal-regulations-canada-1.4164056.

Jackson, A. (2007). From leaps of faith to hard landings: Fifteen years of "free trade." In R. Grinspun & Y. Shamsie (Eds.), *Whose Canada? Continental integration, fortress North America, and the corporate agenda* (pp. 211–33). McGill-Queen's University Press.

Jaffray, H.T. (1941). Canada's banks and war finances. *Canadian Banker, 48*(2), 147–51.

Jamieson, A.B. (1953). *Chartered banking in Canada*. Ryerson Press.
Jarvis, C. (2008, June 18). Birmingham's First American Bank to officially become RBC Bank next week. *Birmingham Business Journal*. https://www.bizjournals.com/birmingham/stories/2008/06/16/daily23.html.
Jeffees, W. (1952, January 11). Finance at large. *Globe and Mail*, 20.
Jenkins, P. (1996). *An acre of time*. Macfarlane Walter & Ross.
Jenson, J. (1989). "Different" but not "exceptional": Canada's permeable fordism. *Canadian Review of Sociology/Revue Canadienne de Sociologie, 26*(1), 69–94. https://doi.org/10.1111/j.1755-618X.1989.tb00413.x.
Jessop, B. (2015). Hard cash, easy credit, ficticious capital: Critical reflections on money as fetishised social relation. *Finance and Society, 1*(1), 20–37. https://doi.org/10.2218/finsoc.v1i1.1369.
– (2016). *The state: Past, present, future*. Polity Press.
– (2018). The world market, "north-south" relations, and neoliberalism. *Alternate Routes: A Journal of Critical Social Research, 29*, 207–28. https://alternateroutes.ca/index.php/ar/article/view/22453.
Johansen, D. (1991). *Property rights and the constitution*. Law and Government Division. https://publications.gc.ca/Collection-R/LoPBdP/BP/bp268-e.htm.
Johnson, L. (1979). Precapitalist economic formations and the capitalist labour market in Canada. In J.E. Curtis & W.G. Scott (Eds.), *Social stratification: Canada* (pp. 89–104). Prentice-Hall.
Johnson, S. (2018, January 16). Beyond the Bitcoin bubble. *New York Times*. https://www.nytimes.com/2018/01/16/magazine/beyond-the-bitcoin-bubble.html.
Johnson, S., & Kwak, J. (2011). *13 bankers: The Wall Street takeover and the next financial meltdown*. Vintage Books.
Joint Canadian Securities Administrators/Investment Industry Regulatory Organization of Canada (CSA/IIROC). (2010). *Dark liquidity in the Canadian market* (Position paper 23-405). Ontario Securities Commission. https://www.osc.ca/sites/default/files/pdfs/irps/csa_20101119_23-405_dark-liquidity.pdf.
Judd, A. (2022, March 16). Hollywood celebrities call on RBC to stop financing BC's Coastal GasLink project. Global News. https://globalnews.ca/news/8687345/hollywood-celebrities-mark-ruffalo-leonardo-dicaprio-rbc-coastal-gaslink-bc.
Julian, P. (2020, June 4). *Letter to Finance Minister from MP Julian*. https://xfer.ndp.ca/2020/MPLetters/Letter%20to%20Finance%20Minister%20from%20MP%20Julian%20-%20June%204%202020%20ENG.pdf.
Jun, M. (2018). Blockchain government: A next form of infrastructure for the twenty-first century. *Journal of Open Innovation: Technology, Market, and Complexity, 4*(1), 1–12. https://doi.org/10.1186/s40852-018-0086-3.
Kain, P.J. (1980). Marx's dialectic method. *History and Theory, 19*(3), 294–312. https://doi.org/10.2307/2504546.

Kalaitzake, M. (2017). The political power of finance: The Institute of International Finance in the Greek debt crisis. *Politics & Society, 45*(3), 389–413. https://doi.org/10.1177/0032329217707969.

Kaljulaid, K. (2019, February 19). *Estonia is running its country like a tech company.* Quartz. https://qz.com/1535549/living-on-the-blockchain-is-a-game-changer-for-estonian-citizens.

Kalman-Lamb, G. (2017). The financialization of housing in Canada: Intensifying contradictions of neoliberal accumulation. *Studies in Political Economy, 98*(3), 298–323. https://doi.org/10.1080/07078552.2017.1393911.

Kaplan, J.J., & Schleiminger, G. (1989). *The European Payments Union: Financial diplomacy in the 1950s.* Clarendon Press.

Kapstein, E.B. (1994). *Governing the global economy: International finance and the state.* Harvard University Press.

Kapur, A., Macleod, N., & Singh, N. (2005). *Plutonomy: Buying luxury, explaining global imbalances.* Citigroup Global Markets.

Karlstrøm, H. (2014). Do libertarians dream of electric coins? The material embeddedness of Bitcoin. *Distinktion: Scandinavian Journal of Social Theory, 15*(1), 23–36. https://doi.org/10.1080/1600910X.2013.870083.

Kastner, L. (2014). "Much ado about nothing?" Transnational civil society, consumer protection and financial regulatory reform. *Review of International Political Economy, 21*(6), 1313–45. https://doi.org/10.1080/09692290.2013.870084.

Kaufman, M. (1985). The internationalization of Canadian bank capital (with a look at bank activity in the Caribbean and Central America). *Journal of Canadian Studies, 19*(4), 61–81. https://doi.org/10.3138/jcs.19.4.61.

Keister, L.A. (2002). Financial markets, money, and banking. *Annual Review of Sociology, 28*(1), 39–61. https://doi.org/10.1146/annurev.soc.28.110601.140836.

Kellogg, P. (2005). Kari Levitt and the long detour of Canadian political economy. *Studies in Political Economy, 76*(1), 31–60. https://doi.org/10.1080/19187033.2005.11675122.

– (2009). Of nails and needles: A reconsideration of the political economy of Canadian trade. *Socialist Studies/Études Socialistes, 4*(2), 67–92. https://doi.org/10.18740/S41W2W.

– (2015). *Escape from the staple trap: Canadian political economy after left nationalism.* University of Toronto Press.

Kiladze, T., & Marotte, B. (2016, April 6). RBC faces tough questions over Panama connections. *Globe and Mail.* https://www.theglobeandmail.com/report-on-business/financial-services-firms-should-be-force-for-good-rbc-chief-says/article29537700.

Kilpatrick, C. (1959). Bank and fund look ahead. *Canadian Banker, 66*(2), 116–21.
Kilpatrick, S. (2010, April 22). Flaherty rejects global bank tax. *Guelph Mercury*, A14.
King, M.R., & Sinclair, T.J. (2003). Private actors and public policy: A requiem for the new Basel Capital Accord. *International Political Science Review, 24*(3), 345–62. https://doi.org/10.1177/0192512103024003004.
Kingston, A. (1998, April). Stealth banker: They say he's quiet and a nice guy (He's also extremely ambitious and about to become Canada's most powerful executive. Underestimate him at your peril). *Report on Business Magazine, 14*(10), 84–94.
Kirton, J.J. (1999). Canada as a principal financial power: G-7 and IMF diplomacy in the crisis of 1997–9. *International Journal: Canada's Journal of Global Policy Analysis, 54*(4), 603–24. https://doi.org/10.1177/002070209905400404.
Klassen, J. (2008). Hollowing out? Myth and reality. *Relay, 22*, 8–11.
– (2009). Canada and the new imperialism: The economics of a secondary power. *Studies in Political Economy, 83*(1), 163–90. https://doi.org/10.1080/19187033.2009.11675060.
– (2014). *Joining empire: The political economy of the new Canadian foreign policy*. University of Toronto Press.
Klassen, J., & Carroll, W.K. (2011). Transnational class formation? Globalization and the Canadian corporate network. *Journal of World-Systems Research, 17*(2), 379–402. https://doi.org/10.5195/jwsr.2011.418.
Klaus, I. (2017). Don Tapscott and Alex Tapscott: Blockchain revolution. *New Global Studies, 11*(1), 47–53. https://doi.org/10.1515/ngs-2017-0002.
Knowles, A.J. (1957). Canadian banking trends. *Canadian Banker, 64*(2), 133–9.
Knox, F.A. (1943). The annual report of the Bank for International Settlements. *Canadian Banker, 50*, 23–6.
– (1945). Bretton Woods. *Canadian Banker, 52*, 31–4.
Kobrak, C., & Martin, J. (2018). *From Wall Street to Bay Street: The origins and evolution of American and Canadian finance*. University of Toronto Press.
Konings, M. (2011). *The development of American finance*. Cambridge University Press.
Kornrich, S., & Hicks, A. (Eds.). (2015). The rise of finance: Causes and consequences of financialization [Special issue]. *Socio-Economic Review, 13*(3).
Krugman, P. (2012). *End this depression now!* W.W. Norton.
Kuczynski, P.-P. (1988). *Latin American debt*. Johns Hopkins University Press.
Kuiper, C., & Neureuter, J. (2022, January 6). *Research round-up: 2021 trends and their potential future impact*. Fidelity Digital Assets. https://www.fidelitydigitalassets.com/research-and-insights/research-round-2021-trends-and-their-potential-future-impact.

Kuntz, P., & Ivry, B. (2011, December 23). *Fed's once-secret data compiled by Bloomberg released to public*. Bloomberg. https://www.bloomberg.com/news/articles/2011-12-23/fed-s-once-secret-data-compiled-by-bloomberg-released-to-public.

Kyer, C.I. (2017). *From next best to world class: The people and events that have shaped the Canada Deposit Insurance Corporation, 1967–2017*. Canada Deposit Insurance Corporation. http://publications.gc.ca/collections/collection_2018/sadc-cdic/CC394-4-2017-eng.pdf.

Lacher, H. (2006). *Beyond globalization: Capitalism, territoriality and the international relations of modernity*. Routledge.

Lagerquist, J. (2022, October 11). *RBC under investigation by Competition Bureau over climate claims*. Yahoo Finance. https://ca.finance.yahoo.com/news/rbc-under-investigation-competition-bureau-over-climate-claims-193221297.html.

Lai, J.L. (2021). A tale of two treaties: A study of NAFTA and the USMCA's investor-state dispute settlement mechanisms. *Emory International Law Review*, 35(2), 259–96. https://scholarlycommons.law.emory.edu/eilr/vol35/iss2/3.

Lall, R. (2012). From failure to failure: The politics of international banking regulation. *Review of International Political Economy*, 19(4), 609–38. https://doi.org/10.1080/09692290.2011.603669.

Lam, E., & Alexander, D. (2014, April 10). *"RBC Nice" pays off amid high-frequency-trading outcry*. Bloomberg. https://www.bloomberg.com/news/articles/2014-04-10/-rbc-nice-pays-off-amid-high-frequency-trading-outcry.

Langille, D. (1987). The Business Council on national issues and the Canadian state. *Studies in Political Economy*, 24(1), 41–85. https://doi.org/10.1080/19187033.1987.11675557.

Lapavitsas, C. (2013a). The financialization of capitalism: "Profiting without producing." *City*, 17(6), 792–805. https://doi.org/10.1080/13604813.2013.853865.

– (2013b). *Profiting without producing: How finance exploits us all*. Verso.

Lapham, L.H. (2018). *Money and class in America*. OR Books. https://doi.org/10.2307/j.ctv62hfv5. (Original work published 1988)

Lash, S., & Urry, J. (1987). *The end of organized capitalism*. Polity Press.

Latour, B. (2020, March 26). Is this a dress rehearsal? *In the Moment*. https://critinq.wordpress.com/2020/03/26/is-this-a-dress-rehearsal.

Lawrence, C.J., & Mudge, S.L. (2019). Movement to market, currency to property: The rise and fall of Bitcoin as an anti-state movement, 2009–2014. *Socio-Economic Review*, 17(1), 109–34. https://doi.org/10.1093/ser/mwz023.

Laxer, G. (2021). *Posing as Canadian: How big foreign oil captures Canadian energy and climate policy*. Council of Canadians. https://canadians.org/BigForeignOil.

Lazzarato, M. (2012). *The making of the indebted man*. MIT Press.

Lebel, R. (1968, January 12). Annual meetings: Royal Bank chief says pacts with US undermining Canada's independence. *Globe and Mail*, B3.

Lehdonvirta, V. (2016, November 21). The blockchain paradox: Why distributed ledger technologies may do little to transform the economy. *Policy and Internet Blog*. https://www.oii.ox.ac.uk/blog/the-blockchain-paradox-why-distributed-ledger-technologies-may-do-little-to-transform-the-economy.

Lenard, P.T., & Straehle, C. (2012). *Legislated inequality: Temporary labour migration in Canada*. McGill-Queen's University Press.

Levine, M. (2022, January 26). Watch out for shadow trading. Bloomberg. https://www.bloomberg.com/opinion/articles/2022-01-26/watch-out-for-shadow-trading.

Levitas, R. (2017). *Where there is no vision, the people perish: A utopian ethic for a transformed future*. Centre for the Understanding of Sustainable Prosperity.

Levitt, K. (1970). *Silent surrender*. St. Martin's Press.

Levy, K.E.C. (2017). Book-smart, not street-smart: Blockchain-based smart contracts and the social workings of law. *Engaging Science, Technology, and Society*, 3, 1–15. https://doi.org/10.17351/ests2017.107.

Lew, B., & Richardson, A.J. (1992). Institutional responses to bank failure: A comparative case study of the Home Bank (1923) and Canadian Commercial Bank (1985) failures. *Critical Perspectives on Accounting*, 3(2), 163–83. https://doi.org/10.1016/1045-2354(92)90009-G.

Lewis, M. (2014). *Flash boys: A Wall Street revolt*. W.W. Norton & Company.

Ligon, C. (2022, October 12). Canadian self-regulatory agency approves first crypto-native investment dealer. CoinDesk. https://www.coindesk.com/policy/2022/10/12/canadian-self-regulatory-agency-grants-approval-to-first-crypto-native-investment-dealer.

Lin, C. (2022, May 3). Physical objects turned into NFTs with blockchain microchips. Fast Company. https://www.fastcompany.com/90748573/the-metaverse-of-things-this-startup-is-using-microchips-to-turn-physical-objects-into-nfts.

Liodakis, G. (2005). The new stage of capitalist development and the prospects of globalization. *Science & Society*, 69(3), 341–66. https://doi.org/10.1521/siso.69.3.341.66525.

– (2010). *Totalitarian capitalism and beyond*. Ashgate.

– (2016). Recent developments of totalitarian capitalism and the evolving world order: Some implications for social movements. *International Critical Thought*, 6(3), 342–58. https://doi.org/10.1080/21598282.2016.1197998.

Lipset, S.M. (1990). *Continental divide: The values and institutions of the United States and Canada*. Routledge.

Livesey, B. (2012). *The thieves of Bay Street: How the banks, brokerages and the wealthy steal billions a year from Canadians*. Random House Canada.

Logan, S.H. (1937). Canada during 1936 reviewed. *Canadian Banker*, 44(2), 141–9.

Lorinc, J. (2022a, April 7). Profiting from inflation: Two new reports show companies are making billions by pushing prices higher. *Toronto Star*. https://www.thestar.com/business/2022/04/07/profiting-from-inflation-two-new-reports-show-companies-are-making-billions-by-pushing-prices-higher.html.

– (2022b, April 26). Meet Freshii's new "virtual cashier" – who works from Nicaragua for $3.75 an hour. *Toronto Star*. https://www.thestar.com/business/2022/04/26/meet-the-freshii-virtual-cashier-who-works-from-nicaragua-for-375-an-hour.html.

Lower, A.R.M. (1946). *Colony to nation: A history of Canada*. Longmans, Green & Company.

– (1958). Theories of Canadian federalism – yesterday and today. In A.R.M. Lower & F.R. Scott (Eds.), *Evolving Canadian federalism* (pp. 3–53). Duke University Press.

Lukacs, M., & Groves, T. (2020, August 24). Private firms pour millions into militarizing police via charities. *The Tyee*. https://thetyee.ca/News/2020/08/24/Private-Firms-Pour-Millions-Militarizing-Police.

Lumsden, I. (Ed.). (1970). *Close the 49th parallel etc.: The Americanization of Canada*. University of Toronto Press.

Ly, M.C. (2017, February 27). *Protecting employees through the temporary foreign workers program*. TheCourt.ca. https://www.thecourt.ca/protecting-employees-through-the-temporary-foreign-workers-program.

Lysandrou, P., & Nesvetailova, A. (2014). The role of shadow banking entities in the financial crisis: A disaggregated view. *Review of International Political Economy*, 22(2), 257–79. https://doi.org/10.1080/09692290.2014.896269.

Macartney, H., & Shields, S. (2011). Finding space in critical IPE: A scalar-relational approach. *Journal of International Relations and Development*, 14(3), 375–83. https://doi.org/10.1057/jird.2011.9.

Macdonald, D. (2012). *The big banks' big Secret: Estimating government support for Canadian banks during the financial crisis*. Canadian Centre for Policy Alternatives. https://policyalternatives.ca/publications/reports/big-banks-big-secret.

Macdonald, D.S. (1976). *White paper on the revision of Canadian banking legislation*. Department of Finance. https://publications.gc.ca/collections/collection_2016/fin/F2-38-1976-eng.pdf.

Macdonald, L. (2020). Stronger together? Canada-Mexico relations and the NAFTA re-negotiations. *Canadian Foreign Policy Journal*, 26(2), 152–66. https://doi.org/10.1080/11926422.2019.1698442

MacDonald, L.R. (1975). Merchants against industry: An idea and its origins. *Canadian Historical Review*, 56(3), 263–81. https://muse.jhu.edu/article/570072.

MacIntosh, R. (1991). *Different drummers: Banking and politics in Canada*. Macmillan Canada.

MacKenzie, D. (2018). Material signals: A historical sociology of high-frequency trading. *American Journal of Sociology*, 123(6), 1635–83. https://doi.org/10.1086/697318.

– (2019). Market devices and structural dependency: The origins and development of "dark pools." *Finance and Society*, 5(1), 1–19. https://doi.org/10.2218/finsoc.v5i1.3015.

MacLean, N. (2017). *Democracy in chains: The deep history of the radical right's stealth plan for America*. Penguin.

Macpherson, C.B. (1962). *The political theory of possessive individualism: Hobbes to Locke*. Clarendon Press.

– (1978). *Property, mainstream and critical positions*. University of Toronto Press.

– (2013). *Democracy in Alberta: Social Credit and the party system*. University of Toronto Press. (Original work published 1953)

Mader, P., Mertens, D., & van der Zwan, N. (Eds.) (2020). *The Routledge international handbook of financialization*. Routledge. https://doi.org/10.4324/9781315142876.

Magna International. (2021). *Annual report*. Magna International Inc. https://www.magna.com/docs/default-source/financial-reports-public-filings/annual-reports/sedar_magna-annual-reportf5ada94159894cf993c6ef2b37b3dd7c.pdf?sfvrsn=4324e5c4_14.

Major, A. (2013). Transnational state formation and the global politics of austerity. *Sociological Theory*, 31(1), 24–48. https://doi.org/10.1177/0735275113477083.

Malcolm, A.H. (1980, June 18). Royal Bank outgrows Canada. *New York Times*, B1. https://www.nytimes.com/1980/06/18/archives/royal-bank-outgrows-canada-royal-bank-outgrowing-canada-fills-world.html.

Malm, A. (2021). *How to blow up a pipeline*. Verso.

Mann, M. (1984). The autonomous power of the state: Its origins, mechanisms and results. *European Journal of Sociology/Archives Européennes de Sociologie*, 25(2), 185–213. https://doi.org/10.1017/S0003975600004239.

– (2001). Globalization is (among other things) transnational, inter-national and American. *Science & Society*, 65(4), 464–9. https://www.jstor.org/stable/40403914.

Marazzi, C. (2010). *The violence of financial capitalism* (K. Lebedeva, Trans.). Semiotext.

Marchak, P. (1985). Canadian political economy. *Canadian Review of Sociology/Revue Canadienne de Sociologie*, 22(5), 673–709. https://doi.org/10.1111/j.1755-618X.1985.tb00388.x.

Marchese, A. (2021, September 17). *Royal Bank of Canada to pay fine over municipal bonds charges by SEC*. MarketWatch. https://www.marketwatch.com/story/royal-bank-of-canada-to-pay-fine-over-municipal-bonds-charges-by-sec-271631886519.

Margaret Thatcher, 1925–2013: British conservative stateswoman. (2016). In S. Ratcliffe (Ed.), Oxford essential quotations (4th ed.). Oxford University Press. https://doi.org/10.1093/acref/9780191826719.001.0001.

Martin, J. (2010). *Relentless change: A casebook for the study of Canadian business history*. University of Toronto Press.

Martin, J., & Srikantiah, A. (2012). *Case study: The Toronto-Dominion Bank and Canada's "little bang" of 1987*. Rotman School of Management. https://www.rotman.utoronto.ca/media/rotman/content-assets/documents/cbh--cdn-biz-his/CBH-TD-Bank-and-the-Little-Bang-of-1987_REVISED.pdf.

Marvin, D.M. (1937). Bank of Canada. *Canadian Banker, 45*(1), 25–33.

Marx, K. (1844, August 7). Critical notes on the article: "The King of Prussia and social reform. by a Prussian." *Vorwarts!* Retrieved 31 July 2024, from https://www.marxists.org/archive/marx/works/1844/08/07.htm.

– (1863). *Theories of surplus-value*. Retrieved 31 July 2024, from https://www.marxists.org/archive/marx/works/1863/theories-surplus-value.

– (1881, March). First draft of letter to Vera Zasulich. Retrieved 31 July 2024, from https://www.marxists.org/archive/marx/works/1881/zasulich.

– (1971). *The Grundrisse* (D. McLellan, Ed. & Trans.). Harper Torchbooks. (Original work published 1939)

– (1978a). The civil war in France. In R.C. Tucker (Ed.), *The Marx-Engels reader* (pp. 618–52). Norton. (Original work published 1871)

– (1978b). Preface to *A contribution to the critique of political economy*. In R.C. Tucker (Ed.), *The Marx-Engels reader* (pp. 3–6). Norton. (Original work published 1859)

– (1991). *Capital: Vol. 1. A critique of political economy* (B. Fowkes, Trans.). Penguin Classics. (Original work published 1867)

– (1993a). *Capital: Vol. 2. A critique of political economy* (D. Fernbach, Trans.). Penguin Classics. (Original work published 1885)

– (1993b). *Capital: Vol. 3. A critique of political economy* (D. Fernbach, Trans.). Penguin Classics. (Original work published 1894)

Marx, K., & Engels, F. (1978a). *The German ideology*. In R.C. Tucker (Ed.), *The Marx-Engels reader* (pp. 146–200). Norton. (Original work published 1932)

– (1978b). *Manifesto of the Communist Party*. In R.C. Tucker (Ed.), *The Marx-Engels reader* (pp. 469–500). Norton. (Original work published 1848)

McBride, S. (2005). *Paradigm shift: Globalization and the Canadian state*. Fernwood Publishing.

– (2011). The new constitutionalism: International and private rule in the new global order. In S. McBride & G. Teeple (Eds.), *Relations of global power: Neoliberal order and disorder* (pp. 19–40). University of Toronto Press.
McCalla, D. (2003). Buchanan, Isaac. In *Dictionary of Canadian biography* (Vol. 11). University of Toronto. https://www.biographi.ca/en/bio/buchanan_isaac_11E.html.
McDowall, D. (1993). *Quick to the frontier: Canada's Royal Bank*. McClelland & Stewart.
McEwen, N. (2006). *Nationalism and the state: Welfare and identity in Scotland and Quebec*. P.I.E.-Peter Lang.
McGregor, J., & Patel, R. (2020, November 21). Canada, UK strike transitional post-Brexit trade deal. CBC News. https://www.cbc.ca/news/politics/canada-uk-transitional-trade-agreement-1.5811269.
McIvor, R.C. (1958). *Canadian monetary, banking, and fiscal development*. Macmillan Co. of Canada.
McKeen-Edwards, H. (2010). Institute of international finance, Inc. In C. Tietje & A. Brouder (Eds.), *Handbook of transnational economic governance regimes* (pp. 355–66). Martinus Nijhoff Publishers. https://doi.org/10.1163/ej.9789004163300.i-1081.282.
McKeen-Edwards, H., & Porter, T. (2013). *Transnational financial associations and the governance of global finance: Assembling wealth and power*. Routledge.
Mckenna, B. (2004, July 13). Canada dips on list of world's 500 biggest firms. *Globe and Mail*, 7.
McLannahan, B. (2018, January 15). Nine banks accused of rigging key Canada lending rate. *Financial Times*. https://www.ft.com/content/2c2df13e-fa1a-11e7-9b32-d7d59aace167.
McMichael, P. (2001). Revisiting the question of the transnational state: A comment on William Robinson's "Social theory and globalization." *Theory and Society*, 30(2), 201–10. https://doi.org/10.1023/A:1011051711918.
McNally, D. (1981). Staple theory as commodity fetishism: Marx, Innis and Canadian political economy. *Studies in Political Economy*, 6(1), 35–63. https://doi.org/10.1080/19187033.1981.11675700.
– (1999, June 1). Turbulence in the world economy. *Monthly Review*. https://monthlyreview.org/1999/06/01/turbulence-in-the-world-economy.
McQuaig, L. (2007). *Holding the bully's coat: Canada and the US Empire*. Doubleday Canada.
– (2022, March 9). Long banned in Ontario, private hospitals could soon reappear. *Toronto Star*. https://www.thestar.com/opinion/contributors/2022/03/09/long-banned-in-ontario-private-hospitals-could-soon-reappear.html.

Menon, N. (2014, June 20). Canada to scale back foreign worker program. *Wall Street Journal*. https://online.wsj.com/articles/canada-to-scale-back-foreign-worker-program-1403296613.

Meredith, P., & Darroch, J.L. (2017). *Stumbling giants: Transforming Canada's banks for the information age*. University of Toronto Press.

Mertins-Kirkwood, H. (2014). *Unmasking the Trans-Pacific Partnership: A critical Canadian political-economic analysis* [Unpublished master's thesis]. Carleton University.

– (2022). *On the offensive: How Canadian companies use trade and investment agreements to bully foreign governments for billions*. Canadian Centre for Policy Alternatives. https://policyalternatives.ca/sites/default/files/uploads/publications/National%20Office/2022/05/On%20the%20Offensive.pdf.

Miliband, R. (1969). *The state in capitalist society*. Basic Books.

Millan, C., & de Rosario, J. (2020, September 8). *She is BlackRock's new star after sealing Argentina's debt deal*. Bloomberg. https://www.bloomberg.com/news/articles/2020-09-08/she-is-blackrock-s-new-star-after-sealing-argentina-s-debt-deal.

Mills, C.W. (1962). *The Marxists*. Dell Pub. Co.

Mirowski, P., & Plehwe, D. (Eds.). (2009). *The road from Mont Pèlerin: The making of the neoliberal thought collective*. Harvard University Press.

MNP Ltd. (2022, April). *MNP Consumer Debt Index*. Retrieved 31 July 2024, from https://mnpdebt.ca/en/resources/mnp-consumer-debt-index.

Monks, R.A.G., & Minow, N. (2011). *Corporate governance*. John Wiley & Sons. https://doi.org/10.1002/9781119207238.

Moore, J. (2001). Capital, territory, and hegemony over the longue duree. *Science & Society*, 65(4), 476–84. https://www.jstor.org/stable/40403916.

Moore, S., & Wells, D. (1975). *Imperialism and the national question in Canada*. Steve Moore.

Morck, R.K., Percy, M., Tian, G.Y., & Yeung, B. (2007). The rise and fall of the widely held firm: A history of corporate ownership in Canada. In R.K. Morck (Ed.), *A history of corporate governance around the world: Family business groups to professional managers* (pp. 65–147). University of Chicago Press.

Morrison, S. (1998a, July 8). RBC and Koch in strategic alliance. *Financial Times*, 16.

– (1998b, July 21). RBC to buy Credit Suisse division. *Financial Times*, 40.

Mozley, H.N., & Whiteley, G.C. (1977). *Mozley and Whiteley's law dictionary* (9th ed.). Butterworths.

Murphy, R. (2017). *Dirty secrets: How tax havens destroy the economy*. Verso.

Myers, G. (1972). *A history of Canadian wealth*. Lorimer. (Original work published 1914)

Nair, M., & Sutter, D. (2018). The blockchain and increasing cooperative efficacy. *Independent Review*, 22(4), 529–50. https://www.jstor.org/stable/26591760.

Nakamoto, S. (2008). *Bitcoin: A peer-to-peer electronic cash system*. https://bitcoin.org/bitcoin.pdf.

Naylor, R.T. (1972). The rise and fall of the Third Commercial Empire of the St Lawrence. In G. Teeple (Ed.), *Capitalism and the national question in Canada* (pp. 1–42). University of Toronto Press.

– (1982). *Monetarism and Canadian policy alternatives*. Canadian Centre for Policy Alternatives.

– (1985). *Dominion of debt: Centre, periphery and the international economic order*. Black Rose Books.

– (1997). *The history of Canadian business, 1867–1914*. Black Rose Books. (Original work published 1975)

Nelson, J. (2012). RBC among nine subpoenaed in Libor probe. *Globe and Mail*. https://www.theglobeandmail.com/globe-investor/rbc-among-nine-subpoenaed-in-libor-probe/article4678432.

Nerbas, D. (2013). *Dominion of capital: The politics of big business and the crisis of the Canadian bourgeoisie, 1914–1947*. University of Toronto Press.

Neuburger, J. (2017, April 20). Arizona passes groundbreaking blockchain and smart contract law – state blockchain laws on the rise. *New Media and Technology Law Blog*. https://newmedialaw.proskauer.com/2017/04/20/arizona-passes-groundbreaking-blockchain-and-smart-contract-law-state-blockchain-laws-on-the-rise.

Neufeld, E.P. (1958). *Bank of Canada operations and policy*. University of Toronto Press.

– (Ed.). (1967). *Money and banking in Canada*. McClelland & Stewart.

– (1972). *The financial system of Canada, its growth and development*. St. Martin's Press.

– (2001). Adjusting to globalization: Challenges for the Canadian banking system. In P. Grady & A. Sharpe (Eds.), *The state of economics in Canada: Festschrift in honour of David Slater* (pp. 325–53). Centre for the Study of Living Standards.

Neveling, P. (2015). Export processing zones, special economic zones and the long march of capitalist development policies during the Cold War. In L. James & E. Leake (Eds.), *Decolonization and the Cold War: Negotiating independence*. Bloomsbury Publishing.

Newman, P.C. (1979). *The Canadian establishment*. McClelland & Stewart.

– (1989). *The acquisitors: The Canadian establishment* (Vol. 2). McClelland & Stewart.

– (1998, May 25). Not all financial CEOs favor bank mergers. *Maclean's*. https://archive.macleans.ca/article/1998/5/25/not-all-financial-ceos-favor-bank-mergers.

– (1999). *Titans: How the new Canadian establishment seized power*. Penguin.
– (2004). *Here be dragons: Telling tales of people, passion and power*. McClelland & Stewart.
The next big thing. (2015, May 9). *The Economist*. https://www.economist.com/news/special-report/21650295-or-it-next-big-thing.
Nichols, S. (2018). Expanding property rights under investor-state dispute settlement (ISDS): Class struggle in the era of transnational capital. *Review of International Political Economy, 25*(2), 243–69. https://doi.org/10.1080/09692290.2018.1431561.
Nikolova, M. (2021, March 12). *Nasdaq fines RBC capital markets for poor market access risk management controls*. FX News Group. https://fxnewsgroup.com/forex-news/exchanges/nasdaq-fines-rbc-capital-markets-for-poor-market-access-risk-management-controls.
Niosi, J. (1981). *Canadian capitalism: A study of power in the Canadian business establishment*. James Lorimer Limited, Publishers.
– (1985). *Canadian multinationals* (R. Chodos, Trans.). Between the Lines.
Noble, K. (1998a, February 2). Big and bigger. *Maclean's*. https://archive.macleans.ca/article/1998/2/2/big-and-bigger.
– (1998b, December 28). Bitterness on Bay Street. *Maclean's*. https://archive.macleans.ca/article/1998/12/28/bitterness-on-bay-street.
Norfield, T. (2012). Derivatives and capitalist markets: The speculative heart of capital. *Historical Materialism, 20*(1), 103–32. https://doi.org/10.1163/156920612X634735.
– (2016). *The city: London and the global power of finance*. Verso.
North, D.C. (1990). *Institutions, institutional change and economic performance*. Cambridge University Press.
Noto, G. (2017, April 27). *JPMorgan Chase latest to leave R3, consortium confirms*. Bank Innovation. https://bankinnovation.net/2017/04/jpmorgan-chase-latest-to-leave-r3-consortium-confirms.
Not-so-clever contracts. (2016, July 30). *The Economist*. https://www.economist.com/news/business/21702758-time-being-least-human-judgment-still-better-bet-cold-hearted?fsrc=scn/tw/te/pe/ed/notsoclevercontracts.
O'Brien, M.E., & Abdelhadi, E. (2022). *An oral history of the New York commune: 2052–2072*. Common Notions.
O'Connor, J.S., Orloff, A.S., & Shaver, S. (1999). *States, markets, families: Gender, liberalism and social policy in Australia, Canada, Great Britain and the United States*. Cambridge University Press.
Office of the Superintendent of Financial Institutions (OSFI). (n.d.). *Our history*. Government of Canada. Retrieved 31 July 2024, from https://web.archive.org/web/20220620204702/www.osfi-bsif.gc.ca/Eng/osfi-bsif/Pages/hst.aspx.

O'Halloran, S., & Groll, T. (Eds.). (2019). *After the crash: Financial crises and regulatory responses*. Columbia University Press.

O'Hara, C. (2021, November 17). Fidelity approved to handle Bitcoin in Canada, clearing path for institutional investors. *Globe and Mail*. https://www.theglobeandmail.com/business/article-fidelity-approved-to-handle-bitcoin-in-canada-clearing-path-for.

Ollman, B. (2003). *Dance of the dialectic: Steps in Marx's method*. University of Illinois Press.

Olsen, G. (2002). *The politics of the welfare state: Canada, Sweden, and the United States*. Oxford University Press.

Onoszko, M. (2018, March 13). Canada's banks facing great threat from consumer debt: Moody's. *BNN Bloomberg*. https://www.bnnbloomberg.ca/consumer-debt-binge-draws-moody-s-warning-for-canadian-banks-1.1025447.

Orcutt, M. (2019, May 3). China's ubiquitous digital payments processor loves the blockchain. *MIT Technology Review*. https://www.technologyreview.com/s/613478/chinas-ubiquitous-digital-payments-processor-loves-the-blockchain/amp.

Orland, K. (2021a, January 8). Canadian banks face conundrum: How to spend a spare $70.4 billion. *Financial Post*. https://financialpost.com/news/fp-street/canadian-banks-face-conundrum-how-to-use-a-spare-55-5-billion.

– (2021b, October 12). Blockchain, AI, Internet of things will change banking, RBC CEO says. *Bloomberg*. https://www.bloomberg.com/news/articles/2021-10-12/rbc-ceo-sees-blockchain-ai-internet-of-things-changing-banking.

Ontario Securities Commission (OSC) (2021, May 25). *OSC takes action against non-compliant international crypto asset trading platform* [Press release]. https://www.osc.ca/en/news-events/news/osc-takes-action-against-non-compliant-international-crypto-asset-trading-platform.

O'Sullivan, M. (2019). *The levelling: What's next after globalization*. PublicAffairs.

Oved, M.C., Heaps, T.A.A., & Yow, M. (2017, December 14). The high cost of low corporate taxes. *Toronto Star*. https://projects.thestar.com/canadas-corporations-pay-less-tax-than-you-think.

Özselçuk, C., & Hardt, M. (2015, March 16). *Interview with Michael Hardt: Empire, sovereignty and new struggles* [Interview transcript]. https://bogazicichronicles.bogazici.edu.tr/sites/bogazicichronicles.boun.edu.tr/files/Interview%20with%20Michael%20Hardt%20%28Ceren%20%C3%96zsel%C3%A7uk%29_0.pdf

Palen, M.-W. (2016). *The "conspiracy" of free trade: The anglo-American struggle over empire and economic globalization, 1846–1896*. Cambridge University Press.

Panitch, L. (1994). Globalisation and the state. *Socialist Register, 30*, 60–93. https://socialistregister.com/index.php/srv/article/view/5637/2535.

Panitch, L., & Gindin, S. (2005). Superintending global capital. *New Left Review, 35*, 101–23. https://newleftreview.org/issues/ii35/articles/leo-panitch-sam-gindin-superintending-global-capital.
– (2012). *The making of global capitalism: The political economy of American empire.* Verso.
Park, L.C., & Park, F.W. (1962). *Anatomy of big business.* Progress Books.
Pasquale, F. (2015). *The black box society: The secret algorithms that control money and information.* Harvard University Press.
Paterson, D.G. (1976). *British direct investment in Canada, 1890–1914.* University of Toronto Press.
Patnaik, P. (2021, July 19). Why neoliberalism needs neofascists. *Boston Review.* https://bostonreview.net/articles/why-neoliberalism-needs-neofascists.
– (2022, January 16). Financial markets under capitalism. *Monthly Review.* https://mronline.org/2022/01/16/financial-markets-under-capitalism.
Patterson, B. (2013). *Update: The Council of Canadians campaign to stop bank mergers in 1998.* Council of Canadians. https://canadians.org/analysis/update-council-canadians-campaign-stop-bank-mergers-1998.
Patterson, E.L.S. (1932). *Canadian banking.* Ryerson Press.
Peters, J. (2022). *Jobs with inequality: Financialization, post-democracy, and labour market deregulation in Canada.* University of Toronto Press.
Peirce, H.M. (2020, February 6). *Running on empty: A proposal to fill the gap between regulation and decentralization* [Speech transcript]. US Securities and Exchange Commission, Chicago. https://www.sec.gov/news/speech/peirce-remarks-blockress-2020-02-06.
Pentland, H.C. (1950). The role of capital in Canadian economic development before 1875. *Canadian Journal of Economics and Political Science, 16*(4), 457–74. https://doi.org/10.2307/137856.
– (1981). *Labour and capital in Canada, 1650–1860* (P. Phillips, Ed.). James Lorimer & Company.
Perez, Y.B. (2015, November 7). *Meet the 25 banks working with distributed ledger startup R3.* CoinDesk. https://www.coindesk.com/meet-the-25-banks-working-with-distributed-ledger-startup-r3.
Pfeffer, A. (2013, April 10). *Rise in foreign temp workers questioned by labour groups.* CBC News. https://www.cbc.ca/news/politics/rise-in-foreign-temp-workers-questioned-by-labour-groups-1.1361027.
Philips, R.H. (1960, December 10). Cuba funds saved by Canadian bank. *New York Times,* 34. https://www.nytimes.com/1960/12/11/archives/cuba-funds-saved-by-canadian-bank-havana-allows-institution-to.html.
Piédalue, G. (1976). Les groupes financiers et la guerre du papier au Canada, 1920–1930. *Revue d'histoire de l'Amérique française, 30*(2), 223–58. https://doi.org/10.7202/303529ar.

Piketty, T. (2014). *Capital in the twenty-first century* (A. Goldhammer, Trans.). Belknap Press of Harvard University Press. (Original work published 2013)
Pistor, K. (2019). *The code of capital: How the law creates wealth and inequality.* Princeton University Press.
Pittis, D. (2015, December 3). Canada's banking bet on the world's 1%. *CBC.* https://www.cbc.ca/news/business/rbc-results-city-national-hollywood-1.3347853.
Plender, J. (2021, January 4). Stress test looms for financial system in 2021. *Financial Times.* https://www.ft.com/content/5df1b07a-b6d0-44ad-8911-2d9be0096a0a.
Plumptre, A.F.W. (1977). *Three decades of decision: Canada and the world monetary system, 1944–75.* McClelland & Stewart.
Polanyi, K. (2002). *The great transformation: The political and economic origins of our time* (2nd ed.). Beacon Press. (Original work published 1944)
Porter, T. (2005). *Globalization and finance.* Polity Press.
– (2010, June 8). *Canadian banks in the financial and economic crisis.* Policy Responses to Unfettered Finance Workshop, Ottawa. https://www.nsi-ins.ca/wp-content/uploads/2012/10/2010-Canadian-Banks-in-the-Financial-and-Economic-Crisis.pdf.
– (2014a). Introduction and overview. In T. Porter (Ed.), *Transnational financial regulation after the crisis* (pp. 1–26). Routledge.
– (2014b). *Transnational financial regulation after the crisis.* Routledge.
Posner, E.A., & Weyl, E.G. (2018). *Radical markets: Uprooting capitalism and democracy for a just society.* Princeton University Press.
Postelnicu, C., Dinu, V., & Dabija, D.-C. (2015). Economic deglobalization: From hypothesis to reality. *E+M Ekonomie a Management, 18*(2), 4–14. https://doi.org/10.15240/tul/001/2015-2-001.
Postmedia News. (2012, April 30). Did Canadian banks receive a secret bailout? *Financial Post.* https://financialpost.com/news/fp-street/did-canadian-banks-receive-a-secret-bailout.
Poulantzas, N. (1975). *Classes in contemporary capitalism* (D. Fernbach, Trans.). NLB. (Original work published 1974)
– (2018). *Political power and social classes.* (T. O'Hagan, Trans.). Verso. (Original work published in 1968)
Powell, J. (2005). *A history of the Canadian dollar.* Bank of Canada. https://www.bankofcanada.ca/wp-content/uploads/2010/07/dollar_book.pdf.
Prashad, V. (2012). World on a slope. *Critical Sociology, 38*(3), 401–3. https://doi.org/10.1177/0896920511434271.
Prisco, G. (2016, December 1). Move over Uber: Blockchain technology can enable real, sustainable sharing economy. Nasdaq. https://www.nasdaq.com/article/move-over-uber-blockchain-technology-can-enable-real-sustainable-sharing-economy-cm716709.

Prudham, S., & Coleman, W.D. (2011). Introduction: Property, autonomy, territory, and globalization. In W.D. Coleman (Ed.), *Property, territory, globalization: Struggles over autonomy* (pp. 1–28). UBC Press.

Puri, P. (2012). "Bank bashing" is a popular sport. In S.J. Konzelmann, (Ed.), *Banking systems in the crisis: The faces of liberal capitalism* (pp. 155–85). Taylor & Francis.

Puri, P., & Nichol, A. (2014). Developments in financial services regulation: A Canadian perspective. *Canadian Business Law Journal, 55*(2), 454–88. https://digitalcommons.osgoode.yorku.ca/scholarly_works/2225.

Quigley, N.C. (1986). The chartered banks and foreign direct investment in Canada. *Studies in Political Economy, 19*(1), 31–57. https://doi.org/10.1080/19187033.1986.11675596.

– (1989). The Bank of Nova Scotia in the Caribbean, 1889–1940. *Business History Review, 63*(4), 797–838. https://doi.org/10.2307/3115963.

Quintana, O.B. (2011). *A new era of seasonal Mexican migration to Canada.* Canadian Foundation for the Americas (FOCAL). https://web.archive.org/web/20220324001427/https://www.focal.ca/en/publications/focalpoint/467-june-2011-ofelia-becerril-quintana-en.

Rabidoux, B. (2012, May 24). The REAL Canadian bank bailout. *Maclean's.* https://www.macleans.ca/economy/business/the-real-canadian-bank-bailout.

Radforth, I. (1986). Logging pulpwood in northern Ontario. In C. Heron & R.H. Storey (Eds.), *On the job: Confronting the labour process in Canada* (pp. 245–80). McGill-Queen's University Press.

Radia, A. (2013, February 13). *Justin Trudeau discloses details about his inheritance.* Yahoo News. https://ca.news.yahoo.com/blogs/canada-politics/justin-trudeau-discloses-details-inheritance-023515379.html.

Rahman, K.S., & Thelen, K. (2019). The rise of the platform business model and the transformation of twenty-first-century capitalism. *Politics & Society, 47*(2), 177–204. https://doi.org/10.1177/0032329219838932.

Rainforest Action Network, BankTrack, Indigenous Environmental Network, Oil Change International, Reclaim Finance, Sierra Club, & Urgewald. (2022). *Banking on climate chaos: Fossil fuel finance report 2022.* https://www.bankingonclimatechaos.org//wp-content/themes/bocc-2021/inc/bcc-data-2022/BOCC_2022_vSPREAD.pdf.

Ranald, P. (2019, September 16). *Suddenly, the world's biggest trade agreement won't allow corporations to sue governments.* The Conversation. http://theconversation.com/suddenly-the-worlds-biggest-trade-agreement-wont-allow-corporations-to-sue-governments-123582.

Raney, T. (2009). As Canadian as possible … Under what circumstances? Public opinion on national identity in Canada outside Quebec. *Journal of Canadian Studies/Revue d'études Canadiennes, 43*(3), 5–29. https://doi.org/10.3138/jcs.43.3.5.

Rao, G.C. (2010). The national question in Canadian development: Permeable nationalism and the ideological basis for incorporation into empire. *Studies in Political Economy*, 85(1), 149–78. https://doi.org/10.1080/19187033.2010.11675038.

Reeve, A. (1986). *Property*. Macmillan.

Reguly, E. (2001, August 1). Quiet exit for "quiet revolutionary." *Globe and Mail*. https://www.theglobeandmail.com/report-on-business/rob-commentary/quiet-exit-for-quiet-revolutionary/article762560.

Renteria, N., & Esposito, A. (2021, September 7). *El Salvador becomes 1st country to adopt bitcoin as legal tender*. Global News. https://globalnews.ca/news/8171521/el-salvador-adopts-bitcoin-legal-tender.

Resnick, P. (1982). The maturing of Canadian capitalism. *Our Generation*, 15(3), 11–24.

– (2005). *The European roots of Canadian identity*. University of Toronto Press.

Reuters. (2014, December 18). RBC to pay US$35 million over U.S. regulator's "wash trading" scheme lawsuit. *Financial Post*. https://financialpost.com/news/fp-street/rbc-to-pay-us35-million-over-u-s-regulators-trading-scheme-lawsuit.

– (2022, January 10). *Taiwan, Canada to start talks on investment agreement*. https://www.reuters.com/world/taiwan-canada-start-talks-investment-agreement-2022-01-10.

Richardson, R.J. (1982). "Merchants against industry": An empirical study of the Canadian debate. *Canadian Journal of Sociology/Cahiers Canadiens de Sociologie*, 7(3), 279–95. https://doi.org/10.2307/3340391.

Roberge, I. (2013). Canada and the global financial crisis: A model to follow? *Interfaces Brasil/Canadá* 13(16), 131–52. https://doi.org/10.15210/interfaces.v13i1.7236.

Roberge, I., Dunea, D.M., & Williams, R.A. (2015). The break-up: Policy network structure and the politics of financial services. *International Journal of Public Policy*, 11(1–3), 1–16. https://doi.org/10.1504/IJPP.2015.068842.

Roberts, T. (2021, May 6). *"Big reset" called for debt-ridden N.L. with release of ground-shaking economic report*. CBC. https://www.cbc.ca/news/canada/newfoundland-labrador/report-greene-recovery-1.6016005.

Robertson, G., Grant, T., Stueck, W., Tait, C., Cryderman, K., & Curry, B. (2013, April 12). The long list of Canadian firms that have sought temporary foreign workers. *Globe and Mail*. https://www.theglobeandmail.com/report-on-business/economy/jobs/the-long-list-of-canadian-firms-that-have-sought-temporary-foreign-workers/article11113782.

Robertson, G., & Kiladze, T. (2012). US regulator accuses Royal Bank of "wash trade" scheme. *Globe and Mail*. https://www.theglobeandmail.com/globe-investor/us-regulator-accuses-royal-bank-of-wash-trade-scheme/article4097931.

Robinson, K.S. (2020). *The ministry for the future*. Orbit.

Robinson, W.I. (2001). Global capitalism and nation-state–centric thinking: What we don't see when we do see nation-states: Response to critics. *Science & Society*, 65(4), 500–8.
– (2003). The debate on globalization. *Science & Society*, 67(3), 353–60. https://doi.org/10.1521/siso.67.3.353.21242.
– (2004). *A theory of global capitalism: Transnational production, transnational capitalists, and the transnational state*. Johns Hopkins University Press.
– (2007). Beyond the theory of imperialism: Global capitalism and the transnational state. *Societies without Borders*, 2(1), 5–26. https://doi.org/10.1163/187188607X163176.
– (2009). Saskia Sassen and the sociology of globalization: A critical appraisal. *Sociological Analysis*, 3(1), 5–29. http://escholarship.org/uc/item/44j854qc.pdf.
– (2012a). Capitalist globalization as world-historic context: A response. *Critical Sociology*, 38(3), 405–15. https://doi.org/10.1177/0896920511434273.
– (2012b). Global capitalism theory and the emergence of transnational elites. *Critical Sociology*, 38(3), 349–63. https://doi.org/10.1177/0896920511411592.
– (2014). *Global capitalism and the crisis of humanity*. Cambridge University Press.
– (2017). Debate on the new global capitalism: Transnational capitalist class, transnational state apparatuses, and global crisis. *International Critical Thought*, 7(2), 171–89. https://doi.org/10.1080/21598282.2017.1316512.
– (2018). *Into the tempest: Essays on the new global capitalism*. Haymarket Books.
– (2020). *The global police state*. Pluto Press.
– (2022). *Global civil war: Capitalism post-pandemic*. PM Press.
Robinson, W.I., & Harris, J. (2000). Towards a global ruling class? Globalization and the transnational capitalist class. *Science & Society*, 64(1), 11–54. https://www.jstor.org/stable/40403824.
Rogers, C. (2018). Global finance and capital adequacy regulation: Recreating capitalist social relations. *Review of Radical Political Economics*, 50(1), 66–81. https://doi.org/10.1177/0486613416666510.
Rollings, N. (2021). "The vast and unsolved enigma of power": Business history and business power. *Enterprise & Society*, 22(4), 893–920. https://doi.org/10.1017/eso.2021.53.
Rooney, K. (2018, April 25). *Nasdaq is open to becoming cryptocurrency exchange, CEO says*. CNBC. https://www.cnbc.com/2018/04/25/nasdaq-is-open-to-becoming-cryptocurrency-exchange-ceo-says.html.
Roos, D. (2017, January 25). Here's how blockchain will eliminate banks and democratize money. *Seeker*. https://www.seeker.com/how-blockchain-will-eliminate-banks-and-democratize-money-2214709749.html.
Rost, B. (2009). Basel commission on banking supervision. In C. Tietje & A. Brouder (Eds.), *Handbook of transnational economic governance regimes* (pp. 319–28). Martinus Nijhoff Publishers. https://doi.org/10.1163/ej.9789004163300.i-1081.238.

Rowlands, D. (1999). High finance and low politics: Canada and the Asian financial crisis. In F. O. Hampson, M. Hart, & M. Rudner (Eds.), *Canada among nations 1999: A big league player?*, (pp. 113–35). Oxford University Press.

Roy, W.G. (1997). *Socializing capital: The rise of the large industrial corporation in America*. Princeton University Press.

Royal Bank boss knocks deposit bill. (1967, January 12). *Toronto Star*, 11.

The Royal Bank of Canada: Addresses made at the annual meeting of shareholders. (1953, January 9). *Globe and Mail*, 8.

Royal Bank report: New Canadian banking records established. (1951, December 20). *Globe and Mail*, 18.

Rude, C. (2005). The role of financial discipline in imperial strategy. In L. Panitch & M. Konings (Eds.), *American empire and the political economy of global finance* (pp. 198–222). Palgrave Macmillan. https://doi.org/10.1057/9780230227675_10.

Rushkoff, D. (2005, September 4). Commodified vs. commoditized. *Rushkoff*. https://rushkoff.com/commodified-vs-commoditized.

Russia sells banker on trade as peace key. (1956, June 27). *Globe and Mail*, 12.

Russia to implement blockchain in state governance. (2019, May 30). *ForkLog*. https://forklog.media/russia-to-implement-blockchain-in-state-governance.

Sakellaropoulos, S. (2018). The theoretical weakness of theses positing emergence of a transnational bourgeoisie and a transnational state: A critique of the views of William Robinson. *Journal of Labor and Society*, 21(4), 579–96. https://doi.org/10.1111/wusa.12369.

Samman, A., Coombs, N., & Cameron, A. (2015). For a post-disciplinary study of finance and society. *Finance and Society*, 1(1), 1–5. https://doi.org/10.2218/finsoc.v1i1.1366.

Sassen, S. (2003). Globalization or denationalization? *Review of International Political Economy*, 10(1), 1–22. https://doi.org/10.1080/0969229032000048853

– (2006). *Territory, authority, rights: From medieval to global assemblages*. Princeton University Press.

– (2007). *A sociology of globalization*. W.W. Norton.

– (2012). Global finance and its institutional spaces. In K. K. Cetina & A. Preda (Eds.), *The Oxford handbook of the sociology of finance* (pp. 13–32). Oxford University Press.

– (2014a). *Expulsions: Brutality and complexity in the global economy*. Belknap Press.

– (2014b). Finance as capability: Good, bad, dangerous. *Occasion*, 7, 1–7. https://shc.stanford.edu/arcade/publications/occasion/debt/finance-capability-good-bad-dangerous.

– (2017). Predatory formations dressed in Wall Street suits and algorithmic math. *Science, Technology and Society*, 22(1), 6–20. https://doi.org/10.1177/0971721816682783

Satgar, V. (2020). Old and new imperialism: The end of US domination? In V. Satgar (Ed.), *BRICS and the new American imperialism: Global rivalry and resistance* (pp. 1–28). Wits University Press.

Savage, L. (2014). From trial to triumph: How Canada's past financial crises helped shape a superior regulatory system. *Journal of Governance and Regulation*, 4(4), 213–48. https://doi.org/10.22495/jgr_v4_i4_c1_p8.

Sawyer, D.C. (2014, October 20). Royal Trustco Ltd. In *The Canadian encyclopedia*. Retrieved 31 July 2024, from https://www.thecanadianencyclopedia.ca/en/article/royal-trustco-ltd.

Schenk, C.R. (2020). The global financial crisis and banking regulation: Another turn of the wheel? *Journal of Modern European History*, 19(1), 8–13. https://doi.org/10.1177/1611894420974252.

Schrauwers, A. (2008). Revolutions without a revolutionary moment: Joint stock democracy and the transition to capitalism in Upper Canada. *Canadian Historical Review*, 89(2), 223–5. https://doi.org/10.3138/chr.89.2.223.

– (2010). The gentlemanly order and the politics of production in the transition to capitalism in Upper Canada. *Labour/Le Travail*, 65, 9–45.

Schwartz, Z. (2019, November 11). RBC exploring cryptocurrency trading platform for investments, in-store and online purchases. *Financial Post*. https://financialpost.com/fp-finance/cryptocurrency/rbc-exploring-cryptocurrency-trading-platform-for-investments-and-online-purchases.

Scuffham, M. (2017, September 27). *Exclusive: Royal Bank of Canada using blockchain for US/Canada payments – executive*. Reuters. https://www.reuters.com/article/us-rbc-blockchain-idUSKCN1C237N.

Seccareccia, M. (2007). Critical macroeconomic aspects of economic integration. In R. Grinspun & Y. Shamsie (Eds.), *Whose Canada? Continental integration, fortress North America, and the corporate agenda* (pp. 234–58). McGill-Queen's University Press.

Seccareccia, M., & Pringle, D. (2020). Money and finance. In H. Whiteside (Ed.), *Canadian political economy* (pp. 320–48). University of Toronto Press.

Securities and Exchange Commission (SEC). (2021, September 17). *RBC charged with failing to give priority to retail and institutional investors in municipal offerings* [Press release]. https://www.sec.gov/news/press-release/2021-179.

Sewell, W.H., Jr. (1996). Historical events as transformations of structures: Inventing revolution at the Bastille. *Theory and Society*, 25(6), 841–81. https://doi.org/10.1007/BF00159818.

– (2010). The empire of fashion and the rise of capitalism in eighteenth-century France. *Past & Present*, 206(1), 81–120. https://doi.org/10.1093/pastj/gtp044.

– (2021). *Capitalism and the emergence of civic equality in eighteenth-century France*. University of Chicago Press.

Sharp, M., & Winter, J. (2021, October 29). Climate activists target banks funding oil and gas in global day of action. *Canada's National Observer*. https://www.nationalobserver.com/2021/10/29/news/climate-activists-target-banks-funding-oil-and-gas-global-day-action.

Shaw, M. (2000). *Theory of the global state: Globality as unfinished revolution*. Cambridge University Press.

Shecter, B. (2012a, June 5). RBC has "concerns" with Maple's TMX bid. *Financial Post*. https://financialpost.com/news/fp-street/rbc-has-concerns-over-maples-tmx-bid.

– (2012b, October 9). Pressure grows for crackdown on high-frequency trading. *Financial Post*. http://business.financialpost.com/news/fp-street/pressure-grows-for-crackdown-on-high-frequency-trading.

– (2013, January 31). TMX-Maple deal demanded perfection. *Financial Post*. https://financialpost.com/uncategorized/tmx-maple-deal-demanded-perfection.

– (2017, January 10). Canada's banks won't see big mortgage losses when interest rates rise, says RBC CEO Dave McKay. *Financial Post*. http://business.financialpost.com/news/fp-street/canadas-banks-wont-see-big-mortgage-losses-when-interest-rates-rise-says-rbc-ceo-dave-mckay.

Shelupanov, A. (2019, April 10). The Mattereum frontier: How we use Ethereum smart contracts to control real world assets. *Medium*. https://medium.com/humanizing-the-singularity/the-mattereum-frontier-351c496e151d.

Shortt, A. (1897). *The early history of Canadian banking: The first banks in Upper Canada*. Journal of the Canadian Bankers' Association.

Shu, C. (2018, April 22). Amazon's new blockchain service competes with similar products from Oracle and IBM. TechCrunch. https://techcrunch.com/2018/04/22/amazons-new-blockchain-service-competes-with-similar-products-from-oracle-and-ibm.

Siltanen, J. (2002). Paradise paved? Reflections on the fate of social citizenship in Canada. *Citizenship Studies*, 6(4), 395–414. https://doi.org/10.1080/1362102022000041240.

Sinclair, S. (2003, June 13). Martin seen as merger friendly. *Globe and Mail*, B3.

– (2015). *NAFTA Chapter 11 investor-state disputes to January 1, 2015*. Canadian Centre for Policy Alternatives. https://www.policyalternatives.ca/publications/reports/nafta-chapter-11-investor-state-disputes-january-1-2015.

– (2018, October 10). USMCA strikes a welcome blow against investor-state dispute settlement. *Behind the Numbers*. http://behindthenumbers.ca/2018/10/10/usmca-strikes-a-welcome-blow-against-investor-state-dispute-settlement.

Singer, J.W. (2000). *Entitlement: The paradoxes of property*. Yale University Press.

Sklair, L. (2001). *The transnational capitalist class*. Blackwell.
Sklair, L., & Robbins, P.T. (2002). Global capitalism and major corporations from the Third World. *Third World Quarterly, 23*(1), 81–100. https://doi.org/10.1080/01436590220108180.
Slaughter, A.-M. (2004). *The real new world order*. Princeton University Press.
Slobodian, Q. (2018). *Globalists: The end of empire and the birth of neoliberalism*. Harvard University Press.
– (2021a). The backlash against neoliberal globalization from above: Elite origins of the crisis of the new constitutionalism. *Theory, Culture & Society, 38*(6), 51–69. https://doi.org/10.1177/0263276421999440.
– (2021b, July 5). Cryptocurrencies' dream of escaping the global financial system is crumbling. *The Guardian*. https://www.theguardian.com/commentisfree/2021/jul/05/cryptocurrencies-financial-system-digital-future.
Smith, A. (2000). On the sources of the general or public revenue of the society. In *An inquiry into the nature and causes of the wealth of nations: Vol. 5. On the revenue of the sovereign or commonwealth*. Adam Smith Reference Archive. https://www.marxists.org/reference/archive/smith-adam/works/wealth-of-nations/book05/ch02b-2.htm. (Original work published in 1776)
Smith, A. (2012). Continental divide: The Canadian banking and currency laws of 1871 in the mirror of the United States. *Enterprise & Society, 13*(3), 455–503. https://doi.org/10.1093/es/khr052.
Smith, J. (2016). *Imperialism in the twenty-first century: Globalization, super-exploitation, and capitalism's final crisis*. New York University Press.
Snyder, J. (2018, June 4). "Not even on the radar screen": Why Big Oil has abandoned Canada's once-promising energy industry. *Financial Post*. http://business.financialpost.com/commodities/not-even-on-the-radar-screen-why-big-oil-has-abandoned-canadas-once-promising-energy-industry.
Soederberg, S. (2000). Political restructuring of exploitation: An historical materialist account of the emergence of neoliberalism in Canada. *Cultural Logic, 3*(2).
– (2002). The new international finance architecture: Imposed leadership and "emerging markets." *Socialist Register, 38*, 175–92. https://socialistregister.com/index.php/srv/article/view/5782.
– (2004). *The politics of the new international financial architecture: Reimposing neoliberal domination in the global south*. Zed Books.
– (2010). *Corporate power and ownership in contemporary capitalism: The politics of resistance and domination*. Routledge.
Sprague, J. (2010). Statecraft in the global financial crisis: An interview with Kanishka Jayasuriya. *Journal of Critical Globalisation Studies, 1*(3), 127–38.

Stadler, J., Mathews, J., Raju, R., Widrig, M., Holly, T.J., & Siew Quan, N. (2017). *New value creators gain momentum: Billionaires insights 2017.* Union Bank of Switzerland; PricewaterhouseCoopers. https://preview.thenewsmarket.com/Previews/PWC/DocumentAssets/488926.pdf.

Stanford, J. (2008). Staples, deindustrialization, and foreign investment: Canada's economic journey back to the future. *Studies in Political Economy, 82*(1), 7–34. https://doi.org/10.1080/19187033.2008.11675062.

– (Ed.). (2014). *The staple theory @ 50: Reflections on the lasting significance of Mel Watkins' "A staples theory of economic growth."* Canadian Centre for Policy Alternatives.

Starrs, S.K. (2017). The global capitalism school tested in Asia: Transnational capitalist class vs taking the state seriously. *Journal of Contemporary Asia, 47*(4), 641–58. https://doi.org/10.1080/00472336.2017.1282536.

States of Jersey. (n.d.). *Moving to Jersey: Money and tax.* Retrieved 31 July 2024, from https://www.gov.je:80/LifeEvents/MovingToJersey/LivingInJersey/Pages/MoneyTax.aspx.

St. Denis, J. (2022, March 17). Snow-washing: Canada's role as a haven for offshore wealth. *The Tyee.* https://thetyee.ca/News/2022/03/17/Snow-Washing-Canada-Role-Haven-Offshore-Wealth.

The steam has gone out of globalisation. (2019, January 24). *The Economist.* https://www.economist.com/leaders/2019/01/24/the-steam-has-gone-out-of-globalisation.

Stempel, J. (2019, March 14). *Nine banks win dismissal of Canadian rate-rigging lawsuit in US.* Reuters. https://www.reuters.com/article/us-canada-rigging-idUSKCN1QV35Y.

Stewart, B. (2020). The rise of far-right civilizationism. *Critical Sociology, 46*(7–8), 1207–20. https://doi.org/10.1177/0896920519894051.

Stiglitz, J. (2008, December 5). Getting bang for your buck. *The Guardian.* https://www.theguardian.com/commentisfree/cifamerica/2008/dec/05/us-economy-keynesian-economic-theory.

– (2009, April 11). A global crisis requires global solutions. *The Guardian.* https://www.theguardian.com/commentisfree/2009/apr/09/global-economy-development.

Stokes, D. (2005). The heart of empire? Theorising US empire in an era of transnational capitalism. *Third World Quarterly, 26*(2), 217–36. https://doi.org/10.1080/0143659042000339092.

Strange, S. (1997). *Casino capitalism.* Manchester University Press.

– (2015). *Mad money.* Manchester University Press. (Original work published 1998)

Streeck, W. (2013). *The politics of public debt: Neoliberalism, capitalist development, and the restructuring of the state* (MPIfG Discussion Paper No.

13/7). Max-Planck-Institut für Gesellschaftsforschung. https://hdl.handle.net/10419/78032.
– (2014). *Buying time: The delayed crisis of democratic capitalism*. Verso.
– (2016). *How will capitalism end?* Verso.
– (2017). The return of the repressed. *New Left Review*, 104, 5–18. https://newleftreview.org/issues/ii104/articles/wolfgang-streeck-the-return-of-the-repressed.
Struthers, J. (2021, August 13). The great depression in Canada. In *The Canadian encyclopedia*. Retrieved 31 July 2024, from https://www.thecanadianencyclopedia.ca/en/article/great-depression.
Sues banks for $7,400,000: Canadian province of Alberta seeks to collect proceeds of bonds. (1910, December 17). *New York Times*, 11. https://www.nytimes.com/1910/12/18/archives/sues-banks-for-7400000-canadian-province-of-alberta-seeks-to.html.
Summers, L. (2014). Reflections on the "new secular stagnation hypothesis." In C. Teulings & R. Baldwin (Eds.), *Secular stagnation: Facts, causes and cures* (pp. 27–38). CEPR.
Suncor. (2021). *Annual report*. https://minedocs.com/22/Suncor_AR_2021.pdf.
Surrey, W.S., & Nash, P.N. (1984). Bankers look beyond the debt crisis: The Institute of International Finance, Inc. *Columbia Journal of Transnational Law*, 23, 111–30.
Sutherland, G. (2014). *Performance and potential: Toronto's financial services sector, 2014*. Conference Board of Canada. https://docplayer.net/12624065-Performance-and-potential-toronto-s-financial-services-sector-2014.html.
Swan, M. (2015). *Blockchain: Blueprint for a new economy*. O'Reilly Media.
Swedberg, R. (2003). *Principles of economic sociology*. Princeton University Press.
Sweeny, R. (1997). Banking as class action: Social and national struggles in the history of Canadian banking. In A. Teichova, G.K. Hentenryk, & D. Ziegler (Eds.). *Banking, trade and industry: Europe, America and Asia from the thirteenth to the twentieth century* (pp. 315–38). Cambridge University Press.
Szalay, E. (2022, May 23). Banks turn to blockchain in search for high-quality trading assets. *Financial Times*. https://www.ft.com/content/f23c990a-913d-4613-8014-f61d35b6e09d.
Tabb, W.K. (2009). Globalization today: At the borders of class and state theory. *Perspectives on Global Development and Technology*, 8(2), 121–38. https://doi.org/10.1163/156914909X423827.
– (2012). *The restructuring of capitalism in our time*. Columbia University Press.
Tapscott, D., & Tapscott, A. (2016). *Blockchain revolution: How the technology behind Bitcoin is changing money, business, and the world*. Penguin.

Tasca, P., & Ulieru, M. (2016). *Blockchain as an institutional technology spearheading an equitable exchange economy*. https://www.researchgate.net/publication/314453374_Blockchain_as_an_Institutional_Technology_Spearheading_an_Equitable_Exchange_Economy.

Tax Justice Network. (n.d.). *Financial secrecy index: Canada*. Retrieved 31 July 2024, from https://fsi.taxjustice.net/country-detail.

Taylor, F.W. (1911). Canada and Canadian banking. *Journal of the Royal Society of the Arts, 59*(3053), 714–27. https://www.jstor.org/stable/41339687.

Taylor, G.D. (2008). *The rise of Canadian business*. Oxford University Press.

Taylor, G.D., & Baskerville, P.A. (1994). *A concise history of business in Canada*. Oxford University Press.

Tedesco, T. (1998, November 5). Liberal MPs say no to bank mergers: Report pulls no punches. *National Post*, A1.

Teeple, G. (Ed.). (1972). *Capitalism and the national question in Canada*. University of Toronto Press.

– (2000). *Globalization and the decline of social reform into the twenty-first century*. Garamond Press.

– (2005). A commentary on Joel Bakan's "The corporation, the pathological pursuit of profit and power." *Socialist Studies/Études Socialistes, 1*(2), 93–107. https://doi.org/10.18740/S44P4H.

– (2007). Honoured in the breach: Human rights as principles of a past age. *Studies in Social Justice, 1*(2), 136–45. https://doi.org/10.26522/ssj.v1i2.975.

– (2011). Notes on the continuing economic crisis. In S. McBride & G. Teeple (Eds.), *Relations of global power: Neoliberal order and disorder* (pp. 227–57). University of Toronto Press.

Teles, N. (2016, April 27). Socialize the banks. *Jacobin*. https://www.jacobinmag.com/2016/04/banks-credit-recession-finance-socialism.

Tencer, D. (2016, November 1). Big Canadian banks' largest shareholders are … each other. *Huffington Post*. https://www.huffingtonpost.ca/2016/11/01/canadian-banks-owned-by-each-other_n_12751158.html.

Teschke, B. (2003). *The myth of 1648: Class, geopolitics, and the making of modern international relations*. Verso.

Teschke, B., & Lacher, H. (2007). The changing "logics" of capitalist competition. *Cambridge Review of International Affairs, 20*(4), 565–80. https://doi.org/10.1080/09557570701680514.

Tett, G. (2021, December 23). What "Squid Game" tells us about the changing face of globalisation. *Financial Times*. https://www.ft.com/content/1a661eb7-960c-4aeb-845a-a4b82c98fc3c.

Therborn, G. (1984). Classes and states: Welfare state developments, 1881–1981. *Studies in Political Economy, 14*(1), 7–41. https://doi.org/10.1080/19187033.1984.11675631.

Thiessen, G. (1999, May 4). *Global financial turbulence and the Canadian economy*. Bank of Canada. https://www.bankofcanada.ca/1999/05/global-financial-turbulence-canadian-economy.

Thomas, D., & Stafford, P. (2021, September 6). London warned of risk of losing status as top financial centre. *Financial Times*. https://www.ft.com/content/852d34ce-dd66-41ab-8610-a2ddcf7981f6.

Thomas, G., & Morgan-Witts, M. (1979). *The day the bubble burst: A social history of the Wall Street crash*. Hamish Hamilton.

Thompson, E. (2017, June 12). *Big banks lobbied officials, MPs, even watchdogs who police them*. CBC News. https://www.cbc.ca/news/politics/banks-finance-lobbying-government-1.4155703.

Tigar, M.E., & Levy, M.R. (2000). *Law and the rise of capitalism*. Monthly Review Press. (Original work published 1977)

Tomba, M. (2013). Accumulation and time: Marx's historiography from the *Grundrisse* to *Capital*. *Capital & Class*, 37(3), 355–72. https://doi.org/10.1177/0309816813502712.

Tomlinson, K. (2013, April 6). *RBC replaces Canadian staff with foreign workers*. CBC News. https://www.cbc.ca/news/canada/british-columbia/rbc-replaces-canadian-staff-with-foreign-workers-1.1315008.

"Too big to fail" bank rules unveiled. (2014, November 10). *BBC*. https://www.bbc.com/news/business-29982181.

Tooze, A. (2018). *Crashed: How a decade of financial crises changed the world*. Allen Lane.

Trichur, R. (2011, September 2). Former MP Ianno to pay OSC $100,000 over trades. *Globe and Mail*. https://www.theglobeandmail.com/report-on-business/former-mp-ianno-to-pay-osc-100000-over-trades/article1360553.

– (2022, March 16). Canada is an international haven for financial crime and the only antidote is transparency. *Globe and Mail*. https://www.theglobeandmail.com/business/commentary/article-canada-marketed-as-a-haven-for-financial-crime-due-to-lax-oversight-of.

Trichur, R., & Steinberg, J. (2015, January 22). Royal Bank of Canada to buy City National for $5.4 billion. *Wall Street Journal*. https://www.wsj.com/articles/royal-bank-of-canada-to-buy-city-national-for-5-4-billion-1421930814.

Tsingou, E. (2007). Transnational private governance and the Basel process: Banking regulation and supervision, private interests and Basel II. In J.-C. Graz & A. Nölke (Eds.), *Transnational private governance and its limits* (pp. 58–68). Routledge.

TSX Inc. (2022). *TSX DRK*. https://www.tsx.com/resource/en/1584/tsx-drk-feature-sheet-2019-08-12-en.pdf.

Turley-Ewart, J.A. (2000). *Gentleman bankers, politicians and bureaucrats: The history of the Canadian Bankers Association, 1891–1924* [Doctoral dissertation, University of Toronto]. TSpace. https://hdl.handle.net/1807/14886.

Tutton, M. (2015, March 12). Nova Scotia offers Royal Bank up to $22M to open financial services centre. CBC News. https://www.cbc.ca/news/canada/nova-scotia/nova-scotia-offers-royal-bank-up-to-22m-to-open-financial-services-centre-1.2991600.

25th anniversary listings: 1970 – definitions defied. (1994, July 1). *The Banker, 144*(821).

Underhill, G.R.D., Blom, J., & Mügge, D. (Eds.). (2010). *Global financial integration thirty years on: From reform to crisis.* Cambridge University Press.

United Nations Conference on Trade and Development (UNCTAD). (2020). *World investment report 2020: International production beyond the pandemic.* United Nations. https://unctad.org/webflyer/world-investment-report-2020.

US will not join CPTPP, but pursue specific trade tie-ups with allies: Gina Raimondo. (2021, November 17). *Toronto Star.* https://www.thestar.com.my/aseanplus/aseanplus-news/2021/11/17/us-will-not-join-cptpp-but-pursue-specific-trade-tie-ups-with-allies-gina-raimondo.

Van der Pijl, K. (2001). Globalization or class society in transition? *Science & Society, 65*(4), 492–500. https://www.jstor.org/stable/40403918.

Van Hasselt, C. (2012, April 30). Group says Canadian banks weren't bailed out. *Wall Street Journal.* https://www.wsj.com/articles/SB10001424052702304505304577376221955392952.

Van Houten, G. (1991). *Corporate Canada: An historical outline.* Progress Books.

Varoufakis, Y. (2011). *The global minotaur: America, the true origins of the financial crisis and the future of the world economy.* Zed Books.

Veblen, T. (2005). *The theory of business enterprise.* Cosimo, Inc. (Original work published 1904)

Veltmeyer, H. (1979). The capitalist underdevelopment of Atlantic Canada. In R.J. Brym & J. Sacouman (Eds.), *Underdevelopment and social movements in Atlantic Canada* (pp. 9–35). Hogtown Press.

– (1987). *Canadian corporate power.* Garamond Press.

– (2013a). The natural resource dynamics of postneoliberalism in Latin America: New developmentalism or extractivist imperialism? *Studies in Political Economy, 90*(1), 57–85. https://doi.org/10.1080/19187033.2012.11674991.

– (2013b). The political economy of natural resource extraction: A new model or extractive imperialism? *Canadian Journal of Development Studies/Revue Canadienne d'études Du Développement, 34*(1), 79–95. https://doi.org/10.1080/02255189.2013.764850.

Vernengo, M. (2022). The inflationary puzzle. *Catalyst*, 5(4), 91–113. https://catalyst-journal.com/2022/03/the-inflationary-puzzle.

Violation Tracker. (n.d.). *Royal Bank of Canada*. Retrieved 31 July 2024, from https://violationtracker.goodjobsfirst.org/parent/royal-bank-of-canada.

Vitali, S., Glattfelder, J.B., & Battiston, S. (2011). The network of global corporate control. *PLOS ONE*, 6(10), 1–6. https://doi.org/10.1371/journal.pone.0025995.

von Finckenstein, K. (1998). *The competition bureau's letter to the Royal Bank and Bank of Montreal*. Competition Bureau. https://www.competitionbureau.gc.ca/eic/site/cb-bc.nsf/eng/01612.html.

Wachtel, H.M. (1990). *The money mandarins: The making of a supranational economic order*. Routledge. (Original work published 1986)

Walby, S. (2013). Finance versus democracy? Theorizing finance in society. *Work, Employment & Society*, 27(3), 489–507. https://doi.org/10.1177/0950017013479741.

Walker, B.E. (1893). Banking in Canada. *Journal of the Canadian Bankers' Association*, 1(1), 1–25.

Walks, A. (2014). Canada's housing bubble story: Mortgage securitization, the state, and the global financial crisis. *International Journal of Urban and Regional Research*, 38(1), 256–84. https://doi.org/10.1111/j.1468-2427.2012.01184.x.

– (2016). Homeownership, asset-based welfare and the neighbourhood segregation of wealth. *Housing Studies*, 31(7), 755–84. https://doi.org/10.1080/02673037.2015.1132685.

Walks, A., & Clifford, B. (2015). The political economy of mortgage securitization and the neoliberalization of housing policy in Canada. *Environment and Planning A: Economy and Space*, 47(8), 1624–42. https://doi.org/10.1068/a130226p.

Wallerstein, I. (2000). Globalization or the age of transition? A long-term view of the trajectory of the world-system. *International Sociology*, 15(2), 249–65.

– (2010). A world-system perspective on the social sciences. *British Journal of Sociology*, 61(1), 167–76. https://doi.org/10.1111/j.1468-4446.2009.01244.x.

Walsh, M., Silcoff, S., & Carbert, M. (2020, April 18). Canada tightens foreign investment scrutiny, citing economic impact of COVID-19. *Globe and Mail*. https://www.theglobeandmail.com/canada/article-canada-tightens-foreign-investment-scrutiny-citing-economic-impact-of.

Walter, T., & Wansleben, L. (2020). How central bankers learned to love financialization: The Fed, the Bank, and the enlisting of unfettered markets in the conduct of monetary policy. *Socio-Economic Review*, 18(3), 625–53. https://doi.org/10.1093/ser/mwz011.

Walters, J.V. (1936). Effects of depression on Canadian banking. *Canadian Banker*, 44, 49–55.

Wark, M. (2019). *Capital is dead: Is this something worse?* Verso.
Warn, K. (2000, September 29). Royal bank of Canada makes foray into US. *Financial Times*, 33.
Waters, R. (2016, May 17). Automated company raises equivalent of $120M in digital currency. CNBC. https://www.cnbc.com/2016/05/17/automated-company-raises-equivalent-of-120-million-in-digital-currency.html.
Watkins, M. (1989). The political economy of growth. In W. Clement & G. Williams (Eds.), *The new Canadian political economy* (pp. 16–35). McGill-Queen's University Press.
– (2007). Staples redux. *Studies in Political Economy*, 79, 213–26. https://doi.org/10.1080/19187033.2007.11675098.
Weiss, L. (1997). Globalization and the myth of the powerless state. *New Left Review*, 225, 3–27. https://newleftreview.org/issues/i225/articles/linda-weiss-globalization-and-the-myth-of-the-powerless-state.pdf.
– (1999). Globalization and national governance: Antinomy or interdependence? *Review of International Studies*, 25(5), 59–88. https://library.fes.de/libalt/journals/swetsfulltext/14965936.pdf.
– (2003). *States in the global economy: Bringing domestic institutions back in*. Cambridge University Press.
Wherry, A. (2022, April 8). Freeland makes a "modern supply-side" bet on Canada's future economic growth. CBC News. https://www.cbc.ca/news/politics/budget-2022-freeland-trudeau-growth-1.6412716.
White, W.R. (1994). *The implications of the FTA and NAFTA for Canada and Mexico* (Technical Report No. 70). Bank of Canada Review. https://www.bankofcanada.ca/1994/08/technical-report-no70.
Whiteside, H. (2012). Crisis of capital and the logic of dispossession and repossession. *Studies in Political Economy*, 89(1), 59–78. https://doi.org/10.1080/19187033.2012.11675001.
Whittington, L. (1999). *The banks: The ongoing battle for control of Canada's richest business*. Stoddart.
– (2014, September 7). EU trade pact could weaken Ottawa's power to regulate banks. *Toronto Star*. https://www.thestar.com/news/canada/2014/09/07/eu_trade_pact_could_weaken_ottawas_power_to_regulate_banks.html.
Williams, G. (1979). The national policy tariffs: Industrial underdevelopment through import substitution. *Canadian Journal of Political Science*, 12(2), 333–68. https://doi.org/10.1017/S0008423900048149.
– (1988). On determining Canada's location within the international political economy. *Studies in Political Economy*, 25(1), 107–40. https://doi.org/10.1080/19187033.1988.11675551.
– (1994). *Not for export: The international competitiveness of Canadian manufacturing*. McClelland & Stewart.

Williams, R.A. (2004). Mergers if necessary. But not necessarily mergers: Competition and consolidation at Canada's "big banks." In R.M. Campbell, L. Pal, & M. Howlett (Eds.), *The real worlds of Canadian politics: Cases in process and policy, fourth edition* (4th ed., pp. 155–213). University of Toronto Press.

– (2006). *Globalisation, deregulation and financial services reform in Canada: Legislating Canada's "superbanks"* [Unpublished doctoral dissertation]. Simon Fraser University.

Willick, F. (2022, May 5). NS scraps non-resident property tax; deed transfer tax to remain. CBC News. https://www.cbc.ca/news/canada/nova-scotia/ns-scraps-non-resident-property-tax-1.6442412.

Willis, A. (2000, August 25). Bankers' ball. *Globe and Mail*. https://www.theglobeandmail.com/report-on-business/rob-magazine/bankers-ball/article22404312.

Wilson, K.G. (2000). *Deregulating telecommunications: US and Canadian telecommunications, 1840–1997*. Rowman & Littlefield.

Wimmer, A., & Feinstein, Y. (2010). The rise of the nation-state across the world, 1816 to 2001. *American Sociological Review, 75*(5), 764–90. https://doi.org/10.1177/0003122410382639.

Wingrove, J. (2014, January 27). Ottawa to revise foreign-worker rules as employers complain of delays. *Globe and Mail*. https://www.theglobeandmail.com/news/politics/ottawa-to-revise-foreign-worker-rules-as-employers-complain-of-delays/article16510288.

Winters, J.A. (2011). *Oligarchy*. Cambridge University Press.

Wolf, E.R. (1982). *Europe and the people without history*. University of California Press.

Wolf, M. (2010, September 14). Basel: The mouse that did not roar. *Financial Times*. https://www.ft.com/content/966b5e88-c034-11df-b77d-00144feab49a.

Womersley, W. (1937). Communism. *Canadian Bankr, 44*(2), 193–202.

Wood, D.R. (2005). *Governing global banking: The Basel Committee and the politics of financial globalisation*. Ashgate.

Wood, E.M. (1998, October 1). Capitalist change and generational shifts. *Monthly Review*. http://monthlyreview.org/1998/10/01/capitalist-change-and-generational-shifts.

– (2002a). Global capital, national states. In M. Rupert & H. Smith (Eds.), *Historical materialism and globalization* (pp. 17–39). Routledge.

– (2002b). *The origin of capitalism: A longer view*. Verso.

– (2003). *Empire of capital*. Verso.

– (2007). A reply to critics. *Historical Materialism, 15*(3), 143–70. https://doi.org/10.1163/156920607X225915.

Woodcock, G. (1989). *A social history of Canada*. Penguin.

Woodman, D. (2022). Generational change and intergenerational relationships in the context of the asset economy. *Distinktion: Journal of Social Theory*, 23(1), 55–69. https://doi.org/10.1080/1600910X.2020.1752275.

Woyames Dreher, V. (2019). Divergent effects of international regulatory institutions: Regulating global banks and shadow banking after the global financial crisis of 2007–2009. *Review of International Political Economy*, 27(3), 556–82. https://doi.org/10.1080/09692290.2019.1675743.

WTF: The federal budget and 50 years of Canadian debt. (2011, March 21). *National Post*. https://nationalpost.com/news/canada/canadian-politics/graphic-50-years-of-canadian-debt.

Yago, K. (2013). *The financial history of the Bank for International Settlements*. Routledge.

Young, K.L. (2012). Transnational regulatory capture? An empirical examination of the transnational lobbying of the Basel committee on banking supervision. *Review of International Political Economy*, 19(4), 663–88. https://doi.org/10.1080/09692290.2011.624976.

Young, K.L., Banerjee, T., & Schwartz, M. (2017, February 3). When capitalists go on strike. *Jacobin*. https://www.jacobinmag.com/2017/02/capital-strike-regulations-lending-productivity-economy-banks-bailout.

Yunker, Z. (2021). *Royal Bank of Canada*. Corporate Mapping Project. https://www.corporatemapping.ca/profiles/royal-bank-of-canada.

Zadikian, M. (2023, May 3). *Cracks forming as more Canadians set to fall behind on debt payments: RBC*. Yahoo Finance. https://ca.finance.yahoo.com/news/cracks-forming-more-canadians-fall-behind-debt-payments-rbc-165533079.html.

Zhou, L., Qin, K., Torres, C.F., Le, D.V., & Gervais, A. (2021). High-frequency trading on decentralized on-chain exchanges. In *2021 IEEE symposium on security and privacy (SP)* (pp. 428–45). IEEE. https://doi.org/10.1109/SP40001.2021.00027.

Žižek, S. (2012, April 24). Occupy Wall Street: What is to be done next? *The Guardian*. https://www.theguardian.com/commentisfree/cifamerica/2012/apr/24/occupy-wall-street-what-is-to-be-done-next.

Index

Abbreviations used in the index are listed on pages xi–xiv.

Abbey, Edward, 225
ABCP (asset-backed commercial paper), 215–16, 219
Abrams, Philip, 22n25
Adkins, L., 25n31, 30n37
Alberta, 76–7, 110n17, 173n56, 247
Alexander, K., 136
Anand, A., 222n124
anticapitalism, 276–8
Atkinson, Ted, 109n16
Atlantic Canada, 56–7, 62n, 146n17, 267n32, 270n38
August, Martine, 268
authority. *See* territory, authority, and rights (TAR)

Bacevich, Andrew, 265–6
Baillie, Charles A., 192n81, 200, 201, 201n94
bailouts, 173–4, 185n74, 217–19, 220–1
Bal, S.S., 32, 75
Banaji, Jairus, 36
Bank Act: origins and importance of, 62–6; 1881 revision, 70–2; 1900 revision, 75; 1908 revision, 78; 1913 revision, 78–9; 1923 revision, 83; 1934 revision, 91n64; 1944 revision, 108; 1954 revision, 110; 1967 revision, 118; 1980 revision, 155–7; 1992 revision, 183–4; and *Finance Act* (1914), 80; and foreign banks, 153n24, 189; and international banking, 112; and near banks, 109; Section 88 powers, 88. *See also Finance Act* (1914)
Bank for International Settlements. *See* BIS (Bank for International Settlements)
Bank of Canada (BoC): origins of, 81, 86–92; asset regulation proposed by, 111n20; blockchain used by, 260n; consumer viewed by, 109n16; corporate banking viewed by, 111; and foreign banks, 155; as lender of last resort, 205n100; monetarist policies of, 142; reserve requirements, 184
Bank of Montreal (BMO): origins of, 50, 51n12, 54; and *Bank Act* (1871), 63–4, 65, 66; and financial crises, 159, 218; global ranking of, 115; as government bank, 55, 81, 82; international banking operations of, 169n48; M&As, 84, 172n52;

Merchants Bank trust company linked to, 73; merger with RBC, proposed, 189–91, 194n84, 199–204; and TSX merger proposals, 236
Bank of Nova Scotia. *See* Scotiabank (Bank of Nova Scotia)
banks. *See* central banks; chartered banks; foreign banks; near banks; *specific banks*
Barnea, A., 274n44
Barrett, Matthew, 190n, 194
Barrow, C.W., 26n32
Baum, D.J., 63n, 66n
BCBS (Basel Committee on Banking Supervision): Basel Accords, 176–7, 207–8, 221–2, 224, 252; and IIF, 207–8; as regulation coordinator, 135n, 138–9, 161, 184, 197. *See also* BIS (Bank for International Settlements)
BCNI (Business Council on National Issues), 148–49, 182. *See also* CBA (Canadian Bankers Association); chartered banks
Bennett, R.B., 77, 87–8, 91
Benson, Edgar, 121n
Bernes, Tom, 196n87
Best, Jacqueline, 141
Beynon, Thomas G., 106n
Bienefeld, Manfred, 178, 274n46
"Big Bang" (British deregulation), 165–8
Big Five banks. *See* chartered banks
Bill C-8, 204–6
BIS (Bank for International Settlements), 116, 135n, 136–8, 142–4, 197. *See also* BCBS (Basel Committee on Banking Supervision); central banks
Bitcoin, 255, 261
Blackburn, Jean-Pierre, 240–1
BlackRock, 162n41
Blankfein, Lloyd, 222

Block, Fred, 77n
blockchain: overview of, 254–5; corporate use of, 258–61; and global capitalism, 262–5; regulation of, 261–2; revolutionary claims about, 255–8. *See also* dark pools; HFT (high-frequency trading)
Blom, J., 161, 208
Blomley, Nicholas, 24–5
BMO. *See* Bank of Montreal (BMO)
BoC. *See* Bank of Canada (BoC)
Borden, Robert, 80, 120n
Bouey, Gerald, 142
bourgeoisie. *See* capitalist class
Breckenridge, R.M., 54, 56, 61, 62, 68n30
Brennan, Jordan, 179
Brenner, Robert, 36, 39
Bretton Woods system: origins of, 97–8, 102–3; collapse of, 123–8; domestic competition increased under, 97, 105, 108–12, 115; Eurodollar markets as escape from, 115–16; and global capitalism, transition to, 96–7, 98–9, 128–9; and nation states, 100–2, 107n. *See also specific institutions*
Brewer, Anthony, 34, 38
Britain: "Big Bang" deregulation in, 165–8; Brexit, 252; global influence of, 103; LIBOR scandal in, 241–2; London Stock Exchange, 165, 235–7; RBC operations in, 211. *See also* Canada–Britain relationship
British Columbia, 78n
Bronfman, Stephen, 267n32
Brown, A.J., 91
Brown, Mary, 215–16
Brown, Wendy, 22n27
Brummer, Chris, 101
Buchanan, Isaac, 70
Burton, Jonathan, 183

Business Council on National Issues.
    See BCNI (Business Council on
    National Issues)
businesses. *See* corporations
Buterin, Vitalik, 255–6, 258
Butterfield, Nathaniel, 72n38

Cain, P.J., 47n3
Calhoun, C., 8n4
Calvert, J., 186
Camdessus, Michel, 196n87
Cameron, Duncan, 184n72
Campbell-Verduyn, M., 224
Canada: banks in development
    of, 31–3, 62–3, 75; and Bretton
    Woods, 99–100; capitalist class
    in development of, 37–9, 46–9,
    96; Confederation, 58–60. *See
    also* Canada–Britain relationship;
    Canada–United States
    relationship; *specific provinces and
    cities*
Canada–Britain relationship: and
    Bank Act (1871), 64; British banks in
    Canada, 120n; and Confederation,
    58–60; and exchange rates, 100; and
    Finance Act (1914), 80; and National
    Policy, 68–9; post-war, 103; pre-
    Confederation, 46–9, 50n9, 52, 57;
    in RBC history, 66, 72–3, 82; and
    trade, 68n31, 252. *See also* Britain;
    Canada
Canada Emergency Response Benefit
    (CERB), 266
Canada–European Union
    Comprehensive Economic Trade
    Agreement (CETA), 249–50
Canada Mortgage and Housing
    Corporation (CMHC), 214–15, 217,
    218. *See also* mortgages
Canada Trust, 204–5
Canada–United States Free Trade
    Agreement (CUSFTA), 180, 182–3

Canada–United States–Mexico
    Agreement (CUSMA), 179–80
Canada–United States relationship:
    bank charters influenced by, 53–4;
    and banking sector competition,
    198n, 201n93, 204n; and Bretton
    Woods, 99–100, 125; and Canadian
    development, 9n5, 15n16, 96n; and
    Confederation, 58; and corporate
    lobbying, 149; and financial crisis
    of 2008, 215–16; and investment,
    85–6, 148, 182n68; and National
    Policy, 67n, 69; in RBC history, 73;
    and trade, 49–50, 51n12, 179–88,
    192. *See also* Canada; United States
Canadian Bankers Association.
    See CBA (Canadian Bankers
    Association)
Canadian Centre for Policy
    Alternatives (CCPA), 217n119, 218,
    247
Canadian Commercial Bank (CCB),
    173–5
Canadian Deposit Insurance
    Corporation. *See* CDIC (Canadian
    Deposit Insurance Corporation)
Canadian Federation of Independent
    Business (CFIB), 191n79, 202n95,
    204n, 239
Canadian Imperial Bank of
    Commerce. *See* CIBC (Canadian
    Imperial Bank of Commerce)
Canadian political economy, 30–1, 33,
    37–9
Canadian Securities Administrators
    (CSA), 233
capital. *See* global capital; national
    capital
Capital (Marx), 21n24, 29, 34
capitalism: banks in development
    of, 28–30, 33–7, 39; corporations
    as transformative of, 20n;
    globalization as part of, in sceptic

344 Index

view, 8–9; history of, 23, 25–6, 44–5. *See also* global capitalism; national capitalism
capitalist class: plutocratic, 229, 244–5; policies in interests of, 140, 145, 182n68; transnational, 10–12, 18n21, 278. *See also* ruling class; working class
Carney, Mark, 222
Carroll, William K., 11n7, 12, 18, 28n, 147n19, 148n21
Carruthers, Bruce, 36
Catalini, Christian, 257n
CBA (Canadian Bankers Association): origins and role of, 71–2, 80, 81; and Bill C-8, 207; on central bank, 87–9; and CETA, 249; on financial crisis of 2008, 217n119, 218; on foreign banks, 122n, 150n; on inflation targeting, 141–2; on revised *Bank Act* (1967), 119–20; on taxes, 199, 268–9. *See also* BCNI (Business Council on National Issues); chartered banks
CCB (Canadian Commercial Bank), 173–5
CCPA (Canadian Centre for Policy Alternatives), 217n119, 218, 247
CDIC (Canadian Deposit Insurance Corporation), 118, 172–3, 175, 205n100, 222
central banks: and BCBS, 138–9; and BIS, 135n, 136n5, 137n, 142–4; and Eurodollar markets, 116; history of, 90; independence of, 141; in Jamaica, 112–13; national financial institutions as beneficiaries of, 103n; role of, 77n, 161–2. *See also* Bank of Canada (BoC); BIS (Bank for International Settlements); chartered banks; foreign banks; near banks
CERB (Canada Emergency Response Benefit), 266

CETA (Canada–European Union Comprehensive Economic Trade Agreement), 249–50
CFIB (Canadian Federation of Independent Business), 191n79, 202n95, 204n, 239
Chant, John, 32–3
chartered banks. *See also* CBA (Canadian Bankers Association); central banks; foreign banks; near banks; *specific banks*
– 1864 to 1944: and BoC, 87; and CBA, 71–2; expansion of, 73n40, 75–7; and national epoch of capitalism, 93–4; pre-Confederation, 49–56; and state policies, 60–1, 62, 64–7, 69–72, 73; structures and relationships of, 27n, 84; and Western Canadian development, 77–9
– 1945 to 1974: competitors of, 108–12, 120–3; and consumer loans, 108; and Eurodollar markets, 116–17, 124–5; international operations of, 112–15, 123; and state policies, 107, 118–19
– 1975 to 2008: and BCNI, 148–9; competitors of, 151, 155–6, 198; CUSFTA viewed by, 183n70; diversified services offered by, 212–15; failures of, 173–5; and financial crises, 159–60, 173–5, 215–21; growth and dominance of, 151–2, 156n30, 177–8; international operations of, 152–3, 178; M&As among, 189, 190–3, 194–5, 199–205, 209; and Olympia & York bankruptcy, 185n74; regulation/ deregulation of, 155–7, 169–71, 175–6, 177, 183–4, 204–6, 221–2; TAR shifts exemplified by, 225
– 2009 to 2022: and consumer debt, 248–9; and COVID-19 pandemic,

269; economic issues viewed by, 237–8, 249, 251, 252; and fossil fuel industry, 273–4; illicit activities of, 241–3; taxes on, 269–70, 271; and TSX merger proposals, 236
Chartered Professional Accountants of Canada, 261
Chodos, R., 153
Chrétien, Jean, 192n81, 195–6, 267n32
Christophers, B., 102–3, 220n123, 226, 272–3
CIBC (Canadian Imperial Bank of Commerce): dark pool regulations viewed by, 238; and financial crises, 159, 218; HFT activities of, 234; international operations and ranking of, 115, 169n48, 194n83; M&As, 172n52, 190, 191n79; and Olympia & York bankruptcy, 185n74
Citibank/Citicorp, 120–1, 156n28, 244–5
Clarkson, Stephen, 187, 193, 207, 207n102, 209
class. *See* capitalist class; ruling class; working class
Cleaver, H., 125, 126n35, 165
Cleghorn, John, 190n, 192, 199n, 203
Clement, Wallace, 10n5, 22n27
climate change, 273–4
CMHC (Canada Mortgage and Housing Corporation), 214–15, 217, 218. *See also* mortgages
Coldwell, M.J., 89n60
Coleman, William, 14, 24, 26, 264
commoditization, 214
common property, movement for global, 277–8
communism, fears of, 89n61
Competition Bureau, 203, 205n99
Competition Policy Review Panel (2008), 209
Cooke, Peter, 160n36

Corbett, P.E., 93
corporate rights: and Bretton Woods, 128, 129; and deregulation, 163, 164–5, 167; and financial crisis of 2008, 213–14; and financialization, 212; and free trade agreements, 179–80, 185–8, 252–4; and globalization, 128, 144n13, 224–6; privatizing exchanges and new, 237; transnational, 27n33. *See also* political rights; property rights; territory, authority, and rights (TAR)
corporations: definitions of, 46n1, 51n11; blockchain used by, 258–9; and Bretton Woods, 105, 123–4; concentration of, 194–5; DAOs compared to, 255; financialization of, 166n44; and free trade agreements, 179–80, 182, 185–8, 249–51; and globalization, 14–17, 163–5, 224–6; history of, 20n, 50–1; taxation of, 145; transnational, 103, 148, 244. *See also specific corporations*
Council of Canadians, 191n79, 202n95, 204n
Courville, Léon, 6
COVID-19 pandemic, 240, 249, 252n, 266, 268
Cox, Robert, 97, 98
Coyne, James, 109n16, 111, 117
CPTPP (Comprehensive and Progressive Agreement for Trans-Pacific Partnership), 251, 253
crises. *See* financial crises
cryptocurrencies, 255, 256, 261–2
CSA (Canadian Securities Administrators), 233
Curry, Nathaniel, 79
Curtiss, C.A., 52n13
CUSFTA (Canada–United States Free Trade Agreement), 180, 182–3
CUSMA (Canada–United States–Mexico Agreement), 179–80

D'Alessandro, Dominic, 193, 205
DAOs (decentralized autonomous organizations), 255–7, 265
dark pools: overview of, 230–2; in Canadian financial sector, 236–8; and cryptocurrencies, 262; HFT and impact of, 233, 237–8; nation-state oversight escaped via, 232–3; RBC activities in, 233–5. *See also* blockchain; HFT (high-frequency trading)
Darrah, D., 269n
Darroch, James, 32, 72n37, 209n, 215n116, 245n, 248
Davis, G.F., 164
Demirovi, Alex, 11n6, 12n9, 271
democracy. *See* liberal democracy; political rights
Deneault, Alain: on early Canadian capitalism, 47–8; on Eurodollar markets, 115, 116–17; on government debt, 144–5; on tax avoidance, 229, 243, 267n32, 270; on tax cuts, 267; on transnational companies in Canada, 16
Department of Insurance (DOI), 175
deregulation: in Britain, 165–8, 168n46; in Canada, 168–72, 204–6; and corporate concentration, 192; and financial crisis of 2008, 213–14; global capitalism characterized by, 163–5; post-Bretton Woods, 128; and TAR, centrifugal dynamic of, 225. *See also* national regulation
Diefenbaker, John, 117
Dijk, Peter van, 270
Dimon, Jamie, 222
DOI (Department of Insurance), 175
Donough, William, 160n36
Dow, A. and S., 213
Downe, Bill, 248

Drainville, A.C., 136, 142
Draper, Hal, 6–7
Dubinsky, Z., 16n17
Duggan, G.H., 91
Duncan, David, 72n38

Eayrs, James, 3
Eichengreen, B.J., 68n31
Eli Lilly, 187n75
Engels, Friedrich, 20, 278
Estey Report, 108n15, 174
Ethereum, 256, 257, 258, 265
Eurodollar markets: overview of, 115–16; and Bretton Woods system, collapse of, 97, 129; and chartered banks, 116–17, 152–3; and international institutions, transformation of, 138, 147; and LDC crisis, 157
European Union, free trade agreement with, 249–50
Evans, J., 50n9

Fairfield, Joshua, 257n
far-right civilizationism (FRC), 276n48
FCAC (Financial Consumer Agency of Canada), 205, 242n8
Feinstein, Y., 104n7
Ferdosi, M., 266n29
Finance Act (1914), 77, 79–80. *See also Bank Act*
financial crises: of 1997–8, Asian, 195; of 2008, 3–4, 5–6, 31, 212–14, 215–24; bank diversification and risk of, 184n71; Bretton Woods collapse and increased frequency of, 126–7; corporate growth as cause of, 225; and international institutions, 161–2, 195–8; LDC debt crisis, 157–60
financial institutions. *See specific financial institutions*

financialization: definitions of, 8n3, 29n36; and anticapitalism, 276–8; in banking history, 29; of blockchain, 258–62; and consumer debt levels, 248–9; corporate rights as key to, 212; and globalization, 30; of social services, 268. *See also* globalization
Financial Stability Board (FSB), 221–2, 223–4
Financial Stability Forum (FSF), 196–7
Finckenstein, Konrad von, 202
Finkel, A., 140n10, 163n42
firms. *See* corporations
First World War, 79–81, 136
FISC (Financial Institutions Supervisory Committee), 175
Flaherty, Jim, 216, 218–19, 220, 221
Flanders, Stephanie, 217n118
Flash Boys (Lewis), 231, 232n, 233–4, 235, 237
Fligstein, Neil, 3, 31
foreign banks: bailouts for, 217, 221; as CBA members, 207; competition with chartered banks, 150–1, 178; deregulation of, 171, 172n52, 189, 192, 206; national regulation of, 120–2, 153n24, 155–7, 183n69. *See also* central banks; chartered banks; near banks
Fortier, Michael, 247
fossil fuel industry, 110n17, 157, 158, 173
Frank, Sam, 256
Fraser, Nancy, 262
Frazee, Rowland, 130, 142, 153, 155, 170
FRC (far-right civilizationism), 276n48
Freedman, C., 183n69
Freeland, Chrystia, 249

free trade agreements: and Bretton Woods, 100, 101, 128; and Canada, 58, 59, 179–83, 185–8, 249–50, 251; continued importance of, 251–2; and corporations, 16, 19, 192, 207; and TAR, centrifugal dynamic of, 224–5. *See also specific agreements*
Friedman, Milton, 4, 142, 143n11
FSB (Financial Stability Board), 221–2, 223–4
FSF (Financial Stability Forum), 196–7
Fuchs, Christian, 7n
Fyshe, Thomas, 73

G7/G8 countries, 127, 163, 193n81, 195n85, 196, 197n89
G10 countries, 176
G20 countries, 196–8, 221
Gans, Joshua, 257n
Gardner, B.C., 88
Garrod, Joel, 17
GATS (General Agreement on Trade in Services), 185–6
GATT (General Agreement on Tariffs and Trade), 101, 181
Geithner, Timothy, 197n
Gemini Trust Company, 258, 262
George, Susan, 40
Germain, Randall, 90, 100–1, 126–7, 128, 159n, 227
German Ideology, The (Marx and Engels), 23n29
Gibson, J. Douglas, 107
Gilbert, C., 268n34
Gill, Stephen, 18
Gilman, Nils, 229
Gindin, Sam, 4, 278
Glassman, Jim, 195
global capital: denationalization of, 133–4; and financial crisis of

2008, 3–4, 5–6; and free trade agreements, 186–8; globalization and financialization of, 244; legal frameworks for, 180–1; lobbying by, 149; making of, 132; mobility of, 15, 27; and nation states, 128, 187–8, 221, 232; post-Bretton Woods liberation of, 127–8. *See also* national capital

global capitalism: anticapitalist struggle against, 276–8; and blockchain, 257–8, 262–5; in Bretton Woods era, 95–7, 98–9, 100–2, 128–9; Canadian examples of, 14–17; and deregulation, 163–5; and Eurodollar markets, 123; and financial crisis of 2008, 3–4, 5–6; institutional support for, 223–4; and international banking, 114n; and international institutions, 127, 161–2; and nation states, 20–1, 254, 270–3; as novel epoch, 10–14, 19, 128, 130–2; and TAR in globalization, 7; and working class, 126n. *See also* financialization; globalization; national capitalism

global cities, 230

globalization: definitions of, 7n; and anticapitalism, 276–8; Canadian examples of, 14–17; and corporate power, 154, 194, 243; and deregulation, 163–5; and Eurodollar markets, 116; and financial crisis of 2008, 3–6; financial institutions as key to, 28–30; and international institutions, 138–9; as novel historical epoch, 7, 10–14, 17–19, 20–1, 23; sceptic views of, 8–9, 20; state–capital conflicts in, 271. *See also* financialization; global capitalism

Godsoe, Peter, 193

Goldstein, Jacob, 230, 237
Goodhart, C.A.E., 139n8
Gordon, Walter, 121
Gordon Report, 120
Gould, E., 185
Graefe, P., 266n29
Great Depression, 86–92, 101, 102
Greenfield, Adam, 262–3
Greer, A., 275n
Grossman, Richard S., 28, 30
Grundrisse (Marx), 13, 21n24
Guénin, H., 268n34
Gupta, Vinay, 264n27

Hager, S.B., 146
Hague, George, 64
Haldane, Andy, 224, 232n
Hann, C.M., 25
Hardt, Michael, 7
Harris, Stephen, 209
Harten, Gus Van, 250
Hartt, Stanley, 169, 170n
Harvey, David, 8, 8n4, 17, 134n, 144, 165, 272n41
Hathaway, T., 273
Hayes, S.L., 116
Hayes, Tom, 241n6
Helleiner, E., 64, 100, 137, 139
Heller, H., 48
Henwood, Doug, 20n, 39, 98, 123–4, 125n34, 146
Heron, J., 108n14
HFT (high-frequency trading), 232, 233–5, 237–8, 260. *See also* blockchain; dark pools
Hincks, Francis, 64, 71n35
Hockin, Thomas, 171, 175
Holt, Herbert, 79, 86, 91
Home Bank of Canada, 83
Hopkins, A.G., 47n3
Houston, Tim, 267n32
Houten, G. Van, 58n20, 87n58, 182–3

Hubbard, P.M., 116
Hudson, Peter J., 49n, 114
Hussan, Syed, 240
Hymer, Stephen, 124n31, 130

Ianno Report, 200–1, 202, 204n
IEX (dark pool), 234n
IIF (Institute of International Finance), 160–1, 207–8
IIROC (Investment Industry Regulation Organization of Canada), 233, 237–8, 261, 262
IMF (International Monetary Fund), 98, 134n, 159n, 161–2, 163, 195, 196n87, 223n
imperialism: and Bretton Woods, 99; and Canada, 9n5, 14, 14n12, 59–60, 69n32, 96n, 148; and globalization, 9, 11; legal framework of, 48n7
institutions. *See* international institutions; *specific institutions*
international institutions: and free trade agreements, 186; global capital and reorientation of, 133–5, 146, 225; lobbying by, 160–1; nation states constrained by, 138; and neo-liberalism, 144n13, 181n66; post-Bretton Woods, 127; regulatory role of, 139n8, 159–60, 161–3, 184, 194–8, 221–4, 229. *See also* Bretton Woods system; *specific institutions*
ISDS (investor-state dispute settlement) mechanisms, 179–80, 187, 249–50, 253n18, 254

Jacobsson, Per, 136–7, 140n9
Jaffray, H.T., 92
James, C.L.R., 113
Jayasuriya, Kanishka, 17n20
Jeffees, W., 104
Jenkins, P., 48n5
Jenson, Jane, 40

Jentzsch, Christoph and Simon, 256
Jessop, Bob, 131, 220, 253
Johnson, Simon, 221
Julian, Peter, 269

Kain, P.J., 13n10, 21n24
Kalman-Lamb, G., 214–15, 215n115, 249
Kastner, L., 225
Katsuyama, Brad, 234, 237
Kelly, Dan, 239
Kenny, Thomas, 74
Keynes, John Maynard, 105, 106, 196n88
Keynesianism, 140n10, 143
King, William Lyon Mackenzie, 82, 83n51, 87, 88
Kinnear, Thomas, 61
Klassen, J., 164, 244
Knowles, A.J., 85–6
Knox, F.A., 98, 101, 134n, 136
Kobrak, C., 100, 123
Koch-Weser, Caio, 197n
Krugman, Paul, 4, 196n88
Kwak, James, 221
Kwinter, Monte, 169
Kyer, C.I., 118n25, 173n56, 174, 222n126

Lambert, Allen Thomas, 118n26
Lamfalussy, Alexandre, 196n88
Langille, D., 149
Lapavitsas, C., 30n36, 38n44, 112n, 212
Lapham, Lewis, 163, 228
Lash, Scott, 27n34
Latour, Bruno, 266
law: blockchain and changes to, 263–4; and capitalism, 25, 27; and deregulation, 165; free trade agreements as, 179n63, 180, 187n75, 249–50; and global capital,

187–8; and imperialism, 48n7; international institutions as source of, 127. *See also* Bank Act; *Finance Act* (1914); national regulation; taxes
Lawrence, C.J., 263
Laxer, Gordon, 246–7
LDC debt crisis, 157–60
LeDrew, Stephen, 199n
Lee, Ian, 271n
Lee, Marc, 247
Lehdonvirta, Vili, 256
Levine, Matt, 263, 264
Levitas, Ruth, 277n
Levy, Karen, 256–7
Lewis, Michael, 231, 232n, 233–4, 235, 237
liberal democracy: and anticapitalist struggles, 276–8; and banks, 88–9, 92, 141; business rights as part of, 201n94; Canadian class structure and, 49n8; free trade agreements as undermining, 181, 182, 187, 251, 252; globalization as undermining, 18–19, 132n, 133–4, 145–7, 225–6, 253–4; government debt blamed on, 143n12; neo-liberal disapproval of, 141n; and post-war international order, 99n. *See also* neo-liberalism; political rights
Liodakis, George, 10n6, 12n8, 12n9
"Little Bang" (Canadian deregulation), 168–73
Livesey, Bruce, 218n, 219
Logan, S.H., 48, 85
London, U.K., 103, 167–8, 252
Lower, Arthur R.M., 66, 68
LSE (London Stock Exchange), 165, 235–7
Lubin, Joe, 257
Lucas, Robert, 143n11

Macdonald, David, 217n120, 218, 220
Macdonald, Donald S., 157, 182
Macdonald, John A., 55n16, 67
Macdonald, Laura, 17
MacDonald, L.R., 37n41
MacIntosh, Robert: on *Bank Act* (1871), 65; on Basel Capital Accord (1988), 177; on Canada–US banking ties, 53n15; on CUSFTA, 183n70; on deregulation, 169n49, 171n, 172n52, 176n58; on foreign financial institutions, 122n, 156n28, 157n31; on government banking, pre-Confederation, 55n16; on international banking centre controversy, 169n48; on LDC debt crisis, 157n32, 158, 158n33; on mortgage lending, 110n18; on near banks, 111n19; on Northland Bank failure, 175n; on Nova Scotia trade, 57n18; on offshore banking centres, 168n47; on politics, 28; on regulation, 111n20; on short-term money market, 112n
MacKay Task Force, 190, 193, 199–200
MacKenzie, Donald, 231, 234, 235n
MacKinnon, Janice, 4–5
MacLaren, Roy, 198
MacLean, Nancy, 144n13
Macpherson, C.B., 275
Major, A., 124n32, 133, 140, 141
Malm, Andreas, 277
Manley, John, 199n, 205n98
Mann, M., 22n27
Maple Group Acquisition Corp., 236
Marchak, Patricia, 15, 20
Maritimes, 56–7, 62n, 267n32, 270n38
Martin, J., 100, 123, 169n49
Martin, Paul, 163n42, 190–1, 195–6, 198–204, 267n32, 271
Marvin, D.M., 92

Marx, Karl: analytical methods of, 13, 21, 25–6; on banking and money capital, 29, 33–7; capital defined by, 254; on centralization and concentration, 150; on freedom and politics, 276; on historical change, 131; on property relations, 20; on the state, 23, 59n22; on working class and bourgeoisie, 278; on world market, 9, 179n61
Masrani, Bharat, 269n
McBride, S., 134–5, 181–2
McDougall, Barbara, 172–3
McDowall, Duncan, *Quick to the Frontier*: as source, 39
– on banking history: *Bank Act*, 65, 66, 78; CCF banking policy, 89n60; Central Gold Reserve, 79–80; consumer credit growth, 108; deregulation, 170; Eurodollar markets, 95; *Finance Act* and credit expansion, 81; urbanization, 108n14; war bonds, 90n62; Western Canada, 79n47
– on RBC history: Caribbean and Latin American expansion, 112, 113–14; deregulation, 170; expansion, 74, 76–7, 82; Great Depression, 91; LDC crisis, 159; M&As, 76; Montreal head office, 84n; National Policy and move to Montreal, 70n33; national regulation, 106n
McKay, Dave: on blockchain, 254, 260–1; on climate change, 273; on consumer debt concerns, 248; on COVID-19 pandemic, 269; on international wealth management activities, 247–8; on NAFTA renegotiations, 251; on oil industry and Canadian competitiveness, 245–6

McKeen-Edwards, Heather, 138, 160n36, 207, 208
McLaughlin, W. Earle, 95, 110n18, 117, 119n26, 121–2, 125n33
McMichael, Philip, 18
McNally, David, 59n22, 238
Merchants Bank. *See* Royal Bank of Canada (RBC)
Meredith, Patricia, 32, 209n, 215n116, 245n, 248
Mertins-Kirkwood, H., 16, 180n64, 181, 251n16, 253n18
Miliband, R., 21n24
Mills, C. Wright, 227
Mills, Greg, 236, 237
monetarism, 142–7
Montreal, 168–9
Montreal Trust, 118
Moorecraft, David, 201
Morck, R.K., 83n50
mortgages and mortgage-backed securities, 110–11, 118, 214–17, 218, 248–9
Mudge, S.L., 263
Muir, James, 103, 104, 111, 112n, 114
Mulroney, Brian, 267n32
multilateral institutions. *See* international institutions
Myers, Gustavus, 3, 32

NAFTA (North American Free Trade Agreement), 180, 185–7, 249–50
Nakamoto, Satoshi, 255
Nasdaq, 258
national capital: *Bank Act* and construction of Canadian, 67; in Bretton Woods era, 102, 107, 115, 128–9; growth and deregulation of, 168; and nation states in global epoch, 240; and property relations, 95; and RBC history, 44–5, 93–4. *See also* global capital

national capitalism: in Bretton Woods era, 98–9, 100–2, 128–9; Canadian, 46–9; free trade agreements as fundamental change to, 253; vs. global capitalism, 95–7, 130–2; and RBC history, 92–3. *See also* global capitalism

National Policy, 67–9, 70n33

national regulation: blockchain used to comply with, 259n; and Bretton Woods, 100–2, 105, 124–5, 126–8; Canadian, 117–18, 120–2, 172–3, 176, 177, 204–6, 222–3; and chartered banks, growth of, 153n24, 153n25; corporate escape from, 115–16, 123, 227–30, 234–43; and financial crisis of 2008, 223–4; and financial innovations, 233, 237–8, 261–4; free trade agreements as limit on, 179–80, 249–51; international institutions as limit on, 127, 133–4, 138, 195–8; in national vs. global capitalist era, 130–2; neo-liberalism opposed to, 144n13; as sovereignty issue, 274n46. *See also* deregulation; law; taxes

nation state: anticapitalist movement concerns with, 276–8; blockchain use by, 260n; and Bretton Woods system, 100–2, 126–8; Canadian, 28, 46–9, 58–60, 75–81, 87; as capability for global capital, 131–2, 177, 179n62, 181, 187n75, 221, 224–6, 240, 270–3; as capability for national capital, 93–4, 95, 105–7, 129, 130–1, 179; central bank as transnationalized element of, 141; and financial crisis of 2008, 3–6, 223–4; fiscal and monetary policy, 139–42, 143–7; and free trade agreements, 179–82, 185–8, 249–54; and globalization, 7, 9, 18–19, 95–7, 227–30; and international institutions, 134n, 135n, 138; and mercantilism, 53n14; proliferation of, post-war, 104; TAR and analytical importance of, 10–14, 17–19, 20–7. *See also* Britain; Canada; territory, authority, and rights (TAR); transnational state (TNS); United States; welfare state

Naylor, R.T.: on American investment in Canada, 85n54; on *Bank Act* revisions (1980), 155, 156; on banks and Western Canadian development, 78n; on Canada–Britain relationship, 48n6; on CBA and competition, 72n37; on chartered companies and class relations, 53n14; on competition in financial sector, 151; on *Finance Act* (1914), 81; on monetarism, 143; on rentier capitalists, 35

near banks: chartered bank acquisitions of, 177–8, 183–4; as competitors of chartered banks, 97, 108–12, 116, 117, 119, 129, 150–1; failures of, 118n25; foreign owned, 122n. *See also* central banks; chartered banks; foreign banks

Neill, Charlie, 44, 81n

neo-conservatism, 272n

neo-liberalism: origins of, 140n10; and Bretton Woods system, 98–9, 126; and far-right civilizationism, 276n48; free trade agreements as central to, 181; and globalization, 8, 132n, 272–3; and government policies and programs, 165, 268; international institutions and rise of, 134n, 136–7; and monetarism, 142–4; public debt as central to, 268n34. *See also* liberal democracy

Nerbas, Don, 84, 88
Neufeld, E.P., 60, 111n20
Newfoundland and Labrador, 146n17
Newman, Peter C., 79n46, 95, 152, 166
Nichols, Shawn, 254
Nixon, Gordon, 205–6, 238
Noble, Randolph, 106n, 190n, 201n93
Norfield, Tony, 103n, 166, 167–8
Norman, Montagu, 88
North American Free Trade Agreement (NAFTA), 180, 185–7, 249–50
Northland Bank, 173–5
Northrup, Jeremiah, 61
Nova Scotia, 56–7, 267n32, 270n38
Nystrom, Lorne, 202

offshore banking: and Bretton Woods collapse, 128; development of, 113, 115n; and Eurodollar markets, 116–17; in Montreal and Vancouver, 168–9; national regulations avoided via, 229–30; and RBC, 240–1; and tax avoidance, 243n, 270. *See also* tax havens
OIGB (Office of the Inspector General of Banks), 83, 174, 175
oil industry, 110n17, 157, 158, 173, 245–7
Olympia & York bankruptcy, 185n74
Ontario, 146n17, 169, 262, 266n29, 268
Orion Bank, 153–4, 172
OSFI (Office of the Superintendent of Financial Institutions), 175, 203, 205, 205nn99–100, 222n124, 242

Panitch, Leo, 4, 19
Park, F.W., 114
Park, L.C., 114
Pease, Edson, 70n33, 80, 81, 90n62
Peihani, M., 222n124

Pentland, H.C., 47n3, 49n8, 60n, 69n32
Pierce, Hester M., 262
Piketty, Thomas, 4
Piron, Stephen, 237
Pistor, Katharina: capital defined by, 25; on ISDS, 179n63, 182n67, 187n75; on law and imperialism, 48n7; on legal code of global capitalism, 27, 179n62, 180
Plumptre, A.W.F., 99
Polanyi, K., 69, 77n
political economy, Canadian, 30–1, 33, 37–9
political rights: and bank notes, right to issue, 70–1; and central banks, 141; class conflict over, 140; and globalization, 133–4, 145–6; and international institutions, 138; labour rights, 240. *See also* corporate rights; liberal democracy; property rights; territory, authority, and rights (TAR)
Porter, Brian, 271n
Porter, Tony: on banks and Canadian development, 14; on Eurodollar markets, 115–16; on G10 and globalizing banks, 139; on LDC debt crisis, 158; on markets and property rights, 26; on property rights and MNCs, 27n33; on transnational financial associations, 138, 160n36, 207; on transnational regulation, 5–6, 139n8, 208, 224
Porter Report, 117–18, 122n, 153n24
Posner, Eric, 258
Poulantzas, N., 18n21
Powell, J., 102n5
Pringle, David, 31, 143n11, 184, 202–3, 214, 248
private property. *See* property rights
property, common, 277

property relations: analytical importance of, 20, 22–5, 46, 275–6; and Bretton Woods system, 102, 128–9; in Canadian history, 59, 60, 148; and deregulation, 164–5, 168; and free trade agreements, 179–80, 253–4; and globalization, 17, 19, 97, 130–2, 224–6, 228; national, and RBC history, 44–5; national, TFWP as way to escape from, 240; and national capital, making of, 95; transnational regulation of, 127

property rights: in anticapitalist movement, 276–8; class conflict over, 140; global, 179n63, 232, 249–51, 257–8, 263, 264–5; national, 22–3, 46–9, 67, 129, 131; and RBC expansion, 82. *See also* corporate rights; political rights; territory, authority, and rights (TAR)

Prudham, Scott, 24, 264

Puri, P.: on ABCP crisis, 216; on bank diversification and risk, 184n71; on Basel II Accord, 208; on chartered banks, growth of, 107; on CMHC, 110n18; on mortgage insurance, 122n; on Olympia & York bankruptcy, 185n74; on regulation, 153nn24–5, 156n29, 222–3

Quebec, 108n13

Quick to the Frontier (McDowall). *See* McDowall, Duncan, *Quick to the Frontier*

Quigley, Neil, 37, 73, 85n54, 103

R3 consortium, 259

RBC. *See* Royal Bank of Canada (RBC)

Reeve, Andrew, 25

regulation. *See* deregulation; national regulation

Rhodes, William H., 162

Richardson, H.A., 79

rights. *See* corporate rights; political rights; property rights; territory, authority, and rights (TAR)

Ritchie, Cedric, 183n70

Robertson, Fraser, 111n20

Robinson, William I.: on capital and capitalism, 12nn8–9, 18n21, 38n42, 213; on deregulation, 164; on government debt and deficits, 146, 147; on LDC debt crisis, 157–8; on offshore capital markets, 154; on TNS, 10n6; on trade agreements, 186

Rogers, Chris, 138

Rollings, Neil, 31

Rose, John, 62–4

Rost, B., 138n

Royal Bank of Canada (RBC): analytical overview, 41–3; globalization exemplified by, 15–16, 28, 30; name changes, 74, 210; sources on, 39–41

– 1864 to 1944: origins of, 56–7, 62; economic and political issues viewed by, 61–2, 81; and Great Depression crises, 90–2; national epoch of capitalism exemplified by, 93–4; state policies and expansion of, 66–7, 72–4, 75, 82–6

– 1945 to 1974: diversified services offered by, 110–11, 119; economic issues viewed by, 104, 108–9, 112n, 117; and Eurodollar boom, 116; global capital transition exemplified by, 95, 97; international operations of, 103, 104, 112–15, 123; and near banks, links with, 109, 118; post-war growth of, 107–8

– 1975 to 2008: economic issues viewed by, 142, 149–50; and

financial crises, 157, 159–60, 162, 219–20; and free trade agreements, 183, 188–9; growth of, 147, 150, 177–8, 184, 189, 194–5; international operations of, 153–5, 157, 168, 169n48, 194n83, 209–12; merger with BMO, proposed, 189–91, 194n84, 199–204; and Olympia & York bankruptcy, 185n74; and regulation/deregulation, 170, 171–2, 177–8, 222; TAR shifts exemplified by, 225
– 2009 to 2022: blockchain used by, 260–1; charitable activities vs. corporate actions of, 273–4; and COVID-19 pandemic, 269; dark pool and HFT activities of, 233–5, 238; illicit activities of, 240–3; and oil industry, 245–7; tax haven operations of, 229–30; TFWP used by, 238–9; and TSX merger proposals, 236; wealth management activities of, 244–5, 247–8
Royal Commission on Banking and Currency (1933), 89–90
Royal Commission on Corporate Concentration (1978), 147–8, 151–2, 155
ruling class: and Bretton Woods, 99–100; in Canada, 9n, 46–9, 50n9, 58n21, 59n22, 96; domestic, and national regulation, 131; and early banks, 52, 65n; notable individuals, 70n34, 79n46; welfare state supported by, 106n. *See also* capitalist class; working class

Sacher, W., 16, 47–8
Sands, Stafford, 113
Sapinski, J.P., 11n7, 18
Saskatchewan, 78n

Sassen, Saskia: on banking and finance, 29, 115n, 166n44, 231n, 233, 237; on bourgeois propertied class, 38n43, 39n45; on Bretton Woods era, 98–9; on capitalist epochs, 49, 93, 133; on foreign worker programs, 240; on free trade agreements, 188; on global cities, 230; on government debt, 147; on inflation targeting, 140–1; on international institutions, 127, 135n; on nation state, analysis of, 44; on TAR and globalization, 7, 13, 17, 23–7, 39, 131, 165. *See also* territory, authority, and rights (TAR)
Satgar, V., 8n4
Schenk, Catherine R., 6, 223
Schrauwers, A., 52
Scotiabank (Bank of Nova Scotia): origins of, 56, 66; economic issues viewed by, 183n70, 238; and financial crisis of 2008, 218; international ranking of, 115, 194n83; M&As by, 84, 172n52
SEC (US Securities and Exchange Commission), 230, 231, 233
Seccareccia, Mario, 31, 143n11, 184, 202–3, 214, 248
Second World War, 101, 102, 107–8
Sewell, William H., Jr., 24n30, 33n39, 36
Sharp, Mitchell, 118n24, 125n33
Shaw, M., 59, 99n, 100n
Siltanen, Janet, 105
Sinclair, Helen, 199
Singer, Joseph W., 22n26
Slobodian, Quinn, 144n13, 180–1, 181n66, 260
Smith, Adam, 130
Smith, Andrew, 47n3, 62, 65, 67
Snyder, J., 14n14

Soederberg, S., 147, 196, 197
Somers, Margaret, 77n
Srikantiah, A., 169n49
state. *See* nation state; transnational state (TNS); welfare state
Steck, Brian, 204n
Stewart, B., 276n48
Stiglitz, Joseph, 4, 134n, 196
stock exchanges: "Americanization" of, 232n; LSE, 165, 235–7; TSX, 234, 235–7. *See also* dark pools; HFT (high-frequency trading)
Storey, R.H., 108n14
Strange, Susan, 166, 167, 194
Streeck, W., 107n, 140, 143n12, 145–6, 145n17, 147
Struthers, J., 86
Summers, Larry, 197n
Swedberg, Richard, 26, 28, 49
Sweeny, R., 51n12, 57n19, 65n, 148, 182n68
Swift, Catherine, 191n79, 204n

Tabb, William K., 6, 8, 30
TAR. *See* territory, authority, and rights (TAR)
Tasca, Paolo, 258
Taschereau, Louis-Alexandre, 120n
taxes: on chartered banks, 269–70; corporate, cuts to, 267; and government debt, 143n12, 145; tariffs, foreign branches as way to avoid, 103. *See also* law; national regulation
tax havens, 113, 229–30, 244, 270. *See also* offshore banking
Taylor, Allan, 160, 170, 171n, 183n70
TD (Toronto-Dominion Bank), 115, 190, 191n79, 194n83, 204–5, 242
Teeple, G.: on Canadian history, 48n5, 67; on capital–state relationship, 22, 50n10, 132n, 145n17, 146n18;
on Eurodollar markets, 116; on inflation targeting, 140; on international banking, growth of, 114n; on Keynes, 106; on transnational institutions, 225; on world market, 179n61
Temporary Foreign Worker Program (TFWP), 238–40
Territory, Authority, Rights (Sassen), 23–4
territory, authority, and rights (TAR): as analytical framework, 7, 23–7, 39. *See also* Sassen, Saskia
– global organization of: and blockchain, 263–5; and Bretton Woods collapse, 126–7; and deregulation, 163–5; and free trade agreements, 178–80, 185–8; and global capitalism, 21, 95–7, 130–3, 178, 224–6, 227–30, 253–4; and international institutions, 135n, 138, 147, 176–7; TFWP as example of, 240
– national organization of: in Bretton Woods era, 128–9, 130–1; Canadian examples of, 55–6, 58–60, 64–70, 77–83, 87, 90, 92; and decolonization, 103–4; French example of, 90n63; national capital as product of, 93–4, 95; and post-war welfare state, 105–7; and RBC history, 44–5, 73–4, 75–7
Teschke, B., 53n14
TFWP (Temporary Foreign Worker Program), 238–40
Theories of Surplus Value (Marx), 33
Therborn, G., 105
Thiessen, Gordon, 196n86, 198
Thomson, Dick, 170n
tipping points, 24, 97, 123, 129
TMX Group, 235
TNS. *See* transnational state (TNS)

Tomba, Massimiliano, 25
Tomkins, Charles S., 83
Tooze, Adam, 197n, 253n19
Toronto, 168–9
Toronto-Dominion Bank. *See* TD (Toronto-Dominion Bank)
Towers, Graham, 92, 109n16, 112–13
transnational anticapitalism, 276–8
transnational state (TNS), 10–14, 10n6, 11n7, 17–19, 21, 128. *See also* nation state; welfare state
Trudeau, Justin, 252
Trudeau, Pierre, 159
Trump, Donald, 251–2
TSX (Toronto Stock Exchange), 234, 235–7
Turley-Ewart, John, 40, 71n35, 73n40
Turner, John, 150n, 158, 173

UBS (Union Bank of Switzerland), 241n6
Ulieru, Mihaela, 258
United Kingdom. *See* Britain; Canada–Britain relationship
United States: and Bretton Woods system, 97–9, 125n34; corporate taxes in, 272; currency of, 124–5; and financial crises, 159n, 215, 219, 221; financial sector of, 115n, 193, 198n, 201n93, 204n, 237–8; and free trade agreements, 185, 251–2; public debt and inequality in, 146; RBC operations in, 82, 84–6, 103, 123, 154–5, 209–10, 212, 245; RBC violations in, 241, 242, 243; regulation/deregulation in, 152, 171, 263–4. *See also* Canada–United States relationship
universal banking, 169n50
Urry, John, 27n34
US Securities and Exchange Commission (SEC), 230, 231, 233

Vancouver, 169
van Dijk, Peter, 270
Van Harten, Gus, 250
Van Houten, G., 58n20, 87n58, 182–3
Veblen, Thorstein, 228
Veltmeyer, H., 62n24
Vernengo, M., 141n
Volcker, Paul, 196
von Finckenstein, Konrad, 202

Walker, Byron Edmund, 71n36, 75, 76n43, 276
Walker, James, 183
Walks, A., 217n118
Wallerstein, Immanuel, 9, 13n11
Walters, J.V., 228–9
WB (World Bank), 98, 114, 134n
welfare state: banks as beneficiaries of, 107; and COVID-19 pandemic, 266; cuts to, 143n12, 146n18, 147, 163n42, 268; and free trade agreements, 186; historical preconditions for, 276; neo-liberal assault on, 125–6, 140n10; TAR and rise of, 105–7. *See also* nation state; transnational state (TNS)
Western Canada, 76–7, 78n, 108–9, 110n17, 173–5, 173n56, 247
Weyl, E. Glen, 258
White, Darryl, 269n
White, W.R., 185
Whiteside, Heather, 217
Whittington, L., 119, 191n80, 194, 202nn95–6
Williams, Glen, 10n5, 38
Williams, Russell, 190, 199
Wilson, Michael, 162, 169–70, 171
Wimmer, A., 104n7
Winters, Jeffrey, 24
Wolf, Eric, 36
Womersley, Wilfrid, 89n61
Wood, Ellen Meiksins, 9, 20, 29n35

working class: and anticapitalist struggle, 277–8; and COVID-19 pandemic, 266; debt levels of, 248–9; and exchange rates, 126n; government debt paid by, 146n18; and inflation targeting, 140; transnational institutions inaccessible to, 225. *See also* capitalist class; ruling class

World Bank (WB), 98, 114, 134n
World War I, 79–81, 136
World War II, 101, 102, 107–8

Yago, Kazuhiko, 137–8
Young, Charles, 156n28
Young, K.L., 208

Žižek, Slavoj, 276–7

www.ingramcontent.com/pod-product-compliance
Lightning Source LLC
Chambersburg PA
CBHW030304140825
31010CB00009B/20/J